Gregory Pittman, Christoph Schäfer et al.

Scribus

Open Source Desktop Publishing
The Official Manual

W0009075

FLES Books

First published in Great Britain by FLES Books Ltd.
www.flesbooks.com

Copyright © 2007/2008 Gregory Pittman, Christoph Schäfer and other contributors mentioned in section 14.6.2 of this manual

Copyright for the cover illustration © 2007/2008 Daniel S. Prien

Copyright for the cover layout © 2008 Christoph Schäfer

Proofreaders: Craig Bradney, Louis Desjardins, Maciej Hanski, Gregory Pittman, Christoph Schäfer

Layout: Christoph Schäfer, Scribus 1.3.3.12

Printed in the United Kingdom and the United States of America by Lightning Source, Inc.

ISBN: 978-0-9560780-0-1

First edition 2009
Reprinted 2009

Preface

What you have in your hands is the result of an amazing journey for a large group of people, and years of dedicated hard work in the realm of Free Software. You have a copy of the first Official Manual for Scribus, the leading cross-platform Open Source Desktop Publishing application. Importantly, this manual is written primarily by users of Scribus – an enthusiastic bunch, drawn together by the selfless interest in helping beginners and experienced users alike.

This is a perfect representation of the spirit that can grow behind an Open Source application. Not only are there the coders that make the actual application, but when a development team is open to a community, it is the users that really make the application what it is. In this case, a manual, written by users for users, is the result of this community spirit.

Feature requests, bug reports, and great ideas from our huge and steadily growing user base have helped us turn a small application with a lot of potential into an application downloaded thousands of times daily, and used to produce magazines, books, flyers and all manners of publications. This manual brings all of that together and should help even the newest user to start from scratch and become productive quickly.

So many times have we had an email along the lines of "unfortunately I can't code but I so wish I could help." Joining the community, helping each other and submitting requests for changes are almost the biggest things one can do to help an Open Source project. Getting a small group of enthusiastic, determined and even forceful writers together to think about writing a book is certainly one of the more adventurous efforts around. Turning the idea into a reality in about 6 months – a real "tour de force" – is even more astonishing!

On behalf of the team of developers of Scribus, I would like to thank all of the contributors, led by Christoph and Greg, for this outstanding support of Scribus and their efforts to educate the Scribus community. Well done, and, like all of the users out there, we'd be glad to meet you, Dear Reader, in IRC sometime soon, or perhaps at the next Libre Graphics Meeting.

Take care, and happy publishing!

Craig Bradney

Scribus Developer

Notes on Usage

- This manual is written with the presumption that you are familiar with the general behavior of the computer and operating system you use, ie. know how to start or close a program etc.

- The main body of text in this manual is set in Liberation Serif. Words in italics are generally referring to menu entries, entries in the context menu or tabs in the Properties Palette. Other text entries in dialogs, buttons etc. are distinguished from the rest of the text by quotation marks.

- References to other chapters or sections are in Futura LT Book.

- Various commands that might be entered on a command line verbatim, as well as command line output or the content of plain text files, like configuration files, are shown in Courier New.

- If hyperlinks or paths to files are hyphenated, an arrow at the end of the line indicates that there is no empty space in the link or path.

- Keyboard shortcuts are always written in PC terminology. If you are using Scribus on a Mac, you should know that the CTRL key is the equivalent of CMD key on an Apple keyboard. In general, the terminology of mouse clicks applies to the use of a two-button mouse with scrollwheel, which is recommended for use with Scribus. Again, if you use a Mac, you should know the equivalent actions for various mouse operations. Unless specifically indicated otherwise, reference to one or more clicks of the mouse will mean a left-button click.

Table of Contents

1   Installation 1
1.1   Scribus on Linux and UNIX 1
1.2   Scribus on Mac OS X 8
1.3   Scribus on Windows 9

2   Scribus Quick Start Guide 13

3   Scribus Basics 25
3.1   Basic Concepts 25
3.2   Workflow and Scribus 30
3.3   The Scribus Workspace 35
3.4   The Help System 37
3.5   Opening, Creating and Saving Documents 39
3.6   There's More Than One Way to Look at a Document 50
3.7   Navigating in a Document 55
3.8   Managing and Laying Out Pages 58
3.9   Working with Frames 62
3.10   Working with Text 70
3.11   Working with Styles 85
3.12   The Story Editor 91
3.13   Working with Images 96
3.14   Working with Shapes and Polygons 104
3.15   Straight Lines and Arrows 113
3.16   Bézier Curves and Freehand Lines 116
3.17   Colors and Gradients 118
3.18   Importing Vector Drawings 123
3.19   Tables 132
3.20   Master Pages 135
3.21   Page Numbering 139

4   Customizing Scribus 141

5   Advanced Features 155
5.1   The Scrapbook 155
5.2   Converting Frames 157
5.3   The Action History 159
5.4   Search and Replace 161
5.5   Attach Text to Path 162
5.6   Importing Text with Custom Text Filters 165
5.7   Typography 173
5.7.1   Fonts and Font Technology 173
5.7.2   Getting and Using Good Fonts 179
5.7.3   Font Preview and Font Management 183
5.7.4   Drop Caps 193
5.7.5   Short Words 195
5.7.6   Hyphenation 198

5.7.7 Special Characters 200
5.7.8 Lists 205
5.8   Placing and Moving Items with Precision 209
5.8.1 Measuring Tools 209
5.8.2 The Properties Palette 211
5.8.3 Using the Keyboard 212
5.8.4 Rotating Items 213
5.8.5 Multiple Duplicate 214
5.8.6 Aligning and Distributing Items 216
5.8.7 Grids 219
5.8.8 Guides 221
5.9   Creating a Table of Contents 224
5.10   Layers 227
5.11   Managing Images 229
5.12   Image Effects 232
5.13   Extended Image Properties 235
5.14   The Barcode Generator 244

6   Colors and Color Management 247
6.1   The Eye Dropper 247
6.2   The Color Wheel 248
6.3   Spot Colors 252
6.4   Color Management 258

7   File Export 265
7.1   Text Export 265
7.2   Bitmap Export 266
7.3   Vector Export 268
7.4   PDF Export 271

8   Printing 285
8.1   The Print Preview 285
8.2   The Preflight Verifier 287
8.3   Local Printing 289
8.4   Booklet Printing 294
8.5   Preparing Files for Commercial Printing 301

9   PDF Forms 305
9.1   Introducing PDF Form Elements 305
9.2   PDF Form Features in Scribus 307
9.3   Enhancing PDF Forms with JavaScript 314
9.4   Emulating Radio Buttons 319
9.5   Annotations and Links in PDF Files.............................. 321
9.6   Viewers for PDF Forms 324

10   PDF Presentations 325

11	The Scripter	333
11.1	Using Scripts	333
11.2	The Python Console	335
11.3	Script Info	337
11.4	Extension Scripts	338
11.5	Scribus Scripts	339
11.6	Scripting Basics	354
12	Tips and Tricks	357
13	Your DTP Toolbox	367
14	Appendices	393
14.1	Installing Scribus from the Command Line on Linux/UNIX	393
14.2	Keyboard and Mouse Shortcuts	396
14.3	Scribus, QuarkXPress™ and InDesign™ Terminology	401
14.4	File Types and Resources Used by Scribus	402
14.5	Useful Links	404
14.6	Copyrights and Licensing	405
15	Glossary	411
16	Credits	429
17	Index	433

1 Installation
1.1 Scribus on Linux and UNIX®

1.1.1 Building Scribus from Source

NOT ONLY have things come a long way with Scribus over the few years of its history, but simultaneously various Linux and UNIX® distributions have become much more user friendly. Several now have automated or semi-automated repositories for downloading Scribus, along with all of its dependencies or auxiliary components.

Many Linux/UNIX distributions offer graphical user interfaces for the management of binary packages. Please read the documentation of your distribution, to learn how to use them. Most Linux distributions are shipped with Scribus these days, and if not, it's available in online repositories. You can also install Scribus packages from the command line. See the instructions in Appendix 1.

If no current package is available for your Linux or UNIX version, you have the option of building (compiling) it yourself. The instructions below will help you learn how to do this.

1.1.2. Tools and Ingredients

For some, the task of building or compiling software is daunting, merely because they haven't done it before. Here we would like to try to allay your fears and break this down into an understandable step-by-step task. Once you have assembled the various tools and ingredients, you may find that building your own up-to-date version of Scribus is very rewarding. For one thing, it allows you to take advantage of various upgrades and bug fixes as they are released and before they are in the stable official version.

Let's go over the components you need other than Scribus first:

- You must have a compiler, and a sufficiently up-to-date one. This is the program that transforms those text instructions into machine-readable binary files. For various UNIX-like operating systems, including Linux, this is gcc (gcc stands for GNU Compiler Collection), and at least a 3.x version – current versions are 4.x. An additional version which may be desirable or necessary is gcc-c++.

- You must have Qt. For Scribus 1.3.3.x, this will be qt-3.3.x, and importantly, you must also have the header files, the various Qt modules that gcc will need to cross-compile Scribus with Qt. These are likely labelled something like qt-devel-3.3.x, but check with your distribution for specifics.

Other essential ingredients:

- Ghostscript: at least 8.15, ideally more advanced, such as 8.60. Ghostscript handles the import of EPS and PostScript files, as well as the print preview.
- Python: at least 2.3 – without Python on your system, the Scripter won't work.
- Freetype: 2.1.7 or higher. This is a library to access font files.
- libxml2: 2.6 or better.
- lcms (LittleCMS): 1.17 or higher, and lcms-devel for color management.
- libtiff: 3.6 or higher and libjpeg for image handling.
- CMake: the program that is used to configure your Scribus build. Support for autoconfig has faded in more recent Scribus versions, in favor of cmake.
- CUPS: the Common Unix Printing System is required for printing with Scribus on Linux and UNIX systems, including Mac OS X.

Recommended or desirable:

- cups-devel: Most Linux and UNIX distributions now use CUPS for printing, but this does not necessarily include the development libraries.
- Python imaging libraries and tkinter: required to run some Scribus scripts.
- fontconfig-devel
- openssl-devel: Some Linux distributions require ssl support for CUPS, notably OpenSUSE/Novell SLED.
- Subversion: Used for obtaining the most up-to-date versions, with the latest bugfixes and enhancements.

Go to http://sourceforge.net/projects/scribus, click the "Download Scribus" button. This should take you to the download page, where you are presented with a list of file choices. Look under "Scribus SVN," where you should find a link to a file called scribus-1.3.3.1x.tar.bz2 (where "x" is number 2 or higher), and click on this, after which you should begin downloading to the location of your choice in your computer.

1.1.3 What's this ".tar.bz2"?

These are extensions which indicate that the directory of Scribus files has first been tarred (using a program called tar) or converted to a single file, then compressed to shrink its size, using a program called bzip2. You can simply extract it like this:

```
tar jxvf scribus-1.3.3.x.tar.bz2
```

Then you will have a directory called `scribus-1.3.3.x` which has the sources. Inside will be everything you need to compile – except for all the other requirements mentioned above.

1.1.4. Now the Fun Begins

The basic process for compiling involves three commands:

```
cmake .
make
make install
```

1.1.4.1 CMake

First enter the directory called scribus-1.3.3.x, using the `cd` command. If you simply wish to compile Scribus with all its basic settings and in the default location (where the binaries and other files will end up after installation), just run

```
cmake .
```

Note that this is the command, `cmake`, followed by a space, then a period/full stop. The period/full stop ensures that CMake runs using the contents of the directory you are in. CMake is the program Scribus uses to check for necessary components in your distribution, and all the requirements mentioned above. Any options present will be noted and adjustments made in how Scribus is compiled – if you lack some optional feature, Scribus will be compiled without that function. You will get a running commentary as CMake finds or doesn't find various things. There may be an error message indicating something is missing, and in the end if something critical is broken or missing, you will get a failure message – one of the things it checks is whether the compiler works properly. If the message isn't understandable, the best thing is to go to Scribus list for help, pasting your error(s) into your email.

The output from CMake is a bit cryptic. In general, if it says that something is missing, it usually means it cannot find the header files for compiling. Here is one kind of error message, in which CMake asks you to set variables:

```
CMake Error: This project requires some vari-
ables to be set,
```

and cmake can not find them.

```
Please set the following variables:
LIBART_LGPL_INCLUDE_DIR
```

A note about security and not wasting your time:
Be aware that there have been instances where altered files have been uploaded to legitimate sites. Sometimes there is a glitch in the download and the file is simply broken in the process. These altered files can cause problems or at least a lot of frustration. The way to ensure your downloaded file is legitimate is to run a checksum program on your downloaded file. On the Scribus download site you should see a label for an md5sum and an sha1sum. These are small programs which generate a unique code based on the actual contents of a file. Most Linux distributions have one or the other, perhaps both. On Sourceforge, there should also be a file ending in .sig, which is a gpg generated signature for the source. This is a very secure means of authenticating the source files. To verify in a terminal:
```
gpg --verify ./scribus-
1.3.3.x.sig ./scribus-
1.3.3.x.tar.bz2
```
Once you have downloaded your file, you can run `sha1sum scribus 1.3.3.x.tar.bz2` in a command line, and this sha1sum checksum will be generated. If it does not match the code on the Scribus site, do not proceed to compile and install – this download is either broken or altered. If you consistently download a file that fails this test, please notify the developers, so this can be fixed.

```
LIBXML2_INCLUDE_DIR (ADVANCED)
LIBXML2_LIBRARIES (ADVANCED)
PYTHON_INCLUDE_PATH
PYTHON_LIBRARY
```

What was needed here (this example from Fedora 8) was the following packages: libart_lgpl-devel, libxml2-devel, and python-devel. Check with your distribution or the Scribus mailinglist to help locate these. Finally, CMake will generate a number of files needed to actually do the compiling.

1.1.4.2 Building

If you've gotten this far, things should be getting simpler. Just enter in the command line,

```
make
```

which tells gcc to compile Scribus. Compiling Scribus will take some time, how much depends on the speed of your CPU and the amount of memory. As make runs, you will get an indicator at the beginning of lines about the percentage of the job that is completed. Either you will reach 100% or one or more error messages will stop the process – again, go to the Scribus list for help if needed.

1.1.4.3 Installing

Now, finally, you're almost finished. If you are installing in the default location, most likely you need root privileges to install, so either become root with the su command or use sudo.

For the former situation after becoming root, type:

```
make install
```

for the latter:

```
sudo make install
```

Installing should be an automatic and rather quick process. Your Scribus binaries should be located in /usr/local/bin, but watching the messages should confirm this.

1.1.4.4 Running Scribus

From a command line, type

```
/usr/local/bin/scribus
```

after which Scribus should run. Setting up a desktop shortcut or a panel launcher to run this command makes things simpler.

Once Scribus is running, check *Help > About Scribus* to verify your version and other installed components. In the "About" tab you can see the following informations:

- The Scribus version, for instance "Scribus Version 1.3.3.12."
- The date of creation of the source files. This date is set by the developers when they create the package.

Next you see the so-called "Build ID." If all necessary components are installed, the Build ID should contain five letters. These letters are abbreviations with the following meaning:

- C (1) = LittleCMS is installed and used by Scribus.
- C (2) = CUPS is installed and used by Scribus.
- T = Libtiff is installed and used by Scribus.
- F = Fontconfig is installed and used by Scribus.
- C (3)/A = Scribus uses either Cairo (C) or libart (A) for on-screen rendering.

Missing library support is indicated by an asterisk. Finally, the version of Ghostscript detected by Scribus is shown in the last row of the dialog.

Scribus Version 1.3.3.12

12 June 2008
Build ID: C-C-T-F-C
Using Ghostscript version 8.60

A detail of the *About Scribus* dialog, indicating the version number, the date of creation of the source files, the Build ID, and the Ghostscript version detected by Scribus

1.1.5 Getting and Using Development Versions

There are several reasons why you may be interested in using a version of Scribus other than the stable, official version:

- There may be one or more bugs impeding some kind of work you need to do, and you know these have been fixed in development versions.
- You may be curious as to what new features have been added beyond the stable, official version.
- You may wish to help in the development of Scribus by looking for and reporting bugs and other problems.

While it is true that if you download a development version and compile and install using default settings, you will replace a previous version, you can actually have more than one operating Scribus version on your system, as will be explained later.

1.1.5.1 Subversion

Currently, Scribus is using Subversion [1] as its version control software. From the users' perspective, Subversion represents a way to gain access to the newest versions of rapidly developing software, as Scribus is. You must have this program installed on your system, and it should be available from your package repository if you do not have it. Running man svn will result in the display of its man page if it is installed. Running svn --version will tell you which version you have. In case it is not obvious, you must be connected to the internet for svn to download and update Scribus.

- Subversion has a host of capabilities, but we will cover just a few here. Let's begin by downloading for the first time the newest development version in the 1.3.3.x series of Scribus.
- cd to the location you wish to download Scribus – you will be creating a new directory with Subversion.
- Run this command:

```
svn co svn://scribus.info/Scribus/branches/
Version133x/Scribus Scribus133x
```

- This creates a directory named Scribus133x, then downloads the latest development version in the 1.3.3.x series. This will take some time.

Later, if you wish to simply update this downloaded version, cd to this new directory, and then just enter:

```
svn up
```

If nothing new is downloaded or updated, you already have the latest version.

1.1.5.2 CMake Options

If what you want to do is use the default location and other settings for Scribus, simply follow the directions outlined above. Be aware that occasionally an update to fix one problem may create another, and ideally one should uninstall an old version before installing another to the same location, otherwise there may be conflicts.

You may want to install elsewhere for this and other reasons, so what follows are some of those possibilities.

Let's say your username is bud. After you make sure you don't already have some directory by the following name, you type:

```
mkdir /home/bud/scribus133x
```

Go back to your download directory if you are not already there. This time when you run CMake, type:

```
cmake . -DCMAKE_INSTALL_PREFIX:PATH=
/home/bud/scribus133x
```

This tells CMake to set up the process to install to /home/bud/scribus133x when you later run make install. Another advantage of installing to your home directory is that you do not need to be root, since you have write privileges to that location. In fact, if you do `make install` as yourself and it works, you cannot possibly have ruined your default Scribus.

You might consider something like this as an alternative:

```
cmake . -DCMAKE_INSTALL_PREFIX:PATH=/opt/
scribus133x
```

the advantage of this being that others using the system can have access to Scribus. This directory `/opt` is one commonly used for user-added software.

1.1.5.3 Developmental Version

You can also download and install the developmental version of Scribus, in a way similar to what is described above. Be aware that development versions are not recommended for important, critical work, since, depending on the development cycle, they can have a variety of problems, including unexpected failures at times. Also be aware that work saved with a developmental version generally will not be able to be opened in the stable version, as the file format will probably be somewhat different.

Currently, the developmental version is 1.3.5svn. With the advent of 1.3.5svn, there are the additional requirements to also have Qt4 (and Qt4-devel), Cairo (and cairo-devel), podofo (and podofo-devel) and boost++. If you want to use the formula editor, you also need to have LaTeX installed. Download it with this command:

```
svn co svn://scribus.info/Scribus/trunk/
Scribus Scribus135
```

Follow the instructions as above to compile. Using the CMake options, you can install 1.3.5svn to its own directory, and thus have access to both stable and developmental versions. For instance, to install a parallel version of 1.3.5svn in your home directory, use:

```
mkdir /home/bud/scribus135svn
```

Then:

```
cmake . -DCMAKE_INSTALL_PREFIX:PATH=
/home/bud/scribus135svn
```

Finally run `make` and `make install` as described above.

[1] http://subversion.tigris.org

1.2 Scribus on Mac OS X

INSTALLING a binary package of Scribus on Mac OS X is quite simple.

1.2.1 Preparations

If you don't have a current version (8.5 or higher) of Ghostscript installed already, download it from Sourceforge, extract the content and move the resulting folder `Ghostscript.Framework` to `/Library/Frameworks`. Scribus should detect Ghostscript automatically.

1.2.2 Installing

1. Now, download Scribus from SourceForge.
2. Extract the downloaded file (with the extension .tgz). You will have a new application called "Scribus.app" available now. You can move this application wherever you want; the Applications folder in your home directory is a good place.
3. Double-click on Scribus.app to launch Scribus.

Two problems may arise:

1. If you have many fonts installed, the first time Scribus starts, it could take up to an hour (but most of the time slightly more than a minute) in order to check all of them.
2. If Scribus doesn't automatically find Ghostscript (and if this happens, you will be warned by an alert), you can set the path to gs (it should be `/Library/Frameworks/`$\searrow$

   `Ghostscript.Framework/bin/gs`) in the "External Tools" tab of the *Preferences*.

1.3 Scribus on Windows

1.3.1 Hardware

To RUN Scribus on Windows, you need at least 512MB memory. More is strongly recommended for larger and more complex documents. Your CPU should be a Pentium III (750MHz) or better.

1.3.2 Software

Windows 95/98/ME are not supported. Scribus won't work on these platforms.

1.3.2.1 Windows 2000

If you are running Windows 2000, you need to have SP4 installed. You also need the GDI+ library, which can be downloaded from Microsoft.

You should also download and install a current version of Ghostscript before you start the installation of Scribus. Scribus will detect the location in most cases. If it doesn't, you can add it in *File > Preferences > External Tools > PostScript Interpreter*. Note that the Ghostscript directory contains two executable (*.exe) files, namely gswin32c.exe and gswin32.exe. If you need to insert the path to Ghostscript manually, you have to choose gswin32c.exe.

When you select the "Extra Fonts" option in the installer, this installs two sets of high-quality, freely distributable fonts. One set is the the URW fonts from Ghostscript. This includes 45 type faces which are commonly included with most Post-Script printers. The second is the Bitstream Vera font family, widely used on Linux and by many of the included templates.

1.3.2.2 Windows XP

The installation on XP is similar to 2000, except that you don't need to install the GDI+ library, which is part of Windows XP.

Use of the Windows standard themes is very strongly recommended. An issue has been known to cause display problems with some third party themes. If you were to encounter this issue, as a workaround we suggest you change the Scribus theme (*File > Preferences > General > Theme*) to "Windows" instead of the default "Window XP" one.

1.3.2.3 Windows Vista

While Scribus runs on Vista, it hasn't been tested extensively on this platform. There may be some glitches, and users are encouraged to make the developers aware of Vista-specific issues.

1.3.3 Installation

Installing Scribus on Windows:

A

B

C

Installing Scribus on Windows is hardly any different from other installations on this platform. The most current version can be downloaded from Sourceforge. Scribus and all required libraries (except GDI+ for Windows 2000) are all in one installation file called "scribus-1.3.3.x-1-win32-install.exe" (where x is the current version). Download the file to your hard drive and double-click on it. Note that you need to have Administrator privileges to install Scribus. After a few seconds, you'll see the welcome screen. Simply click "Next" to continue.

The next step is to choose the components that are going to be installed. You have the choice between Scribus itself (required), additional fonts (see above) and a desktop shortcut (a link to the Scribus executable file on the desktop). You can also determine whether a default set of shortcuts for all users will be installed **(A)**.

After selecting the components you can select an installation directory. There's probably no reason to change the default setting, unless you want to install Scribus to a non-standard place, for example, on a separate partition or hard drive **(B)**.

The last choice you have to make before you start the installation is to define a folder in a Start Menu for Scribus shortcuts. You shouldn't change the default values in this dialog **(C)**.

After clicking the "Install" button, Scribus will be installed, which may take some time.

Once Scribus is installed, you can click the "Finish" button. If you don't want to start Scribus immediately or make sure Windows doesn't open a text editor to display the README file, uncheck both boxes in this dialog.

When you have finished the installation, you'll see an entry called "Scribus 1.3.3.x" in the program list of the Windows "Start" menu, where x is the Scribus revision number (eg. 1.3.3.12) An arrow indicates that the entry has sub-entries. There are five sub-entries:

- *qtconfig*: This is a configuration program for the Qt toolkit which is used by Scribus. You can change some aspects of the visual appearence of Scribus here.
- *Readme*: A click on this entry will open a plain text file that contains some basic information about the Scribus version you have installed.
- *Scribus 1.3.3.x*: This will start Scribus just like any other program on Windows.
- *Scribus 1.3.3.x (console)*: If you click here, Scribus will be started from a Windows command line. This is especialy useful if you wonder why a certain font is not available in Scribus. Scribus checks all installed fonts during startup and it will show an error message if a font is rejected due to quality issues.
  - *Uninstall* lets you remove Scribus from your computer. You will need Administrator privileges to do this.
  - *Website* opens www.scribus.net in your default browser.

qtconfig
Readme
Scribus 1.3.3.12
Scribus 1.3.3.12 (console)
Uninstall
Website

1.3.4 Uninstalling, Installing More Than One Version

Once you have installed Scribus, when you later install a newer version, you will be asked whether you wish to uninstall the older one. If you choose not to uninstall, you will then have two versions of Scribus to choose from, since the newer version will by default go into its own directory.

2 Scribus Quick Start Guide

BEFORE we start explaining Scribus in depth, it might be useful to get a feeling for the way Scribus works. For that purpose, you can learn how a simple front page of a magazine for an imaginary Rembrandt exhibition is being created. If you want to follow the description provided here, you need:

- the Gentium [1] and Bitstream Vera Sans [2] fonts installed on your computer.
- Rembrandt's self-portrait from Wikimedia. [3]
- the Scribus logo from your Scribus install directory.

This is what we want to achieve:

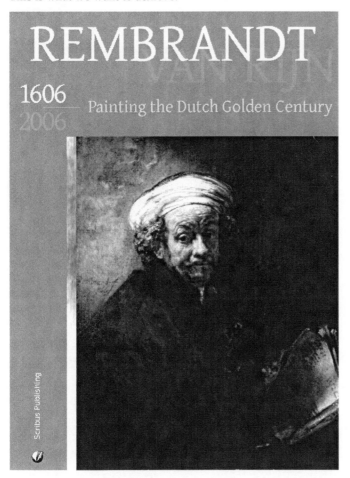

Step One: Creating a Document and a Page Background

You probably know what happens if you create a new file in a word processor: the program you're working with creates a new page and you can start typing. If a new page is necessary, the word processor will create a new one. This won't work in Scribus (or most other DTP programs). To create a new page, you have to tell the program to do exactly that. The main purpose of a DTP software is to give you a maximum of control over design and content of your document. So we click *File > New*, and Scribus brings up the following dialog:

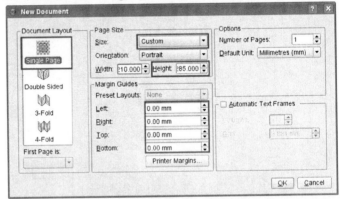

For our cover page we will choose a single page layout. Set the page size to "Custom" and change the default value for height to 285 mm. This is going to be about the same as US Letter size. The cover page won't need any margins, so that we use 0 mm as the value for all page margins. Leave the rest of the default settings as they are.

After clicking the "OK" button, Scribus creates a new page:

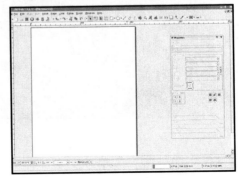

Next, we need a gray background for our page. Click on the white rectangle in the menu bar or simply press S on the keyboard. Yes, you're reading correctly, pressing S doesn't mean anything will be "typed" on the page. To type, you need a special environment called text frame, as you will see below. In this case, we need a shape, thus the keyboard S command.

Your mouse pointer now turns into a rectangle with a + on its upper left corner. Click and hold the mouse button, then drag the + across the page and let up – you have just created a shape. Size, position and color don't matter here, as we will soon change them.

If you haven't clicked somewhere else on screen, your new rectangle is still selected, which means it is outlined in red dots and so-called handles at each corner and the middle of a line. Now use *Windows > Properties* or press F2 to bring up the Properties Palette, which is the Swiss Army Knife of Scribus. You will learn a lot more about its use later. For the time being, let's stay in the default tab of this dialog, which is called *X, Y, Z*. The more complex a document is, the more useful it is to give each object a unique name. It will make it easier to find and to select it later on. Not surprisingly, we'll call our shape "Background."

Next, we make our rectangle match the size of the page. Remember the values we chose for the page? Insert them here, but first don't forget to click on the chain symbol to the right of the boxes for changing the values for width and height. If you try to do this without unlinking that chain, you will see that a change in one value changes the other in a proportional way, and it will seem like you are forever stuck, which you will be until you unlink that chain.

Now that our rectangle has exactly the size of our page, you need to make sure that it matches the page borders by setting its X and Y positions to 0.000 – if you just delete what is there and replace with 0, then press Tab or Enter, Scribus will make the decimal point and other zeros for you.

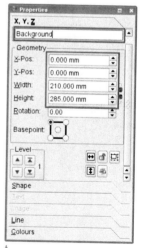

The Properties Palette with the values for the "Background" shape.

By default, Scribus uses black as the color for shapes, which is not what is needed here. Provided our shape is still selected, we use the Properties Palette again to assign a new color to it. For that purpose we use the *Colors* tab. From the list select "Grey41" as the fill color.

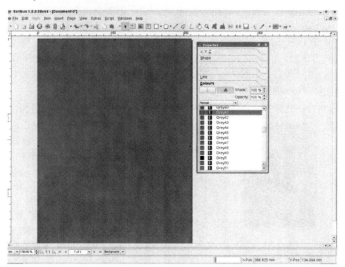

By clicking the lock icon in the Properties Palette you can protect each item against further changes.

Each shape and each frame in Scribus has a border. In the case of shapes the default color is always black. Since we don't want any color for our frame border, click on the symbol with the pen and select the color "None," which is always at the top of the list.

Our page background is now finished. To make sure it isn't changed unintentionally, return to the *X, Y, Z* tab of the Properties Palette and click on the "lock" symbol, so that our background is protected from any further changes.

Step Two: Inserting the Cover Picture

Now that the background has been created, you need to place the cover picture. You may be accustomed to inserting images directly in your word processor, but in Scribus they are inserted in a container (called a frame). For images, or, more precisely, for bitmap images, we have to create an image frame by clicking on the image frame icon in the toolbar or by pressing I (as in image) on the keyboard. Draw your image frame as you did with the rectangle and go to the *X, Y, Z* tab of Properties Palette again.

Rename this image frame "Rembrandt1," and for width and height enter the values as shown in the screenshot on the right. Our cover picture needs to be placed exactly in the lower right of our page. How can this be achieved? Actually, it's quite simple. We know the X and Y coordinates of our page, namely 210 mm and 285 mm. So you can enter these values in "X-Pos" and "Y-Pos," but wait! Not so fast. Before you do that, first change the basepoint of our object. When you set 0.000 values for the background shape, the values were for the upper left of the page. But our image will have to align to our lower right page margins, so we change the basepoint to lower right before we enter the X and Y values. Also, fix the size of our image frame by locking it.

To make our design a bit more stylish, let's add an edited copy of the image frame. We won't see much of it, just a small stripe on the left. Use *Item > Multiple Duplicate* for this operation, because it allows us to enter precise numbers for horizontal and vertical shift. We need one copy, and for "Horizontal Shift," insert -6 mm, as you want to place the copy on the left of the cover image:

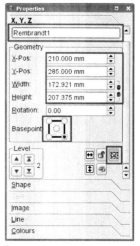

Here we changed the basepoint of the image frame and entered the correct values for its placement. We also protected it against a change of size.

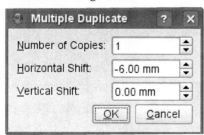

Since the new image frame is a copy of "Rembrandt1," there is no need to change its size, and the position has been determined by the copying action. Assign the name "Rembrandt2" to the frame, but there's another problem: The new image frame is placed on top of the frame for the cover picture. The solution is to move it behind the cover picture. So far, 3 items have been created, and each new object is placed on top of the others. Therefore, we simply move the copy one level down, ie. behind "Rembrandt1."

Now we have to become a little more serious and bring in content from outside of Scribus into our document. To load our cover picture into "Rembrandt1," right-click on the frame and click on "Get Image."

This will open a file dialog, but, as is usual with exhibitions, there are a huge number of images with similar names in one directory. How can we identify the correct file? Houston, we have a problem! Not. Fortunately, Scribus offers a preview in its file dialog for images:

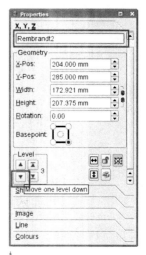

The levels of items on a page can be changed in the *X, Y, Z* tab of the Properties Palette.

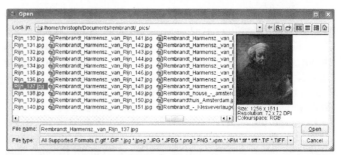

Now that we have identified the correct version of the file, click on the "Open" button or just double-click, but what's that?

It seems obvious that the size of the image and the size of the image frame are not identical twins, but fortunately, the Properties Palette will come to our rescue and force them to behave as if they were. In the *Image* tab check "Scale to Frame Size" and "Proportional" and our cover picture will be perfectly placed.

The next thing we need is a copy of the "Rembrandt1" content in "Rembrandt2." Right-click on "Rembrandt1" and click *Contents > Copy.* Then right-click on the visible stripe of "Rembrandt2" and click *Contents > Insert.* The result is everything but spectacular, so that you will need to apply some magic to "Rembrandt2." Once again, use the right mouse button to bring up the context menu, this time to bring up the "Image Effects" dialog.

In the "Image Effects" dialog, let's go all out and apply four different effects to the

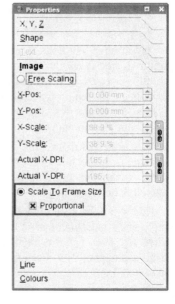

image: invert, blur (values are Radius: 7.0 and Value: 5.0), grayscale, and brightness (set to -43):

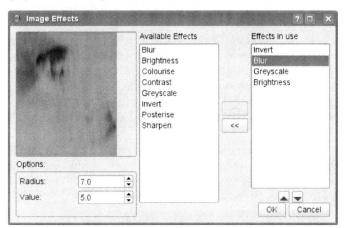

The context menu of an image frame with the option "Image Effects" selected.

Now, that looks a lot better, doesn't it?

Step Three: Adding Text

Next, let's tell our audience who the hero in the image is. For that purpose, create a text frame by clicking on the text frame icon in the toolbar or by pressing the T key – surely you're seeing this pattern now. You can create this frame by dragging, just as you did with the shape. It should be big enough to contain the text as shown below. Then double-click on the text frame and type REMBRANDT. Next, click somewhere else on screen and select the text frame again by clicking on it (single click).

Open the Properties Palette (F2) and click on the *Text* tab. In the font selector choose the "Gentium" font, set the font size to 97 pt and choose the text color "White" for Rembrandt's name. The result should look like this:

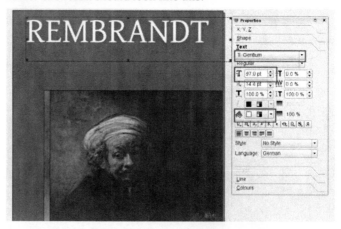

So far, our cover looks OK, but a bit boring. Time to add some tasteful features. Historical facts are on our side when we try to accomplish our task: Rembrandt was the man's (admittedly uncommon) first name, while his surname was "van Rijn." So create another text frame, double-click and type VAN RIJN. Choose the same font and the same font size as in the first text frame, but instead of "White" select "Pink2" as the text color. "What?" you say, "Pink? Rembrandt would shoot you on the spot!" Sure he would have, if he wouldn't have seen where we're going with this, but we're not finished yet. Switch to the Color tab and set "Shade" to 50% and "Opacity" to 20%. Better now? We told you so, and even Rembrandt is happy with the result – you can almost see him smile.

Finally, move the "Van Rijn" frame one level down, behind the "Rembrandt" frame:

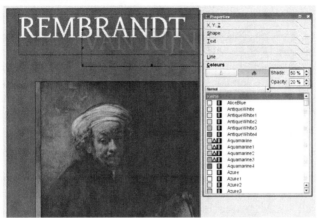

Now add 3 other text frames and insert the texts "1606," "2006" and "Painting the Dutch Golden Century." Use the Gentium font for all text frames. The numbers need a font size of 53 pt and the text one of 31 pt. Select the text colors "Bisque1" for "1606," "Chocolate2" for "2006" and "Gold" for "Painting ..." After what you've learned so far, this should already be easy. Here's a design tip: Notice how pleasing this looks, even though we are using different colors and sizes, when we use the same font for all these text elements.

In the *Line* tab of the Properties Palette you have all options for lines available, except for the line color, which is set in the *Color* tab.

To finish our title, draw a straight line by clicking on the line icon in the toolbar and dragging with the mouse. Draw your mouse from left to to right and press Ctrl while you drag to make sure the line is exactly horizontal. Then open the Properties Palette and switch to the *Line* tab. Set the line width to 0.5 pt, then open the *Colors* tab. Here you open the color list for lines (pen icon) and select "WhiteSmoke" from the list.

Finally, move our line halfway between the "1606" and the "2006" text.

Step Four: Adding the Publishing "Company"

The final steps include adding an imaginary publishing company and its logo. We'll decide in modesty to call the company "Scribus Publishing." That way, we need not rack our brains about a logo, but can simply use the Scribus logo. You'll find it in the folder ~/share/scribus/icons, where ~ is your Scribus installation directory. The filename is scribusicon.png.

Now create a small image frame at the bottom of our page, between the page border and the cover image(s). Make sure the fill color of the image frame is set to "None," because we are going to import an image with a transparent background. Then, as with our first image, we import the icon via right-click > *Get Image*. To prevent the icon's colors from interfering with the colors chosen for our layout, open the "Image Effects" dialog, as explained in step two. Setting the image to "Grayscale" and raising the contrast makes sure the logo won't "disappear," and at the same time it won't clash with the rest of our colors.

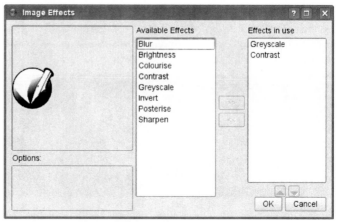

To add our company name, create a text frame somewhere, call it "ScribusPublishing" in the *X, Y, Z* tab of the Properties Palette and enter the text "Scribus Publishing." Choose "Bitstream Vera Sans" as the font, set the font size to 13 pt and the font color to "Grey97."

Finally, rotate the text frame 90 degrees. The *X, Y, Z* tab of the Properties Palette is the right place to do this. Just change the value for "Rotation" to 90.

Now use the mouse to move the rotated text frame to a position above the Scribus logo. Then click *File > Save*, enter "Rembrandt-tp" as the file name and click "OK." Voilà! You just successfully created your first document in Scribus. It wasn't that hard, was it?

[1] http://www.sil.org/~gaultney/Gentium

[2] http://mirror.cs.wisc.edu/pub/mirrors/ghost/GPL/current/⤸
ghostscript-fonts-std-8.11.tar.gz

[3] http://commons.wikimedia.org/wiki/⤸
Image:Rembrandt_Harmensz._van_Rijn_137.jpg

3 Scribus Basics

3.1 Basic Concepts

3.1.1 Metaphors in Desktop Publishing

MANY computer programs are digital versions of real world tools. For instance, a word processor is the digital metaphor of a typewriter, and a presentation program is the metaphor of the way transparent plastic slides used to be produced. Even if computer technology may offer more intelligent ways to solve problems, it makes sense for software manufacturers to use familiar terms and familiar-appearing screen features when they design user interfaces. A good example is the use of tabulators. The easiest way to create a table with a typewriter was the use of tabulator stops. Nowadays, each word processor can create tables, yet the tabulators are still there. In Desktop Publishing (DTP) software the metaphors are even more pervasive than in many other programs.

3.1.1.1 Page-Based Layout

The most obvious metaphor in a page layout program is the page itself. Since a text file generated by computers may not ever be printed, pages don't exist in text editors. In contrast, word processors generate files designed to be printed out, so virtual pages are created by the software and added automatically, which is more or less the same as inserting a new sheet in a typewriter. Conceptually, the number of pages expands (length, formatting) to fit the amount of text.

In a DTP program, each page exists individually, since layout designers are accustomed to working this way – it's the equivalent of a blank sheet on a table. One may certainly plan a design having multiple pages, but nonetheless the planning is considered page by page. Content has to be added and placed with a particular purpose in mind, therefore it generally won't work automatically, even if there are some repetitive or recurrent elements. Moreover, the digital metaphor of the table is the scratch space around a page, which means you can drag content off the page for later use, just as you could do with snippets on a paper sheet.

3.1.1.2 Frames

To place content on a page, DTP programs like Scribus use another digital version of a very old concept. In letterpress printing typesetters used a tool called composing stick to create a text by assembling movable type. The composing stick was a metallic frame, and therefore, content in a page layout program is inserted into frames. With software, frames can also contain images.

Compared to traditional page layout, the possibilities to work with frames in DTP software are quite sophisticated and allow for more creativity, as you will learn later on. Frames can be inserted, resized and moved around, and even the type of content can be changed. Here, the difference from a word processor or an image editing program becomes more obvious.

3.1.1.4 Levels and Layers

If you add images and text to a real sheet, you do it sequentially, and if you place an object on top of another, the objects have a stacking order. Levels and layers in Scribus are the metaphors of this stacking process in real world documents. Moreover, just as you can use a transparency film for some of these objects and cover the original sheet with the film, Scribus can use variably transparent objects in levels and layers. Something opaque on that film blocks the view underneath, and this happens also with Scribus.

In Desktop Publishing and drawing programs, levels and layers allow for this layering process, and with added flexibility.

Level means that each item that is added to a document is automatically placed at the top of the stacking order of all existing objects. Even when items do not overlap, each will have its own level. The stacking order is always a sequence, and the object, which has been created or imported lastly, is always on top of the other ones. One of the advantages of DTP software, compared to physical design, is that the order can be changed easily.

A layer in Scribus is an entire collection of objects on levels that can be moved as a unit above or below other layers. Although it might at first seem superfluous to have both processes, as one begins to divide a project into collections of objects or perhaps makes different versions of the same document, you'll realize you can have all of this in one single Scribus file, then for different versions have certain layers visible or invisible, print or not print, creating a whole family of PDFs. See the section Layers for more details.

3.1.2 Some Basic Concepts

In Scribus most operation modes are quite streamlined, ie. they can be applied to almost every item on a page, and sometimes even to a page itself. Below you get to know some of those basic concepts.

3.1.2.1 The Context Menu

If you have used OpenOffice.org/StarOffice or any other word processor, you probably already know how useful a right click with the mouse can be, as many sensible options related to certain types of content are easily available – without having to leave the canvas and using the menus instead. This kind of menu is called a context menu. In Scribus, the options of the context menu are more extensive than in many other programs.

3.1.2.2 The Properties Palette

The Properties Palette is a kind of "command center" in Scribus. It's a dialog, with which you can change almost every aspect of a selected item. You can open it via *Windows > Properties* or by pressing the F2 key. To work with Scribus, the use of the Properties Palette is essential. See Working with Frames and subsequent sections for a detailed description.

3.1.2.3 Styles

Styles are an incredible facility that can really speed up workflow – every Scribus user is advised to learn about them. Although word processors like Word or OpenOffice.org/StarOffice provide styles, they are rarely used by most users. A style is a set of properties that are given a name (that's why the term "Named Styles" is widely used), and can be applied to any appropriate object. In Scribus 1.3.3.x there are two or three styles, depending on your point of view: Paragraph styles and line styles are definitely styles in the aforementioned sense, but colors can also be regarded as styles, because when the properties of a color (values, color space) are changed in the colors dialog, they will change for all items which use that color. For more information about styles and colors, see Working with Styles and Colors and Gradients.

3.1.2.4 Configuration

DTP programs need to be highly configurable, and Scribus is arguably at least as configurable as any you'll see. This can be confusing and even a bit daunting for beginners, but advanced users do appreciate the opportunity to adjust the software to their various needs. Therefore, it's recommended that even beginners have a look at the chapter Customizing Scribus.

3.1.2.5 Shortcuts

Users of programs like Photoshop and programmers who use Emacs or vi(m) share one experience: Using the keyboard allows for more working speed than using the mouse – and it might even be better for your health. For this reason, most actions in Scribus can be attached to a keyboard shortcut. These shortcuts are freely configurable, so that you can adjust them to your needs. Be careful as you choose, though, to avoid clashes between the default shortcuts of your operating system or your desktop environment and your personal Scribus shortcuts. For more information, see Customizing Scribus and Keyboard and Mouse Shortcuts.

3.1.2.6 Open File Formats

Scribus is an Open Source program, which means the source code is open. In fact, it's not just the source code that's open, but also the file format. The file format of Scribus 1.3.3.x is based on XML, which means that SLA files can be opened in a text editor without any issues, and they can also be edited that way.

Apart from using an open file format internally, Scribus also relies on other publicly documented and open file types. Among them are HTML, SVG, OpenDocument, PostScript and PDF.

Scribus also supports some closed formats, like Microsoft Word or Adobe Photoshop's PSD, but support is limited to publicly available documentation.

While the support of these commonly used but non-public formats can be useful in certain circumstances, Scribus favors open and documented standards and also encourages their use whenever possible.

3.1.3 The Concept of Workflow

"Workflow," used in connection with a production/printing process, has a very special meaning. In many cases (and especially in corporate environments), people trust a word processor to create text and layout at the same time, and there has to be a high level of trust considering the limited flexibility you have with these programs. This approach by and large will result in poor quality and unprofessional design.

A well-designed workflow can help to prevent the usual corporate missteps. The fundamental rule is this: Use the right tool for the job. Word processing programs are great for editing text, doing spell-checking, and applying some basic formatting. This is fine for writing letters and other simple text documents, but let's be explicit and emphatic – word processors are not the appropriate tools to prepare something for serious, professional printing. The same goes for image editing software or vector drawing programs – both can do some limited layout work, but their purpose and point-of-view are different.

If you want to work seriously, you should use a layout program like Scribus to assemble the parts and pieces produced by specialized programs – and "assemble" is the key word here. A DTP program is the equivalent of a final assembly in an industrial process. All of the creative work done by others is going to be assembled in one piece here. The major and only difference from a factory, and really where much of the satisfaction comes from, is that the way the pieces get assembled allows for creativity and aesthetics.

That being said, the best workflow is to keep creative processes apart. Authors should write their text in a text editor or a word processor, photographers and image editors should finish their work before submitting it to a project, and the same goes for artists. Even if you are the author, the image editor, and the artist all rolled into one, you will do your best work by focusing on each ingredient of the layout as an individual piece. The final step will be the assembly of the different pieces of work in a DTP program like Scribus, where you can then produce a print-ready PDF or PostScript file.

3.2 Workflow and Scribus

AS ALREADY noted in the previous chapter, a good DTP workflow is one of the keys to your success. While this is true for many kinds of production environments, in DTP a well thought-out workflow is essential. Below you find some useful hints which may help you to organize your work and to prevent as many frictions and points of failure as possible.

3.2.1 Rule Number One: Communicate

Always keep in mind that successful layout and print is the result of communication and interaction between human beings. Computers can help with achieving a given task, but during the process from idea to print it's the people in front of the screens who count. Since hardly anyone involved has a detailed overview of all parts of the process, it's essential to communicate openly and probably often.

3.2.2 Keep Creative Processes Separated

Many people are used to editing documents (especially in collaborative office environments) in a quite chaotic way. While it looks easier in the beginning to let various people write copy, proofread, and format text, as well as inserting or moving images, this will almost certainly end up with an unprofessional layout.

In a well thought-out workflow, text editing, proofreading, image and vector drawing creation are kept separate from each other. It's up to the one who's doing the final layout (you) to assemble all the different pieces. Make sure you received final copies of all texts, images etc. If you're working commercially, let authors and other creatives sign a so-called imprimatur, a guarantee that the delivered version is final and approved for release.

The reason is simple: Once you've finished a document, even changing a few letters or the size of an image frame may change the whole layout, and in the worst case you would need to start from scratch. Requiring an imprimatur is not a sign of distrust, it's just an effective means to create trust and to impose discipline on all participants in a workflow.

3.2.3 Use Local Project Folders

While it's possible to edit Scribus files in shared network folders, it's better to work with local copies, since as we all know, networks can occasionally be undependable, and thus you guarantee access to a project file when the local network is down.

You should also create separate project directories that contain all the data (text files, images etc.) that you need. To improve your workflow even more, put those content files in subdirectories. Having all content available in one project directory with its subdirectories will make it easier to copy all content to another hard drive, a USB stick or a network. Since Scribus stores relative paths to external content, the latter will be found, even if the project directory has been moved somewhere else.

3.2.4 Don't Bite More Than Scribus Can Chew

If you're working on a huge project, it is recommended that you split up your project into smaller chunks. As a rule of thumb, a single file shouldn't exceed about 30 pages, especially if it contains much text or lots of high-resolution images, as this will result in slow performance in Scribus.

Once you've finished all files, you can adjust the page numbering as described in **Page Numbering**. The use of master pages (as described in **Master Pages**) will help you to keep a consistent layout throughout the final document.

3.2.5 Help Your Writers

If you don't give your writers a few guidelines, chances are good they will make your life harder, albeit with the best intentions. Most writers are working with a word processor, but this kind of of program is quite different from a text editor or a layout application. Here are some hints that will save you and your writers a lot of time:

- Do not use hyphenation in texts that will be imported into a layout program. Ever! Just like automatic line breaks, whether or not to hyphenate will be decided by Scribus, so this is quite unnecessary.

- Other word processing options like page breaks or automatic numbering should also be avoided. They may disappear during import or even create some ugly artefacts.

- Create a style guide for the authors. Explain what quotation marks will be used, how text is going to be emphasized etc.

- Explain the difference between a hyphen and en/em dashes, since the typographic uses are different, and need to be consistent.

• If your authors are using OpenOffice.org, StarOffice or any other ODF compliant word processor, you can create an example file with the paragraph styles that will be used in your Scribus document. They can then use them for their texts, and the styles will match those you are going to use in your Scribus document. If they use another word processor, you can either ask them to create a PDF with all the formatting information and then save as plain text (in this case you will have to re-create the formatting yourself). Or you can open their files in OpenOffice.org/StarOffice and save them as ODT from within Writer.

3.2.6 Use Appropriate Bitmap Formats

Many people think their neatly blinking GIF file or the web-optimized progressive JPEG (a JPEG version that partially displays as it is downloading in a web browser) they use for their website can also be used for professional printing. The opposite is true, and these files should be avoided at all costs in a print workflow. An exception to this occurs whenever you are creating a PDF for the web, where low resolution graphics are the norm.

If you're going to print commercially, you are well advised to use TIFF files whenever possible, as this format is well-tested in print workflows. Native Photoshop files or EPS files (more precisely: bitmap files contained in an EPS file) should also work without issues. It's also possible to use JPEG files in print workflows, but be aware that JPEGs become worse each time they're opened and re-saved by an image editor. It's better to convert an existing JPEG file, eg. from a digital camera, to TIFF before you consider editing it. You should also note that saving a low-resolution GIF or JPEG file as a TIFF with a higher resolution won't improve the quality at all. No matter how you slice it, the print result will look bad.

If you need to work with bitmap files that contain screenshots or line art, the PNG format is probably your best choice. Logos and other images with large single-colored areas can often be converted to vector files by using pstoedit or GSview (see the section GSview for more information). Their print quality will be dramatically enhanced if converted to vector files.

While this subsection hopefully made you aware of the risks and potential points of failure, there is also some good news. While other DTP programs may ask you to import images in the CMYK colorspace if the exported PDF or EPS file(s) are used for offset printing, Scribus will convert the colorspaces for you, depending on the output target you choose. See PDF Export for more information.

For more information about the image formats supported by Scribus, see Working with Images.

Importing Content into Scribus

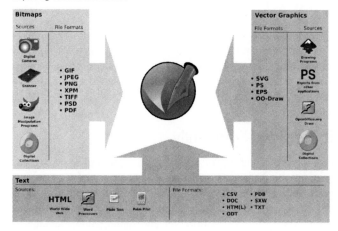

3.2.7 Don't Waste Resources

A properly organized workflow can save time and prevent headaches, and furthermore is easier on physical resources like disk and memory space, even energy usage.

While it's possible to mask or transform images in Scribus, it's better to use an image editing program for those tasks whenever possible. For instance, if you import an image into Scribus and then mask it, so that only a small part of it is visible, Scribus will nevertheless export the whole image into a PDF or EPS file. This means that a printer or a Raster Image Processor (RIP) will have to process the whole image, not just the visible part. While this may be acceptable if a document contains only one image, it's going to become a problem when there are many pictures at high resolution. Processing time is still a real issue in modern printing.

You can try this yourself by creating a document with only a few pages and some high-resolution images: Print this document to a PostScript file and start the clock ... You'll notice that the operation is not only taking a lot of time, but also that your computer will become very slow at times, because the operation requires a lot of CPU and memory capacity. This, in turn, means a lot of electrical power, which could have been saved by using the right tool for the job earlier in the process. Even if you don't think "green," you will appreciate the extra time gained for fine-tuning your document by reducing masked or hidden pixels to a minimum.

3.2.8 Ask Your Printer

As described in Preparing for Commercial Printing, talk to your printing company before you start your layout. Their demands may directly influence the way you need to handle a Scribus document from the beginning. See Rule Number One above – remember that your printer is part of the workflow team.

3.2.9 Save Frequently

In case you haven't noticed with other programs, saving your changes regularly can avoid data loss in case of a crash (yes, even Scribus may crash once in a while). In Opening, Creating and Saving a File you find all necessary information about the different AutoSave and emergency backups in Scribus.

3.2.10 Use Templates

If you are working on projects with a recurring design, like eg. newsletters, you should use templates. Create a sample file with all the necessary content like logos, fixed headlines (eg. imprint) and guides, then use *File > Save as Template*. This will help you to achieve a consistent layout in every issue.

3.2.11 Don't Ignore the Preflight Verifier

While there is an option in the *Document Setup* and the *Preferences* to ignore the warnings of the Preflight Verifier, you shouldn't enable it. The Preflight Verifier will detect errors you may easily overlook and will thus help you to prevent problems downstream. Some of these warnings are simply informational, yet still good as a reminder about your layout and content.

3.3 The Scribus Workspace

3.3.1 The Layout of the Workspace

THE SCRIBUS WORKSPACE basically consists of five elements, the menu bar, the toolbar, the canvas and the status bar. These elements are supplemented by dialogs that can appear and disappear on the canvas. The Properties Palette is the most important dialog in Scribus.

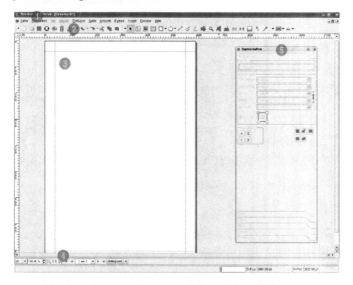

1. The menu bar, containing menus from *File* to *Help*.

   Note: A potential source of confusion exists in 1.3.3.x and earlier versions of Scribus. There is a menu item *Style*, which is simply an alternative way to individually apply some of the features described below. It can be easily confused with the concept of line and paragraph styles. For that reason we will ignore this menu in this manual.

2. The toolbar for important operations. It consists of four groups of buttons, from left to right: File Actions, Edit, Tools, PDF Forms.

3. The Scribus canvas consists of the document pages and the surrounding space, the scratch space. You can drag items with the mouse to the scratch space for later use. On the left and on top it shows rulers for precise measurement.

4. The status bar. As you would expect, it shows the coordinates of the mouse pointer, and it also has a progress bar for longer operations like opening large files. On the left, you can set the

unit for the rulers or choose another zoom level. You can also navigate in the document and between layers.

5. The Properties Palette. It can be opened/closed by pressing F2.

3.3.2 Rearranging the Icons

"Out of the Box," Scribus arranges its toolbar horizontally across the top of the screen. But you can change this at any time.

• New, Open, Save, Close, Print, Preflight Verifier, Export to PDF:

• Undo, Redo, Cut, Copy, Paste:

• Select, Insert Text Frame, Insert Image Frame, Insert Table, Insert Shape, Insert Polygon, Insert Line, Insert Bézier Curve, Insert Freehand Line; Rotate, Zoom, Edit Content, Story Editor, Link Text Frames, Unlink Text Frames, Measure, Copy Properties, Eyedropper:

• Insert PDF Fields, Insert PDF Annotations:

Each of these groups, including the basic seven, has a faint dotted mark to its left, indicating its beginning. You can click on any mark in any group and move it to any place on the canvas. If you click on the arrow beside the faint dotted mark, you can decide whether and where the button group will dock to and what the orientation of the group will be on canvas (horizontal or vertical).

If you dock it either on the left or right margin of the page, the group will appear vertically. If you move two groups and they don't quite line up together, you can right-click the group and select "Line Up."

Another convenient feature of Scribus is the scratch space, the ability to define big areas on all sides of the active page area which you can use as a playpen. If you move the toolbars to the left, right or bottom and you have substantial scratch space defined in those areas, the icons will be displaced from your working area; you may find this inconvenient.

3.4 The Help System

3.4.1 The Help Browser

IT'S NOT easy to use a versatile program such as Scribus without any guidance and tips. Scribus basically offers two different built-in kinds of assistance for its users. The first one is the Help Browser. You can open it via *Help > Scribus Manual* from the menu bar or by pressing the F1 key.

The Help Browser consists of two display fields. On the left, you can navigate through the tree structure of the documentation. On the right, you can read about the selected topic:

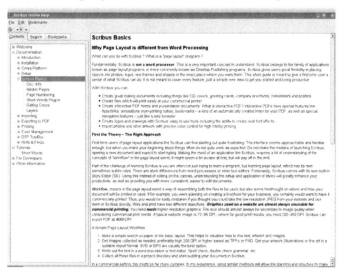

The Help Browser isn't just useful for reading the help files. You can also do a full text search in the available documentation if you click on of the "Search" tab on top of the tree view.

You can also use the menu bar or a keyboard shortcut for the same purpuse: Click *Edit > Find* or press Ctrl+F on the keyboard. To continue searching for the same word, use F3; to go back to a previous entry of a word, press Shift+F3. The only difference with this kind of search is that the Help Browser will bring up a separate dialog, where you can enter the word you want to search for:

Another helpful feature of the Help Browser is its ability to create bookmarks, which allows you to find important information more easily. It works exactly as in most web browsers: either you click *Bookmarks > Add Bookmark* in the menu bar or you press Ctrl+D on the keyboard or you click the "New" button at the bottom of the "Bookmarks" tab. This will bring up a dialog where you can enter a name for the new bookmark, as you can see on the left.

The bookmark will show up in the "Bookmarks" tab on top of the tree view.

To delete a single bookmark or all bookmarks, use *Bookmark > Delete or Bookmark > Delete All* in the menu bar or use the buttons at the bottom of the "Bookmarks" tab:

3.4.1 Tooltips

Another important help feature in Scribus are tooltips. If you want to benefit from them, make sure they are enabled. To check this, go to *Help > Tooltips* and see if the entry is marked by a checkbox.

Tooltips in Scribus are different from other programs in that they are often quite extensive. Many important details are presented to you when you hover your mouse pointer over buttons and fields in Scribus, as you can see on the image below.

3.5 Opening, Creating and Saving Documents

3.5.1 The Start Dialog

WHEN YOU start up Scribus, you will be shown a dialog with three tabs, "New Document," "Open Existing Document," "Open Recent Document."

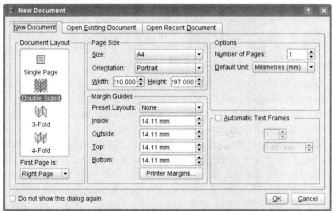

The first tab allows you to create a new document. The other two tabs make it possible to open a Scribus document which has been saved earlier. Once the startup dialog has been closed, it is possible to access "Open," "Save" and "New" actions using the file menu's and toolbar's entries. In addition, there are also template documents that can be opened using *File > New from Template*. It is also possible to save one's own documents as templates using *File > Save as Template*.

In *File > Preferences > Miscellaneous*, you can choose to not automatically be shown this startup dialog.

3.5.2 Supported File Formats

For opening and saving, the only file format fully supported by Scribus is its own SLA (Scribus Layout) format. It's the only format with which everything is guaranteed to be placed exactly where it was originally placed. However, the *File > Open* dialog has options to open a few other vector based formats. Importing and exporting other formats than SLA (and its older incarnation called SCD [Scribus Document]) will be explained later on.

3.5.2.1 SLA Files

An SLA file is a regular text file having a style similar to XML. To save space, the SLA file can be compressed with gzip, resulting in the file extension SLA.GZ. Scribus will automatically uncompress these gzipped SLA files, but it's also possible to unzip the file with a program like WinZIP or Ark.

Backward Compatibilty:
You will always be able to load SLA files from an older version of Scribus. For example, 1.3.3.x versions can load files generated by 1.2.x, 1.1.x, and even older Scribus versions. What you cannot do, in contrast, is load a 1.3.3.x file in Scribus 1.2.x.

Scribus is a rapidly evolving program, with each version providing more features. This has required several changes to the SLA format, the result being that older Scribus versions cannot open SLA files from newer ones. However, it is part of the development process to ensure that newer versions can always load SLA files from older versions.

This is especially important to understand if you are one of the many Scribus users who wants to work or experiment with development versions, obtained via Subversion and then compiled on your computer. As of this writing, 1.3.3.x is considered the current stable version, or more precisely, version series. Bugfixes and other minor enhancements are taking place in this series. SLA files can be freely exchanged back and forth between all 1.3 versions up to 1.3.3.x. If you wish to experiment with later development versions (1.3.4 or later), perhaps help with finding bugs and other problems, be sure to make a copy of an old SLA file to experiment with, since 1.3.4+ will make the file unusable for 1.3.3.x and earlier versions. Also, you may want to turn off Autosave to avoid losing old work.

In case you mistakenly saved a file in the 1.3.4+ format, you can use a trick to get the content back to 1.3.3.x: Group all items on each page and send the groups to the Scrapbook, then open 1.3.3.x and create a new document in 1.3.3.x. Currently, 1.3.3.x and 1.3.4+ share the same Scrapbook, so that you can drag the items back into the 1.3.3.x document.

3.5.2.2 Vector Formats

The dialog *File > Open* in Scribus also provides an option to open several vector based formats. Supported formats include SVG, PostScript, EPS, OpenDocument Graphics (ODG) and OpenOffice.org Draw files (SXD). Opening files of these types has some limitations (See Importing Vector Drawings). It's also good to note that Scribus cannot open and edit PDF files, but it can use them with some limitations.

3.5.2.3 The File Dialog in Scribus

At the first launch, Open and Save dialogs will default to the document directory set in *File > Preferences > General*. Successive open and save actions will open the file dialog in the directory that was last used for the action. The save dialog will have an additional option to compress a SLA file. If this option is enabled, the file will be saved with the extension .SLA.GZ.

3.5.2.4 The Open File Dialog – Advanced Features

The Dialog *File > Open* is more than just a tool to open files. Instead, it offers some advanced features.

In the field labeled "Look in:" you can see the path to your current directory. All folders and all files Scribus can open are listed here. It's possible to narrow down the number of listed files by selecting a single file type in the dropdown list at the bottom.

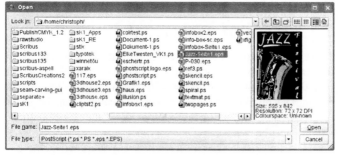

On top right you see 6 buttons with the following functions:

- *Back* will move to the previous directory. It's only available if you navigated in the file system before.
- *One directory up* will move to the parent directory of your current folder.
- *Create New Folder* will create a new directory in the current folder.
- *List View* lists all folders and files that Scribus can open without further information.
- *Detail View* changes the display, as all files will be listed in one column. In addition, more informations about files and folders, namely size (in kilobyte), type (file or folder), date (date of file creation) and attributes (permissions like read or write).
- *Preview File Contents* enables the display of file informations or previews for some, but not all supported file types. The preview capabilities work as follows:

- *SLA, SCD*: No visual preview. The document title and the author are listed if they are stored in *File > Document Setup > Document information*. The Scribus version that created the document will also be shown.

- *SLA.GZ, SCD.GZ*: No preview and no document informations will be shown.

- *OpenDocument Drawing, OpenOffice.org Drawing, SVG, PostScript*: No preview and no document informations will be shown.

- *EPS*: A preview will be displayed if the EPS contains a preview image. Scribus also shows the size, the resolution of the preview image and the color space of the preview image.

- *PDF*: A preview will be displayed. Scribus also shows the size, the resolution and the color space of the file.

- *Move to the Document Directory* moves to the default directory for your documents. On Linux and UNIX systems this is the home directory, on Windows your "Personal Files" folder. The default directory for Scribus documents can be changed in the Preferences.

3.5.3 Opening a Document

There are three options for opening a Scribus document. If the document has been worked on recently, it is likely that you will find an entry for it in the *File* menu's *Open Recent* submenu. The number of recent documents shown can be set in the "General" tab in *File > Preferences*. If the document cannot be opened with the *Open Recent* menu, it's possible to open it using *File > Open*. This will bring up a regular file dialog, so that you can browse for your Scribus document and open it by selecting and clicking on the "Open" button. The last option for opening a Scribus file is to have the SLA file format associated with Scribus, so that double clicking on an SLA document will start up Scribus and open the document. It may be the case that your operating system does not allow gzipped SLA files to be handled by Scribus. In this case you will need to open SLA.GZ files using *File > Open* in Scribus.

The open action inside Scribus can be triggered using three different methods:

- using *File > Open*.
- using the "Open" icon in the Icon Bar.
- using the keyboard shortcut CTRL+O.

3.5.3.1 Revert to Saved

Revert to Saved is a special case of opening a document. The *Revert to Saved* action can be found in the *File* menu. The function makes it possible to reload the last saved version of the currently opened document. This can be a good work-around when Scribus' still limited undo and redo functionality has failed to recover an error that has been made. To get the most out of this feature, you will need to save your document in relatively short intervals. All your changes done after the last save action will be lost when running *Revert to Saved*. As might be expected, if you have made no edits since the last saving, this option will be nonfunctional.

3.5.4 Creating a New Document

Creating a new document in Scribus can be accomplished either by beginning with a blank page, or with a template. A few templates are included with your Scribus distribution, but you can also create your own.

Clicking on *File > New from Template* (keyboard Ctrl+Alt+ N) will show a dialog with some choices of layouts: a brochure, two newsletters, and a presentation. See below for details about templates.

You can always begin a new document using whatever the default settings are, but for many tasks it will be better if you think through the requirements of your layout job before beginning your document. While it is possible to change the document details afterwards, you will find it easier and less frustrating if you already have made some of the choices for your document, such as page size, layout and margin widths.

If you find yourself using a particular document size, layout style, or certain font most commonly, make these your default settings. See *Customizing Scribus* for more information. If you make similar documents with only some small variations in layouts, consider creating templates you can reuse and modify for future documents – this will be covered later in this section.

3.5.4.1 New Document Dialog

The *New Document* dialog is of course what you see when you first start Scribus, along with tabs to choose existing documents. The default values you see in the dialog can be set in *File > Preferences*.

This dialog can also be brought up later by clicking *File > New*, the "New" icon on the toolbar, or keyboard Ctrl+N.

"Document Layout" controls the page setup inside Scribus. The first option "Single Page" will create pages in a single column, one page per row. The "Double Sided" option will create a regular magazine type layout where pages are set in pairs (two pages per row). With the second, third and fourth option it is also possible to control the first page dropdown box where one can tell Scribus the position of the first created page. For a regular left-to-right magazine the first page would be a right one.

Keep in mind that with "Double Sided", "3-Fold", and "4-Fold", you are still creating individual pages, printed or exported to PDF as individual pages. These multiple-page selections only apply to the layout appearance in Scribus, so you can see the juxtaposition you desire for whatever reason. A commercial printer, of course, will be able to take those individual pages and arrange them in the end format you desire. In contrast, if you want to create a 3-fold brochure that you plan to print yourself – ie. a brochure printed on a single sheet of stock and then folded – you should create a single page landscape document of the appropriate size, then use guides to indicate the folding points. How guides are used is explained in **Grids and Guides**.

Inside the "Page Size" frame are general options for the page size. Scribus includes a wide range of preset paper formats that can be selected from the "Size" dropdown list. If no suitable format is available, there is also an option to create a custom page size by inserting custom values for width and height in the spin boxes below the dropdown lists.

Once you are done with the page size, set margins with the spin boxes in "Margin Guides." Scribus can also query your printer driver for a possibility to automatically adjust the margin settings and offer you to change them with the "Printer Margins ..." button. If you have selected any other page layout than "Single Page" the margin selection will be: "Inside," "Outside," "Top," "Bottom" instead of "Left," "Right," "Top," "Bottom." If you conceive of a book as your final product, inside will be the side closest to the binding, outside the farthest away. There are a few preset margin schemes to be used with the double-sided, 3-fold and 4-fold layout options. These presets are controlled by selecting the desired scheme from the "Preset Layout" dropdown list and by altering the width of the inside margin. Scribus will then automatically calculate the other margins based on the inside margin's value and the selected margin scheme.

"Options" include the number of pages which are initially created (1–10,000) and the default measuring unit for the document. You will not need to know the actual number of pages in the final document yet, because pages can be easily added to a document using the *Page* menu after the document has been created.

The last section, "Automatic Text Frames," can be used to create a text frame, bounded by the margins, for every page of the document. These automatic text frames will also be linked, so that the text will flow from one frame to another. This option also enables selection of the number of columns (1– 99) and the gap between them. Also note that if you later insert additional pages, these too will have frames automatically created and linked.

Once you are happy with the values, click the "OK" button. Scribus will create your document, and you may begin to add content. There are some additional document options not covered by the "New Document" dialog, which can be set in *File > Document Setup*. This is covered in Customizing Scribus.

3.5.4.2 New From Template

Whenever you will be serially creating documents with a number of recurrent, similar or identical features, such as graphics, headers, titles, and even content, document templates can greatly ease the layout work. In addition to actual content, a template can also include paragraph and line styles and a custom color set.

The *New from Template* dialog can be opened by using the *New from Template* menu entry in the *File* menu. This will open up a dialog with three sections:

The left-most section lists the template categories. Scribus includes a basic set of categories that can be localized. It's also possible to create your own categories with the *Save as Template* option as described later on. The middle column shows thumbnails of the templates that belong to the selected category, and the right-most column has details about the currently selected template. Instead of details it is also possible to show a larger screenshot of the template by clicking on the image button above the details. To open a template, double-click on the thumbnail or select a template and click "OK." It is also possible to remove templates from the template dialog by using the template's context menu's "Remove" entry.

There are only a few default templates, and these are admittedly of limited scope, but are mainly included as illustrations of how they might be used. As you will see further in this chapter, creating and editing your own is quite easy, since it only involves creating your own layout, then saving as a template.

3.5.5. Saving a Document

The second section in the *File* menu is reserved for save actions which include *Save, Save as, Save as Template* and *Collect for Output*. In addition to the *File* menu's save actions there are two additional save actions more hidden from the user. These are "Autosave" to automatically save your document at a given interval and "Emergency Save" which is trying to save your document in a case of sudden crash. If you have done some changes to your document and have not saved it yet but are closing the document or Scribus you will be shown a pop up dialog asking if you would like to save the document before it's going to be closed.

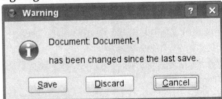

3.5.5.1 Save and Save As ...

Save actions will save all unsaved changes that have been done since it was opened or saved the last time. If the document has not been saved when the save action was triggered, the *Save as ...* action will be run instead. The *Save as ...* action will bring up a file dialog, letting you choose a directory and a filename for the currently opened document. These actions always save the currently shown document. If there are many documents open at the same time, you will be prompted to save any unsaved documents.

Note that in 1.3.3.x versions of Scribus a bug that managed to remain undiscovered for quite some time occasionally causes the program to indicate changes to a file when in reality there had been none. If you are sure you didn't change anything, you can ignore the warning displayed by Scribus when you close a document. Of course you can also save the file again, as this won't harm your work. If you think you may incidentially save some changes you don't want to save, you should use "Revert to Saved" as described above.

The save actions will save the file in the native Scribus SLA file format. If you want to save your document in some other file format like PDF or EPS, see the chapter File Export. One thing to note with the SLA file format is that it does not save the images inside the file, but only links to the used images. The links will point to the original place from where they were imported to Scribus. Vector graphics, however, will be converted to Scribus' internal vector format and those are a part of the SLA file.

As of Scribus versions 1.3.3.x, the paths to images are relative ones, from the location of the Scribus file itself. The downside of this is that, if you move this file to another location – for example using your computer's copy utility, the file will likely not be able to load your images, since the links will be broken. One way of preventing this problem is by keeping a file and its images in its own separate directory. Another is by using *File > Collect for Output* as we will see next.

3.5.5.2 Collect for Output

To avoid the problem of broken image links, it's possible to use *Collect for Output* from the *File* menu. This will be necessary if you want to share your work with someone else and need to send it to another Scribus installation along with its images. This will copy all the images and the Scribus document to a single directory. It's important to understand that with *Collect for Output* you are not just creating a file, but a directory with a collection of files inside. Once you name the directory and click "OK," the default action is to create the directory if it does not already exist, then save the Scribus file and its images inside. If you later load new images into the document, you will need to repeat Collect for Output.

The dialog for picking a directory includes two additional options compared to a regular file dialog. It is possible to compress the collected Scribus document and to include used fonts in the output directory. If you are unsure whether another Scribus installation using your saved directory will have all the necessary fonts, check the "Include Fonts" option. Beware of possible licensing issues with fonts if you decide to include them, though.

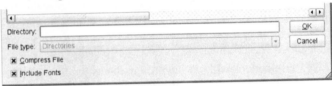

3.5.5.3 Save as Template

The *Save as Template* action in the *File* menu is similar to *Collect for Output*. The first step, like *Collect for Output*, is to choose a directory where the template and additional files will be collected. Next you will be shown a new dialog where some metadata can be inserted. You will get the metadata dialog in its full size by clicking the "More Details" button. Once you are done with the metadata, clicking "OK" will finalize the saving of the template. From now on, your template will be shown in the *New from Template* dialog that can be opened from the *File* menu. Note that while it's possible to save disk space by saving the template as a compressed SLA.GZ file, it will also copy all image files used in a document to the template folder. Depending on the size of the original images, this means they might very well occupy a lot of storage space on your hard drive, as Scribus doesn't compress them. Scribus will also generate two preview images in PNG format, but those are very small and shouldn't be any cause for concern.

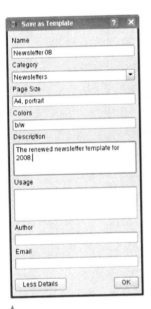

The *Save as Template* dialog with the elected option "More Details".

Templates can contain anything that can be stored in a normal Scribus file, including document settings, styles, colors, layers etc. There is no inherent limitation to the number of pages in a template, but generally it is best to limit to the smallest number of pages that can describe all expected unique variations.

By default, the *Save as Template* dialog will open your template directory, which is set in the *Preferences*. If you have not

set any template directory, the default is the "template" directory in your personal ~/.scribus folder. Before saving a document as a template, it should, in any case, be saved as a new
document, and it can remain there without being added to the
templates gallery.

3.5.5.4 Autosave

Scribus can save your document automatically at a given interval, with a default of every 10 minutes. The "Autosave" option
and its interval can be set in *File > Preferences > Document*
for future documents, and for the current document in *File >
Document Setup > Document*.

Autosave saves your document regularly and creates a copy
of the previous version adding the extension ".bak." If you
need to recover a previous version, you will need to rename it
with an SLA extension, so that it will be recognized by Scribus.

3.5.5.5 Emergency Save

In case of an emergency – eg. Scribus crashing for any reason
or being closed by the operating system – Scribus will try to
save the document. The emergency save will use the same directory where the document was originally stored or, if it hadn't
been saved yet, the emergency save will be done to the current
working directory. The file saved in case of emergency is easy
to recognize, because its file extension is sla.emergency.
Just as with backup files, it will need to be renamed to end
with ".sla" to be recognized by Scribus, yet even then there is
no guarantee that this file can be opened. In such a case you
will have to reload the last saved version.

3.6 There's More Than One Way to Look at a Document

3.6.1 Document Windows

Cascading Windows

IF YOU have opened more than one document, you can switch between them by using the *Windows* menu. All open documents are listed at the end of the menu. This method isn't that useful if you want to switch faster between open files. In this case, you can either tile or cascade the document windows via *Windows > Cascade* or *Windows > Tile*.

As you will learn by reading this manual, Scribus is highly configurable, and this is also true for viewing options. The most relevant tab in the *Preferences* and *Document Setup* is "Display." Some of the options you find here are also accessible from a menu and will be explained below. Here, we want to focus on the options related to the canvas. These options are placed in the lower part of the dialog.

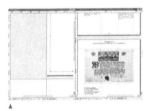

Tiled Windows

In the *Preferences* and the *Document Setup* you can set the minimum scratch space, which means the space between the borders of the Canvas and a page at a zoom level of 100%.

"Gap between Pages" is the displayed distance between single pages in a document. Note that this will only change the display of the document in Scribus; it has no influence whatsoever on the display of exported PDF files in a PDF reader.

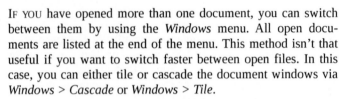

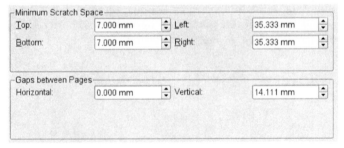

In the *Preferences* you can also adjust the display size, ie. put a ruler on the screen and adjust to match. The new size will be the zoom level 100% in new documents. This only works for new files, not for the current one.

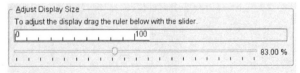

3.6.2 Page and Document Options

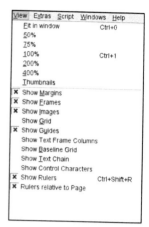

Most options in the *View* menu are related to the display of pages or documents. *Fit in Window* (Ctrl+0) reduces the zoom level, so that each page can be fully displayed. The following list of zoom levels is self-explaining, and *Thumbnails* sets the zoom level to 20%.

The next section of the menu contains options to switch on or off certain elements of a document or the canvas. In the image on the right you see Scribus's default settings:

- *Show Margins*: By default, Scribus will indicate the page margins with blue lines. If you don't want to see the lines to get a general impression of a whole page, you can switch the display of margins off and on here.

- *Show Frames*: Just like with margins you can switch off the black dotted lines that indicate frame shapes to get a better impression of the final page. Note that selected items will nevertheless be indicated by red dotted lines and handles.

The display option *Show Margins*.

The display option *Show* Frames.

- *Show Images*: See below.

- *Show Grid*: Scribus provides two grids that can help you placing items with precision. You can switch those grids on and off here. For more information about grids, see Grids and Guides.

- *Show Guides*: Guides are lines that can help you placing items with precision. By default, guides are visible. For more information about guides, see Grids and Guides. The picture on the right shows a page with grids and guides visible.

A page with visible grids and guides.

The color of margins, guides and grids, as well as the values for the grids can be configured in the "Guides" tab of *Docu-*

ment Setup for the current document and in the *Preferences* for all future documents:

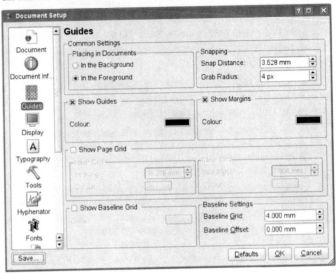

Further document related options can be found in the *Document Setup/Preferences* in the "Display" tab:

- Clicking on the button with the caption "Color" brings up a color selector. For instance, you can choose a page color which emulates a paper color other than white.

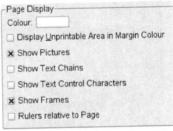

- "Display Unprintable Area in Margin Color": To better distinguish the margins from the print space, you can visualize them by checking this option in the "Display" tab, as you can see in the image on the left.

3.6.3 Text Options

Some viewing options in the *View* menu relate only to text frames.

- *Show Text Frame Columns*: If you are using columns, you can make the inner column borders visible here.

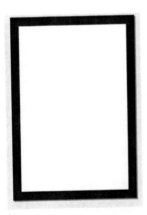

A page with a white print space and margin space in a dark color.

- *Show Baseline Grid*: The baseline grid is a special grid that is used to determine the line spacing (for more information about the baseline grid, see Working with Text). You can make it visible here. By default it is not displayed.
- *Show Text Chain*: If text frames are linked, the link can be indicated by arrows that also show the direction of the text flow (for more information about the linking of text frames, see Working with Text). You can make them visible here. By default they aren't displayed.
- If you want to see the control characters (special symbols for empty spaces, line breaks etc.) in text frames, you have to use *View > Show Control Characters*:

A page with the baseline grid set to visible.

1am,∘arcu∘risus∘dapibus∘diam,∘nec∘sollicitu
∂an∘massa∘nulla,∘volutpat∘eu,∘accumsan∘et,
∂rat∘porta∘justo.∘Nulla∘vitae∘turpis.∘Praesen
r∘sit∘amet,∘consectetuer∘adipiscing∘elit.∘Ut∘
s∘molestie∘dolor.∘Integer∘quis∘eros∘ut∘erat∘
issim.∘Integer∘orci.∘Fusce∘vulputate∘lacus∘
o∘nec∘mi∘laoreet∘volutpat.∘Aliquam∘eros∘p∂
que∘cursus,∘placerat∘convallis,∘velit.∘Nam∘

3.6.4 Document Preview

To hide all guides, grids, frame markers and so on in one go, you can press F11 on the keyboard.

3.6.5 Image Options

Scribus provides some useful viewing options for images, most of which are related to performance.

If you want to focus on working with text or vector graphics, you can switch the display of images on or off altogether by using *View > Show Images*. To switch the display for a single image on or off, use *Image Visible* in the context menu.

You can also change the display resolution of images. By default, Scribus uses a reduced resolution for performance reasons, which is called "Normal Resolution." You can change this in the context menu under *Preview Settings*. Your further options are the full resolution and a very low resolution. The default behavior can be changed in *File > Document Setup > Tools > Image Frames* for the current document and in the respective tab in *File > Preferences Tools > Image Frames* for future documents.

If you edited the image in an external image editing program, you have to use *Update Image* in the context menu to see the changes made to the image. If you open a Scribus file, all images will be updated automatically.

3.6.6 Zooming

Beside the list box for the measuring units of the rulers you find several functions to change the display size of the document. In the spin box you can enter a zoom level. If you click on the magnifier buttons, the zoom level shown in the spin box will be either doubled or halved by default. You can change this behavior in *Preferences/Document Setup* in the "Tools" tab by clicking on the magnifier icon and by changing the value for "Stepping" (see Customizing Scribus).

By clicking on the button with the caption "1:1", the zoom level is reset to 100%.

Another versatile tool is the direct zoom tool in the icon bar. You can activate it by clicking on the magnifier icon or by pressing Z on the keyboard. The mouse pointer will then turn into a magnifier. Clicking with the left mouse button on the canvas will magnify the area you clicked on, right-clicking does the opposite. It's also possible to magnify a certain area, like a word or an image, precisely by drawing a "rubberband" rectangle around it while in zoom mode. Scribus will then make the selected part of the page fit the screen. Again, using the right mouse key does the opposite. Clicking on the magnifier icon a second time or on any other icon will deactivate direct zoom.

If you are using a wheel mouse, you can zoom in and out of the canvas by pressing Ctrl and scrolling the wheel.

3.7 Navigating in a Document

SCRIBUS files can contain many pages, which in turn may contain many objects. Scribus provides some powerful tools to navigate in complex documents.

3.7.1 The Page List

The easiest way to access a particular page is to use the page list in the status bar. If you click on the arrow, you will be presented a list of all pages in a document. To jump to a page, simply select its number in the list.

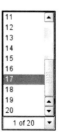
The page list

You can jump page-by-page, to the first page, or to the last page by clicking the arrows to each side of the page list. As you can see yourself, the PgUp and PgDn keys only move by part of a page.

3.7.2 The "Arrange Pages" Dialog

Another way to access a page is to open the dialog *Windows > Arrange Pages*. In the field titled "Document Pages" you can see all pages in the document, represented by a symbol and the page number. Note that the page numbers displayed in this dialog are the ones you assigned to them in the *Document Setup*, for instance, if you used I, II, III, –, 1, 2, 3 as a numbering scheme, you will see I, II, III, 1, 1, 2, 3 in the field.

The dialog *Arrange Pages*

If you click on one of the page symbols, Scribus will select the respective page and display it on screen. For more information about this dialog, see **Managing and Laying Out Pages**.

3.7.3 The Document Outline

If you want to access single items quickly without scrolling and selecting, you can use the document outline (*Windows > Outline*). The dialog offers a hierarchical tree view of the document and its items. It starts with the file name, then master pages are listed, followed by normal pages and their content. The items on each page are listed in their stacking order (their levels). If you click on a page, Scribus will select the page and display it. If you click on a master page, Scribus switches into the editing mode for master pages and displays the selected page. If you click on an item on a page, Scribus will jump to the page, select the item and display it. To ease navigation, it might be appropriate to attach specific names to items in the *X, Y, Z* tab of the Properties Palette.

The document outline

3.7.4 Bookmarks

Sometimes it makes sense to navigate between particular objects in a document, for instance between two remote text frames that require heavy editing. In such a case, it's advisable to employ bookmarks. Note that only text frames can be used as bookmarks.

To create a bookmark, select a text frame, and bring up the context menu with a right click. Then choose *PDF Options > Is PDF Bookmark*:

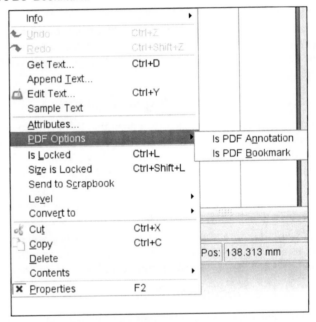

The text frame is now "bookmarked." If you open the bookmarks dialog (*Windows > Bookmarks*), you'll see that the first words in the text frames are used to identify the content. Clicking on a bookmark lets Scribus select the respective text frame and display it. Note that bookmarks are listed in the order they were created rather than the order they are in the document. If you need to change the order, you can move the entries in the "Bookmarks" dialog with the mouse. You can also create different sublevels of bookmarks. Just drag the bookmark you want to be at a lower level than another by dragging it with the mouse on the entry for the higher level and then choose "Insert Bookmark" from the pop-up dialog.

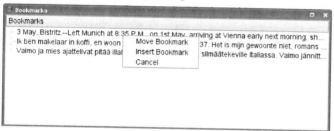

Scribus bookmarks will also be exported to a PDF file. In Adobe Reader you have the option to use PDF bookmarks (*View > Navigation Tabs > Bookmarks*) for navigation purposes as you can see in the screenshot on the right.

If you don't want to export your Scribus bookmarks to the PDF file, use the context menu to uncheck the label "Is PDF Bookmark."

PDF bookmarks in
Adobe Reader 7

3.8 Managing and Laying Out Pages

DESKTOP PUBLISHING is all about creating and laying out pages, which means you need to have full control over the pages in a document. This comes at a price users have to pay when they need more pages than expected. In contrast to word processors, a DTP program won't add pages automatically. You have to do this yourself. The same goes for unneeded pages: they won't just disappear automagically – it's up to you to delete them. On the other hand, this means you have the desired control over your document. Scribus offers all the required tools to manage and to lay out pages.

3.8.1 Adding and Deleting Pages

To insert a new page, use *Page > Insert ...* In the dialog you can insert the number of new pages, as well as their position: at the end of the document or before or after a particular page.

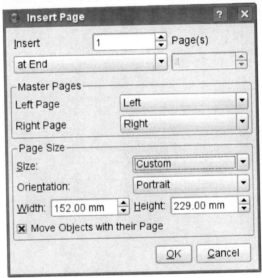

You can also select master pages for the new pages, as well as determine their size and orientation. The option "Move Objects with their Page" makes sure that all objects stay on a page when it changes its position in a document. This may not always be what you want, for instance if you just wish to insert a page between existing ones, but keep the content at the same position.

Pages can also be imported from other Scribus files by using *Page > Import* ... First you have to choose the SLA or SLA.GZ file that contains the page(s) you want to import. By clicking "Change" you will open a file dialog to select the file. Next you have to specify the page(s) you want to import. You can use a range of pages (eg. 1–3), single pages (eg. 2, 5) or mix both modes (eg. 1, 3–6). Finally you have to decide whether you want the imported files to replace existing ones or to be added as new pages. In the first case you have to uncheck "Create Pages(s)". In the second case you have to specify where the pages will be placed, just like in the *Insert* dialog:

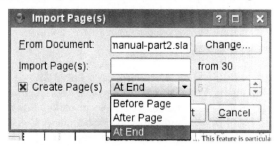

Another possibility to create new pages is to copy existing pages by using *Page > Copy* ... This feature is particularly useful if you need to use similar items on many pages, while being able to edit them. Remember, objects on master pages can't be edited from a normal page. By copying existing pages you can work around this issue.

Copying a page in Scribus

It's also possible to move an existing page to another position. Use *Page > Move* ... The dialog is almost identical to the *Copy* dialog:

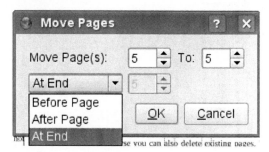

Of course you can also delete existing pages. Use *Page > Delete* ... for that purpose. The dialog expects you to specify a range of pages. If you want to delete a single page, you have to insert the same number in both spin boxes.

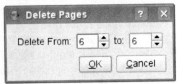

Some of the operations described above can also be executed in *Windows > Arrange Pages*. For instance, you can easily move a particular page to another position by dragging it with the mouse. You can also delete a page by dragging its symbol to the trash bin icon.

3.8.2 Laying Out Pages

Any page basically consists of two parts, the print space and the page margins. The relationship between these two parts is one of the first design choices you have to make. Other basic decisions are page size and the type of document, for instance the choice between a single-page or a double-sided document.

In general, you made your choice when you created a new document, as described in the section Opening, Creating and Saving Files. But what if you change your mind or a single page needs a different layout?

In case you want to change the basic layout of the whole document, you have to use *File > Document Setup*. In the "Document" tab you can change the layout as explained in the section about creating and saving files:

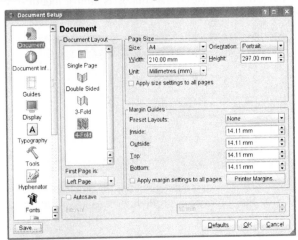

To change the layout of a single page, go to *Page > Manage Page Properties ...* or by using the context menu for pages (right-click on an empty part of the page), which will present you the same options as the *Document Setup*, except that they will apply only to the selected page:

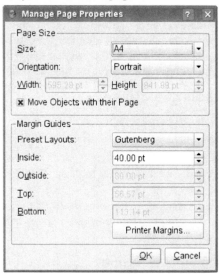

The *Arrange Pages* dialog presents some layout options as well. If you look at the image below you'll notice that the display of pages in the field in the middle depends on the type of document. You can change this document type in the drop-down list "Document Layout." You can also decide, which page type (left, right, middle) will be the first page. Finally, you can also apply master pages, as described later on in the section **Master Pages.**

3.9 Working with Frames

MOST of the items used in a document use one kind of frame or another. These include text frames, image frames, shapes, and polygons

In many cases, these will be used in a straightforward manner, yet depending on a special desired effect, there may be a need to convert from one type to another. These advanced features will be discussed later. In this section, we will cover the ways of manipulating frames that these have in common.

3.9.1 Creating a Frame

There are 3 ways to create a frame:

- Selecting from the menu: *Insert > (type of frame)*.
- Clicking on a toolbar icon.
- Keyboard shortcuts: T for Text, I for Image, S for Shape, P for Polygon.

Any one of these activates your mouse, so that pressing down the left button begins the frame at one corner, letting up determines its opposite corner.

3.9.2 Selecting a Frame

In order to work with frames they must be selected. When a frame is created, it is automatically selected, which is signified by having a dotted red outline, plus small red squares at the corners and at the midpoint of each side, used for resizing the frame. To unselect a frame, click anywhere outside it. To select again, click anywhere inside it. If you should have a situation in which you wish to select a frame which is completely underneath another frame, one way to select would be to lower the level of the overlying frame – see the context menus below or the *X, Y, Z* tab in the Properties Palette. Alternatively, hold down Shift+Ctrl and you can toggle between the frames with subsequent clicks.

3.9.3 Context Menu

Clicking with the left mouse button simply selects an object, but with the right button there also appears the context menu, which allows the selection of many common operations particular to that frame type. These operations are covered in the individual chapters on each kind of frame.

3.9.4 Deleting a Frame

You can delete a selected frame by pressing the Del key, selecting "Delete" from the context menu, or Ctrl+X. None of these will ask for confirmation, and the frame and its contents will simply disappear, but it is recoverable with undo. If you use Ctrl+X, Ctrl+V will recover the frame and contents in the same position it had occupied.

3.9.5 Cut, Copy and Paste

As just mentioned, cutting (Ctrl+X, *Edit > Cut*, or from the context menu) deletes a frame but copies it and its contents to the clipboard. Copying (Ctrl+C, *Edit > Copy*, or from the context menu) saves to the clipboard without deleting. Paste (Ctrl+V, *Edit > Paste*, or from the context menu) retrieves from the clipboard to the same coordinates as the original, but importantly, to whatever page is currently selected.

3.9.6 Duplicate, Multiple Duplicate

This sounds like a combination of copy and paste, and in a sense it is, since the frame is also copied to a buffer. Duplicate (*Item > Duplicate*, or Ctrl+Shift+Alt+D) copies and then immediately pastes with a default offset of +10 points in each of the X and Y coordinates – if the document's units are something other than points, the distance will still be equivalent to 10 points.

Multiple duplicate (*Item > Multiple Duplicate*) creates one or more copies, and allows the offset to be adjusted. In addition, once the offset has been changed, duplicate will use the new offset throughout the current session of Scribus. Since the frame is copied to the clipboard, the duplicated frame will be used for paste as well. See Multiple Duplicate for further information.

3.9.7 Resizing, Repositioning Frames

The quickest way to resize and reposition your frame is with the mouse: click and drag inside the frame to reposition. Resizing is done by clicking on the red rectangular control points at the corners and sides, then stretching or shrinking as desired. For greater precision, use the Properties Palette – if not visible, activate this with *Windows > Properties* (keyboard: F2). In the Properties Palette, you will see a number of tabs: *X, Y, Z, Shape, Text, Image, Line*, and *Colors*.

A selected frame can also be repositioned and resized strictly with the arrow keys. Simply pressing the arrow keys moves the frame in the expected direction (eg, the up arrow moves the frame up). Holding down Ctrl will move in tens of page units, holding Shift tenths of units.

If you hold down the Alt key, you can enlarge the frame: up arrow moves the top side, down arrow the bottom, right arrow the right, and left arrow the left side. Holding down Shift-Alt shrinks the frame, but note these differences: up arrow moves the bottom side, down arrow the top, right arrow the left side, left arrow the right.

If you are working with a shape, you will see that these apply to the bounding box of the shape, however, a rotated shape can be resized in a more complex fashion.

3.9.8 Grouping of Frames

If you have frames in a particular layout and want to manipulate them, meanwhile maintaining their relative positions, you can group them. The first step is to select all of the frames you want in your group, and depending on your needs can be done in various ways:

- If you want to select all the frames in your document (not likely if you have more than one page), click *Edit > Select All* (Ctrl+A).
- If your frames are in a contiguous area, with none that you don't want selected, then simply click-drag your mouse around them.
- Hold down the Shift key, and click the frames one-by-one.

Once you've done this, you may find you can, by clicking carefully in between frames, move this group of selected frames around, but you run the risk of clicking only one and having the relationship ruined. Better to select *Item > Group* (Ctrl+G), at which point your group will stay a group until you ungroup them with *Item > Ungroup* (Ctrl+Shift+G).

What you find now is that when you go to the *X, Y, Z* tab of the Properties Palette, the various spinboxes for positioning and rotation now apply to your group as a whole. Width and height for the group's members can be adjusted all at once. Line and fill colors, and line properties can also be adjusted to be the same for the whole group. Some other functions, such as manipulating any images or shapes will generally not apply to all images or shapes in the group – usually you will find that only one member of the group is edited. Just as with individual frames, a group can be deleted, cut, copied, and pasted. A group can be copied to the Scrapbook. The Scrapbook is covered in its own section.

There is a special operation on shapes and polygons, *Combine Polygons*, which is discussed in Working with Shapes and Polygons.

3.9.9 Properties: X, Y, Z

As seen in the images below, we have very precise control over the position, size, and rotation of our frames on the page. What may not be so obvious is that these two images show information about the same frame, with the same size and position on the page. The reason the X and Y coordinates are different is that the basepoint has been changed from the upper left corner of the frame in the first image to the lower right in the second. Thus we can use a basepoint at whatever position helps us place the frame properly on the page:

The basepoint also determines the point around which rotation takes place when using the "Rotation" spinbox.

Here you can adjust position, size (note that the width/height

Names of Items:
Please note that while you can rename items in the *X, Y, Z* tab of the Properties Palette, you cannot use empty spaces in those names. The reason is that they are also used in the PDF exporter for the field names in PDF forms. As you will learn in the **PDF Forms** chapter, these forms can embed JavaScript in PDF files, and the names of the respective text frames are referenced in the JavaScript code. Since JavaScript doesn't permit the use of empty spaces in item names, you can't use those spaces. A workaround is to use underscores, eg. "title_box_1."

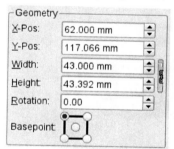
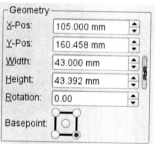

ratio can be linked or unlinked with the chain icons on the right), and rotation. If you rotate an item with the mouse, by clicking the "Rotate Item" icon on the toolbar, rotation works differently: Here, the rotation depends on the position of the mouse pointer. If you click on a corner of a frame and then move the mouse, the opposite corner will be the center of the rotation. Clicking anywhere else and moving the mouse uses the center of the object as the pivotal point.

Change the level of an item in relationship to others by using the arrow buttons, seen to the left of the following image – either one level at a time or all the way to the top or bottom. The adjacent number denotes which level the currently selec-

The "Level" buttons in the X, Y, Z tab of the Properties Palette (on the left)

ted object is on.

Here are some useful keyboard shortcuts for levels, when you have a frame selected (and not in Edit Contents mode):

• PgUp/PgDn: Move frame up/down one level.

• Home: Move frame to top level.

• End: Move frame to bottom level.

In the cluster of buttons to the right, the two leftmost allow flipping of the frame horizontally or vertically. You can lock the all of the characteristics of a frame (picture of a lock) or its size only. The middle button at the bottom allows or prevents the frame from being printed or exported.

3.9.10 Properties: Shape

In the *Shape* tab, we begin to see differences depending on the type of frame. For all frames, you can edit their shape, a quick method being to click the top button and select from a table of shapes, but you can also click "Edit Shape ..." to edit the shape of a frame like a vector drawing. You can also round the corners of your frame inwards or outwards by applying positive or negative values in the spinbox:

3.9.11 Text Flows Around Frame

Another feature common to all frames is at the bottom of the *Shape* tab, where you can elect to have text flowing around a frame – this will apply when you have a text frame behind the frame for which this is selected. When you check this box, the default behavior is for text to flow around the frame.

When a frame is created, the frame, the bounding box, and the contour line will coincide with each other. The easiest way to see the difference between the frame and the bounding box is to rotate the frame – you must then move the frame with the mouse to see its bounding box, which is always a rectangle. The frame rotates, but the bounding box will continue to have horizontal and vertical sides, enlarging to indicate the X and Y coordinate space that the frame takes up. The contour line moves with the rotation of the frame, but it is actually a second frame that can be edited separately in the "Edit Shape" dialog, activated from the *Shape* tab in the Properties Palette. Check "Edit Contour Line" and you can change the contour line like a vector graphic to then use it for flowing text. For example, one could have a circular text flow around a rectangular frame.

To learn more about editing shapes, which is the same process and same dialog as "Edit Contour Line," read Working with Shapes and Polygons.

Here we show these separate structures: bounding box (large square, would be a dotted red line on your screen), contour line (irregular shape slightly larger than image, in blue

on screen when being edited), and image frame boundary (dotted black line at image boundary). As shown here, the contour line can fall outside the bounding box.

You can choose which one of these to have text flow around, the default being the image frame boundary.

Text frames show in the mid-portion of the tab the ability to set the number of text columns within the frame, gap between columns, and the distances of the text from the edge of the frame. You can also manage tabulators – see Working with Text.

3.9.12 Properties: Line

For a frame, the line properties apply to the border of the frame. In order for the border to show, it must have a line color assigned, which has to be set in the *Color* tab of the Properties Palette. By default, text and image frames have no line color,

shapes and polygons are set to black. The thickness, the type of line and the type of edge are adjusted in this tab. Five types of lines and three types of edges are available.

3.9.13 Properties: Color

As mentioned above, text and image frames have no default line color. The fill color is "None" for text and image frames. Although it may seem nonsensical for a frame with an image to have a fill (background) color, it may be that the frame is larger than the loaded image, in which case this color will fill the balance of the frame space. You can also assign a shade (saturation) and opacity of the line or fill color, and for fill, various gradients types can also be selected. In this case you will select two or more colors for the gradient fill – appropriate widgets will appear. While Scribus allows for changing opacity in any document, when you export to PDF, only PDF versions

1.4 or later allow for transparency.

One thing to note when you are changing the opacity of a text or an image frame via the *Color* tab is that the opacity is always changed for the whole frame, not just the background color. Thus, if you set the opacity to, say, 20 %, your text or your image will also become "pale" and partially transparent. As a workaround, you can place a shape behind the text or image frame as a frame without content (see below), then set fill color and opacity as desired. The only thing to take care of here is that the fill color of the text or image frame is set to "None," so that they're transparent.

The other tabs of the Properties Palette will be described in the following sections.

3.9.14 Magic Wand

If you have a frame selected, you will see a magic wand, or perhaps only a star on a stick in the toolbar. Its tooltip will tell you that it copies item properties. At this time, it will copy only a frame's line and fill colors from one frame to another, regardless of frame type. Click the wand a second time or another tool on the toolbar to deactivate it.

3.9.15 Frames Without Content

There is also a potential use for a frame with nothing or almost nothing in it. A page-sized frame could give the background of the layout a color or an image. An empty frame with only its border showing creates an empty box, a box which might be transparent inside, have text flow around it, have an opaque or only partially opaque color. Sometimes an otherwise invisible frame helps to control text flow in an easier way than working with existing frames on the page. For these purposes, a frame could be of any type, since all frames can be used in this manner. Such minimalist frames can allow for some interesting effects.

3.10 Working with Text

3.10.1 Single Text Frames

TO CREATE a text frame, click the text frame icon on the toolbar, menu item *Insert > Text* Frame, or use the keyboard shortcut: T. Then click-drag-let up to make your frame.

3.10.2 Automatic Text Frames

Unlike other kinds of frames, text frames can be inserted automatically when you create a new document. To the right hand side of the *New Document* dialog there is a checkbox for automatic frame creation, where you specify the number of columns and the gap between them. You can also initially indicate a number of pages. Any additional pages that you might insert later will continue with this same automatic scheme, in which a text frame will fill the page up to the preset margins. When there are multiple pages, the frames will be automatically linked. Relinking manually created frames is not supported with a chain of automatically created frames.

On the left you see the context menu introduced in Working with Frames, obtained by right-clicking inside a text frame.

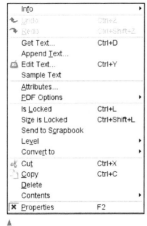

The context menu for text frames.

- *Info* will give you some information about the content of the frame: the number of paragraphs, the number of words, the number of characters and its export/print status

- *Undo* will undo the last operation on the frame itself. Operations which cannot be undone are deleting the frame or clearing or editing its contents.

- *Redo* gives you an opportunity to revert an undo, in case you change your mind.

- *Get Text* of course will be used to load a text file into the frame, generating a file dialog. If you use this option for a frame which already has content, that content will be replaced, but you will be warned.

- *Append Text* allows for adding to already existing text in the frame.

- *Edit Text* brings up the Story Editor.

- *Sample Text* gives you a choice of sample texts: the classic Lorem ipsum, and many other language variants.

- *Attributes*: A frame may have a number of attributes which can be used for various purposes, such as generating a table of contents.

- *PDF Options* allows for conversion of the frame to a PDF annotation or PDF bookmark for PDF export.

- *Is Locked* will prevent editing of the frame in all respects.
- *Size is Locked* locks only the size of the frame.
- *Send to Scrapbook*: The Scrapbook is a folder where text frames and other content can be saved, and reused. Sending to Scrapbook does not delete the frame from the current document. Moreover, it will also make it available in other documents. See The Scrapbook.
- *Send to Layer* will only be present if you have more than one layer in your document, and allows you to move the frame to a different layer – you are presented with a list of choices.
- *Level*: Use this to move this frame toward the surface (top) of the current layer or toward its bottom.
- *Convert to* allows conversion to other frame types, but there are limitations, denoted by a choice being grayed out if not possible for the current frame. For example, a text frame in a series of linked frames cannot be converted.
- *Cut, Copy, Delete* are conceptually self-explanatory, but what happens depends on what mode you are in. In Select Item mode, the frame and contents will be cut, copied, or deleted. In the editing mode, this applies to any highlighted text.
- *Contents > Clear* allows for deleting the text from the frame. It cannot be undone, but you will receive a dialog, asking for confirmation.
- *Properties* simply shows/hides the Properties Palette.

3.10.3 Entering/Editing Text in the Frame

3.10.3.1 The Story Editor

The Story Editor is the easiest way to enter text directly from the keyboard. With the text frame selected, click the Story Editor icon on the toolbar, select *Edit > Edit Text ...*, or use the shortcut Ctrl+Y. It is also an option in the context menu ("Edit Text").

The many features of the Story Editor are covered in its own chapter. For this brief introduction, just note that a large array of text features are completely under your control in the Story Editor, including font family and font face, color, spacing, kerning, justification, and more. Changing a setting will only modify text that you have selected (highlighted) and any subsequently entered text. Its most important function within Scribus, however, is the possibility to apply and change paragraph styles easily.

Take the time to learn how to create and use styles, also in its own chapter, which will save time when you are repetitively using a specific set of text features.

3.10.3.2 Editing from the Main Page

Click the "Edit Contents of Frame" icon on the toolbar (keyboard: E). Double-clicking inside the frame will also activate this mode. When you click inside the frame, you will see a blinking vertical cursor where you may add, remove or edit text as you are used to from text editors or word processors. You may also select (highlight) text and change the highlighted text features in the *Text* tab of the Properties Palette. As you can see the choices are analogous to those in the Story Editor.

You can enter text directly from the keyboard, and also by using the context menu > *Append Text …* to add to the text from a file. Context menu > *Get Text …* will replace the text in the frame.

3.10.3.3 Editing All the Text in the Frame

It's possible to manipulate the appearance of text in a frame by simply selecting the frame and using the Properties Palette. The text itself cannot be edited by this method, but font type and features can be, as well as applying styles. If not already selected, click the "Select Item" icon on the toolbar (keyboard: C). Note that if you are in the editing mode, pressing C will enter text (the character "c") in the frame – simply clicking outside the frame, then inside switches to Select Item mode. At this point, if you make changes in the Text tab of the Properties Palette, all visible text in the frame will be modified.

While you cannot enter text directly from the keyboard, you can use context menu > *Append Text …* to add to the text from a file. Just as you can in the editing mode, context menu > *Get Text …* will replace the text in the frame.

3.10.3.4 Inline Objects

While in the editing mode (double-click on frame, click the icon on the toolbar, or keyboard: E), you can add graphics and other items as you would with letters in your frame: For example, you can select an image frame, copy it (context menu > *Copy, Edit > Copy*, or keyboard: Ctrl+C), then put your cursor where you want the graphic to be inserted, then *Edit > Paste* or Ctrl+V to insert it wherever you want. You can also insert any other Scribus object like a text frame, a line, a Bézier curve, a shape, or an imported vector drawing as an inline object. A known limitation is that borders of cells in tables (see Tables) remain invisible if a table is placed as an inline object.

Since an inline graphic is treated like a character, this will work best when the font size and image size are roughly in the same scale. To rescale an inline object, you have to place the cursor in the text frame before the graphic, press Shift and the left arrow key to select it. Then go to the *Text* tab of the Properties Palette. Now you can use the tools described below for scaling the width and the height of glyphs to resize the object, as well as the "Offset to Baseline" option for vertical placement and "Word Tracking" for horizontal placement. Note that text won't flow around inline objects, so that you have to create the space around them by using the space bar for creating a horizontal distance and the return key for vertical distances.

Lorem ipsum dolor sit amet, consect adipisc✔ing elit. Ut a sapien. Aliqua purus molestie dolor. ⬚Integer quis posuere dictum. Curabitur dignissim. Fusce vulputate lacus at ipsum. Quis nec mi laoreet volutpat. Aliquam ero scelerisque quis, tristique cursus, pla convallis, velit. Nam condimentum. mauris. Cu⬚rabitur adipiscing, m⬚ dictum aliquam, arcu risus dapibus d sollicitudin quam erat q⬚his ligula. massa nulla, volutpat eu, accumsan e eget, odio. Nulla placerat porta justo. turpis. Praesent lacus.V✔estibulum

Here we see some Scribus icons inserted randomly in sample text.

To remove an inline object, simply treat it like any other character in your text frame: Place the cursor before it and press the Del key, or place it behind the object and press the backspace key. Note that there is one important difference between regular characters/glyphs and inline objects: While characters in a text can be copied and pasted in a text frame and between text frames, this doesn't work with inline objects. You will always have to copy the item outside the frame to be able to paste it into a text frame.

3.10.4 Loading Text from a File

Load text from a file from the context menu > *Get Text*, or from the menu *File > Import > Get Text*. You may also append text (*Get Text* will replace whatever is already in the frame). Plain text files may also be loaded into the Story Editor.

The default behavior of the file dialog is to automatically sense the type of file from its extension, then load its contents appropriately, but you may also specify a type of file to reduce the number of files you see in the dialog.

File name:		Open
File type:	All Supported Formats (*.csv *.doc *.html *.htm *.odt *.pdb * ▾)	Cancel
Importer:	Automatic ▾ ☐ Import Text Only	
Encoding:	UTF-8 ▾	

3.10.4.1 Comma-Separated Values Files

There is a built-in filter for comma-separated values (CSV), which can be the output from a spreadsheet or a database. They are most often automatically generated by other software, yet since they are simple, could be done manually. In Scribus, if you are not planning on stripping out the text, you will need to indicate what you want Scribus to do with the comma separated values.

The import dialog for CSV files

Scribus will assign a default format (or style) for your CSV data, once you indicate in the pop-up dialog what the field separators are. Tab stops will be created as needed for the number of fields per line. See below for a description of editing styles – the names of these styles will take the name of the frame and append "-CSV_data," so for example, a frame named "Text5" will create a style "Text5-CSV_data." This allows you to easily edit this style later and apply it to all the imported data in that frame.

Here is an example of a table imported from a database output. What you see here is that for the header line a bold style is set using the default font for the frame, and while the tab stops are actually the same as the columns below, they are center type rather than left as the rest of the columns are. Therefore, expect that adjustments in the assigned stops will be necessary.

Letter	Numeric	Name
à	&#224;	&agrave;
á	&#225;	&aacute;
â	&#226;	&acirc;
ã	&#227;	&atilde;
ä	&#228;	&auml;
å	&#229;	&aring;
æ	&#230;	&aelig;

3.10.4.2 HTML Files

Upon import, the importer will create paragraph styles which correspond to the HTML markup. Bold, italics and monospace text and alignment are also supported. Below is a listing of the HTML markup supported – both upper and lowercase tags:

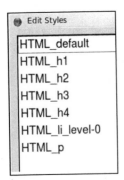

Styles imported from an HTML file

- body, div, a: Text must be within the <body> tags.
- p and br: Corresponding to paragraph and line breaks.
- h1 to h4: Correspond to heading sizes 1 to 4.
- ol, ul, li: Corresponding to ordered or unordered lists.
- pre and code: Corresponding to pre-formatted text and source code listings. These will be converted to text using the fixed pitch font Courier.

- b, u, i, em, strong, sub. sup, del, u: Text formatting is converted to the corresponding font styles. Note that your default font must have all of these font faces available to Scribus.

Did you know...

From Wikipedia's newest articles:

- ...that **Wo Hing Society Hall** *(pictured)* is one of two existing **Chinese Society Halls** left on the island of Maui?

- ...that **Dick Rifenburg** was a Michigan high school state champion in basketball and track & field, but was drafted to play professional American football?
- ...that *Ancient Qumran: A Virtual Reality Tour* is a computer-generated film that presents in 3-D a theoretical reconstruction of the ancient Khirbet Qumran site?
- ...that the first **Trk receptor**, which regulates synaptic strength and plasticity in neurons, was originally identified as part of a fusion gene with the cytoskeletal protein tropomyosin, forming an oncogene in colon and thyroid cancers?
- ...that in the wake of the Yen Bai mutiny of Vietnamese soldiers in the French colonial army, **large numbers of Vietnamese troops who had served in France were sacked** because it was felt that overseas travel made them more inclined to rebel?
- ...that the specifications for the U.S. Navy's World War II icebreakers were so imposing that **Western Pipe & Steel** was the only shipbuilder to bid?

Archive - Start a new article...

Here is an example showing part of a saved page from Wikipedia. One must save the source as an HTM or HTML file, then import into a frame – simply use *Get Text*. Similar to the above example, paragraph styles are created. Below we see the result in Scribus. As you can see, there is an attempt to implement simple text styles such as bold or italics, but not font type. Links are shown in blue text. Bullets are changed to hyphens in the list structure shown. Tables will not be imported with any kind of a tabular structure. Much of the metadata and formatting information will be left out, but in a complex web page expect extraneous text.

Did you know...

From Wikipedia's newest articles:

img., alt: Wo Hing Temple src:
http://upload.wikimedia.org/wikipedia/en/thumb/5/5e/Wo_Hing_Temple.JPG/100px-Wo_Hing_Temple.JPG

- ...that **Wo Hing Society Hall** (pictured) is one of two existing **Chinese Society Halls** left on the island of Maui?
- ...that **Dick Rifenburg** was a Michigan high school state champion in basketball and track & field, but was drafted to play professional American football?
- ...that *Ancient Qumran: A Virtual Reality Tour* is a computer-generated film that presents in 3-D a theoretical reconstruction of the ancient Khirbet Qumran site?
- ...that the first **Trk receptor**, which regulates synaptic strength and plasticity in neurons, was originally identified as part of a fusion gene with the cytoskeletal protein tropomyosin, forming an oncogene in colon and thyroid cancers?
- ...that in the wake of the Yen Bai mutiny of Vietnamese soldiers in the French colonial army, **large numbers of Vietnamese troops who had served in France were sacked** because it was felt that overseas travel made them more inclined to rebel?
- ...that the specifications for the U.S. Navy's World War II icebreakers were so imposing that **Western Pipe & Steel** was the only shipbuilder to bid?

If you check "Import Text Only" in the "Get Text ..." dialog, Scribus will import the text without formatting and without creating any paragraph styles.

3.10.4.3 Importing OpenDocument Text and Open Office.org Writer documents

The importer for Writer imports only the text contained in a file. Thus, a compound Writer document with tables or charts will not be imported in its entirety. Tables, charts or other embedded objects need to be placed into their own Draw file, exported and then imported into Scribus separately.

The singular most important issue to take into consideration for hassle-free OpenOffice.org Writer import is well chosen usage and correctly applying of styles in OpenOffice.org. Doing so will greatly reduce the amount of time needed within Scribus to format and style text. Any special paragraph styles in your Writer file will automatically be imported into your existing Scribus document.

Here are the steps necessary to import an OpenOffice.org Writer file or an OpenDocument Text file:

1. Select the text frame.
2. Right click > *Get Text ...*
3. Select your OpenOffice.org document. The importer will recognize the type of OpenOffice.org file (SXW or ODT).

This will import all the text in your source document. In case there is not enough space in your frame or set of linked frames, you can also add and link them later. You should easily be able to import 10, 20 or even 50 pages of text in one go. While as much as 600 pages have been imported during testing, the practical limit is probably not more than a chapter's (15–30 pages) worth of text for performance reasons.

When importing text from OpenOffice.org there are four important options, which need to be carefully considered:

- *Update Paragraph Styles*: This option will tell Scribus to change the formatting of any created styles in your Scribus document to follow those in the OpenOffice.org document.
- *Merge Paragraph Styles*: This option looks at the actual attributes (fonts, size) of the OpenOffice.org file and merges styles which have common attributes. This can help to eliminate differently named, but similar styles.
- *Use document name as a Prefix for Paragraph Styles*: This is self-explanatory, but can be useful for sorting styles when importing from several documents.

- *Do Not Ask Again*: Here you should be cautious, as this last option will make your choices permanent. If you inadvertently checked this option and want to revert it, open the file prefs13.xml in the hidden folder `./scribus` in your home directory (or in `Documents and Settings` on Windows) with a text editor. Search for the text string `<attribute key="ask-Again" value="0"/>`, change the 0 to 1 and save the file. Now the import dialog will show up again.

The import dialog for ODT and SXW files

Here is an example importing part of the introduction from "Origin of Species" by Charles Darwin, to which some font types and styles have been artificially applied. The two font types (Liberation Serif and Luxi Sans) have been correctly used, and features such as center justification, bold, and italics have been applied as well.

> INTRODUCTION.
>
> THE nature of the following work will be best understood by a brief account of how it came to be written. During many years I collected notes on the origin or descent of man, without any intention of publishing on the subject, but rather with the determination not to publish, as I thought that I should thus only add to the prejudices against my views. It seemed to me sufficient to indicate, in the first edition of my '**Origin of Species**,' that by this work "light would be thrown on the origin of man and his history;" and this implies that man must be included with other organic beings in any general conclusion respecting his manner of appearance on this earth. Now the case wears a wholly different aspect. When a naturalist like Carl Vogt ventures to say in his address as President of the National Institution of Geneva (1869), *"personne, n'ose plus soutenir la création au moins, n'ose plus soutenir la création indépendante et de toutes pièces, des espèces,"* it is manifest that at least a large number of naturalists must admit that species are the modified descendants
>
> In consequence of the views now adopted by most naturalists, and which will ultimately, as in every other case, be followed by other men, I have been led to put together my notes, so as to see how far the general conclusions arrived at in my former works were applicable to man. This seemed all the more desirable as I had never deliberately applied these views to a species taken singly. When we confine our attention to any one form, we are deprived of the weighty arguments derived from the nature of the affinities which connect together whole groups of organisms—their geographical distribution in past and present times, and their geological succession. The homological structure, embryological development, and rudimentary organs of a species, whether it be man or any other animal, to which our attention may be directed, remain to be considered; but these great classes of facts afford, as it appears to me, ample and conclusive evidence in favour of the principle of gradual evolution. The strong

In the original ODT document, only one paragraph style was used, "Text body." On import to Scribus, two styles were created, "origin-example_P2" for the initial heading, and "origin-example_Text_20_body." Even though the font changed in the next paragraph, Scribus did not create a new paragraph style, since this was not done in OpenOffice.org Writer. Instead, the new font was applied to the previous style, just as it was in the original ODT file.

As with HTML files, checking "Import Text Only" in the "Get Text …" dialog, lets Scribus import the text without formatting and without creating any paragraph styles.

3.10.4.4 Word File Import

In order for Word (DOC) files to be imported, and for that matter to be acknowledged as existing in the dialog, you must have installed the program antiword. Consult your distribution to find and install this – it will come with your Windows installation of Scribus automatically.

Word files will be stripped of formatting. A workaround for this would be to save from Word as HTML or load the DOC file into another application such as OpenOffice.org Writer, then save to SXD, ODT or HTML format.

3.10.4.5 Aportis Doc PDB documents

Aportis Doc files (PDB) may also be imported. Like those processed by antiword, they will be stripped to plain text. Unlike DOC files, no additional software is needed.

3.10.4.6 Text Filters and Text Files

You can also create your own filters, used to tell Scribus which style to apply to a given paragraph. See Importing Text with Custom Text Filters for detailed information.

Finally, for plain text files, one can simply import the text into the frame. This will be automatic for files ending in TXT but if the file has some other extension, specifying this action will help.

Note that not all "plain text" files are the same, since each text file is stored in a specific "encoding." You may not notice this if you are importing text that only uses the letters of the Latin and English alphabet, but as soon as a text file contains any special characters like umlauts, they won't be recognized correctly if the wrong encoding is used for import. You can select the correct encoding in a dropdown list at the bottom of the file dialog for text import. If you don't know the correct encoding, you will have to experiment.

3.10.4.7 Sample Text

There are also the special files of "Lorem ipsum" text, that can most easily be accessed via context menu > *Sample Text*. Scribus has this in several language versions, in addition to the original Latin-like version. Lorem ipsum is used as arbitrary text, for assessing typographic aspects of a given font, justification, and other features which may help in making decisions as a layout is being developed.

3.10.5 Linking One Frame to Another

Text may be continued from one frame to another, on the same page or different pages.

Before linking

After linking – arrows show the path of text flow

Here are the steps:

- Select the first frame
- Click the "Link Text Frames" icon on the toolbar (keyboard: N)
- Click the second frame – that's it.
- Continue clicking to continue linking further frames. Remember that the links go in the order that you click from one to the next. When you are finished, click the "Select" icon to stop linking.
- To add more frames later, create the new frames, select the last of the linked frames, then click the link icon, then the new frame(s) you want to link to. Newly added frames always are appended at the end.
- Be sure to unselect the "Link Frames" icon or click on the canvas when you are finished, since this will interfere with normal operations while selected.

Note that frames can be linked before or after they have any content. On the document, you can tell when a frame is linked, because its border will have a solid dark red line for its border.

3.10.6 Unlinking Frames

Unlinking text frames is operationally similar – click the first frame, then the "Unlink" icon in the toolbar (keyboard: U), then the frames to unlink.

3.10.7 Text Columns

In the middle of the *Shape* tab in the Properties Palette is a block labeled "Distances." Here is where we can set the number of columns in a text frame. Columns can be set before or after text is entered. "Gap" refers to the space between columns, and "Top," "Bottom," "Left," and "Right" refer to the empty space between the text and the borders of a frame. These spaces may become necessary when we are applying a color and a stroke to the frame border.

Lorem ipsum dolor sit amet, consectetuer adipiscing elit. Ut a sapien. Aliquam aliquet purus molestie dolor. Integer quis eros ut erat posuere dictum. Curabitur dignissim. Integer orci. Fusce vulputate lacus at ipsum. Quisque in libero nec mi laoreet volutpat. Aliquam eros pede, scelerisque quis, tristique cursus, placerat convallis, velit. Nam condimentum. Nulla ut mauris. Curabitur adipiscing, mauris non dictum aliquam, arcu risus dapibus diam, nec sollicitudin quam erat quis ligula. Aenean massa nulla, volutpat eu, accumsan et, fringilla eget, odio. Nulla placerat porta justo. Nulla vitae turpis. Praesent lacus.Vivamus neque velit, ornare vitae, tempor vel, ultrices et, wisi. Cras pede. Phasellus nunc turpis, cursus non, rhoncus vitae, sollicitudin vel, velit. Vivamus suscipit lorem sed felis. Vestibulum vestibulum ultrices turpis. Lorem ipsum dolor sit amet, consectetuer adipiscing elit. Praesent ornare nulla nec justo. Sed nec risus ac risus fermentum vestibulum. Etiam viverra viverra sem. Etiam molestie mi quis

metus hendrerit tristique. Vivamus neque velit, ornare vitae, tempor vel, ultrices et, wisi. Cras pede. Phasellus nunc turpis, cursus non, rhoncus vitae, sollicitudin vel, velit. Vivamus suscipit lorem sed felis. Vestibulum vestibulum ultrices turpis. Lorem ipsum dolor sit amet, consectetuer adipiscing elit. Praesent ornare nulla nec justo. Sed nec risus ac risus fermentum vestibulum. Etiam viverra viverra sem. Etiam molestie mi quis metus hendrerit tristique. Cum sociis natoque penatibus et magnis dis parturient montes, nascetur ridiculus mus. Maecenas tortor metus, pellentesque nec, vehicula vitae, suscipit sed, quam. Aenean scelerisque sodales tortor. Sed purus. Curabitur turpis est, bibendum tristique, porttitor tempor, pulvinar vitae, tortor. Nullam malesuada dapibus orci. Vivamus aliquet tempus velit. Curabitur interdum posuere risus. Duis egestas, ipsum sit amet molestie tincidunt, ligula libero pretium risus, non faucibus tellus felis mattis sapien.

Because of the way that a font may be placed on its baseline, adjusting the offset to baseline can be useful for evening out the top and bottom spaces. This text shows good alignment of the text in both columns, obtained by setting "Align to Baseline." See the settings in *Text* tab for further help with these. Baseline grid spacing for the current document can be changed in *File > Document Setup > Guides*.

Like many things in Scribus, there is more than one way to accomplish a columns structure, and you may use more than one in the same document.

et, wisi. Cras pede. Phasellus nunc turpis, cursus non, rhoncus vitae, sollicitudin vel, velit. Vivamus suscipit lorem sed felis. Vestibulum vestibulum ultrices turpis. Lorem ipsum dolor sit amet, consectetuer adipiscing elit. Praesent ornare nulla nec justo. Sed nec risus ac risus fermentum vestibulum. Etiam viverra viverra sem. Etiam molestie mi quis

scelerisque sodales tortor. Sed purus. Curabitur turpis est, bibendum tristique, porttitor tempor, pulvinar vitae, tortor. Nullam malesuada dapibus orci. Vivamus aliquet tempus velit. Curabitur interdum posuere risus. Duis egestas, ipsum sit amet molestie tincidunt, ligula libero pretium risus, non faucibus tellus felis mattis sapien.

Lorem ipsum dolor sit amet, consectetuer adipiscing elit. Ut a sapien. Aliquam aliquet purus molestie dolor. Integer quis eros ut erat posuere dictum. Curabitur dignissim. Integer orci. Fusce vulputate lacus at ipsum. Quisque in libero nec mi laoreet volutpat. Aliquam eros pede, scelerisque quis, tristique cursus, placerat convallis, velit. Nam condimentum. Nulla ut mauris. Curabitur adipiscing, mauris

pede egestas nibh, sit amet posuere metus tortor id enim. Donec at sem. Vestibulum in lectus ut diam lacinia lacinia. Maecenas sit amet nulla. Suspendisse vel dolor. Nunc hendrerit elit vitae quam. In nonummy velit nec lorem. Etiam rhoncus felis a turpis. Aliquam vel nulla. Ut nonummy, nisl non sodales iaculis, mi tellus viverra diam, eget euismod dui turpis at mi. Class aptent taciti

In the graphic at the bottom of the previous page, to the right we see the bottom of the two-column frame introduced above, and the top of two frames, aligned with the top frame and linked, so that text flows from one to the next – we can see they are linked because they are outlined in solid pale red on your screen (these red lines will not show when the document is printed or in the PDF). We are using page guides and the margins to help us align these new frames with the above columns, and even though these frames are linked, you can see that each can have independent left and right spaces, so lining up our text with the top frame is quite easy. Using "Align to Baseline" is especially necessary when we generate two columns with separate frames and when the tops of the frames are not aligned.

3.10.8 Tabulators

3.10.8.1 Editing Tabs from the Properties Palette

Clicking on the "Tabulators" button in the *Shape* tab of the Properties Palette brings up the "Manage Tabulators" dialog, the central feature being a ruler for your frame in the appropriate units. Stretch out the dialog or scroll along the ruler as needed. Left-clicking along the ruler adds new stops, the active stop being highlighted in red. To highlight and adjust an existing stop, carefully place the cursor over the stop until the cursor turns into a double-sided arrow, then left-click. Now see that you can either manually adjust its position or use the spinbox to do "Position" more precisely.

Appearance of stops on the ruler: Left, Right, Period/Full Stop, Comma, Center. Period and Comma are indistinguishable.

Tabs may behave in various ways. A typical, typewriter-like tab stop behaves like the stops labelled left – pressing the tab key jumps to the stop, and subsequently entered text appears to the right of the stop in a left-to-right fashion. A right stop, in contrast, will enter text which builds to the left of the tab stop, still in a left-to-right fashion. Period (full stop outside the United States) and comma are used to align around the decimal point or comma respectively (in many countries, commas are used in numbers where English uses decimal points, and vice-versa) – in essence each will build text to the left until you type the appropriate character, then build to the right. The "Center" type of stop centers entered text on the stop, until you press the tab key once again. Right-clicking a tab stop will toggle through the choices.

Left-click and drag a stop off the ruler to delete an individual one, "Delete All" is self-explanatory. Press "OK" to save stop positions.

3.10.8.2 Editing Tabulators from the Main Page in the Editing Mode

Here we see a closeup of a text frame near the ruler in the main screen. The frame is in editing mode. What we see here is that replacing the black numbers and ticks in the ruler are new ones (blue on your screen), corresponding to a ruler for the frame – in this example the units are in points.

We also see our tab stops indicated in black, the one on the left is a left stop and the other is period. Just as in our "Manage Tabulators" dialog, we can manually move this with the left mouse button or toggle through types of stops with a right click on a stop symbol. Drag the tab stop off the ruler to delete it. Enlarging the view helps to place stops with more precision.

3.10.8.3 Editing Tabs as a Feature of a Style

This is covered in the chapter Working with Styles.

3.10.9 Textflow Around a Frame

Use this to determine what happens with text underneath the selected frame. Flow can be around the frame, the bounding box, or the contour line. See Working with Frames for further information.

3.10.10 The Text Tab of the Properties Palette

The *Text* tab of the Properties Palette shows the font family, and just under it the font face. These font subtypes must be included in the font description, since Scribus does not make artificial ones if they do not exist. Incidentally, there is a small symbol to the left of the name indicating its type. OpenType fonts are indicated by a blue "O," TrueType fonts by a red "T," and PostScript/Type 1 fonts by a green "1."

Next we see two columns of spinboxes:

- *Font size*
- *Line spacing*
- *Width* – deviation from standard

- *Offset to baseline of characters*
- *Kerning*
- *Height* – deviation from standard

Notes:

- *Offset to baseline of characters* allows for placement of glyphs at a set distance from the baseline grid.
- *Line Spacing*: If you click-hold the icon to the left of the spin-box, you are offered a choice of fixed linespacing, automatic linespacing, or align to baseline grid. When you adjust font size, linespacing automatically changes to 120% of the font size or any other value you set in *File > Document Setup > Typography.* Fixed linespacing allows you to then independently adjust linespacing, automatic linespacing does not, as it uses the values stored in the font. Align to baseline grid keeps the linespacing according to the baseline grid, adjustable in *File > Document Setup > Guides.*
- *Kerning* adjusts the space between individual letters. The space will be changed between two letters if the cursor is placed between them. If three or more letters are selected, the space will change between all of them.

The *Text* tab of the Properties Palette

Now we have colors:

- *Line* (only applies to outline and shadow, and these will use the same color), and
- *Fill* (body of a character)

  For both "Line" and "Fill," click the percentage to select a degree of shading (saturation) from a list, or choose "Other ..." to enter a value between 0 and 100.

Under these is a row of buttons, from left to right:

- *Underline*: Click-hold to adjust displacement and line width.
- *Underline Words Only* (not intervening spaces): Click-hold to adjust displacement and line width.
- *Subscript*: Position and size are editable in *File > Document Setup > Typography.*
- *Superscript*: Position/size editable in *File > Preferences/File > Document Setup > Typography.*
- *All Caps*: For all letters uppercase glyphs will be used.
- *Small Caps*: Uppercase letters will get a large cap for the capitalized letter, and lowercase letters a small one. Note that these small caps are just resized uppercase letters. You can get better typographical results if you use a special small caps font face (often indicated by the letters "SC" in the file name).
- *Strikethrough*: Click-hold to adjust displacement and line width.
- *Outline*: Click-hold to adjust linewidth.

- *Shadow*: Click-hold to adjust X-Offset and Y-Offset.
- *Right to Left Writing*: Completely mirrors the direction of all characters in a text frame, no matter where the cursor is placed.

Next are justification choices: Left, center, right, full, and forced full. With forced full, even partially filled lines will be fully justified.

3.10.11 Resizing a Text Frame and its Content

Sometimes it may be necessary or desirable to adjust the size of a text frame and the text in it at the same time. Instead of resizing the frame and then changing the font size in the Properties Palette, Scribus offers a useful shortcut for this operation: Press Ctrl+Alt on the keyboard and resize the frame with the mouse pointer. Frame size and font size will change with infinite variability. If you also change the shape of the text frame by making one side shorter or longer, the shape of the glyphs will also change, ie., the font scaling will change as you can see below:

scaled text

scaled text

scaled text

Above we see the original text frame, then a proportionally scaled version and finally a text frame whose width has been has been enlarged more than its height. Scribus applied the new ratio of width and height to the text.

3.11 Working with Styles

3.11.1 Styles – Why and What They Are

IN SCRIBUS, styles are a collection of features which are given a name, and thereby can be used and reused. Paragraph styles pertain to text, and will be discussed in this chapter. Line styles apply to drawn lines, and therefore will be discussed in the chapter on straight lines and arrows. Styles allow you to achieve a consistent appearance in your document, without having to reset a complex set of features repeatedly. In addition, you can save them and then reuse in another document. Finally, after they are created, editing them will then make the changes wherever they are applied once they are saved.

3.11.2 Where They Are, How to Make Them

Like many other features in Scribus, there are several paths to styles, both using them and also creating them. If you are going through this manual in sequential fashion, or have simply just started using Scribus on your own, you may be aware of them from the *Text* tab in the Properties Palette, where there is a button to apply styles. In a new document this will be labelled "No Style," since none have yet been created. As you will easily find out, when you click this button, you can apply styles, but not create or edit them from there.

While it might seem that the *Style* menu item might be the route to making/editing styles, this is rather unfortunately named, and in the development versions, the menu item has been removed to avoid this confusion. Instead, click on *Edit > Paragraph Styles* (Alt+E, then P from the keyboard), and you are presented with a dialog such as this one:

If you have no styles, this dialog will be empty, so to make a style, click "New."

This is obviously a complex dialog, so we will describe it bit by bit. At this point, we will just mention that the bottom window of sample text is strictly for a preview of your font and its characteristics. Note that the preview may slow down your creation of a new style, depending on your CPU. Therefore you can switch it off in the checkbox on top of the preview window.

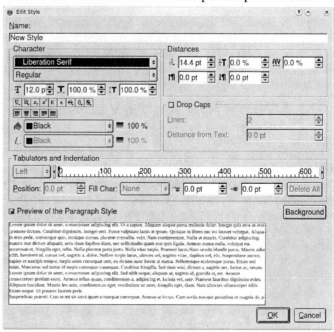

3.11.2.1 Name and Character

At the top is the name automatically created for this new style. Change to your liking. Just below this to the left we have a "Character" section. With a slightly different layout, this corresponds to settings in the *Text* tab of the Properties Palette, which has been described earlier.

From top to bottom, we have:

- Font name, and just under it the available font faces.

Next a row of spinboxes for size, width, and height respectively. Width and height are for deviations from the standard features for that font size.

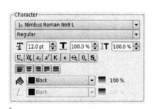

The character/font options in the dialog for paragraph styles.

Under these is a row of buttons, whose functions have been described in the previous section. From left to right:

- *Underline*
- *Underline Words Only* (not intervening spaces)
- *Subscript*
- *Superscript*
- *All Caps*
- *Small Caps*
- *Strikethrough*
- *Outline*
- *Shadow*

Next are justification choices: left, center, right, full, and forced full. Finally in this section we have colors: fill (body of a glyph), and line (stroke of a glyph).

To the right of each color selector is a percentage. Click and hold to choose a shading ("Saturation") from a list or enter a custom value ("Other ...").

3.11.2.2 Distances

Let's cover these spinboxes left to right, by row:

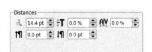

The spacing options in the dialog for paragraph styles.

- *Line Spacing*: As you will see, when you change the font size, line spacing changes automatically with a size change, at 120% of the font size (the % increase is changeable in the *Document Setup* or the *Preferences*). You can then change line spacing independently, but if you go back and change the font size again, line spacing will revert to 120% of the new size. If you click and hold the icon to the left of the spinbox, you can choose fixed linespacing, automatic linespacing, or align to baseline grid. Automatic linespacing removes the ability to independently change linespacing. Align to baseline grid may be needed to align lines of text in columns within a text frame or even between separate frames. See also Working with Text.

- *Offset to Baseline of Characters*: The baseline itself is a document property set in the *Document Setup,* but where the characters are placed in relationship to the document's baseline is a feature of the style.

- *Kerning* is a relative adjustment of the distances between individual characters for this style as a whole.

- *Spacing above the paragraph*: Line spacing will specifically apply to the spacing between lines within a paragraph, and is the default spacing between paragraphs. This setting allows customization of the space above the paragraph, for this particular style.

- *Spacing below the paragraph* is analogous to the above setting. Note that the spacing below one paragraph will be added to the spacing above the next paragraph, dependent on its style.

3.11.2.3 Drop Caps

Drop caps are the first letters of a text which are bigger than the rest. In old books they are often colorful and artistic paintings. Scribus has a built-in function to achieve this effect in the paragraph styles dialog.

The drop cap options in the dialog for paragraph styles.

Click the checkbox to activate drop caps. Specify the number of lines the drop cap will cover, and the distance from the drop cap to the text just to the right of the drop cap. Note that the drop cap won't adapt to the linespacing if you have adjusted the text to the baseline grid.

These are the only parameters for the built-in feature, but see Drop Caps for alternative and much more flexible ways to create drop caps.

3.11.2.4 Tabulators

Tabulators were also covered in Working with Text, as we worked our way through the *Shape* tab of the Properties Palette. Here we will just briefly review the process for making tabs. The first step to making a tab stop is to click on the ruler. By default you will create a left tab stop. Once you have done this, you can then change the type to the choices seen here, and more precisely place the tab with your mouse or the "Position" spinbox.

Left, right, and center tab stops are straightforward. Period (full stop outside the USA) obviously can be used for lining up decimal numbers. Since much of the world uses a comma as a decimal separator, this explains the choice "Comma."

Keep clicking the ruler to add more tab stops, drag them off to delete. As noted in Working with Text, you can also edit tab stops in the main window in the editing mode of text frames.

Finally, in "Fill Char" there is the ability to assign a character other than the default empty space in between tab stops. "Custom" can be any individual character you assign. You have to insert this character with the keyboard behind the colon after selecting "Custom."

Inserting a custom fill character, in this case "#", as shown above, will result in a fill of the distance between the starting and the end point of a tabulator.

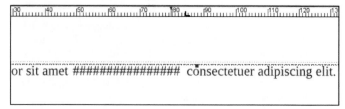

3.11.2.5 Indentation

There are two aspects to indentation – what happens to the first line, and what happens to the rest (body) of a paragraph. In Scribus, each can be adjusted independently, though for obvious reasons everything must happen within the boundaries of the text frame.

Perhaps a bit hard to recognize, but the top ruler shows the default placement of indentation markers, all the way to the left of the ruler. There are two separate markers, best seen when they are separated such as in the bottom ruler. The top, downward-pointing marker is for the first line, the bottom, upward-pointing marker is for the rest of the paragraph, and the spinboxes for each show -20.0 and 30.0 points, respectively. The units here correspond to the units you are using for your document. In case it is not apparent, the measurement for the first line is always a relative distance from the marker for the body.

3.11.2.6 A Final Word: Background

When you change a font's color in *Edit > Paragraph Styles*, the preview display font color will change. If this is a very pale color, visibility can be enhanced by clicking the "Background" button just above the text display window to obtain a better contrast.

3.11.3. Using Styles From Another Document

On the right is our *Edit > Paragraph Styles* dialog once again. You may have noticed the "Import" and "Save" buttons, and you may think these are complementary operations – well, not quite.

When you click "Save," your styles are saved to the document you are working on. What happens when you click Import is that a file dialog comes up to identify a saved SLA file from which to import its styles. The styles from that document can be imported for your use in the current one.

Look below to see the dialog from which you can import all or some of those styles, meanwhile making sure there are no name conflicts.

Scribus lists all paragraph styles it found in another SLA(.GZ) or SCD(.GZ) file in the import dialog for styles.

Here is a tip on how to make efficient use of the import feature. For styles which you may use frequently in many of your documents, create an SLA file which is empty, except for containing a number of different styles for importing to other documents – this can be a great timesaver.

You can also copy text frames with applied styles to the Scrapbook. Dragging such a frame to the canvas in a new document will automatically add all styles stored in the frame to the document.

"Duplicate," in case it's not obvious, can be used to save time by only slightly modifying an existing style.

3.12 The Story Editor

3.12.1 Introduction

LET'S JUMP ahead a bit just to show you an inkling of where this section is going. We will show how to get there and beyond later.

The Story Editor Window

To the right is the Story Editor, as we learned in *Working with Text* opened by creating or selecting an existing text frame, then using the context menu > *Edit Text ...*, clicking the Story Editor icon on the toolbar, choosing *Edit > Edit Text ...* from the main menu, or keyboard Ctrl+Y.

Below our picture of the Story Editor is another one showing what we see after we save our work and go back to our document. The top paragraph shows what happens if we just begin entering text – we use the default style parameters, called "No Style" in the Story Editor and various buttons within in Scribus, such as in the *Text* tab of the Properties Palette. What we have done subsequently is to create two styles, "Example1" and "Example2," as described in the text body for each. Finally, in the last paragraph we started with "No Style," then highlighted the paragraph (by dragging the cursor over the text) then manually changed parameters here in this Story Editor dialog. The screenshot shows these manually set parameters – we know they are for this paragraph since the cursor is in this paragraph – see the middle of the word "text."

As you can see, in the Story Editor there is little to reflect the actual appearance of the text – in this example only centering is seen – so we must rely on the small box to the left to see which style has been applied, and in addition, many parameters are shown in the various buttons and spinboxes at the top – move the cursor to the paragraph you wish to view these settings.

3.12.2 Story Editor – From Menu to Styles

The Story Editor dialog is complex, so here we will describe its contents in something of a north to south direction.

File

- *New* clears all text from Story Editor. If you have any text, it will ask to confirm. This and other changes do not apply to the text frame until you save and exit or update the frame.

- *Reload from File* will only apply after you have made edits that you have not saved to the frame, and in essence will undo those edits in the Story Editor.

- *Save to File ...* allows you to save your text to a file. An appropriate dialog will open. Note that the text will be saved without formatting.
- *Load from File ...* loads text from a plain text file. Plain text files do not contain any formatting, so this is not the same as importing formatted text via context menu > *Get Text ...*
- *Save Document* allows you to save the entire document while still in the Story Editor.
- *Update Text Frame and Exit* and *Exit Without Updating Text Frame* are self-explanatory and apply to exiting the Story Editor, not the document.

Edit

- *Select All* selects (highlights) all text in the frame. One can partially select by using the mouse or holding down Shift and using movement keys: arrows, Home, End, PgUp, PgDn.
- *Cut, Copy* apply to highlighted text.
- *Paste* applies text previously cut or copied.
- *Clear* applies to highlighted text, not the entire contents.
- *Search/Replace ...* applies not only to the text, but also many of its features, and styles. See the section Search and Replace.
- *Edit Styles ...* allows editing styles and creating new ones as described in the previous chapter.
- *Fonts Preview* will give you a visual appearance of the fonts in your system which Scribus is aware of. See Font Preview and Font Management.
- *Update Text Frame* updates the text frame in the document from the Story Editor without closing it.

Insert

- Inserting special characters is covered in detail in the section Special Characters.

Settings

- *Background* opens a dialog to choose the background color of the display in the Story Editor. This does not affect the background color of your text frame.
- *Display Font,* similar to "Background" only affects the display in the Story Editor. Do notice that you can choose to show strikeout and underline when these font features are selected in the Story Editor font effect buttons.
- *Smart Text Selection* shows it is selected by a checkbox being filled. The default behavior (unchecked) will highlight a word which is double-clicked, and also following spaces and tabs up to the next printable character or end of the line. With smart text selected, a double-clicked word highlights only the characters of the word, no preceding or following spaces. Triple-clicking

behaves the same with either setting – an entire line is highlighted, but note this is display-dependent. A line's limits depend on the size of the Story Editor dialog, and represents only the length of the line in the current dialog size.

Now we'll move down to the icons. These icons simply are shortcuts to selected operations from the menu, from left to right:

- *Clear Text from Frame* – same as *New* above
- *Load from File*
- *Save to File*
- *Update Text Frame and Exit*
- *Exit Without Updating Text Frame*
- *Reload Text from Frame*
- *Update Text Frame* – without exiting
- *Search/Replace*

Next we see a button and 3 spinboxes:

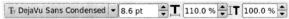

Click the button to the left to choose your font. To its immediate right the unlabeled spinbox selects font size, the middle spinbox adjusts width in percentage of the standard font size, and the right spinbox height, again as percentage.

Next we have choices for justification, and styles:

The icons are self-explanatory:

- *Left justification*
- *Center justification*
- *Right justification*
- *Full justification*
- *Enforced full justification* – even short lines will be fully justified.

The "Style" button merely allows applying an existing style to an existing paragraph. It is not a means to editing styles.

The next row of buttons have labels (and tooltips) that should help remembering their purposes:

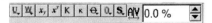

From left to right:

- *Underline*: This will underline text and all intervening spaces. Click to select, click and hold to bring up a small dialog for adjusting line thickness and distance from text.
- *Underline Words Only*: Underlines words only. Spaces are not underlined. This also has the click and hold option for the same purpose.
- *Subscript*: Various subscript parameters are set in *File > Document Setup/File > Preferences > Typography*.
- *Superscript*: Again, parameters are set in *File > Document Setup/File > Preferences > Typography*.
- *Caps*: All letters will be capitalized.
- *Small Caps*: Uppercase letters are large caps, lowercase letters are (artificial) small caps. If your font has built-in small caps or a font file with a small caps font face, that would be a better alternative.
- *Strikethrough*: Click and hold for adjustments of line width, position. You will need to experiment to understand the settings.
- *Outline*: Click and hold to set line width as a percentage.
- *Shadow*: Click and hold to select X and Y displacement – again as percentages. The shadow color will be the same as outline if both are used. Shadows in Scribus are simply a duplication of the letter "behind" it, with a monochrome color, and sharp edge. Opacity can be set.
- *Kerning* (spinbox) is a bit out of place here, but allows for adjusting the distance between characters, and can be applied to one or many at a time.

Lastly, there are two sets of color adustments, each operating in an identical fashion.

- The left sets the line color, applied to outline and shadow. If neither outline nor shadow is selected, the line color button will be inactive, as seen here.

- The right sets the fill color of the font, its main color. Click the button to choose the color, then click and hold the percentage to be able to choose shading (saturation) from a list or set your own ("Other …"). This brings up a dialog to enter a number from 0 to 100. Numbers less than 0 become 0%, greater than 100 become 100%.

3.12.3 Text Entry and Using Styles

One can certainly use the Story Editor without either making or using styles, in which case to the left you will see the label "No Style" for each paragraph entered. How is a paragraph defined? Simply put, a paragraph begins either with the beginning of the block of text or a press of the Return key, and ends with the next Return key press or the end of the entire text block. So each time the Return key is pressed a new label is created, the previous style carried over to the next paragraph.

Check the font and other features set, as indicated above, change any you wish, and begin typing or load your text from a file. If you wish to continue entering text with a different font or other features, make any desired changes in settings, then continue typing – changes made apply only to newly entered text. In order to change settings for previously entered text, highlight it by holding down Shift and using arrows or other movement keys, or use the mouse to select. Changes to settings will modify only the highlighted text. Use either of the update methods (with or without exiting) to save any changes to your text frame.

If you do use styles, they are very easy to apply or change in the Story Editor. Click on "No Style" or whatever the current style is to the left of the text area. See the screenshot to the right.

You can click "Edit Styles..." to bring up the styles dialog, taking us to the process explained in the Working with Styles chapter for creating and editing styles.

Otherwise, click the arrow and you get a list of style choices if any exist. Click on your choice, and that style is applied to that entire paragraph. Remember it will not be applied to the actual text frame until you update.

To apply a single style to the whole text, use *Edit > Select All* or use Ctrl+A on the keyboard. Then select a style from the dropdown list in the toolbar of the Story Editor.

3.13 Working with Images

To CREATE an image frame, click the image frame icon on the toolbar, or from the main menu: *Insert > Image Frame*, or press "I" on the keyboard. Click-drag-let up on the document to create your frame. A new, empty frame will show a black cross from the diagonals – a sign that it has no image.

3.13.1 Context Menu: Image Frames

The context menu of image frames

Here is the context menu introduced in Working with Frames, obtained by right-clicking inside an image frame.

- *Info* will give you some information about the image – the name of the file, its resolution in pixels per inch (PPI), the actual PPI as contained in the document (not to be confused with the display PPI of Scribus), its colorspace (eg, RGB or CMYK), and whether export/print is enabled.

- *Undo* will undo the last operation on the frame. An operation which cannot be undone is clearing its contents.

- *Redo* gives you an opportunity to revert an undo, in case you change your mind.

- *Get Image ...* of course will be used to load an image file into the frame, generating a file dialog. If you use this option for a frame which already has content, that content will be replaced. Image types which can be loaded into an image frame are GIF, JPG, PNG, XPM, TIFF, PSD, EPS, and PDF.

- *Image Visible* is a checkbox to choose not to display the frame's image by unchecking. You might do this to speed up working with a document, by eliminating the time to refresh the screen when scrolling in the document. This will only affect the display, not whether the image is exported to PDF or printed. A frame which has an image, yet is not being shown will have a red cross from the diagonals.

- *Preview Settings* allow for low, normal, and high resolution displays. Lower resolutions speed up screen refreshes. This does not affect the resolution in the final PDF or a print.

- *Image Effects* allows for a limited scope of non-destructive image alterations. See the section Image Effects.

- *Edit Image ...* will load your image file into an external image editor, such as GIMP. This will be a destructive edit. If your image source cannot be edited (PDF, for example), this choice will not appear in the context menu. You can set the path your image editing program of choice in *File > Preferences > External Tools*.

- *Update Image* will refresh your image frame on the screen and makes only sense if it had been edited in an image editor while the Scribus document is open.

- *Adjust Frame to Image*: If you have just loaded the image, the size is determined by the image frame. Choosing the option will enlarge or shrink the frame to the current size of the image. If you have previously selected "Scale to Frame Size" in the *Image* tab of the Properties Palette, the scaling of the image will remain constant, and the frame adjusted accordingly.

- *Attributes*: A frame may have a number of attributes which can be used for various purposes, such as generating a table of contents. This is discussed elsewhere in the manual. While it's not possible to use image frames for a table of contents, you can save other other attributes, like eg. the creator of the image.

- *Is Locked* will lock the frame in all respects – its contents, size, position, and other features.

- *Size is Locked* locks only the size of the frame.

- *Send to Scrapbook* will send a copy of this frame to the Scrapbook. The Scrapbook is a folder where frames and other content can be saved, and reused. Sending to the Scrapbook does not delete the frame from the current document. Moreover, it will also make it available in other documents. See The Scrapbook.

- *Send to Layer* will only be present if you have more than one layer in your document, and allows you to move the frame to a different layer – you are presented with a list of choices. See the section about layers.

- *Level*: Use this to move this frame toward the surface (top) of the current layer or toward its bottom.

- *Convert to* allows conversion to other frame types, but there are limitations, denoted by a choice being grayed out if not possible for the current frame.

- *Cut, Copy, Delete* are conceptually self-explanatory – the frame with its contents will be cut, copied, or deleted.

- *Contents > Copy* copies the image contents to the clipboard.

- *Contents > Paste* pastes the copied image contents to a new frame, in the same relative X and Y position (relative to the frame) and same scaling as from the frame where it was copied.

- *Contents > Paste Absolute* pastes the image contents at the same scaling as the original, but with its original X and Y coordinates with respect to the document's coordinates. One might use this for a special effect, where one part of an image appears in one frame and some other part in a separate image frame elsewhere. You can even do this absolute pasting to a frame on another layer.

- *Contents > Clear* allows for deleting the content of the frame. It cannot be undone, but you will receive a dialog, asking for confirmation.

- *Properties* simply shows/hides the Properties Palette.

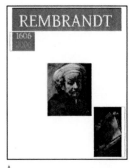

Contents > Paste Absolute of a copied image to 3 other Frames

3.13.2 Some Notes About Image Formats

There are two basic kinds of image formats: bitmap and vector. Bitmap graphics in one way or another have assigned a
point of image data as a certain color, so the image is a collection of tiny colored dots – pixels on the screen. Although printing machinery can have very high densities of these dots (DPI,
or dots-per-inch), computer monitors are severely limited, and
typically will show about 90 PPI (pixels per inch). In order to
visually see the quality of an image on a monitor, one must use
high magnification, and even then it will depend on the rendering capabilities of the software. Excessively high resolution on
the screen markedly increases the rendering time whenever the
screen refreshes. Some compromise is required, depending on
your computer specification, however the default usually suf-
fices.

Scribus has 3 display modes: low, normal, and high resolution, as shown in the section on the context menu > *Preview
Settings* above. Ultimately, however, you will need to view the
final PDF to check the true resolution of your document, although printing directly from Scribus can give a rough impression.

Vector graphics consist of a list of instructions for drawing
the image on the screen, and adjust to the size of the display or
other output. High quality fonts, ie., those which are not bitmap fonts for computer screens, are a form of vector graphic.
In theory, there should be unlimited resolution of such images,
but again, this is software dependent.

3.13.3 Supported Bitmap Formats

Let's begin by saying that TIFF (Tagged Image File Format)
and PNG (Portable Network Graphics) are the recommended
bitmap formats when choice is available.

- *TIFF* (Tagged Image File Format) is a format widely used for a
  variety of purposes, not only publishing, but also image transmission such as faxes. In its basic incarnation it is a one-for-one
  format, with each pixel represented by a data value, and thus for
  large images the files can be quite large. Every widely used image graphics program will be able to use TIFF. It also has an option for lossless compression (lossless meaning that no data is
  lost with compression or decompression). If it has a drawback it
  is that there are different versions of TIFF files, some of inferior
  quality, and one only finds this out after you use the image. In
  general, it is hard to go wrong with TIFF, but keep in mind that

the image quality is dependent on source – we certainly don't expect much from a fax machine. TIFF supports transparency, the CMYK colorspace and ICC color profiles. For special TIFF files exported by Adobe Photoshop see below.

- *PNG* (Portable Network Graphic) is a lossless compression format designed in part as an alternative to the patent encumbered GIF format, but also as an alternative to the complex TIFF format. One of its advantages is the ability to show transparency, but in addition, PNG does a better job than other formats where there are large areas of monochrome color and sharp transitions from one color to another. Therefore it is much preferred for things like screengrabs, images of text, and line art, where there is such a characteristic. The PNG format doesn't support the CMYK colorspace, but it can store ICC color profiles.

- *JPEG* (Joint Photographic Experts Group) is a lossy compression format, meaning that in the process of compression and decompression some information is lost. Consequently, every time it is loaded into an image manipulation program, uncompressed, then saved (compressed) again, information is progressively lost. It is worth mentioning here that Scribus only displays and uses the file, so no further information is lost in Scribus, unless you edit the file in an external editor (context menu > *Edit Image ...*). It cannot support transparency, but tends to do a better job than PNG where there are smooth gradients in color, thus it's in common use for photography. Most cameras support JPEG, though high-end cameras allow one to choose TIFF as the format. Thus, JPEG images are ubiquitous, and there will be times when you must use them – it will do no good to convert a JPEG image to TIFF, for example, since the information is already lost. If you plan to manipulate the image, however, this may be a good idea, so that further data is not lost. If you use JPEG in Scribus, try to use a scaling of 300 DPI or greater if possible (see below) – you can easily get by with less if your output medium is on a computer screen, such as a presentation or if your file is designed for the Web. The JPEG format supports the CMYK colorspace and ICC color profiles.

Beware of Progressive Files
TIFF, PNG, JPEG can use a technique called "Interlacing." It is a means to transfer an image gradually while using a slow network connection. Users will first see a low quality preview that slowly improves. If you want to print your images, make sure you're not working with progressive files!

- *GIF* (Graphics Interchange Format) is worth mentioning only because it is widely used on the internet. It is proprietary and uses a lossless compression. Images are only 8-bit, and you are limited to 256 colors. GIFs will produce unsatisfactory results in print publishing and should be avoided at all costs if the output is intended for commercial printing. The GIF format neither supports the CMYK colorspace nor ICC color profiles.

- *XPM* (X PixMap) is a simple format mainly used in computer screen icons and splashscreens. While 256 colors may be possible, in many cases there will be 128 or fewer. It is a text-based format and thus easy to edit – if you understand it. The XPM format neither supports the CMYK colorspace nor ICC colorspace profiles.

- *PSD* (Photoshop Document) format, as the name implies, was designed for use with Adobe Photoshop, and therefore contains the information needed by Photoshop to save image files for editing in Photoshop – transparency, clipping paths, alpha channels, spot colors, and duotone settings. Scribus does have its own native capabilities to import PSD files from version 6 and earlier – the latest version of the PSD format which is publicly documented. Files saved from newer versions should work without major issues, but they may have file format features which are not publicly documented.

  Scribus generally will import 8-bit Grayscale, RGB and CMYK PSD files without issue. It will also import PSD files with normal layers and will display the individual layers. Adjustment layers and effect layers are not yet supported. In this case, Scribus will fall back to using a "flattened" version of the file.

  Where you need to include CMYK plus Alpha transparency, the current workaround is to export a Photoshop PDF, then import into an image frame. The trade-off is that importing the PDF will require more memory and is slower to export, as it must be filtered through Ghostscript.

  Layered TIFFs saved from Photoshop are often not handled well by other TIFF readers and importing applications. This is because Photoshop actually embeds PSD type layers in a private tag. Scribus will attempt to read the PSD layers info and make this also accessible to the Extended Image Properties dialog. Text and vector layers within this private tag are not yet supported.

  Scribus in almost all cases will automatically detect the encoding wether it is ASCII, Binary or Binary with JPEG. It will also handle both PSD and TIFF files, no matter what byte ending is used – PPC Mac/SPARC or PC. Thus, you need not care whether a PSD or TIFF file from Photoshop has been created on a PowerPC-Mac or on a newer Mac or the Windows platform respectively. See Extended Image Properties for more information about special features for PSD files.

- *PDF* (Portable Document Format): While the PDF format doesn't actually qualify as a bitmap format, it is mentioned here, because Scribus can import a PDF only by loading it into an image frame. During that process it will rasterize, or convert it to a bitmap, using Ghostscript. Thus, you have the same considerations as far as image quality is concerned. There are settings to maximize this resolution in your final product. As of this writing, Scribus can only import the first page of any PDF document, so you must use other software – both open source (Free) and proprietary choices are available – to break a PDF into single page documents before importing.

- *EPS* (Encapsulated PostScript) files, similar to PDFs, can be imported into an image frame, and like PDFs will be rasterized. One would ideally want to import an EPS directly as a vector graphic, but depending on its contents, this may not be possible. See the section Importing Vector Drawings for further details.

3.13.4 Loading an Image into a Frame

When you first create an image frame, it will be blank except for a black "X" drawn from opposite corners, denoting the fact that there is no image.

Load an image from the context menu (right-click in frame) > *Get Image* (keyboard: Ctrl+D), from the menu *File > Import > Get Image* (or its keyboard equivalents). By default, the image will be loaded at its native size, with the upper left corner of the frame the upper left corner of the image.

It is conceivable that you may be able to simply resize the frame, but most likely you will need to adjust scaling of the image. If you know the final size you want the frame to be, follow the directions in **Working with Frames** then go to the *Image* tab of the Properties Palette.

Note that you can only load images with a color depth of 8 bit per channel into Scribus. While this is in a sense a limitation, it also helps to prevent problems with commercial printers, as many, if not most Raster Image Processors can only handle 8-bit images. Moreover, with current printing technology the use of 16-bit images won't result in a higher quality than 8-bit files.

3.13.5 Properties: Image Tab

If your frame is already the correct size, click "Scale to Frame Size." Subsequent adjustments in frame size will adjust scaling to continue to fill the frame size. Clicking back to "Free Scaling" will allow you to crop edges, reposition, or change scaling.

While it might at first seem difficult to make a frame of the precisely needed size but at a certain width or height, try this sequence:

1. Make your frame of the appropriate width or height – let's say you want a width of 300 points.
2. Load the image.
3. Click "Scale Image to Frame" in the tab of the Properties Palette.
4. Adjust height so that width dimension is filled.
5. Right click for the context menu, select "Adjust Frame to Image."

3.13.6 Scaling and Repositioning the Image

With the mouse on the frame:

1. Hold down Shift+Ctrl+Alt. Now clicking and dragging inside the frame will allow you to adjust the position of the image inside the frame (the frame stays in place). As soon as you let up on the keys, you go back to moving the frame.

2. Double-click the frame, or click on the "Edit Contents of Frame" icon on the toolbar (keyboard: E) – note that this will not happen if "Scale to Frame Size" is selected. This works like holding down Shift+Ctrl+Alt, except that you stay in the image-moving mode until you click back to Select Item on the toolbar, or click outside the frame.

You cannot resize the image directly with the mouse on the frame. Use the *Image* tab of the Properties Palette in "Free Scaling" mode instead:

- *X-Pos, Y-Pos*: These refer to the offset of the image (left upper corner) inside the frame.

- *X-Scale, Y-Scale, Actual X-DPI, Actual Y-DPI*: linked by default, click the chain to unlink.

Left: X-Pos, Y-Pos at 0,0 Middle: at 10,10 Right: at -10,-10

Note that changing the DPI settings doesn't change the actual resolution of an image, but just the size on a page. Do not attempt use the DPI option to achieve a higher quality output as it does not resample the source image but simply resizes it. Technically, changing X-/Y-Scale and changing Actual X-/Y-DPI is the same, just with two different units to choose from. You shouldn't be surprised that setting a lower DPI value will result in a higher percentage and thus in an enlarged image: a lower resolution without removing pixels creates a larger image in the frame.

3.13.7. Spreading Images over Many Pages

In Scribus you can spread an image over more than one page. For instance, if you want to use an image with a landscape as a background for two facing pages, you can create one image frame and draw it across the page boundaries. When you export your file to PDF, Scribus will automatically cut the image frame in the middle. Note that to use this feature reliably, you have set the gap between pages to zero in *File > Document Setup > Display*. This feature works for facing pages as well as for vertical spreads.

3.14 Working with Shapes and Polygons

SHAPES AND POLYGONS are two kinds of vector-drawn figures available in Scribus, and once created, can be manipulated in identical ways. It's worth mentioning here that if you import vector drawings such as SVGs from other sources, you will be able to edit these within Scribus, but in many cases, making your vector drawings within Scribus will save time.

▲
Screengrab of maximally en-larged shape – on the prin-ted page these edges will be absolutely crisp, within the limits of the printer res-olution.

A major advantage of vector-based graphics, and something of great value in publishing, is that they can be magnified almost infinitely and still have sharp edges.

3.14.1 Creating a Shape

The default shape is a rectangle, initially seen in the icon. The icon actually has two parts, the main area to the left, and to the right an arrow indicating where to click for a drop-down menu for selecting your shape as seen in our graphic. Click your choice, and you should see that the toolbar icon shows your se-lected shape, and it will be highlighted. As with other frames, click-drag to position and size your shape as desired. To make additional shapes of this same type, click the icon again, or choose *Insert > Shape* from the menu, or use the keyboard shortcut S.

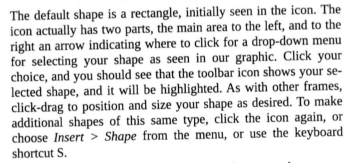

▲
Drop-down selector for Shapes

In contrast to text and image frames, the rectangle you see around your selected shape is a bounding box. A bounding box is a rectangle which delineates the horizontal and vertical boundaries of your shape, plus all of its elements. As we get to editing, you will see how this can actually be larger than the shape itself. If you change the line properties, or the fill color, these will apply to the shape, not the rectangular bounding box. See Working with Frames for explanations of basic frame manipulation common to all frames.

3.14.2 Creating a Polygon

In mathematics, a polygon can be any closed shape made up of straight lines. In Scribus, polygons are regular polygons hav-ing 3 to 999 sides, even though a polygon with 999 sides will likely be hard to differentiate from a circle, even at high magni-fication.

Click on the toolbar icon, select *Insert > Polygon* or use key-board shortcut P to get a default polygon. The default polygon has 4 sides (even though the icon always shows a pentagon) until you change its properties in the dropdown dialog, activated similarly to the dialog for phapes. Click the arrow, then "Properties ..." to bring up the polygon properties dialog shown here.

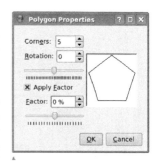

The properties dialog for polygons

Select the number of corners (or sides if you prefer to think of it that way), and as you will see your basic polygon will have equal length sides. Rotation of the figure (-180 to 180 degrees) is adjusted with the spinbox or the slider, with a visual preview as you adjust. In addition, by checking "Apply Factor" you can cause the sides to become folded inward (concave) or outward (convex) – again, the preview shows what you are doing. As the examples show, small percentage changes will make dramatic differences.

In contrast to the changing shape icon, the polygon icon always will show a pentagon.

Apply Factor: -50%, -25%, 0, 10%, 25% respectively (min -100%, max 100%)

3.14.3 Context Menu: Shapes

Here is the context menu brought up by right-clicking inside a shape or polygon. As you see, we have fewer choices than with text or image frames.

The context menu for shapes and polygons

- *Undo* will undo the last operation on the frame. Operations which cannot be undone are deleting the frame or changing the gradient
- *Redo* gives you an opportunity to revert an undo, in case you change your mind.
- *Attributes*: A shape may have a number of attributes which can be used for various purposes.
- *Is Locked* will lock the shape in all respects – its size, position, and other features.
- *Size is Locked* locks only the size of the frame.
- *Send to Scrapbook* will send a copy of this item to the Scrapbook.
- *Send to Layer* will only be present if you have more than one layer in your document, and allows you to move the item to a different layer – you are presented with a list of choices.

105

- *Level*: Use this to move this item toward the surface (top) of the current layer or toward its bottom.

- *Convert to* allows conversion to other frame types, but there are limitations, denoted by a choice being grayed out if not possible for the current frame. Conversion of a shape to a text or image frame allows for interesting effects. In contrast, conversion of image or text frames to a polygon will lose the display of the content, but if you then convert back to its former type, its content will be available again.

- *Cut, Copy, Delete* are conceptually self-explanatory.

- *Properties* simply shows/hides the Properties Palette.

3.14.4 Shapes and Polygons: Vector Drawing

Like special vector drawing programs, Scribus has the ability to dramatically edit both shapes and polygons, but before we get to actual editing, let's talk about how a program uses information to draw these figures. For polygons, ie. closed figures made up of straight lines, all one needs to know are the points representing the corners and then draw straight lines from one to the next, such as the square on the left. These corners in vector drawing are called nodes.

On the left, the circled dots (which are blue on your screen) represent these nodes, which we can then move independently to change the shape of our polygon. This is the most simple way of editing shapes beyond resizing or rotating as it has been described in Working with Frames.

Circles and other curved shapes add the challenge of describing and controlling the curves of various parts of the shape, so we obviously need something more than just nodes.

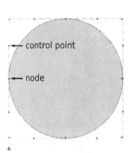

Circle showing nodes in blue on screen, control points in magenta on screen. Red squares on screen are related to the bounding box.

That something is called a control point in vector drawing. In the circle on the left we see our blue nodes as before, but also magenta-colored control points. Less obvious are the blue dotted lines connecting a control point to its node. Each node in a closed figure will have two control points, affecting the line or curve on opposite sides of the node. So in our circle, imagine these control points mathematically pulling out the portion of the curve which is attached to the next node. It is important to realize that the final curve represents the interaction of four pieces of information: the two nodes at the ends, and the control points of each node which control the curve. In addition, while it may appear that our square above only had nodes, the control points are indeed there, but superimposed on the nodes, thus exerting none of this mathematical pull and a straight line results from one node to the next.

Now that you know this, you can begin to understand how we might transform a figure with straight lines and sharp corners into one with no corners and rounded contours, and vice versa.

3.14.5 Properties: Shape > Edit Shape

When you click "Edit Shape" in the *Shape* tab or double-click on a shape/line, you bring up this dialog. As with most dialogs and buttons in Scribus, there are tooltips for the different functions. Let's start by working our way down this dialog – we'll talk about the basic editing of nodes and control points first.

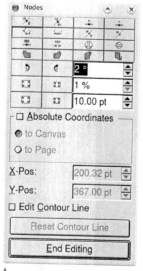

The "Edit Shape" dialog

In the first row:

- *Move Nodes* allows for click and drag to move a node.
- *Move Control Points*: Same for control points. If a control point coincides with a node, you cannot see it. Click and drag the node and you will pull out one control point. Click and drag again and you will pull out the other.
- *Add Nodes*: Click along the line of the shape to add more nodes.
- *Delete Nodes*: Since you cannot have control points without nodes, these will disappear too.

In the second row:

- *Move Control Points Independently*: Applies only when the "Move Control Points" button is active. Each individual control point moves without affecting its partner.
- *Move Control Points Symmetrically*: Applies only when the "Move Control Points" button is active. The two control points at a given node will align themselves in a straight line, passing through the node and remain equidistant from it.
- *Reset Control Points*: As of this writing, this works with difficulty and without dependability. Therefore its use is discouraged.
- *Reset this Control Point*: The currently selected control point resets to coincide with its node.

If "Absolute Coordinates" is checked, the numbers apply to a reference to 0,0 for the page, otherwise 0,0 is the left upper corner of the bounding box. If no node or control point is selected these will be inactive (gray).

On the following page we see an edited, distorted, and unhappy-looking circle. The set of control points in the upper right of the shape have been moved independently, and the upper left set moved symmetrically. As you can see, moving symmetrically easily allows for more smooth curves through the

Here we see some spinboxes for precisely positioning the nodes and control points.

node, while independent positioning allows for a sharper transition at the node.

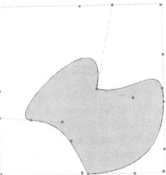

Also demonstrated here is the bounding box principle mentioned earlier, that the bounding box defines the space required by all of the shape's elements, including in this case the control points. This is important to know if you are considering "Text Flows Around Frame" using the bounding box as the delimiter, and also if there may be a problem in case your bounding box extends beyond the document's edge, even though the shape does not.

This is also a point at which it is worth mentioning that in many cases it will be wise to edit a copy of your shape. For example, if you used a complex sequence of changing various nodes and control points, you may find it impossible to retrace back to some former state, even using undo in the main window. As you can see there is no undo in the "Edit Shape" dialog.

3.14.6 Edit Shape Dialog – Part 2

Let's go back now to the next two rows of buttons in our "Edit Shape" dialog, starting with the 3rd row:

- *Open a polygon or cuts a Bézier curve.*
- *Close this Bézier curve.*
- *Mirror Path Horizontally* is self-explanatory and will not be explained further.
- *Mirror Path Vertically* is self-explanatory and will not be explained further.

The first two are complementary, and unless you have an open curve, the "Close ...." button will be inactive. Here we see the results of opening this circle at the top node, shifting a node upward (there are now two where there was one), then finally closing the curve. As you can see, this makes creation of a discontinuous curve easy.

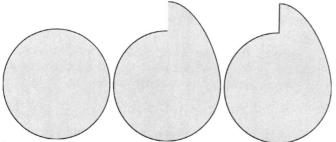

In case you hadn't already anticipated, you can also use the "Close this Bézier Curve" button to turn a Bézier curve into a closed figure.

The 4th row are all skewing operations: left, right, up, and down. The graphic more easily shows the results than one can verbally describe. As you can see, for horizontal skewing, the top of the figure goes left or right, for vertical skewing, the right side goes up or down, but the opposite sides go in the opposite directions. Each click of the button skews a small amount – these results represent about 15 clicks each, and each beginning with the right triangle shape at far left.

Skewing, left to right: none, left, right, up, down. Before skewing, each lighter-colored triangle started out coinciding with the underlying dark triangle.

3.14.7 Edit Shape Dialog – Finale

"Edit Contour Line" (not shown here, but shown on p. 107) allows you to edit the contour line of a frame, which can be used as the delimiter for text flow around a frame. Once you activate this checkbox, the editing process is identical and uses the same process that is described in this chapter for editing shapes and polygons – the contour line becomes visible and shows nodes and interconnecting lines.

↺	↻	2 °	⇕
⊡	⊡	1 %	⇕
⊡	⊡	10.00 pt	⇕

The top row of this section of "Edit Shape," "Rotate the Path Counter-Clockwise" and "Rotate the Path Clockwise" perhaps only need mention that "path" refers to the entire vector graphic you are editing. The spinbox to the right can be set from 0 to 180 degrees (no decimals), and represents the number of degrees the path will be moved each time you click the button.

The next two rows allow for proportionally enlarging (left button each row), or shrinking (right button each row). Like the rotation buttons, the amount of change is an incremental value indicated by the spinbox, either in percentage or number of page units – points in this screenshot. Percentages can be 0 to 100.

Be careful with changes in page units – the value in the spinbox can be quite large, and even negative numbers can be entered. Once again, undo may or may not be your salvation.

3.14.8 Fill Rules

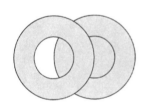

In the *Shape* tab of the Properties Palette you can choose between two so-called fill rules, even-odd and non zero. Fill rules are geometrical rules, which determine how a shape is filled. While in most cases the selected fill rule won't make any notable difference for a user, some shapes require a choice as to which rule will be applied. Below you see the "donut" shape from the shape selector. The left shape uses even-odd, wheras non zero is applied to the right one; as you can see, the central area in the left shape is transparent, not filled.

3.14.9 Combining and Splitting Polygons

If there is any feature of vector drawing manipulation in Scribus where the adage, "Make copies of your graphics to experiment with" applies, this is it. As we will see, results can be variable. It is also safe to say that undo is unhelpful.

The basic idea of "Combine Polygons" (also applies to shapes, or mixtures of polygons and shapes), is to take some overlapping vector drawings on different levels, and combine them into a single vector drawing. In the process, the final drawing can only have a single fill color, and a single line color, and we see an interesting effect in the areas of overlap.

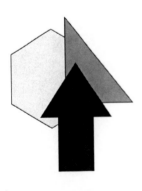

Let's start with an arbitrary series of a polygon and two shapes. As you can see on the left, the hexagon is on the bottom, then the triangle, then the arrow on top.

The operation for combining polygons is to:

• Select all the polygons/shapes you wish to combine

• Click *Item > Combine Polygons* from the Menu

But we can select these polygons in two different ways:

1. Click-drag completely around the figures with the mouse.

2. Hold down Shift, then click frames sequentially.

Original – before combining

On the right we see what we get with these two methods:

- Method 1: Drawing a rubberband around with the mouse to select them all, then choosing *Item > Combine Polygons*.

- Method 2: Shift-clicking in this order: triangle > hexagon > arrow, then *Item > Combine Polygons*.

What happened here was that in the first instance, the fill and line colors come from the bottommost frame – the hexagon, and in the second, from the first frame clicked – the triangle. Shift-click selecting will pick the first frame for the colors used in the combined polygon.

As far as concerns undo, you can reasonably expect that if you undo after combining polygons, you will split them up, but the colors will stay with the single choices from the combined figure. Clicking "Undo," and especially multiple undos after splitting polygons results in changes that are strange and unpredictable, with polygons moving about the page and changing size.

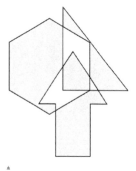

Method 1

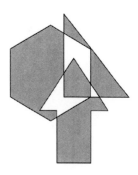

Method 2

3.15 Straight Lines and Arrows

STRAIGHT LINES are simple Scribus objects with a starting point and an end point. You can create straight lines by using *Insert > Line* in the menu bar, by clicking the button "Insert Line" in the toolbar or by pressing "L."

Click the icon, then click-drag to draw the line; let up to finish the line. If you hold down Ctrl while drawing, your line will rotate in steps of 15 degrees: 0, 15, 30, 45, and so on.

It's also worth pointing out that these lines can only be simple ones – two points connected by a line. For a series of points connected by lines, you will need to use Bézier curves.

In the *Line* tab of Properties Palette you can control the properties of lines and convert them to arrows:

- *Basepoint*: The basepoint can be set to left point or to end points. In the first case, you can edit the line's properties like width in relation to the left point; in the second case you can adjust the X and the Y values of both end points separately. You'll find these properties in the *X, Y, Z* tab of the Properties Palette, not in the *Line* tab. Note that the setting of the basepoint is always valid for all lines in the current document.

- *Type of Line*: Different kinds of lines like solid, dotted and some more:

The *Line* tab of the Properties Palette

Line types and arrowheads in Scribus

- *Start Arrow and End Arrow*: Both sides of a line can be decorated with various kinds of shapes: arrows, squares and triangles on both end are possible. Each shape is available in three sizes: large (L), medium (M) and small (S). They always have the same color as the line itself. The image shows three lines with an arrow as starting point and a square as endpoint. From top to bottom in size large, medium and small:

- *Endings*: The shape of the endings of a line. Flat, square and round cap are possible. With a flat cap, the line ends abruptly at its end point, while square and round cap are adding a "cap" to the end of the line, having a rectangular or round shape. The im-

Line Endings

age to the left illustrates the three types of endings: all three lines are exactly of the same type, except for the endings. The first one has a flat cap, the second one a square and the third one a round cap:

Note that you can also apply these kinds of endings to the corners of shapes and polygons.

3.15.1 Line Styles

In the lower part of the *Line* tab of the Properties Palette is a listbox for applying a line style to a line. You can create and edit these line styles via *Edit > Line Styles*:

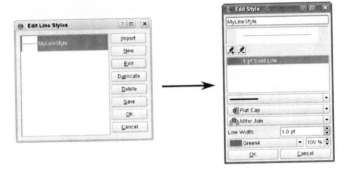

- *Import* imports existing line styles from other Scribus files.
- *New, Edit and Duplicate* all open a dialog like the one on the right side of the screenshot above. Here you can change the properties of the selected line style as described above.
- *Delete* removes the selected style.
- *Save* saves all line styles to the document.
- *OK* accepts the current settings and closes the dialog.
- *Cancel* closes the dialog without saving the changes.

3.15.2 Customizing the Relationship between Line and Arrow Size

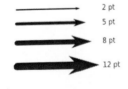

Automatcially adjusted arrow-heads

If you use the automatic adjustments in the *Line* tab of the Properties Palette, you will see that after you assign an arrow style, adjustments in line thickness cause an automatic change in arrowhead size, illustrated here.

It's entirely possible that this size ratio doesn't suit you, so here is how to modify this behavior. First, adjust your line thickness so that the arrowhead size is correct. Now, create a line style, via *Edit > Line Styles*.

Keeping it simple for this example, on the right are the settings for a 6 pt solid black line style, which we then save and assign to our line – you will see our new line style "Sixpointsolid" appearing as a choice at the bottom of the *Line* tab in the Properties Palette.

And below the settings you see the final result, with our new line style applied to all but the smallest arrow.

Note that if you change color and/or opacity of the line style, this will be applied to the arrowhead in the Scribus display. However, when you export to PDF, the arrowhead will have the color as defined in Properties > *Colors* > *Line Color*.

3.15.3 Shapes as Arrows

There is another fast way to create arrows in Scribus: the Shape menu contains some predefined arrows. These can be edited in the same way as other shapes. See Working with Shapes and Polygons.

3.16 Bézier Curves and Freehand Lines

3.16.1 Bézier Curves

A BÉZIER CURVE in Scribus is created as a combination of several straight lines, where the end point of the actual line is the starting point for the next one. Use *Insert > Bezier Curve*, the button "Insert Bezier Curve" from the toolbar or press B for creating a new Bézier curve.

The cursor changes to a cross now and starts to create a straight line. With a second click, the line is finished. With a third click, another line is drawn between the end point of the first line and the actual position of the cursor. Every next click adds one more line to the Bézier curve. Pressing the ESC button or the right mouse button ends adding new lines and finishes the Bézier curve. The Bézier curve shown below consists of three points. Incidentally, you can make perfectly horizontal or vertical lines by holding down Ctrl as you move your mouse.

In contrast to straight lines, a Bézier curve can have a fill color.

You can see the flexibility of this tool by click-dragging to cause the line from the last point in a particular direction, rather than simply clicking individual points. Expect this to require some practice (also known as trial and error) before you can use this feature proficiently.

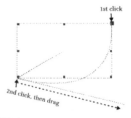

What you see as you go ...

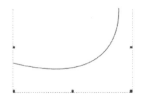

Result after clicking right mouse button

A Bézier curve, like all Scribus shapes, can be edited via *Shape > Edit Shape* in the Properties Palette or a double-click. If "Move Control Points" is activated, the straight lines of the Bézier curve can be transformed into curves.

A straight line converted to a Bézier curve

See the chapter on shapes and polygons for more details about editing shapes, including Bézier curves. It's also good to be aware that there is a way to transform an open curve into a closed shape, pointed out in that chapter.

3.16.2 Converting Bézier Curves

Bézier curves can be converted to text or image frames (context menu or *Item > Convert to …*), but you will likely find them hard to work with except when the curve has been converted to a shape which has been closed.

3.16.3 Freehand Lines

Freehand lines in Scribus are similar to drawing with a pen on a piece of paper. Use *Insert > Feehand Line*, the button "Insert Freehand Line" in the toolbar or press F on the keyboard to create a new freehand line:

Click on the document and hold down the mousebutton to draw the freehand line. Releasing the mouse button stops drawing. You have to press F again to continue adding more lines to your drawing. On the right you can see a complex example of a freehand drawing:

Drawing something like this requires much skill. Note that the lines drawn with the Freehand Line tool are not initially Bézier curves. However, if you select them in the Shape tab of the Properties Palette and select "Edit Shape," you can edit them as Bézier curves, although expect this to be a complex exercise, since invariably many nodes will have been created. A simple straight line cannot be edited as a curve.

3.17 Colors and Gradients

3.17.1 Line and Fill Colors

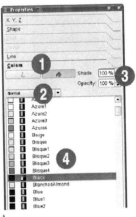

The *Colors* tab of the Properties Palette

THE COLORS of Scribus objects are applied via the *Colors* tab in the Properties Palette. For frames and shapes, Scribus distinguishes between the line color and the fill color. The fill color is used to fill the area which is surrounded by the object's borders. The line color is the color of a text or image frame's border or the outline of the shape. If the border's width is set to "0" in the Line tab of the Properties Palette, changing the line's color will have no visible effect. Also, a line with the color "None" will be invisible, regardless of its width.

A straight line and freehand lines can only have a line and not a fill color. However, as you can see in the section Bézier Curves and Freehand Lines, Bézier curves can have a fill color. The two buttons in the middle of the tab ("Edit Line Color Properties" and "Edit Fill Color Properties") **(1)** can be used to switch between line color and fill color.

The select box **(2)** under the two buttons controls the kind of color which is used on the object. If it is set to "Normal," the selected color is simply applied. The other selections are defining various kinds of gradients.

Here is something important to know as you make lines thicker, not just in shapes, but also in frames: All of these squares have the same dimensions as defined in the *X, Y, Z* tab of the Properties Palette, and the thin line also has this same "Y-Pos" value. If you increase line thickness, you'll see that it spreads both outwards and toward the center of the square, so in effect the visual boundary of the square becomes larger, and simultaneously the content of a frame is encroached upon.

3.17.2 Shade and Opacity

With the spin boxes, shade and opacity can be set from 0 to 100% **(3)**.

3.17.2.1 Shade

The shade in Scribus is similar to saturation. A fully saturated color is at 100%, and whatever hue the color has will be the most intense. At 0% the shade will be a neutral gray color. The example shows a black rectangle at decreasing levels of shade from left to right:

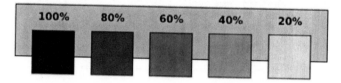

3.17.2.2 Opacity

The opacity, like its opposite term transparency, defines how much of the background behind the actual object can be seen. If set to 100%, nothing of the background shines through the object. In contrast, an opacity of 0% results in a transparent object. The example shows a gray rectangle in the background and in the foreground a black one at different levels of opacity:

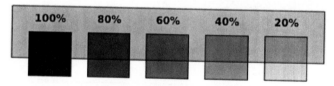

3.17.3 Applying Colors

A simple click in the list of colors **(4)** selects this color and applies it to the object's line or area, depending on what is selected. If you want to add more colors or edit existing ones, this can be done in *Edit > Colors*.

3.17.4 Editing Colors

The Scribus file format has a section in which available colors for a document are saved. You begin with a default list when you begin a new document, but since this list can be edited, each document can have its own particular list.

Scribus is shipped with a number of predefined color sets. If these are not sufficient, you can edit existing colors and add new ones. Go to *Edit > Colors*:

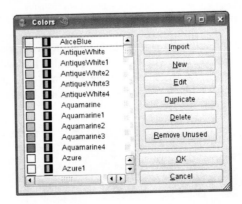

- *Import*: With this function you can import colors from other documents into the existing one.

- *New and Edit*: Change existing colors or create new ones:

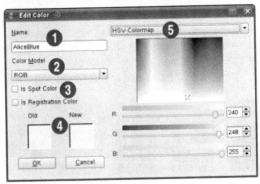

1. Name of the color.

2. The color model, RGB, CMYK or web safe RGB.

3. Spot and/or registration color. For information about spot colors, see the section Spot Colors. Registration marks are used in offset printing to check if all four process colors are printed to the same space on a printing sheet. In most cases these marks look like bull's eyes. Only if these marks on the final sheet are 100% black and there's no offset in any of the process colors, the print run went correctly. It is highly recommended to use only one registration color with the values for C, M, Y and K all set to 100!

4. Preview of the edited color, compared to the old one.

5. Different choices of predefined color lists or a generic HSV color selector.

- *Duplicate*: Duplicates the selected color.

- *Remove unused*: Deletes all colors from the list that are not used in the current document.

3.17.5 Managing Color Sets

If you open the dialog *Edit > Colors* when no document is open, you'll get some more options to change the existing color lists:

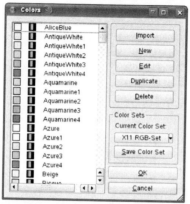

Select an existing color set via "Current Color Set." Change or edit colors as described above – a click on "Save Color Set" saves the edited color set. A click on "Save Color Set" asks for a new name, so that you can create new color sets.

3.17.6 Gradients

Scribus objects can be filled with gradients, which are smooth transitions from one fill color to another. Between these start and end colors, there can be one or more color stops. Gradients can be only applied to fill colors, not to line colors.

The dropdown list in the middle of the Color tab of the Properties Palette offers several kinds of gradients. If a gradient is selected, the gradient editor appears under the dropdown list.

Editing a gradient in the Properties Palette

Selecting the arrows at the start or end of the gradient, and clicking in the list of colors applies a new color to the gradient. The arrows can be moved away from the start or end point with the mouse pointer. As a result, the selected color moves within the gradient. The select box "Position" under the gradient allows for exact control of the position of a color stop (on your screen the selected stop is highlighted in red). Add a new stop by left-clicking between existing stops - you will see the mouse pointer become a "+" when it is positioned properly.

Adding a gradient stop in the Properties Palette

The new stop can be assigned a third color, and so on. Dragging an arrow outside the gradient's area deletes the gradient stop.

There are two special kinds of gradients, namely "Free Radial Gradient" and "Free Linear Gradient." These permit editing the gradient directly on canvas:

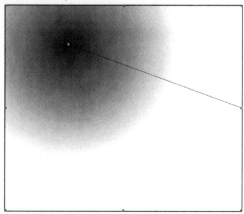

The spin boxes "Shade" and "Opacity" also work in gradients as described above. When a color's opacity is set to 0%, it is completely transparent. Here, a gradient from "Black" to "White" is applied. The end color's opacity is set to 0% and the text frame below can be seen:

Here are some examples of gradients. From left to right: A horizontal gradient, a vertical one, two diagonal ones and one radial gradient.

3.18. Importing Vector Drawings

3.18.1 SVG

ALTHOUGH SVG [1] was not exclusively designed with printing in mind, it does have some major advantages: it is vector-based, and fully documented (World Wide Web Consortium [W3C] recommendation), so that it can be regarded as an open and useful alternative to EPS, AI and CDR. SVG supports vectors of course, but also bitmaps, text, effects, scripting, and animation, and has subparts written to make it more reliable for certain kinds of outputs such as small screens (mobile phone, PDA ...), or pre-press (SVG::print). Scribus supports the SVG specifications 1.0 and 1.1 to some degree.

The development of SVG started between 1998 and 2000, when Adobe and Sun (with PGML) on the one hand and Macromedia and Microsoft (with VML) on the other hand were unable to muster enough support for a W3C recommendation for either form of markup language. As a result a new format was created, incorporating elements of both PGML and VML, which quickly won approval. SVG 1.0 was completed in 2001, and SVG 1.1 in 2003. SVG Tiny (for mobile devices) became a recommendation in 2006. As of this writing, the final version of SVG 1.2 is expected to be published soon.

SVG is not yet as widely used as some other vector formats (EPS, AI, SWF), mostly because of the lack of software able to create or display all current features. Now that all browsers (except for Internet Explorer, which still needs a special plug-in) support it by default, things have begun to change, so that it should begin to be seen as a mature alternative to proprietary formats (note that Adobe Illustrator and CorelDraw support SVG, and Inkscape even uses SVG as its native file format).

3.18.1.1 Advantages

SVG

- is an open standard
- is platform-independent
- is XML-based like the Scribus or OpenDocument formats
- supports color management
- is light-weight

Furthermore, there are free software programs that have good SVG support, especially Inkscape.

Whenever you are creating logos, icons, charts, maps, or other documents that need to be dynamically resizable, SVG can be your format of choice.

3.18.1.2 Importing SVG

From the menu, select *File > Import SVG ...* SVG files can have the file extension .svg/.SVG and .svgz/.SVGZ (the z indicates a compressed version of SVG). In contrast to bitmap images, you do not need to create a frame. Scribus will convert the SVG file to a native vector drawing instead. Depending on the content, you may get a message telling you, that some features may not be implemented in Scribus. In most cases, however, you won't notice any difference between the SVG in a drawing program and in Scribus. Click on the page to place the SVG drawing. Moving and resizing are similar to what you see with frames, but most SVGs will consist of a number of vector graphic elements, much like a group of polygons.

3.18.1.3 Known Issues

SVG is a complex and evolving standard. Some features aren't yet fully supported in Scribus, and others, like animation, will never be – for obvious reasons. Presently, some deficiencies include:

- Some text styles
- Some gradient styles
- Masking and clipping
- Embedded images
- SVGs which are not well-formed. If all tags and structures are not correct or the SVG is corrupted in some other way, the plug-in may crash.
- Animations, multi-media and "extensions" or proprietary tags within SVG, which can only be viewed with certain viewers.

3.18.1.4 Modifying SVG drawings

Since SVG files are natively supported, this means that:

- Colors of the imported SVG will be added to the color list of the document. Their names will begin with "FromSVG," so that you can re-use those colors for other objects.
- SVG paths can be modified in Scribus after "ungrouping" (context menu or *Item > Ungroup*) the imported vector item, and then clicking the "Edit Shape" button of in the *Shape* tab of the Properties Palette. See Working with Shapes and Polygons for more details on editing vector drawings in Scribus.

It is recommended that text in vector graphics should always be converted to outlines in the program that creates them, either with the tools available for that purpose or during export.

3.18.2 PostScript/EPS

The PostScript file format played a major role in the Publishing Revolution, together with the Apple LaserWriter and Page-Maker. While PostScript is actually a full-fledged programming language like, for example, C, C++ or Java, its main purpose – even today – is to describe pages and their content (text, drawings, images etc.) as well as "translating" them to a printing device. Even though other "page description" languages, like GDI/GDI+ in Windows, have been developed and succeeded for many consumer devices, PostScript is still ubiquitous in professional printing. The very popular PDF format, used by Scribus for output, is a close relative of PostScript, the main difference being that PostScript is first and foremost designed for printing, while PDF adds and continues to add lots of other ingredients to the sauce, like, for instance, scripting, hyperlinks, forms etc.

Encapsulated PostScript (EPS) is a subset of the PostScript format made to exchange PostScript data between applications. EPS can be considered as a special kind PostScript file format that describes a single page (or a part of it) and also contains (optionally) a preview image of its content.

The last major update of the EPS specification was released in 1992 [2], and the latest PostScript specification is from 1997 [3]. Since then, PDF has become an alternative standard, so that EPS has consequently lost some its importance. Nonetheless, the use of EPS remains widespread, so being able to manage this format is still essential in DTP.

PostScript files usually have the file extension .ps/.PS. Most EPS files use .eps/.EPS, but there are also some other (older) extensions, namely .epsf/.EPSF, .epsi/.EPSI, .ept/.EPT, .epi/.EPI, .eps2/EPS2, .eps3/.EPS3. If you want to use files with those extensions, you have to rename them to *.eps or *.EPS – otherwise, Scribus won't recognize them.

3.18.2.1 EPS Import in Scribus

To improve your chances of successfully importing EPS/PS files it helps to have three ingredients:

• An EPS/PS file which is conformant to the published specifications. Not all applications export EPS files with the same level of fidelity, nor do all embed fonts properly.

- The latest Ghostscript available for your platform.
- Where an EPS file has fonts embedded, ensure that Ghostscript's font paths are set up correctly. This is mostly for those using Linux or UNIX with X-Windows. Windows and Mac OS X users will not need to worry so much about font configuration with Ghostscript.

There are two basic methods of importing EPS files and both have pluses and minuses. The first and most often preferred method is to import the EPS into Scribus as native objects via *File > Import > Import EPS/PS*. The second is simply importing the EPS file into an image frame. This means the file will be rasterized or turned into a bitmap like a TIFF or JPEG. This method may be the only possibility if the EPS file has embedded images.

3.18.2.2 Importing Hints

A recommended way to import EPS/PS files into Scribus is to simply create a new document via *File > Open*. Select "PostScript" from the dropdown under "File Type" in the file dialog. Then directly import the EPS/PS file. This creates a new document in which the page size is automatically calculated from the EPS bounding box. A bounding box in an EPS file is a rectangle that describes the actual size of the graphical content. Save this temporarily as a SLA file.

Then, re-open the target document for import. Create a new layer and then use the page import function to import your newly created document into the new layer in your existing document. This prevents any of the imported elements from disturbing existing objects and allows you to place the file where you want with precision.

3.18.2.3 Other EPS/PS Hints

- If you are using Adobe Illustrator 9.0+, it is recommended that you save in Illustrator 7 or an older format. The reason is that Illustrator 9.0 or later actually uses PDF as a native format and embeds quite a bit of Adobe-specific information into in the EPS which can cause difficulties when importing.
- You are well advised to separate images from vector and import only the vector artwork as EPS, if possible. See below.
- Scribus can import multi-page PS files via *File > Open*. Scribus will create as many pages as the PostScript file contains, but for PostScript files which are purely text this is not recommended. Currently, text is converted to outlines on import. If you need the text contained within the PostScript file you can use GSview

to extract the text or the command line tool `ps2ascii` which comes with Ghostscript. This tool works on Windows and OSX as well.

If your platform supports it, GSview is recommend above all other PostScript viewers for diagnosing and previewing Post-Script. While the display is not color managed, it will generally help to diagnose issues with importing in Scribus.

3.18.2.4 Importing EPS as Native Scribus Objects

Importing EPS as Scribus native objects, when possible, does have some advantages. First, they are all vectors, so file size and exported PDF size are relatively small. It makes them resolution independent, so they can be re-scaled without losing crispness in printing. As a bonus you can edit the graphical elements like lines, polygons and curves natively.

To import an EPS file as a native Scribus Object, click *File > Import > Import EPS/PS* and select the EPS. If you have previews enabled in the file chooser, large complex EPS file may take some time to render. Then left-click to drop the cursor where you want to place the file. Once dropped on the canvas, the EPS file objects are grouped. You will need to ungroup them to edit individual objects. To scale an imported EPS proportionally, select the lower right corner and Ctrl+left click drag up or down as needed.

3.18.2.5 Importing EPS Files with Embedded Raster Graphics

Scribus can import EPS files which contain embedded raster graphics (bitmaps). However, this works best with Ghostscript 8.50 or later, and there are some limitations:

- Image mask doesn't work correctly
- Clipping paths are ignored
- Importing will create one file (a TIFF) for each bitmap and there can be many within an EPS. If you seem to run out of disk space after importing many EPS files, you should check your home directory/your Personal Files folder for TIFF files starting with "Document" or the name of the file(s) you imported the EPS files into.

3.18.2.6 Importing EPS as an Image

When you wish to import an EPS into Scribus and it has a mix of text, images and vector, importing the file as an image is the only real option. Importing in this manner, provided the fonts are correctly embedded, usually works very reliably and will maintain fidelity to the CMYK colors defined in the EPS. On initial import, Scribus will ignore any embedded preview bitmaps and will generate its own low resolution preview of the EPS. If nothing displays, this is a hint something is not working correctly in the import and needs closer inspection. When exporting to PDF, the EPS will be rerun through Ghostscript and it is embedded into the PDF, so do not be surprised about long PDF export times or high memory usage.

3.18.2.7 Troubleshooting EPS Import

As mentioned above, EPS export quality from other applications can vary widely. Some applications like to add their own ingredients – unfortunately. The first step for testing a failed import is to open the file in GSview, then press M to watch the messages from Ghostscript while it attempts to open the file. When you have a failure in GSview, the messages can be sometimes cryptic, but they are a helpful pointer to see what but they are a helpful pointer to see what the problem may be.

3.18.3 OpenOffice.org Draw/ OpenDocument Graphics

OpenOffice.org Draw is one of the modules of the OpenOffice.org suite. It is a general-purpose vector drawing program similar to Adobe Illustrator or Inkscape. It can export drawings in a large variety of formats, but before version 2.0 it used its own native SXD (StarOffice XML Drawing) format, and since version 2.0, OpenOffice.org Draw's default file format is the ISO standard OpenDocument Graphics (ODG). Just like OpenOffice.org Writer and OpenDocument Text files, OpenOffice.org Draw and OpenDocument Graphics files are sets of XML and other files, like images, which are compressed in a single file. Scribus can import both file formats, but you have various choices, depending on the content. The most promising of them are native SXD/ODG import and exported EPS files from OpenOffice.org Draw.

For most drawings, import of native files works very well. Very complex Draw files have been tested, which imported flawlessly. In some cases, especially with gradients, it may be preferable to test exporting EPS, with the settings listed below. You should check both methods for best quality not only on screen in Scribus, but also after export to PDF. Load into Adobe Reader and compare at high magnification.

3.18.3.1 Caveats

- It is important to note that Draw 3D objects do not export well, as they are limited to screen resolution. They do not print well in most cases and will appear pixellated (read: really ugly) at print resolutions. They should be avoided in vector drawings that are designed for printing.

- Not all shapes in OpenOffice.org Draw 2.x are supported. Contours and callouts do not currently work natively. The workaround is to go *Edit > Select All* in Draw and then right click the selection, then choose *Convert > To Curves* or *Convert > To Polygon* depending on the kind of content.

- Most curves, polygons and Bézier shapes are imported without issues. The same applies for star shapes, ellipses and markers – a type of line with arrows.

- Text effects, especially those from the "Fontwork Gallery" should be avoided in preference to doing them natively in Scribus which has very versatile text effects. Many OpenOffice.org Draw and ODG text effects won't be imported at all and in the worst case may trigger a Scribus crash.

- If you aren't sure whether a font you use in an SXD or ODG file is available on a system, or if you use "faux" bold or italics (see *Typography*), you are advised to to convert text to curves in Draw: Select the text in your SXD/ODG file, then click *Modify > Convert > To Curve* in Draw's menu bar.

3.18.3.2 Importing Formulas

The most reliable way is to save your formula as desired and close Math. Then open OpenOffice.org Draw and create a new file. Then click *Insert > Object > Formula*. You will have a tiny embedded square on Draw's canvas, and Draw will launch Math automatically. In Math, select *Tools > Import Formula* and browse to your saved formula. Then press Esc to quit the editing mode for formulas. The embedded formula is now scalable in Draw with the context menus (you may have to unlock the size in the dialog "Position and Size," which is available from the context menu). Save this Draw file, then export as EPS and import into Scribus. The formulas and text will import as a grouped objects of scalable vector items. Any text is imported as outlines as well. This will result in formulas which will print with very high quality and little worries when exported as PDF. Saving the Draw file and attempting to import the Draw file with embedded objects will fail, as Scribus cannot access those object directly.

You can also use OpenOffice.org Draw to import complex tables from Writer or Calc into Scribus. See the section about tables for more information.

3.18.3.3 EPS Export in OpenOffice.org Draw

Below are the recommended EPS export settings for all versions of OpenOffice.org Draw:

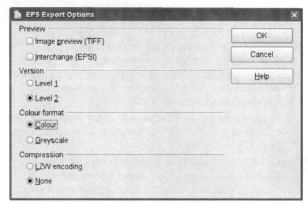

By using these settings and a recent Ghostscript (8.50 or higher), you might encounter at most minor difficulties importing files from OpenOffice.org. Even then, ungrouping the import and minor touching up is easily done. The most noticeable issue is some lines on charts or freehand lines, which are too thin when viewed as imported EPS in Scribus, but a quick adjustment of the size of the line with the Properties Palette sets things right.

3.18.4 WMF

Given the availability of superior formats, WMF (Windows Metafile) vector graphics should be of little to no significance in the realm of professional printing, yet they are nonetheless ubiquitous in the Microsoft-dominated "Office" world. Sooner or later Scribus users are therefore likely to need a way to import them. Scribus doesn't support WMF yet, but actually it doesn't need to, since there are two easy workarounds for the issue.

WMF files were introduced with Windows 3.0, and they're closely tied to the Windows Graphics Layer (GDI). They are 16-bit files and thus their capabilities are quite limited compared to formats like PS/EPS/SVG. There is an extended version of the format that uses 32 bit, called EMF (Enhanced Metafile), but like its 16-bit twin, it does not so far play any role in professional graphics design.

Option 1: Inkscape

Inkscape's import of WMF is quite mature, and most WMF files can be imported without issues. If you absolutely need to get a WMF file into Scribus, open it with Inkscape and save it as Inkscape SVG. The resulting SVG will import flawlessly into Scribus.

Option 2: OpenOffice.org/StarOffice

Some WMFs cannot be imported correctly by Inkscape. In these cases you can use OpenOffice.org or StarOffice. As "Office" applications they offer perfect support for WMF files.

Begin by creating a new OpenOffice.org/StarOffice Draw file. Then use Insert > Picture > From File to import your WMF file. The next step is crucial: Use the context menu and apply "Break." This is the equivalent of "Ungroup" in Scribus or a vector drawing program. If you forget this step, OpenOffice.org/StarOffice will embed the graphic as an embedded WMF file, and Scribus will not be able to import it.

Once the drawing is ungrouped or "broken up," export the selection as EPS or SVG, after which Scribus will import the result without issues in most, if not all cases.

[1] http://www.w3.org/Graphics/SVG/
[2] http://partners.adobe.com/public/developer/en/ps/5002.EPSF_Spec.pdf
[3] http://partners.adobe.com/public/developer/en/ps/PLRM.pdf

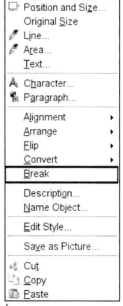

"Breaking" or ungrouping a WMF file via the context menu in OpenOffice.org Draw

3.19 Tables

3.19.1 Inserting Tables

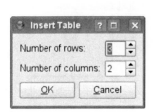

To INSERT a table, you can either click on the table icon in the toolbar, press the A-key, or use *Insert > Table*. Click-drag, then let go to create a new frame the way you are used to from other frame types. A dialog will show up, where you can enter the number of rows and columns of the table. Scribus will now create a new table.

3.19.2 Editing Tables

To edit a cell in the table, you have to double-click just like in any other text frame, since tables are, in many respects, just grouped text frames. You may even find a use for ungrouping them (*Item > Ungroup*) to move or resize individual elements.

To change the size of a row or a column, you can change the values for a single cell in a row/column in the X, Y, Z tab of the Properties Palette (in theory, you could also drag with the mouse, but this doesn't work well).

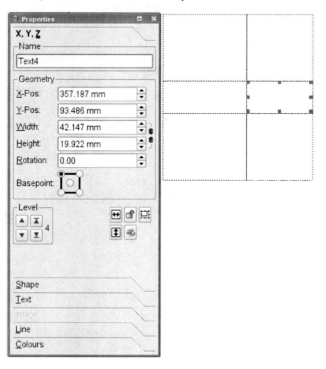

Since table cells are simply grouped frames, applying or changing the line properties of a table or a cell is a bit complicated in Scribus 1.3.3.x. Here are the necessary steps for different tasks:

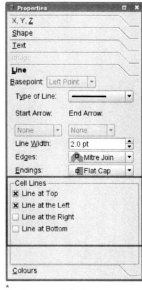

The *Line* tab of the Properties Palette when a table cell is selected

- If you want to apply the same color and line properties to all cells of a table, you have to ungroup and then immediately regroup it. Then you can select a line color in the *Color* tab and a line style in the *Line* tab of the Properties Palette. Please note that you won't be able to select a single cell anymore, once you ungrouped and regrouped the table.

- If you want to change the borders of a single cell, select it with a double-click. Then go to the *Line* tab of the Properties Palette, where you see a list of the borders: Line at top, at the left, at the right and at bottom. You can check for each side whether a color and a line style will be applied. Note that it's impossible to apply different colors or line styles to each of the four lines.

- If you want to apply a color and a line style only to the outer borders of a table, you have to use the step described before and change each cell individually, so that only one or two lines are colored.

It's also possible to change the size and the shape of single cells. Just select a cell and use *Shape > Edit Shape* in the Properties Palette. Now you can modify the cell like a single frame:

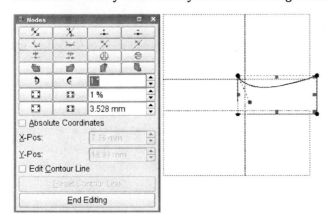

3.19.3 Converting Cells

As stated above, cells in tables are text frames. If you want to use images in a table, you have to convert the cells/text frames to image frames. This works just like any other conversion of frames by using the context menu.

The picture below shows a table with images and text:

An alternative approach to creating tables is described in the section Multiple Duplicate.

3.19.4 Creating and Importing Complex Tables

If you need to have more complex tables, here is a workaround:

1. Create your table in either OpenOffice.org Writer or Calc.
2. Copy the table only (in other words: not the whole spreadsheet in Calc) to the clipboard, create a new OpenOffice.org Draw document, and paste from the clipboard.
3. Export the selection to EPS.

If you plan to edit the content of tables you want to import, you always have the option to export a table as CSV (comma separated values) files from a spreadsheet program. You should note, though, that all formatting will be lost, since CSV is a plain text format. See Working with Text for hints about importing those.

3.20 Master Pages

3.20.1. Why Master Pages?

As SOON as you consider using many objects (common headers, logos, background, page numbers etc.) in the same places throughout your document, you will be well advised to use master pages. You'll avoid some unnecessary drudgery and save much time this way.

If you think of a page as a transparent sheet, a master page is an underlay with some fixed elements. You can place and arrange many items on the sheet, but you can't change the underlay. Each master page may include static text, images, shapes, lines, and so on. These will then appear on all pages to which the master page is applied, after which the items which vary from page to page are added on one or more other layers. Typically these elements of a master page will include running headers and footers, as well as other decorative features. These elements can be both items which will print, such as headers or page numbers, and those which will not, such as guides and margins.

There is no inherent limitation to the number of master pages within a document or what kind of page they describe, but each document page can only have one kind of master page applied to it.

On the right you see a master page for an exhibition catalogue. It contains a page header and placeholders for page numbers (page numbers will always be displayed with #-characters on master pages). The page also uses guides. All of it will appear on each page that uses this master page, but it can't be "touched" on a normal page. If you need to edit some or all of the recurring elements on a page, you should use create a normal page, which can serve as an editable template (a template as in the common meaning of the word, not as described in Opening, Creating and Saving Documents). You can even create a separate document that contains all "template" pages you need and then import them as required. See Managing and Laying Out Pages.

3.20.2 Creating and Editing Master Pages

Whenever you see this "Edit Master Pages" dialog on screen you are in the editing mode for master pages only. Delete this dialog and you return to the normal editing mode.

In the dialog you see the default master page "Normal." It is created when you create a new document. It's always present and cannot be deleted – the delete button will be disabled if the master page "Normal" is selected. "Normal" can be edited, even though it's better to leave it empty to be able to insert new empty pages.

The editing dialog for master pages provides four buttons. Their function is (from left to right):

- Add a new master page.
- Duplicate an existing master page.
- Import master pages from another document.
- Delete the selected master page.

The "New Master Page" dialog

If you click on the button for the creation of a new master page, another dialog is displayed. You have to enter a name for the master page. Other options depend on the type of the document:

- In single page documents, there are no further options available.
- In double-sided documents, you have to decide whether you want to create a master page for a left or a right page.
- In 3-folded documents, you have to decide whether you want to create a master page for a left, a middle or a right page.
- In 4-folded documents, you have to decide whether you want to create a master page for a left, a middle left, a middle right or a right page.

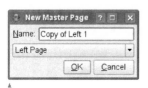
The "Copy Master Page" dialog

If you find that you need a master page similar to an existing one, click on "Duplicate" to clone the selected master page rather than starting a new one from scratch. In our example above, the text in the headers had to be changed for each section of the exhibition, thus, copying the original master pages was a real time-saver.

The dialog for duplicating a master page is almost identical to the one for new master pages. The only difference is the default name of the new page.

To rename a master page, simply double-click on the entry

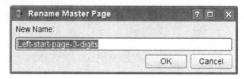

in the list. This will bring up a dialog, in which you can enter another name for the page:

The "Convert to Master Page" dialog

Another way to create a new master page is to convert an existing page into a master page. To create a master page from a normal page, click on the page (to select it), then use *Page > Convert to Master Page*. The dialog that will be displayed is almost identical to the ones described above, except that the default name for the new page is "New Master Page."

You can also import a master page from another document by clicking on *Import Master Pages from Another Document* button, which opens an import dialog.

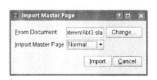

The "Import Master Page" dialog

Next, click on the button "Change ..." to select a document containing the master page you would like to import. Choose a master page from the drop-down list and click the "Import" button.

3.20.3 Applying Master Pages

To apply an existing master page to a page or a range of pages, use *Page > Apply Master Page ...* or *Apply Master Page ...* from the context menu (right-click on the page). This brings up a multifunctional dialog:

The "Apply Master Page" dialog

In the drop-down list in the upper right you can select a master page. Now you can apply the master page to the:

- Current page
- Even pages
- Odd pages
- All pages
- and you may apply to a range of pages.

Perhaps not surprisingly, the option "Even pages" can only be selected when the document has more than one page. Also, applying to a range of pages only applies when you have selected "All pages."

Another way to apply a master page (especially to single pages) exists in the Arrange Pages dialog. If you open *Windows > Arrange Pages*, Scribus shows all available master pages in the upper field. You can switch on a thumbnail preview for those pages if you click with the right mouse button on one of the entries.

Applying master pages in the "Arrange Pages" dialog

To apply a master page to a particular page, drag it with the mouse over a page symbol.

When you insert a new page (*Page > Insert*), you open up a dialog, in which you can choose to add one or more pages, choose the place of insertion, and in addition decide whether these new pages will contain master pages. Depending on the type of the document, you can apply different styles to different page types, for instance left and right pages:

If you try to apply a master page with a different page size than the selected page, you will note that the size doesn't change. This is a deliberate limitation, as it makes no sense to apply a master page with a different size to an existing page.

3.21 Page Numbering

PAGINATION in Scribus is quite different from word processors. It's a bit more difficult, but at the same time more flexible.

3.21.1 Inserting Page Numbers

Inserting a page number in Scribus is quite easy. Simply create a new text frame, double-click to turn into the edit mode, and enter Ctrl+Alt+Shift+P (it might not work with some keyboards, but you can choose your own shortcut in the Preferences) or use *Insert > Character > Page Number*. On master pages (see previous section), the page number will be indicated by a # – this is a special character, and not the same as inserting the character "#" from your keyboard.

You need to insert one placeholder for each digit of the page number, ie. # for 1–9, ## for 10–99, ### for 100–999 etc.

On the right is a depiction of how your page numbering will align from page to page, using a scheme in which we have used ## for 1–99, and also right-justified in the text frame. As you can see, in spite of right-justification, the single digit uses the left-hand #, so there is a space afterward. If you want to have the last digits of the page numbers aligning (eg, the 1 of page 1 aligning with the 8 of page 28), you will need separate page numbering for each number of digits.

Page 1
Page 11

3.21.2 Automatic Creation of Page Numbers for Each Page

If you want to let Scribus add page numbers automatically for each page, you can use master pages (*Edit > Master Pages*). Create a master page for left and right, and add a text frame with placeholders for the page number (Ctrl+Alt+Shift+P). Then apply these page templates to all pages in your document. You will need separate master pages for pages 1–9, 10–99, 100–999 etc.

3.21.3 Changing the Numbering Scheme

To change the numbering scheme, you need to open the Document Setup dialog. In "Sections" you can now create numbering sections for your document (see Screenshot). Let's assume you have an introduction on the first three pages that you want to be numbered with capital letters, and your text starts at page 5 with 1. Page 4 will not have a number at all. The first section is already there. You can enter a name for it in the "Name" column. In the "From" column enter "1" and in "To" enter "3". Choose "A, B, C" as a style, and the "Start" value is "1". To add new sections, simply add a new row by clicking "Add." For page 4 the values are: "From" = 4, "To" = 4, "Style" (doesn't matter here), "Start" (doesn't matter here). It's important that you uncheck "Shown" in the second column. For the main text, the values are: "From" = 5, "To" = (insert the number of pages you need), "Style" = 1, 2, 3, and "Start" = 1. That's all, your document will be paginated as desired.

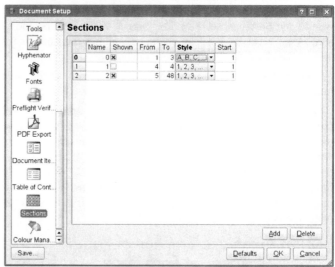

4. Customizing Scribus

File > Preferences and *File > Document Setup* are closely related, though not identical, since there are some settings unique to *Preferences,* and one ("Document Information") unique to *Document Setup.*

Preferences are either application wide settings, or those that will be used for future documents. Therefore, if you are creating a document at the time, most changes in *Preferences* will not take effect until you create a new document. *Document Setup* does the opposite, affecting the current document, but does not make permanent changes for the next time you create a new Scribus document. *Document Setup* is, of course, only accessible when a document is open.

If you find yourself wondering why a particular font comes up when you make a text frame, or certain colors are used for a new shape, the answer to that, and the means to change these behaviours is found in this chapter. Until you get more accustomed to Scribus, not all of these items will be clear, but you can come back to this chapter as you explore Scribus.

This chapter will mainly focus on *Preferences,* but will point out differences, when any exist, for *Document Setup.*

4.1 Opening Preferences

You can find the *Preferences* in the menu bar: *File > Preferences.* Similarly, there is *File > Document Setup.* When you select *File > Preferences,* you are presented with a screen that includes a scrolling list of 18 items on the left side. We'll go through them from top to bottom.

In the *Preferences,* as well as in the *Document Setup* dialogs, there's a row of buttons at the bottom that are visible in all categories, "Save," "OK" and "Cancel," "OK" and "Cancel" being self-explanatory. "Save" lets you save the settings of a document or Scribus for use on another system or for backup purposes. For example, to use this feature, you might click on "Save" and enter the filename scribus13.rc.

If you later want to use or reuse those settings, close Scribus, enter the directory `~/.scribus` (in Windows this can be found in `\Documents` and `Settings\User-Name\.scribus`), rename the file scribus13.rc, for instance to scribus13.rc.bak, then copy your saved scribus13.rc file to this directory. Scribus will now use the new settings as default

In the *Document Setup*, there is a fourth button called "Defaults." If you click on it, the current document will load the settings from the *Preferences*.

We'll now go through different tabs one by one in the rest of this chapter.

4.2 General

- *Language* applies to the language used in various menus and dialogs in Scribus. It does not affect the default hyphenation language, since this is derived from the language settings of the operating system and/or the desktop environment. Changes made here will be applied immediately when you click "OK."
- *Theme* affects the way Scribus looks and, to some degree, works on your system. It's dependent on the way Qt (the UI toolkit that's used for creating Scribus) is configured for your system. For Windows users, only Windows themes are available, for Linux user only the themes from Qt for Linux etc.
- *Font Size* (Menus), *Font Size* (Palettes), *Wheel Jump* are self-explanatory – just play around to find the appropriate settings for your environment.
- *Recent Documents* adjusts the number of documents to choose from with *File > Open Recent*.
- *Paths* sets the default directories for various Scribus needs – documents, ICC profiles (will only be possible if your version is compiled to use these), scripts if you have Python installed on your system, and document templates. If none of these are set, there are default locations, depending on where Scribus is in-

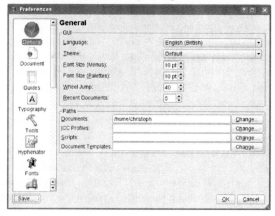

stalled on your system. An additional path for ICC profiles can only be set if no document is open.

There is no "General" category in *Document Setup*.

4.3 Document

"Document Layout" choices are "Single Page," "Double Sided," "3-Fold," and "4-Fold." It's important to realize that for each of these layouts, you are working with individual sheets, so that when you export to PDF or print from Scribus, the 4-fold layout will display or print as four separate pages. One purpose is to have these layouts side-by-side in your workspace so that you can see how it will look in a book or some other form. Another is that with a double-sided layout, for example, you will have left pages and right pages, with the various margins perhaps being different for these two, and if you use master pages, there will likely be left and right master pages.

"Page Size" allows choosing from a wide array of standard formats and also custom sizes. If you are changing your page size with *Document Setup* while you are working on a document, you will need to check "Apply Size Setting to All Pages" to change already existing pages. Also in this block you can choose portrait or landscape orientation, and the units of display for your page (Points, Millimeters, Inches, Picas, and Ciceros). If you change the settings for width or height of the page, the format will automatically change to "Custom."

"Margin Guides" varies according to the document layout.

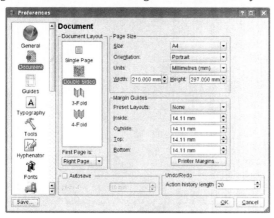

- With a single page layout, you cannot choose a preset layout, and your margin guides are left, right, top, and bottom.
- With double sided, 3- and 4-fold layouts, you can choose for a preset layout such as Gutenberg, Magazine, Fibonacci, Golden Mean, and Nine Parts. In any of the multipage layouts, left and right become inside and outside margins, since for example whether the inside is on the left depends on which page it is. Middle pages have both left and right margins the same.
- Printer margins will allow you to set guides according to the published margins for printers on your system.

If you choose to use Autosave, you can set the interval for it.

You can also set the number of levels of undo/redo. This option is not present in *Document Setup*.

4.4 Document Information

This is present only in Document Setup. It allows the entry of various metadata about your document, which will be saved with the file.

In the "Document" tab, the first three fields can contain information that can be read by PDF viewers and specialized indexing software. On the screenshot below you see how Adobe Reader 7 displays the inserted data in the Dialog *File > Document Properties*.

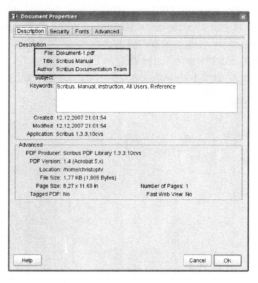

The field "Description" and all the other fields in the second tab are a subset of the Dublin Core Metadata Element Set (DCMI).

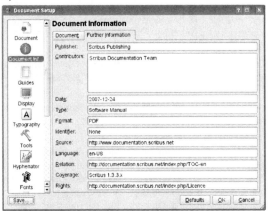

Below is a list of the DMCI's definitions of the metadata [1]:

- "Description": "An account of the resource. Description may include but is not limited to: an abstract, a table of contents, a graphical representation, or a free-text account of the resource."

- "Publisher": "An entity responsible for making the resource available. Examples of a Publisher include a person, an organization, or a service. Typically, the name of a Publisher should be used to indicate the entity."

- "Contributors": "An entity responsible for making contributions to the resource. Examples of a Contributor include a person, an organization, or a service. Typically, the name of a Contributor should be used to indicate the entity."

- "Date": "A point or period of time associated with an event in the lifecycle of the resource. Date may be used to express temporal information at any level of granularity. Recommended best practice is to use an encoding scheme, such as the W3CDTF profile of ISO 8601 (W3CDTF)."

- "Type": "The nature or genre of the resource. Recommended best practice is to use a controlled vocabulary such as the DCMI Type Vocabulary (DCMITYPE). To describe the file format, physical medium, or dimensions of the resource, use the Format element."

- "Format": "The file format, physical medium, or dimensions of the resource. Examples of dimensions include size and duration. Recommended best practice is to use a controlled vocabulary such as the list of Internet Media Types (MIME)."

- "Identifier": "An unambiguous reference to the resource within a given context. Recommended best practice is to identify the resource by means of a string conforming to a formal identification system."

- "Source": "The resource from which the described resource is derived. The described resource may be derived from the related resource in whole or in part. Recommended best practice is to identify the related resource by means of a string conforming to a formal identification system."

- "Language": "A language of the resource. Recommended best practice is to use a controlled vocabulary such as RFC 3066 (RFC3066)."

- "Relation": "A related resource. Recommended best practice is to identify the related resource by means of a string conforming to a formal identification system."

- "Coverage": "The spatial or temporal topic of the resource, the spatial applicability of the resource, or the jurisdiction under which the resource is relevant. Spatial topic may be a named place or a location specified by its geographic coordinates. Temporal period may be a named period, date, or date range. A jurisdiction may be a named administrative entity or a geographic place to which the resource applies. Recommended best practice is to use a controlled vocabulary such as the Thesaurus of Geographic Names (TGN). Where appropriate, named places or time periods can be used in preference to numeric identifiers such as sets of coordinates or date ranges."

- "Rights": "Information about rights held in and over the resource. Typically, rights information includes a statement about various property rights associated with the resource, including intellectual property rights."

4.5 Guides

In "Common Settings," "Placing in Documents" allows for guides to be covered up by page content (background) or show as if on top (foreground). "Snapping Distances" applies when *Page > Snap to Grid* or *Page > Snap to Guides* are selected. "Grab Radius" determines the size of the area in which you can select object handles.

"Show Guides," "Show Grid," "Show Baseline Grid," and "Show Margins" are all features that can also be selected and deselected from the menu (under View). These allow your choice for default behaviour, and for changing spacing and colors for these various tools. The baseline grid is used to align to baseline for text. See Working with Text for more about this.

The grid consists of two parts, the major and the minor grid. You can't switch them on or off independently, but you can change the color and the space between the grid lines separately. If you don't want to see one of the grids, set its color to the page color, which will be white in most cases. Alternatively, you could set the distance between lines at or larger than the longest page dimension.

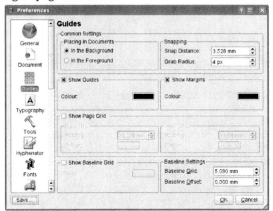

If you change these settings in *Document Setup,* you will find that they will be present for the document you have saved with those features every time it is opened, regardless of the settings in *Preferences.*

4.6 Typography

Here is where we set the default behaviour for placement and sizing of subscript, superscript, underline, and strikethrough. Also, the relative size of small caps is set here.

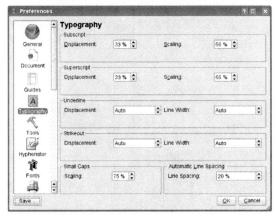

When you change font size in the *Text* tab of the Properties Palette or in the Story Editor, there is an automatic change in line spacing – "Automatic Line Spacing" set at 20% will make line spacing 120% of the font size. For example, a font size of 10 pt will have a line spacing of 12 pt if automatic line spacing is used. You can enter a value between 0% and 100% in all fields of this dialog.

4.7 Tools

Here we have a number of subcategory settings for the default behaviours.

- *Text Frame Properties*: Font (type), size, text tolor, and text stroke apply to the text itself (text stroke is the outline or shadow if selected). "Fill Color" and "Stroke Color" apply to the text frame: its fill and line colors. Each color has an adjustable saturation/shading. We can also set a default tab fill character and default tab interval (when tabs are used automatically rather than set separately in the *Shape* tab of the Properties Palette) – see Working with Text and Working with Styles. Finally, we can set a default number of columns and the gap between them. The text field at the bottom of the dialog displays a preview of the text properties.

- *Image Frame Properties* begins with allowing for free scaling or "Scale Image to Frame Size" when an image is loaded, with subsettings. As with text frames, fill color and shading can be selected. If the image has an embedded clipping path this can be used. "On Screen Preview" applies only to the appearance of images on your screen while using Scribus, not to resolution when printing or exporting to PDF. It might be a good idea to use "Scale Image to Frame Size" and maintain the aspect ratio; this means you will always see the whole image when you import it. You can free-scale it later. See Working with Images.

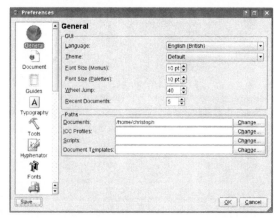

- *Shape Drawing Properties*, just as for text and picture frames, allows for default colors and saturation, and in addition the line style and line width. These settings also apply to polygons.
- *Polygon Drawing Properties* shows the same settings we see when Polygon > Properties is brought up on screen from the toolbar, so that default settings can be made. By default, the polygon tool will create a diamond shape. If you want to have something else as the default, you can change it here. See Working with Shapes and Polygons.
- *Line Drawing Properties*, as one could anticipate, adjust default color, shading, line style, line width, and presence or absence of arrows at each end. See Working with Shapes and Polygons.
- *Magnification Level Defaults* has to do with behavior when the magnification tool is selected (left click larger, right click smaller), and also when increase or decrease magnification icons are clicked at the bottom of the screen. See There's More Than One Way to Look at a Document.

4.8 Hyphenator

The settings presented here are straightforward in themselves, however may require some experimenting to understand fully. Hyphenation is not activated by default. See Hyphenation.

4.9 Fonts

- *Available Fonts* shows you the fonts which Scribus located when it started up. You can deselect any you do not want to use to shorten the number of choices in various dialogs.
- *Font Substitutions* allows for automatic use of a different font when a file requests one not on your system. This is also useful when, as can happen, the name of a font changes in some way.
- *Additional Paths* will allow Scribus to find fonts in non-standard locations on your system. If you know you have fonts that Scribus is not finding, this may be your solution.

For more information, see Font Preview and Font Management.

4.10 Preflight Verifier

This dialog has several modes (profiles), perhaps not immediately apparent. PostScript applies to either printing directly from Scribus or saving to a PostScript file from the print dialog. When Exporting to PDF, there are options for PDF 1.3, PDF 1.4, PDF 1.5, and PDF X-3 versions, and each will have its own collection of behaviours when the Preflight Verifier runs. At the bottom, one or more of these profiles can be removed, or added back later ("Add Profile"). Select "Ignore all errors" at your own peril.

Note that you can check for items which may not apply to the output, for example, transparency in PDF 1.3, where this is not supported. Furthermore, you can check for things which are supported, such as transparency in PDF 1.4. Check for placed PDF Files is to serve as a reminder that PDFs incorporated into Scribus will be rasterized (converted to a bitmap), not that this will fail in an absolute sense.

For more information, see The Preflight Verifier.

4.11 Color Management

Generally speaking, you should activate color management if you can, even though some commercial printers do not want color management active. Read the various tooltips on these settings for help. Also check the Color Management section.

4.12 PDF Export

These are the various settings for defaults when you click the Save as PDF ... icon, or *File > Export > Save as PDF ...* from the Menu.

For more information, see the section PDF Export.

4.13 Document Item Attributes

This panel allows to add user defined attributes to document items. Currently it's only used for the generation of a table of contents, but users can add arbitrary metadata here (eg. "author," "date," "license" ...)

You only define the keys (names) of the attributes here. The values are defined via the corresponding action in the context menu of each item.

4.14 Table of Contents and Indexes

This defines how a table of contents is assembled from individual document items. The items which make up section headings must be marked with specific attributes.

The "Index" pane is a placeholder for a future extension of Scribus.

For more information, see Creating a Table of Contents.

4.15 Sections

This is present only in *Document Setup*. It allows to divide the document into different sections with each having their own numbering scheme for page numbers (eg. i, ii, iii, ... ix for the preface, 1, 2, 3 ... for the main text). See **Page Numbering**.

4.16 Keyboard Shortcuts

A number of shortcuts are built into Scribus, which may be altered and others added as desired. At the bottom, entire collections of shortcuts can be exported or imported. See **Keyboard Shortcuts**.

There is no "Keyboard Shortcuts" category in *Document Setup*.

4.17 Display

- *Page Display* allows for changing these various options, none of which affects the output from Scribus to printer or to PDF.
- *Scratch Space* adjusts the space around your document, also usable for temporary placement of various objects.
- *Gaps between Pages* like these other settings, only applies to applicable distances in the workspace.
- *Adjust Display Size* is adjusted with a small visual for the ruler at the top of the workspace.

See also **There's More Than One Way to Look at a Document**.

There is no "Display" category in *Document Setup*.

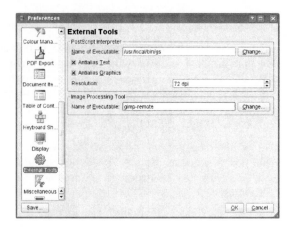

4.18 External Tools

Here is where you can make sure that Scribus is finding your Ghostscript executable, or finds the desired one where more than one exists. "Antialiasing" only applies to the display, as does "Resolution."

You may also choose which image processing software to use, such as GIMP, Krita or Cinepaint. When you choose *Edit Image ...* from the context menu, the program indicated here is started. If you are using GIMP, note that you should insert "gimp-remote" on Linux/UNIX and OS X and "gimp-win-remote" on Windows to prevent opening a new instance of GIMP each time you use the function from the context menu.

There is no "External Tools" category in *Document Setup*.

4.19 Miscellaneous

- "Always ask before fonts are replaced when loading" determines if Scribus will ask you whether fonts that are used in a document, but not installed on your system, should be replaced. Don't switch this off unless you know what you're doing!

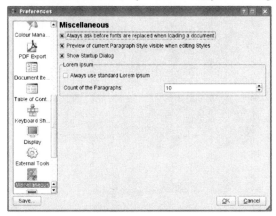

- "Preview of current Paragraph Styles when editing Styles" lets you switch the sample text in the paragraph style dialog on or off. This is recommended if your computer has a slow CPU or video card.

- The startup dialog normally comes up when you start Scribus, asking you to choose between "New Document," "Open Existing Document," or "Open Recent Document." This is the place to change this behavior. See also Opening, Creating and Saving Documents.

- "Lorem Ipsum" allows you to bypass the sample text dialog and simply enter a standard Lorem Ipsum with the number of chosen paragraphs.

There is no "Miscellaneous" category in *Document Setup*.

4.20 Plug-ins

If you know which of these you will not be using, startup can be shortened by not loading various plug-ins.

There is no "Plugins" category in *Document Setup*.

4.21 Short Words

See Short Words.

4.22 Scripter

See The Scripter.

[1] http://dublincore.org/documents/dces/

5 Advanced Features

5.1 The Scrapbook

SOMETIMES, items like logos will be used more than once in a document. If you don't want to search your hard drive each time you need such a file, you can copy it to the Scrapbook for later use. You can think of the Scrapbook as a special folder or a library in which you can store all kinds of objects you need for a project for unlimited reuse. It's similar to the collection of shapes shipped with Scribus, except that the content is defined by the user. It's also much more flexible in that everything that can be placed on a page can also be stored in the Scrapbook or a Scrapbook file.

To copy an item to the Scrapbook, select it, open the context menu and click *Send to Scrapbook*. You can also use *Item > Send to Scrapbook* from the menu bar.

This will bring up a new dialog where you have enter a name for the new Scrapbook item.

Now you can open the Scrapbook via *Windows > Scrapbook*.

To get an item from the Scrapbook back to your document, you can simply drag it with the mouse to the position you want it to be placed. What you are doing is placing a copy of the saved item in your document, which means that the Scrapbook still contains your item, and you can drag and drop as many copies as you wish. One thing you should beware of is the fact that every Scrapbook item, independent of its type (text frame, image frame, line etc.), stores all the fonts that are used in the document from which you copied it, as well as all colors that are available in this document. If you insert this item into another document, all colors will be added to to it, and all fonts stored in with the object will be marked as "used in this document" and thus appear in the "Font" tab in the PDF export dialog.

In the Scrapbook you can rename or delete items by selecting them with the right mouse button.

The Scrapbook dialog has only one menu item called *File*:

- *New* will create a new tab in the dialog. Please note that you will have to select a directory on your hard drive, not a single file in the file dialog that opens when you click New. If you later copy items to this new Scrapbook, they will be stored in the

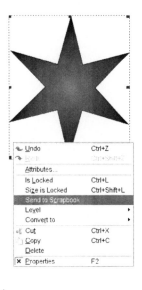

Sending an item to the Scrapbook with the context menu

The *File* menu of the Scrapbook dialog

155

chosen directory. Each Scrapbook is displayed in a separate tab. Also, each item you copy to the Scrapbook will be stored in the folder you selected (or in the folder ~/.scribus/scrapbook in your home directory if you use the default Scrapbook "Main"). Every Scrapbook item consists of a text file with the extension SCE and a bitmap file in PNG format, which is used for the preview in the Scrapbook dialog,

- *Load* will open an already existing Scrapbook directory.
- *Save As* lets you save a Scrapbook in another directory. Please note that you have to choose a directory.
- *Import Scrapbook File*: Scribus stores information about files and other objects (like text frames) in Scrapbooks in a library file. Scribus library files use the extention SCS. You can load such a file (and thereby a Scrapbook) by using this menu entry.
- *Close* will close the displayed tab in the Scrapbook.

If you are sharing a Scrapbook or single Scrapbook files between different computers, you will sometimes be asked to replace a font, even if your Scrapbook item is an image. You will also note that lots of new colors are added to your color list. This is no malfunction of Scribus or a mistake on your side. Rather, a Scribus Scrapbook file stores all font and color data of the Scribus file from which it was copied to the Scrapbook. If you later use the item on another system, which doesn't have a particular font installed, the font replacement mechanism is activated.

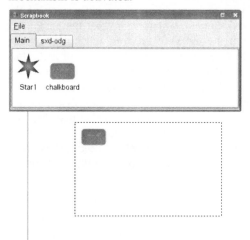

Here, a Scrapbook item called "chalkboard" has been dragged to a page.

5.2 Converting Frames

5.2.1 Simple Conversions

WE ARE using this term to apply to a situation when you are working with a frame type and decide you want it to have some other content. Thus, text frames and image frames can be converted back and forth. Even though the text or image may disappear, if the type is switched back, you will see your text or image reappear.

Converting a text or image frame to a polygon is also a simple process, and your text or image is no longer displayed. As we shall see, converting polygons to other frame types is typically done for a specific purpose.

5.2.2 Conversions for Effect

One of the more common reasons for converting frames is to use a text or image frame that has something other than the default rectangular shape. One can certainly use *Shape > Edit Shape* in the Properties Palette, but in many cases one would like to use something that can be easily generated by *Insert > Shape* or *Insert > Polygon*. In this case, you can make your shape, then convert to a text or image frame, then enter text or load an image.

Another common operation is "Attach Text to Path" – covered in its own chapter. For our purposes here, we will merely restate that in order for a shape or polygon frame to be used in "Attach Text to Path" it must be converted to a Bézier curve. The "Attach to Path" operation causes the original frame to be hidden, though its contour can still be edited as explained in the section Attach Text to Path. Also see A Rising Sun Text on Path and Creating a Tiled Image in the Tips and Tricks chapter.

5.2.3 Conversion by Necessity

Some fonts may not be able to be embedded, which may relate to some characteristic of the font, or there may be licensing issues that do not allow embedding, since embedding means including font descriptors in the final PDF.

In this case, "Convert to Outlines" is your solution. You can wait to do this when you export to PDF, but there may be instances when you will do this in advance. This will convert each character in your text frame to a shape, so on exporting to

PDF, only vector shapes are in the document, not special font data. As might be expected, this can interfere with later extracting the text from the PDF. Please be aware of the fact that you can't revert a conversion to outlines yet. Also, special characters like automatic hyphens will not be converted to outlines and simply vanish after the conversion.

A side effect of a conversion to outlines is a marked increase in saved file size, perhaps 25 to 30 times or more. There will be less difference in PDF sizes.

There are also some interesting effects achievable by combining polygons of your outlines and conversion of your outlined text to an image frame. See Filling Text With an Image and Text Over Images in the Tips and Tricks chapter.

This diagram below shows the possible conversions for various frame types.

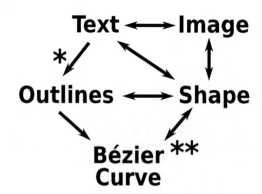

* Text to outlines is irreversible.
** Bézier to text or image frames is feasible, but can be hard to work with.

5.3 The Action History

ACTION HISTORY is a list of recent actions that can be undone. Bring this up with *Windows > Action History.* Every action which can be undone will be appended to the list, so on a simple level, it allows you to view these operations. Actions are listed top-to-bottom from oldest to newest, with the most recent one highlighted at the bottom of the list.

Warning: Not all actions in Scribus are recorded by the undo framework yet. This means that a user will not be able to undo every action he has made – for example, at this time most of the text edit mode actions will not be added to this list.

5.3.1 Undo and Redo

As we can see in the image above, "Polygon2: Set fill color" is the most recent action, which is why it is highlighted as the window opens. Either clicking "Undo" or pressing Ctrl+Z will undo this action. However, it will not disappear from the list, but the highlighted selection will move up the list, and the main screen display will show the document's prior state. At this point, "Polygon2: Set line style" becomes an action which we can redo, this button becoming active, or we can press Shift+Ctrl+Z to return to our original state.

We can also use the mouse to select (highlight) any prior state, and again you will see that all subsequent actions remain in the list and can be redone. One might choose to then save the document in one of these prior states, as desired.

If you wish to replace some actions, ie. truly delete them, click back to a former state, then return to your document to carry out a new editing operation. At this point, you will see all later actions disappear from the list, to be replaced by your new edit action.

Also note that the Action History only refers to the currently open document. When you close the document, the history goes away, and when you reopen it, there is a clean history slate. While this looks like a severe limitation, it actually makes a lot of sense, because otherwise the Action History, which is actually a logbook of your work, would have to be stored in the SLA file. Given that working on a layout means thousands of operations, such as inserting and editing text, creating vector drawings, importing and editing images etc., storing all those actions would result in huge files. Even if you would delete all content and all pages but one in a SLA file, it

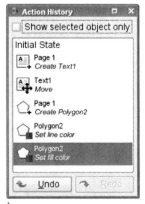

The Action History

could still be some megabyte or even gigabyte in size, depending on the number of previous editing operations. Moreover, as many users of MS Word already found out, storing older file contents and editing stages may result in severe issues regarding privacy and confidentiality.

5.3.2 Item Action Mode

Something else to note is that, in its basic state, the Action History is a global indicator, showing all actions for all objects. You can restrict the undo/redo operation to a selected object by either choosing from the menu *Edit > Item Action Mode* or by clicking the checkbox in the Action History labelled "Show selected object" only. Thus undo and redo will operate only on the selected object.

The same goes for right-clicking on an item or a page, as undo/redo actions in the context menu only apply to the selected item/page.

A limitation of Item Action Mode is that it in effect starts a new individual item history when it is activated, or when switching from one object to another. Prior actions on all objects will still be available by turning off Item Action Mode.

5.4 Search and Replace

AN ADVANCED tool for searching and replacing or reformatting
in text frames is *Edit > Search/Replace*. While the elements of
the dialog are self-explanatory, you should be aware of the fact
that it's an extremely versatile tool. That's because you can't
just search for and replace identical content or properties, but
use the tool to do this "asymmetrically." For instance, you can
search for all instances of text formatted in a certain font and
replace them with new text in another font and another font
color. You can also specify if you want to perform a search for
a whole word (ie. a text string separated from other text by
spaces) and if the search will be case sensitive or insensitive.

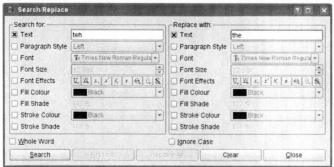

Please note that you have to find at least one matching instance
in the text before you can start the replacement. In other
words: you need to click on "Search" before you can use "Replace" or "Replace All."

You should also be aware of the fact that you can use this
tool only for a single text frame or linked text frames, not for
the whole document.

5.5 Attach Text to Path

5.5.1 First Steps

LOOKING at this first screenshot, we see an arbitrary line and a text frame with a quote from Louis Pasteur. The text frame is a usual text frame, created at an arbitrary location on the page, then the Story Editor has been used to enter this text. You can attempt to set the font and size this text properly, but as we'll see, this isn't worth spending too much time on, since we can edit these features later.

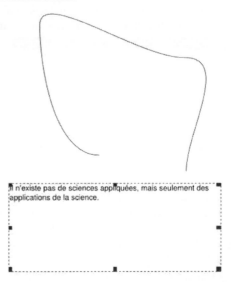

This particular line was made from a circle shape, converted to a Bézier curve (context menu > *Convert to* > *Bezier Curve* or *Item* > *Convert to* > *Bezier Curve*), broken, then edited to the form you see here. Even if you do not edit your shape or polygon, it is important to convert to a Bézier curve for text on path to work.

5.5.2 Now, the Magic

Next, select both the curve and the text frame – the easiest way may be to outline with the mouse using the left mouse button as a "rubber band" in "Select Item" mode. Alternatively, hold down Shift while left-clicking with the mouse on each item.

Now click on *Item* > *Attach Text to Path*, and you get the result here (shown after resizing text to fill the line).

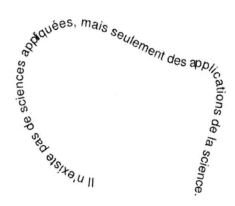

In a sense this works, but it's not so visually attractive. Do you see how some of the letters are bunched together, as in "appliquées" and "applications"? It may be a visual trick, but we want it to be legible as well.

5.5.3 Editing the New Item

To fix these uneven letter placements, click on the item, then open the Story Editor. There you will see our text, fully editable. We can resize the font, and adjust the spacing of the individual words or even parts of the words. Remember, you don't have to close the Story Editor to see your changes – just click on "Update Text Frame" or use Ctrl+U (not "Update Text Frame and Exit"). Make sure the Story Editor is placed and sized, so you can see your updates.

Another way to edit the text properties is to use the *Text* tab in the Properties Palette, that offers even more options to change the visual appearance of the text. All text features except alignment and line spacing (which would not make much sense here) are available for text on path!

In addition, once you have closed the Story Editor, you can go to *Properties > Shape > Edit Shape ...* or double-click on the item and edit your shape as desired while the text is attached. At right, you see the end result.

The *Shape* tab in the Properties Palette also shows special properties, which are only available for text attached to path:

- *Show Curve* lets you make the curve (the path) visible or invisible. This may or may not work as well when you are attaching to a shape or polygon.

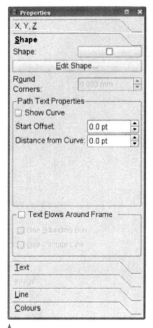

The *Shape* tab of the Properties Palette for text attached to path

- Start Offset sets a value for the distance of the text from the beginning of the curve. If you are attaching to a closed figure, the "beginning" of the curve is somewhat arbitrary, so expect to adjust this setting to get it to start where you want – positive and negative values are possible.
- *Distance from Curve* sets a value for the distance of the text from the curve. If you want to place text below the curve, enter a negative value.

To detach a text from a curve, use *Item > Detach Text* from Path.

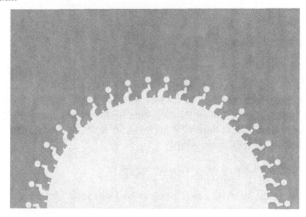

What's this doing here? Check A Rising Sun on a Path in the Tips and Tricks chapter to find out.

5.6 Importing Text with Custom Text Filters

5.6.1 Introduction

IMPORTING "raw" text is another way of getting style information into Scribus – if that information is expressed in some sort of structured text format. If you have created or looked at any HTML code, you have seen structures such as `</head>` and `</strong>`. These structures are generic, and depend on some application applying actual font and formatting information. In the early years of computer-assisted typesetting, input typists might be asked to include codes such as `[it]` for italic and `[h1]` for a level one heading. This sort of thing is often referred to as "tagged text," and commercial page layout programs have elaborate definitions of tagging languages which allow an input typist to access virtually any style when the text is imported into the program. Scribus allows you to do the same, with the advantage that you can invent your own tagging language and make it as simple or complex as you need.

Creating a document with a consistent look of the paragraph formatting is much easier than you may think. The secrets for success are document templates, paragraph styles, and text filters, not to mention writers who don't mind just a little extra work for the good of the project you are working on. The basic idea is that you tag text to be imported in a way that makes use of paragraph styles you have already set up. Once you have tagged the text, it will then be possible to create a text import filter which will automatically apply paragraph styles to the imported text using the tags in the text file. Before we get to the tagging process, let's step back to the beginning of setting up the document, since this is integral to being able to use these tags.

5.6.2 Creating a Document Template

If you have a need to use the same layout repetitively it's a good idea to create a document template. Within a document template you will have all your paragraph and line styles set up and all static graphics and texts so that you will be able to concentrate on setting up the new content instead of creating the non-changing parts of the publication each time you make a new issue. The details of creating and using a document template can be found in the chapter Opening, Creating and

Saving Files. For our purposes here, we will just outline the process.

The document template is done the very same way you will create any other document in Scribus. The only difference is that you will not want to have anything single-issue-specific in the template, so you will for example leave all the text frames for articles empty. What you want to have in the template are all the items that will stay untouched from one issue to another. One such item is paragraph styles you use to set up the articles, so that you can guarantee that all the text paragraphs will be formatted the same way in every issue of your publication.

5.6.3 Setting Up Paragraph Styles

Paragraph style creation is described in depth in the chapter Working with Styles. In the sample document we have set up three paragraph styles called H1, P1 and P2. H stands for headers and the style H1 should be applied to all article headers. The P styles are for paragraphs. P1 will not have the first line indented and should be used for the first paragraph after the header. The P2 style has the first line indented and will be applied to all other paragraphs in the article.

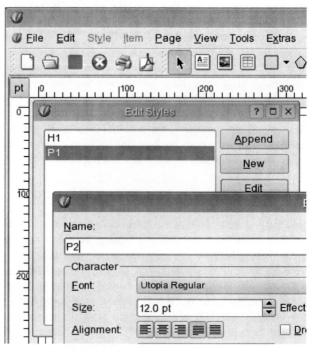

5.6.4 Setting Up the Text Filter

Now it is time to create the text filter you will be using when importing articles to your layout. The idea behind the filter is that you can filter the incoming text, then carry out some Scribus operation. In this example we will be applying paragraph styles (H1, P1 and P2) to the text based on the tags that can be found in the imported text. The filters will work by having your writers prepend every paragraph they write with \P1 and \P2 and headers with \H1. Here the \P1, \P2 and \H1 are the tags and will be used to apply paragraph styles, and the tags themselves will be stripped from the text in the process. Using tag names similar to style names helps you keep track of what you are doing.

At this point we'll go on to create the filter. The filter editor can be accessed via *File > Get Text ...* or via the context menu > *Get Text ...* This brings up a file dialog where at the bottom you will see a dropdown box for the importer. The default importer for a text file is an importer which will get the text to a text frame as it is. Here we need to select the "Text Filters" importer from this dropdown menu. Now browse to your article file, select it, and click "Open," which brings up the text filter editor.

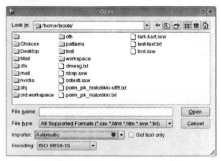

Now with the "Create Filter" editor open, create the first filter part, which will apply paragraph style H1 to all paragraphs that have been "tagged" with \H1. From the first dropdown box select "Apply." This will change the look of the filter part to match the apply function. The second dropdown box will show "Paragraph Style," and the third dropdown box should be empty and writable. The third writable dropdown box is reserved for the paragraph style that will be applied. It is possible to enter a non-existent paragraph style, in which case Scribus will create that style based on the default settings of for text formatting. You see that you can set up filters before you create the styles if you wish. Here we want to use one of the styles we just created, and as a convenience, the existing paragraph styles can be found in the dropdown box. Select H1 from there or type it in the text area of the dropdown box. Since we know that the texts we will be using are tagged, select "paragraphs starting with" from the fourth dropdown box. In the fifth dropdown box type insert the tag name \H1. The last dropdown box should be left to its default remove match, to remove the tag from the text when it is being imported (Note that to remove matching text strings you must not check this option. Leave the box unchecked instead).

Repeat the above steps for the paragraph styles P1 and P2 using the tag names \P1 and \P2. You can create a new filter by using the plus sign on the right side of every existing filter entry – as you might suspect, clicking the minus sign will delete an associated filter part. Once you have set up all three filter parts, you should type in the name for the filter in the text field at the bottom right corner. This will save the filter in the configuration file prefs13.xml in your .scribus directory, so that it will always be available from the dropdown menu in the top right corner. This means that text filters are not document-specific and are not saved with the document, but rather with your Scribus settings.

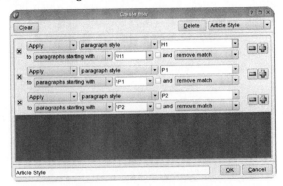

5.6.5 Save the Document Template

Once you have set up the paragraph styles, save your template (*File > Save as Template*), calling your template document a name that suits you. Before saving the document, remember to clear the content of the text frame you used for the filter creation.

5.6.6 Using the Document Template and the Filter

Now we are ready to use our new template. When it is time to start working on a new issue of your publication, select *File > New from Template* from the menu to bring up this dialog:

The template for the article

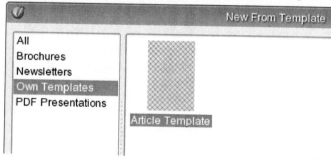

Once you have opened the template, create a text frame or select one of the existing text frames in the template if you included those in your template design. Right click on the text frame, then choose *Get Text ...* from the context menu. In the dialog choose "Text Filters" from the "Importer" list and choose your appropriately tagged text file. In the filter editor choose the filter you created from the top right corner's dropdown box if it is not already visible and click "OK." At this point you should soon have a nicely formatted article inside your text frame and you can start fine tuning the layout.

Note that you cannot yet define tags for character effects like bold and italic. Scribus does not artificially create such effects, and until character styles are available in Scribus, you will have to do such changes in Scribus itself.

5.6.7 Other Text Filter Options

As you can see in the screenshot below, the text filter can do a lot more. For instance, you can remove all instances of text strings from an imported file. You can use this option to remove tags in HTML files that can't be read by Scribus. Or you could spend some time on creating an import filter for XML file types like docbook, so that all XML tags get stripped during import.

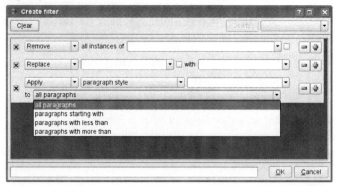

Similarly you can use the "Replace" feature to replace certain text strings during import. This is particularly useful if you are working with texts in different spelling systems or typographical rules. For example one could strip all instances of "ß" and replace them with "ss" in German text that will be published in Switzerland. It's also possible to replace certain quotation marks, for instance „ and " in a German text from Germany with « and » for Switzerland.

The "Apply" feature has also more options than described above, since paragraph styles can be applied to:

- all paragraphs.
- all paragraph starting with a certain text string (as in our example above).
- all paragraphs with less than a certain number of text (useful for the content of tables and lists).
- all paragraphs with more than a number of words.

5.6.8 Regular Expressions

The Text Filter incorporates a powerful feature, which is familiar to many programmers and more experienced users of text editors and word processors, namely the concept of the "regular expression" or "regexp."[1] You probably already know how to use a simple sort of regular expression when you use an asterisk (*) as a substitute for any character in a search, or the simple replacements explained in the previous paragraph, but regular expressions allow for much more complicated searches and replacements.

Entire books have been written about this topic, and we won't go into detail. But notice the box between the search and replacement fields in the dialog. If you check it the search field is taken to be a regular expression. (If the contents of the search field are not expected to be a regular expression, don't check the box.)

Here are two additional lines in the text filter which deal with the problem of correctly converting inch marks to correct typographical quotes. Briefly explained, in the first field, "([a-zA-Z0-9]) means "search for an inch mark followed by any alphabetic character or digit. Store that character in your memory." In the second field, "\1 means "insert an open double-quote followed by whatever character you just stored in your memory."

In the second field, ([a-zA-Z0-9,.])" means "search for any alphabetic character, digit, comma, or period which is followed by an inch mark. Store the found character." In the replacement field, \1" means "insert the stored character followed by a close double quote."

These are not very sophisticated regular expressions; given the versatility of this feature, you are advised to consult a separate resource. Since Scribus uses the regexp functions of the Qt library, the excellent Qt documentation [2] might be a good place to start. However, even though regular expressions are beyond the scope of this manual, you find a list of some less sophisticated ones at the end of this section. These expressions can easily be used even without formal training in computer science.

5.6.9 Closing and Saving

To remove all filters, press the "Clear" button in the upper left corner of the filter dialog. Note that if you delete filters in an existing filter "style" and click "OK," the style will be empty, as all changes to existing filters are saved immediately after clicking "OK."

[1] http://www.regular-expressions.info
[2] Linux users can easily install the Qt documentation with the help of their package manager. Mac OS X and Windows users can consult the documentation available on http://www.trolltech.com/qt.

List of Regular Expressions

Element	Meaning
Any character	Represents any single character unless it has a special meaning in combination with another special character.
\	The backslash indicates that the character that follows it is a normal character, not a regular expression, unless "\" in combination with a certain character has a special meaning (see below). For instance, if you want to search for a Dollar sign in a text, you have to use "\$", since "$" has a special function in regular expressions as explained below.
.	Represents *any single* character. For instance, "T.m" will find "Tim" and "Tom".
^	A caret followed by characters will only find the characters if they are *at the beginning* of a paragraph. For instance, "^Scribus" will be found if a paragraph starts with "Scribus".
$	A Dollar sign is the opposite of a caret: It only finds characters if they are *at the end* of a paragraph. For example, "Scribus$" will be found if a paragraph ends with "Scribus".
*	Finds *zero or more occurrences* of the characters *in front of* the asterisk: "th*e" will match "the", "he", "le", "xyze" etc.
+	Finds *one or more occurances* of the characters *in front of* the plus sign: "th+e" will match "the", but also "thhte".
?	Finds *zero or one occurances* of the characters *in front of* the question mark: "t?e" will match "the", "he", "le".
\t	Backslash plus t will find any *tabulator*.
\r	Backslash plus r will find any *paragraph break*.
\d	Backslash plus d will find any *digit*.
\D	Backslash plus D will find any *non-digit*.
\s	Backslash plus s will find any *whitespace*.
\S	Backslash plus S will find any *non-whitespace*.
\n	Backslash plus n will find the nth *back reference* (see the example in the text above).
\b	Backslash plus b will find a *word boundary*. For instance, "\bwith\b" will find all instances of "with", but not "within" or "without."
\B	Backslash plus B will *ignore word boundaries*. For example, "\Bwith\B" will find "within" and "without", but not "with."
[]	Square brackets are used to find *any character contained within the square brackets*. For instance, "[A,R,Z]" will find all instances of uppercase A, R and Z.
[-]	The hyphen is used to define *a range of characters within square brackets*. For example, "[0-9]" will find all digits. It's the same as "\d".
[^]	A caret within square brackets will *exclude* the content within the brackets from the search. For instance, "[^x,y,z]" will exclude each instance of lowercase x, y and z from the search.
\xHHHH	Backslash plus x immediately followed by a *four-digit hexadecimal number* will find the *special character as specified in Unicode*.
{ }	Curly brackets are used for *quantifiers*. For instance, "wel{2}" will find "well".
{ , }	A comma in curly brackets is used to define the *minimum* and the *maximum* of instances of a character. For instance, "wel{1,2}" will find "well" and "weld." If one one the numbers is missing, the comma indicates either the minimum or the maximum of occurances: "yyy{3,}" will search for three or more ys, and "yyy{,3}" will search for one, two or three ys.
( )	Parentheses are used to group elements.
|	The bar symbol is used to define *alternative search terms*. For instance, "(autumn|fall)" will either search for "autumn" *or* "fall".

5.7 Typography

5.7.1 Fonts and Font Technology

5.7.1.1 Fonts

FONTS are the key ingredient in print publishing. They display the personality of the document – stately, playful, hard-sell, etc.

But they can also be difficult to deal with. There are a number of different font formats; some work better than others. There are hundreds of thousands of fonts available. Some of them are painstakingly crafted by professionals; others are amateur productions created with relatively inexpensive tools. If you're sending a job to press, you don't want to find out when your brochure ships that its fonts look awful. This section is intended to help guide you through the maze – what font formats work, or work better than others; what foundries produce fonts of reliable quality; and how to manage fonts and find characters.

5.7.1.2 Fonts as Intellectual Property

Font foundries claim that fonts are "intellectual property." The web has many sites that describe font piracy policies, but debate continues on exactly what it is about fonts that can be covered by copyright. Whether these claims are valid will depend on the jurisdiction you are living in. For instance, while fonts seem to be recognized as "software" (not as a piece of art) in U.S. case law, which means they are protected by copyright law, German courts have refused to grant copyright protection for fonts, either as a piece of art or as software. Independent of the jurisdiction end users who don't create fonts themselves should consider the license that comes with the font as valid

You can embed fonts when you are printing to a PostScript file or by creating a PDF file. In Scribus, *File > Preferences > Fonts* as well as the PDF export dialog there are check boxes to let you decide whether you want to embed the font. This is a difficult legal hurdle, and frankly, many well-meaning users ignore it. Some vendors of fonts include a special number called "fsType Flag" in their TrueType and OpenType font files (it's not available in Type 1 fonts) to indicate the embedding permissions or restrictions for their fonts. Programs that can read this number will refuse to embed those fonts in a PDF or Post-Script file. Scribus does currently ignore it, so that you'd better read the license of a font before you decide to embed it.

There are many "free fonts" on the Web, and some of them are included in Scribus. Free (as in "gratis") fonts are not always completely free. Some have restrictions, such as not to be used in a commercial publication. If the license doesn't permit embedding a font in a PDF or PostScript file, you still have the option to convert it to outlines. See PDF Export.

You should also be aware of issues caused by many gratis (and some commercial) fonts. They may look good on screen but bad when printed on a press. If you find some of these, it's better to delete them rather than suffer again. The corollary is to pay attention to which fonts you are using, so you can meaningfully identify these problems when they occur.

5.7.1.3 Kinds of Fonts

Here are some kinds of fonts you will find on your system:
- PostScript Type 1
- TrueType
- OpenType

PostScript Type 1 fonts were an important part of the Desktop Publishing revolution, along with the Apple Laserwriter, the first output device using these fonts. Other font types are also defined in the PostScript language specification but are rarely encountered. The most common was Type 3, made by font-creation tools like Fontographer. Most Type 3 fonts have been created before 1990, because until then only the Type 3 specification had been released by Adobe. When Adobe published the Type 1 specification in 1990 [1], the Type 3 format became more or less obsolete. Type 3 fonts are generally of lower output quality on screen and in print than Type 1 fonts, especially at low resolutions. Another, still encountered, is Type 42, which is essentially a Type 1 wrapper for TrueType fonts.

A PostScript Type 1 font has two major parts: the printer font and the screen bitmap font (plus information about font metrics and kerning). Font files with extensions PFA and PFB are Type 1 printer fonts, PFM files contain the font metrics. The major downside of Type 1 fonts is that they can only include 256 characters.

TrueType fonts [2] have been available for almost a decade, but they were generally scorned by pre-press users, who often reported production problems with them. This distaste has largely gone away as fonts and printer technology have improved. Like PostScript fonts, TrueType fonts are "scalable," meaning that they are mathematical outlines that can be scaled in whatever increments your application supports, eg. 10.25 points, 10.2625 points (Note for trivia fans: the TrueType font project was initially code-named "bass" [as in the fish] because a bass can be scaled). They stand alone – they are complete in themselves and don't need separate screen and printer components.

OpenType, a joint venture of Microsoft and Adobe [3], is an extension of the TrueType specification which adds support for Type 1 data. An OpenType font may contain TTF, Type 1, or both; the differences are resolved at output to a printer, Raster Image Processor (RIP), or PDF file. The development of Open-Type was intended to end the "font wars" between the two font developers. As implied by their components, OTF fonts are fully scalable.

There's another important thing to know about TTF and OTF fonts: Both formats have the capacity of containing many more characters than Type 1 fonts. They support an emerging international standard called Unicode, which provides the possibility of accessing some 65,535 characters. If you are using, for instance, Adobe fonts, those with "Pro" in their name include Central European (CE) glyphs; those with "Std" in the name do not. Note that OTF fonts with TrueType content often continue to use the TTF file extension, while OTF mostly indicates Type 1 content in an OpenType file.

OTF fonts may use a different approach than Type 1 or TrueType fonts to define the distance between two adjacent letters (kerning pairs). The Freetype2 library used by Scribus to access font informations can't read the OTF kerning informations, so that they won't be available in Scribus. There is, however, a workaround for the issue.

If you have FontForge (see the section FontForge) installed your system, you can open the OTF file with it.

- Go to *File > Generate Fonts.* This will bring up a file dialog.
- Select "OTF (CFF)" as the export format and click on "Options."
- Under "TrueType" check "OpenType" and "Old Style 'kern'" then click "OK."
- In the file dialog click "Save."

Making kerning informations in OTF fonts available via FontForge

Now your OTF font contains kerning pairs that can be read by Freetype2.

Two other use typical cases for the use of FontForge with Scribus are related to PDF files for screen-only or web display. OpenType fonts can't be embedded in Scribus and are converted to outlines, so that PDF files that use them can't be searched for text content. It's possible to convert an OTF font to a TrueType font with FontForge, to make the PDF file searchable. Another issue with OTF fonts may arise with certain sans serif fonts like Arial or Myriad. Lowercase "l" glyphs often look ugly on screen if an OTF version is used. Converting to TTF or Type 1 (PostScript) can resolve the issue, as you can see on the screenshots below. Beware, though, that the font license may not permit such a conversion.

3 May, Bistritz.—Left Munich at 8:35 P.M., on 1st May, arriving at Vienna early next morning; should have arrived at 6:46, but train was an hour late. Buda-Pesth seems a wonderful place, from the glimpse which I got of it from the train and the little I could walk through the streets. I feared to go very far from the station, as we had arrived late and would start as near the correct time as possible. I find that the district he named is in the extreme east of the country, just on the borders of three states, Transylvania, Moldavia, and Bukovina, in the midst of the Carpathian mountains, one of the wildest and least known portions of Europe. I was not able to light on any map or work giving the exact locality of the Castle Dracula, as there are no maps of this country as yet to compare with our own Ordance Survey Maps; but I found that Bistritz, the post town named by Count Dracula, is a fairly well-known place. I shall enter here some of my notes, as they may refresh my memory when I talk over my travels with Mina. I had to hurry breakfast, for the train started a little before eight, or rather it ought to have done so, for after rushing to the station at 7:30 I had to sit in the carriage for more than an hour before we began to move. I read that every known superstition in the world is gathered into the horseshoe of the Carpathians, as if it were the centre of some sort of imaginative whirlpool; if so my stay may be very interesting. (Mem., I must ask the Count all about them.)

3 May, Bistritz.—Left Munich at 8:35 P.M., on 1st May, arriving at Vienna early next morning; should have arrived at 6:46, but train was an hour late. Buda-Pesth seems a wonderful place, from the glimpse which I got of it from the train and the little I could walk through the streets. I feared to go very far from the station, as we had arrived late and would start as near the correct time as possible. I find that the district he named is in the extreme east of the country, just on the borders of three states, Transylvania, Moldavia, and Bukovina, in the midst of the Carpathian mountains, one of the wildest and least known portions of Europe. I was not able to light on any map or work giving the exact locality of the Castle Dracula, as there are no maps of this country as yet to compare with our own Ordance Survey Maps; but I found that Bistritz, the post town named by Count Dracula, is a fairly well-known place. I shall enter here some of my notes, as they may refresh my memory when I talk over my travels with Mina. I had to hurry breakfast, for the train started a little before eight, or rather it ought to have done so, for after rushing to the station at 7:30 I had to sit in the carriage for more than an hour before we began to move. I read that every known superstition in the world is gathered into the horseshoe of the Carpathians, as if it were the centre of some sort of imaginative whirlpool; if so my stay may be very interesting. (Mem., I must ask the Count all about them.)

Be aware that the file names you see in your font folder(s) are not necessarily the same as you will see in the Scribus font menus. The name displayed in the application is stored within the font itself. If you scroll to the far right of the available fonts list in *File > Preferences > Fonts*, you will see the name as it shows up in the source font folder. For example, what may show up in your font list as Nimbus Roman No9 L Regular may be stored as `/usr/X11R6/lib/X11/fonts/URW/ n0210031.pfb`. These odd names are a heritage of the old DOS/Windows 8+3 naming restriction for files.

A variation in Adobe fonts is Multiple Master fonts. These allow you to use Adobe tools to create new "instances" of the base font by modifying one or more characters. They are not used much now; the tools for manipulating them are not available in Scribus, but instances of the MM font can be created by using the command line utilities `mmafm` and `mmpfb` from the lcdf type tools. [4]

Another special font format that can't be used by Scribus yet is Adobe's CID (Character Identifier) format, which is a container format for Asian (especially Chinese, Japanese and Korean) characters. Since these scripts may use thousands of different symbols, Adobe created the composite CID format to include more than 256 PostScript glyphs per file.

5.7.1.4 Mac Fonts

OS X knows two additional font types which are related to the old Macintosh specific "file forks." In short, files are divided into a data fork (the normal file) and additional resource forks. Traditionally, font data have been stored in the resource fork, but this practice isn't used much in OS X any more. Still, some fonts like "Times" continue to use this format:

```
-rw-r--r--   1 root   wheel          0 Mar 28  2005 Times LT MM
```

As you can see, the listing shows a size of 0 bytes, since the data fork is empty. These files can only be copied with special tools that convert it to BinHex format. There's the fondu utility, which helps to convert these fonts to formats that work on other platforms. [5]

Later, Apple introduced the dfont format, which is basically the same format as resource fonts, except that all font data is in the data fork:

```
-rw-r--r--   1 root   wheel   1624875 Mar 21  2005 Times.dfont
```

While normal Linux distributions will probably not install those fonts, Scribus is able to use them if they are found in the font path. It is also possible to use fondu to convert these fonts to a suitable format for other platforms.

Newer fonts on OS X are all in OpenType or TrueType format, both of which work as-is on Linux/UNIX and Windows.

Font format support in current operating systems:

	Type 1	Type 1 (Mac)	TrueType	OpenType	Multiple Master	dfonts (Mac)
Linux/UNIX with Freetype2	yes	no*	yes	yes	yes**	only Scribus*
Mac OS X	no	yes	yes	yes	only with Adobe Type Manager Deluxe or InDesign	yes
Windows 2000/ XP/Vista	yes	no*	yes	yes	only with Adobe Type Manager Deluxe or InDesign**	no*

* Mac font formats can be converted to other formats with fondu.

** Only on the command line with mmafm and mmpfb.

5.7.1.5 Typographic Niceties

"Artificial" fonts (Adobe calls them "faux" fonts) are mathematically modified to produce variations such as italic and bold.

Some programs, particularly word processors, employ this technique; Scribus does not. This decision was made by the developers though some users still want artificial fonts available in Scribus. If your fonts do not have actual italic, bold, bold italic, condensed, etc., Scribus will not attempt to create them, as artificial fonts can cause enormous problems in a pre-press environment.

The techniques used by Scribus for subscript, superscript, outlined – you can create "faux" bold glyphs by enlarging the font outline and using the same color as the glyph – and small caps (available via the Properties Palette or paragraph styles) are safe but aesthetically not optimal. Especially with "scaling width of characters" you will have to experiment to see what's acceptable.

SMALL CAPS
SMALL CAPS

The difference between scaled small caps (top) and real small caps (bottom) is bigger than most people think.

Typographic purists will point out that, for example, small caps generated by scaling are not the same as "true drawn" small caps. Here's an example: Note that in true small caps, the vertical elements are thicker than those in the Scribus scaled version. There are similar issues with other kinds of characters: ligatures, fractions, superscripts and subscripts. The Adobe OpenType User Guide describes them in detail. [6] It's possible to access these characters with *Insert > Glyph* or *Insert > Ligature*, but that takes a lot more time than just typing. You have to really want them.

We have almost always used here the term "character" as it is popularly understood. But font experts will make a differentiation between "character" and "glyph." An "A" is a character, in a sense, an abstraction, applying to the first letter of the alphabet. A glyph is the particular letterform(s), which make up that character in a particular font – for example, a small cap A or a "decorated" A. A serif font and a sans serif font each have their own glyph to denote the same character. A character may be made up of more than one glyph, eg. an accented character, or two characters might be represented by a single ligature glyph, like fi instead of fi.

[1] http://partners.adobe.com/public/developer/en/font/T1_SPEC.PDF
[2] http://www.truetype-typography.com/ttspec.htm
[3] http://www.microsoft.com/typography/otspec
[4] http://www.lcdf.org/type/
[5] http://fondu.sourceforge.net
[6] http://www.adobe.com/type/opentype

5.7.2 Getting and Using Good Fonts

5.7.2.1 General

THERE ARE hundreds, maybe thousands of places to get fonts on the web. If you google "fonts," you will get several paid ads for sites selling fonts and dozens more showing fonts for sale.

A well-made and well-designed font takes a lot of skill and time to build, especially an OpenType font with possibly thousands of glyphs.

Many fonts now available in digital form originated in the world of metal type or other now seldom-used forms such as filmstrips. So the fonts you buy today, like Garamond or Clarendon, may have histories going back hundreds of years.

If you know where to look, you'll be able to find some excellent fonts for free or even Free. Beware, though, that it's highly unlikely (yet) that a free/Free font provides all the font faces of a commercial font offering. Even though a project like the Open Font Library is attempting to change this, you probably can't avoid buying a commercial font for some purposes any time soon.

Below is an annotated list of sources for free/Free, cheap and commercial fonts.

5.7.2.2 Sources

- There are some great freely licensed URW fonts from Artifex (makers of Ghostscript and GhostPCL) that are well worth grabbing. There are some good quality fonts in there, like Clarendon, URW Bookman, and Antique Olive. They are shipped with the Windows version of Scribus. [1]

- The Gentium font family provides excellent serif fonts under the SIL Open Font License. It supports Unicode, but so far, only regular and italic are complete. [2]

- Linux Libertine is an Open Source project, which is working on a Free alternative to proprietary serif fonts, especially Times/Times New Roman. It offers different font faces in OTF format. As of this writing, regular and italic are complete, bold, bold italic, underlined and small caps will work for most European languages. [3]

- Liberation is a set of fonts created on behalf of Red Hat, Inc. It is intended to serve as a replacement for the Microsoft fonts Times New Roman, Arial and Courier. It is distributed under the GPL v2 plus exception. Liberation Serif has been used for the continuous text of this manual. [4]

- Jos Buivenga is maintaining a website called exljbris. His carefully crafted fonts are available for gratis use in Type 1, TrueType and OTF format. One of them, Fontin, has been used for the cover of this manual. [5]

- The very prolific and very gifted type designer Manfred Klein has put a huge collection of high-quality TrueType fonts on the web at his Fonteria. Perhaps the best thing about Klein's selection is the large number of good text fonts that take off in subtle ways from classical serif faces. He offers the fonts "free for private and charity use. They are even free for commercial use – but if there's any profit, please make a donation to organizations like 'Doctors Without Borders.'" [6]

- TypeOasis, the site that hosts the Fonteria, has nice work by other designers, too. [7]

- Some free TrueType fonts can also be downloaded from Schriftgrad which also hosts a good glossary on typography/printing/DTP in German. [8]

- http://fonts.goldenweb.it/index_file/l/en is a directory with 20,590 free TrueType fonts of mixed quality.

- http://www.webpagepublicity.com/free-fonts-g.html contains 6500 TTF fonts, also free as in beer.

- Valery Friedman hosts a list of his Free Quality Font Top 25 with some excellent fonts. Updates in Smashing Magazine. [9]

- Gerrit van Aken offers links to some excellent fonts and also provides reviews (German). [10]

- Pedro Reina has listed 189 freely available fonts, all of them Type 1, TrueType, PC/Mac. [11]

- Luc Devroye has a regularly updated list of font foundries and designers, including those offering free quality fonts. [12]

- The MS Core TrueType fonts might be useful too, though they're not really designed for print use. [13]

- With Vista, Microsoft has introduced a new set of Core Fonts. To make them available on older versions of Windows, you need to install the PowerPoint viewer 2007. The EULA explicitly forbids the use of the fonts on any other operating system.

- Fry Fonts offers some popular fonts like Apple Garamond or Coca Cola in TrueType format for free download. [14]

- If you can get hold of an older printer driver CD from c. 2000, you may find a collection of high quality Adobe Type 1 fonts, including "classics" like Garamond on it.

- The Linux Box offers an archive with 6760 True Type fonts for free download. Beware of its size, though: it's huge (157.7 MB). [15]

- Another place worth looking at is the German TeX Users Group (TUG). It provides some free high quality Type 1/TTF/Open Type fonts. [16] Similarly, the Comprehensive TeX Archive Network (CTAN) offers a wide range of excellent fonts. Previews are available. [17]

- For using Chinese fonts under Linux, Gentoo developer Alastair 'liquidx' Tse, has written a guide on Gentoo Linux Chinese Fonts HOWTO. Worth to check it out. [18]

- An affordable source for fonts is the German manufacturer of the multi-platform office suite Softmaker Office. They offer one "font of the month" for free download. If TrueType fonts are sufficient for your work, you can buy a CD-ROM with 10,000 fonts [19]. In case you need professional grade fonts, they are offering 6000 TrueType and Type 1 fonts. [20]

- Corel WordPerfect has the TTF fonts and CorelDraw has the TTF plus PS fonts. At least this is true for WP 8/9 and Draw 8/9. The fonts are in their own folders and can be copied WITHOUT installing the product anywhere. Despite rumors to the contrary, CorelDraw fonts are high quality Bitstream fonts which have been used by pre-press folks for years without incident.

- Fontshop [21] is also a good place to go, but you might have a look at Linotype [22], Lucasfonts [23] and maybe Fontfabrik [24] (they only retail) as well. They are all German companies offering some really nice fonts, that unfortunately aren't affordable for everybody.

- Adobe Systems does not have a long history of building fonts, but it was a pioneer in development of digital fonts, first with PostScript fonts, now with OpenType faces. A number of fonts ship with Adobe products, and others may be purchased online. And if you have an ample budget, you can buy from Adobe its OpenType Font Folio: more than 2200 fonts on a CD. Adobe also used to offer a "Type on Call" CD with its applications; you could install the font and buy an unlocking key. It has discontinued this, and if you have a Type on Call CD, you can throw it away.

- Fonts.com is associated with Monotype Imaging, a long-time supplier of fonts from metal to digital.

- Myfonts.com offers fonts from Bitstream, Linotype and URW, all well-established developers of quality fonts.

- There are many other less well-known foundries; if you want to experiment, most offer fonts in the $20 range.

[1] http://mirror.cs.wisc.edu/pub/mirrors/ghost/GPL/current/ ghostscript-fonts- std-8.11.tar.gz
[2] http://www.sil.org/~gaultney/Gentium
[3] http://linuxlibertine.sourceforge.net
[4] http://www.redhat.com/promo/fonts
[5] http://www.josbuivenga.demon.nl
[6] http://www.moorstation.org/typoasis/designers/klein

[7] http://www.moorstation.org/typoasis/typoasis1.htm

[8] http://www.schriftgrad.de/Menueleiste/Xdownload.htm

[9] http://www.alvit.de/blog/article/20-best-license-free-official-fonts

[10] http://www.praegnanz.de/essays

[11] http://apostrophiclab.pedroreina.net

[12] http://cg.scs.carleton.ca/~luc/latest.html

[13] http://corefonts.sourceforge.net/

[14] http://www.fryfonts.com/

[15] http://thelinuxbox.org/files/fonts.tar.gz

[16] ftp://ftp.dante.de/tex-archive/fonts/

[17] http://www.ctan.org/tex-archive/fonts/

[18] http://dev.gentoo.org/~liquidx/chinesefonts/

[19] http://www.softmaker.de/megafont.htm

[20] http://www.infinitype.com/features_en.htm

[21] http://fontshop.de/

[22] http://linotype.com

[23] http://fontfabrik.com

5.7.3 Font Preview and Font Management

5.7.3.1 The Font Preview

ONCE you have installed more than a handful of fonts on your system, you may need to preview the fonts available to you. Scribus comes with a versatile font previewer. You will find it in the *Extras* menu:

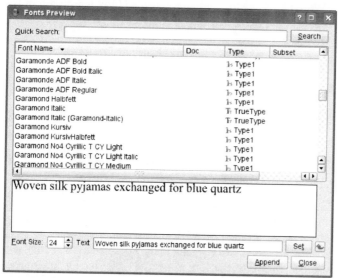

On top of the font list you see a search field. You can use it for searching the names of fonts. For instance, you can insert "garamond" if you want to list only fonts whose name include this string, or you can list all regular font faces by entering "regular." Note that the search isn't case sensitive.

Below the search field you see a font list. It consists of 5 columns:

- *Font Name*: This is a list of fonts available to Scribus. They are listed in alphabetical order, the names displayed are the ones stored in the font files. You can switch the display from ascending to descending by clicking on the caption of the column (the arrow will indicate the order).

- *Doc*: Fonts used in your document are marked with a check mark here.

- *Type*: Indicates the font type (Type 1, TrueType or OpenType).

- *Subset*: Shows whether the font is being subset during export to PostScript or PDF (see below).

- *Access*: Indicates whether a font is system-wide installed or only available to you.

Next you will see a field in which the font is previewed by using a sample text. You can change the preview font size as well as the sample text. To change the sample text, you can edit it in the "Text" field. After you inserted the new text, you have to click on the "Set" button. If you want to return to the default sample text for your language, click on the button with the "Undo" arrow.

With the "Append" button you can add the font to a font selection in the Style menu, which we decided to ignore, as explained above.

5.7.3.2 Font Installation

Scribus will load and use fonts from three sources:

- System fonts are the fonts which are normally installed on your system. See below for installation instructions. When you install a new font, you need to restart Scribus, if you want to use it.

- The Scribus *Preferences* allow to specify additional font paths. If you put any font file in any directory of this path, Scribus will detect it on startup.

- Additionally, when you open a document, Scribus will look for its fonts in the same directory as the document. This makes it possible to work with documents that where collected for output, without installing additional fonts on your system.

Scribus is really picky about fonts, so sometimes a font will not load owing to the font detection code finding internal errors in the font. This is not a bug, this is a feature. Scribus will not load and will ignore bitmap fonts (which are totally unsuitable for publishing), fonts with internal format errors (while most applications will use those fonts, Scribus rejects them since they tend to create havoc at the print office) and fonts without a Unicode encoding (most notorious examples are some Symbol fonts). If you wonder why a font that's installed on your system isn't available in Scribus, you can start Scribus from the command line using the command `scribus -fi` (`scribus.exe -fi` on Windows and OS/2), where the parameter "fi" means "font information." Scribus will then list all the fonts it has found and whether they passed the font test, if they are duplicates and why it didn't load a font.

5.7.3.3 Linux/UNIX

The usual locations for system-wide fonts in a Linux/UNIX environment are `/usr/share/fonts` and/or `/usr/local/share/fonts`. These fonts are available to all users.

Individual users have their own private font directory, in their home directory: `~/.fonts`. It's possible to install fonts by simply copying them manually to either of these directories. But there are graphical front ends for font installation as well.

5.7.3.4 KDE

For KDE users, the best way to install and delete fonts is to use the Font Installer which is part of the KDE Control Center, under "Administration." If you are an ordinary user, you can use this installer to add and delete fonts in your own font directory. If you switch to Administrator Mode (requiring a password), you can install and delete fonts for all users.

In either mode, when you click on the "Add Fonts" button, you then navigate to a source of fonts. You can select individual or multiple fonts, then press the "OK" button. A progress bar charts the installation process, and reminds you at the end that the new fonts will probably not be available to open applications until you close them and restart. This is generally true of font-consuming applications. Note that when you start Scribus and look at the bottom of the "splash screen," you will see a note about "initializing fonts"; this is the process by which Scribus comes to recognize newly-installed fonts. (The same is also true if you add a new font path to Scribus.)

5.7.3.5 Gnome

To install fonts in Gnome, open Nautilus and type "fonts:///" in the adress bar. Then you can copy your fonts to the folder.

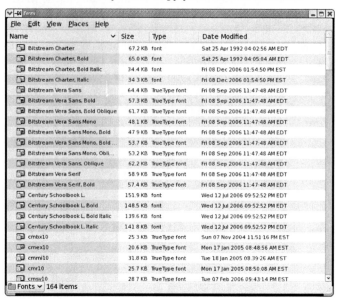

5.7.3.6 Fontmatrix

As of this writing, an Open Source font manager for Linux/UNIX, Fontmatrix, is evolving quickly, and it's already quite usable. Originally developed for Linux Systems, it's also being ported to Mac OS X and Windows. [27]

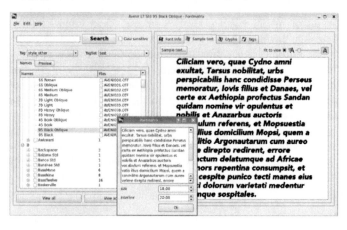

Its features are:

- It can read almost every bit of the internal workings of a font which are human readable, eg. copyright, encodings etc.
- It shows a sample text as a font preview.
- It can examine glyphs.
- It's possible to activate and deactivate fonts.
- It permits the tagging of fonts and to collect the tags.
- It can generate fontbooks (PDF files with font informations and sample text).
- It can start FontForge to edit a font file.
- It can load and activate fonts from network resources, including the internet.

5.7.3.7 Windows

According to Microsoft [28], the recommended way to install new fonts in Windows is the following:

1. Click "Run" in the Start menu.
2. Type `%windir%\fonts`, and then click "OK" or press the "Enter" key.
3. On the File menu, click "Install New Font."
4. Select the source directory that contains the fonts you want to add.
5. Select the font files you want to add. To select more than one font at a time, press and hold down the CTRL key while you click each font or press the Shift key to select a range of fonts.
6. Check "Copy Fonts To Fonts Folder."
7. Click OK.

There is, however, an easier way to install fonts in Windows, as you can just copy/move the font files to the folder `Windows\Fonts` on Windows XP or `WINNT\Fonts` on Windows 2000. In both cases you need to have Administrator privileges. Note that this might not work with Type 1 fonts.

5.7.3.8 Mac OS X

On OS X, Scribus automatically recognizes all fonts installed in the standard locations (`/Library/Fonts`, `/System/Library/Fonts`, `/Users/name/Library/Fonts`) paths. To install a new font in Mac OS X, simply copy the font files to either of those directories except `/System/Library/Fonts`, to which not even root has write privileges. Fonts in `/Library/Fonts` will be available to all users, those in `/Users/name/Library/Fonts` only for the respective user. Additional font paths for Scribus can be configured in the Scribus *Preferences.*

5.7.3.9 OS/2, eCOMstation

Not surprisingly, the OS/2 way of installing fonts is similar to Windows:

1. Open the "OS/2 System" folder.
2. Open the "System Setup" folder.
3. Open the "Font Palette" object.
4. Select "Edit fonts."
5. Click the "Add" button.
6. In the resulting "Add Font" dialog, type the path to the folder that contains the font(s).
7. Select any file in the left "Font files" pane or press Ctrl+/ to select all the font files.
8. Click the "Add" button.
9. Close the "Edit font" dialog and all other folders.

5.7.3.10 Font Management in Scribus

Scribus has its own internal font management tools. If you go to the the "Fonts" dialog in the *Preferences* or the *Document Setup* (depending on whether you want to do document-specific font management or general font management in Scribus) you see three tabs.

The first tab is called "Available Fonts." It lists all fonts Scribus found and accepted during launch. You may not see all of your installed fonts, depending on their quality. Scribus is quite picky with fonts, and it may reject some suspect files to prevent problems downstream.

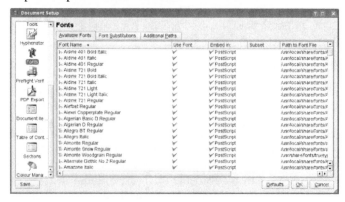

The tab consists of 5 columns:

- *Font Name*: This is a list of fonts available to Scribus. They are listed in alphabetical order, the names displayed are the ones stored in the font files.

- *Use Font*: If you uncheck a font here, the font won't be available to you. By default, all fonts are available. It is possible to do this when a document is open, but you will see no effect on your font menus until you quit Scribus and then start it again. When Scribus is launched, one of the things that happens is initialization of the font system; at this point, the changes you made before quitting take effect.

- *Embed in*: If you uncheck a font here, the font won't be embedded in PostScript files made with Scribus. By default, all fonts will be embedded. If you don't embed a font, you are counting on the user's printer having exactly the same font installed.

- *Subset*: This option will prevent fonts from being embedded in PostScript and PDF files. You won't be able to select them for embedding in the PDF export dialog. By default, all OpenType fonts are selected for subsetting, as they can't be embedded for technical reasons. Scribus will also subset fonts instead of embedding if they contain too many glyphs or if you try to embed TrueType fonts in PostScript.

- *Path to Font File*: As the caption says, you can see the path to a font file in this column.

The next tab is called "Font Substitution." The functionality of the font substitution varies, depending on the kind of operation you execute. If you open a Scribus file that uses a font, which is not available on your system, you have to substitute this foreign font with one from your collection. For that purpose, you will be shown a dialog that lets you choose a replacement for the original. By default, Scribus shows the standard font selected in *Document Setup/Preferences > Fonts*. You can also decide to make this substitution permanent.

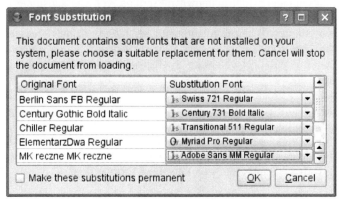

If you don't make it permanent, you will have to make the decision each time you open the document, which may not be what you want, considered the risk of destroying a layout by inadvertently using a wrong font substitute. By checking "Make these substitutions permanent," you will store them. If you decide to make your substitutions permanent, this information will be stored in the *Preferences* and in the *Document Setup*, where you can either delete the substitution(s) by selecting it with the mouse and pressing the "Delete" button, or you can select another font for replacement. Any changes in the *Preferences* will not affect the layout of your current document if you load it again.

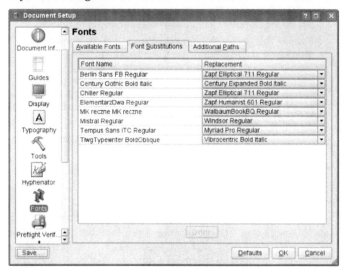

If you import an ODT or SXW file (see Working with Text) that contains a font unknown to Scribus, you can substitute it as well, but there is no option to make it permanent, as the replacement will be stored automatically in both *Preferences* and the *Document Setup* – even if you close the dialog without clicking "OK." If you want to change the substitution for future documents, you have to do this in the *Preferences*. Changes in the *Document Setup* will only affect the current document. Your options for changes are to either delete the substitution or select another replacement font as described in the previous paragraph. Note that any changes you make will only affect future imports of ODT and SXW files; text that has already been imported won't change its formatting.

There are two things you should be aware of when you import an ODT or SXW with unknown fonts. First, as you learned in Working with Text, while Scribus will import existing paragraph styles, text within a paragraph that uses a different font will be treated like other formatting options, for instance text color or underlined. Thus, Scribus will ask you for a replacement of the font, independent of the paragraph style. However, Scribus will not create a different paragraph style, only the individual formatting, even if it's just an empty space that uses a different font.

The second issue is one that may result in problems with your text layout in Scribus. OpenOffice.org and other word processors permit the creation of so-called "faux" font faces like bold or italic. As already mentioned in Fonts and Font Technology, Scribus does not support this feature to prevent pre-press issues. If Scribus detects a faux font face in an ODT or SXW file, it "assumes" that there was an existing font face in use that's just missing on your computer. For instance, the popular free Gentium font currently only consists of regular and italic font faces. If you format text using Gentium as bold in a word processor and save it in ODT or SXW format, Scribus will ask you to select a substitution for the font "Gentium Bold," which simply doesn't exist (see the screengrab below). There is no easy solution to this issue. Your best options are probably to import the text without formatting (see Working with Text) or to use another font in the word processor. You could also replace the faux bolds or italics with the regular font face and later change the font settings for the paragraph styles you imported, but that's probably too much trouble.

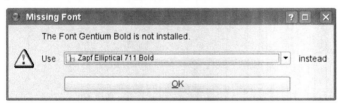

Please note that the font substitution works only with OpenOffice.org Writer and ODT files. If you import OpenOffice.org Draw or ODG files that contain text in a font that's not available on your system or that uses faux font faces, Scribus will automatically replace them with the default font for text frames. In this case you should convert the text to curves before you import the drawing into Scribus (see Importing Vector Files for instructions).

To add new paths to fonts that aren't stored in the standard directories of your operating system, you have to use the tab "Additional Paths." By clicking on "Add," you open a file dialog to browse for the respective directory. This may be useful for testing a font before you install it on your system. Note that you can only add new font paths if no document is open.

5.7.4 Drop Caps

THE METHODS described below are a little more flexible than the built-in features for drop caps in paragraph styles, and also allow for some more effects.

- Create a text frame and load your text. Adjust the font, size etc. as you please.
- Delete the first letter of your text.
- Create a new text frame (we'll call this frame "initial") and type the letter you have deleted in the other frame.
- Set the size of the text frame "initial" to a high value. Remember, it contains only one letter!
- Change the text frame "initial" via *Item > Convert To* to outlines. If necessary, the drop caps's size can be changed like a drawing.
- In the *Shape* tab of the Properties Palette enable "Text Flows around Frame" and then "Use Bounding Box" on the "initial" frame.
- Now just move the "initial" frame, so that its position is in the upper left corner of the original text frame. The text in the frame will flow around it:

W eit hinten, hinter den Wortbergen, fern der Länder Vokalien und Konsonantien leben die Blindtexte. Abgeschieden wohnen Sie in Buchstabhausen an der Küste des Seman-

- The look of the drop cap can be changed in many ways. Here are some examples.
- A second drop cap behind the first one. After some color changes we have a shadow:

W eit hinten, hinter den Wortbergen, fern der Länder Vokalien und Konsonantien leben die Blindtexte. Abgeschieden wohnen Sie in Buchstabhausen an der Küste des Seman-

- Filled with a gradient:

W eit hinten, hinter den Wortbergen, fern der Länder Vokalien und Konsonantien leben die Blindtexte. Abgeschieden wohnen Sie in Buchstabhausen an der Küste des Seman-

- Last, but not least: the outlines can be converted to an image frame:

Weit hinten, hinter den Wortbergen, fern der Länder Vokalien und Konsonantien leben die Blindtexte. Abgeschieden wohnen Sie in Buchstabhausen an der Küste des Seman-

5.7.5 Short Words

5.7.5.1 What the Short Words Plug-in Does

SHORT WORDS for Scribus is a special plug-in for adding non-breaking spaces before or after abbreviations or single-letter words.

These short words are specific to every language's typographic rules, eg. according to Czech, Polish, and Slovak typographical standards, it is not allowed to leave one letter conjunctions at line ends if the line contains more than 25 characters. A common issue in all languages is in regard to measure and weight units, where for obvious reasons non-breaking spaces should be put in-between the preceding numbers and the units. Last but not least, there are plenty of abbreviated academic degrees, military ranks etc., which should not be separated from their owners.

Although the Scribus team cannot individually address every one of these national standards, one of the Scribus core team developers, Petr Vaněk, decided to provide Scribus users with a plug-in, that can be easily customized to meet one's specific needs.

5.7.5.2. How it Works

The screenshot below shows a sample text containing a short word before applying non-breaking spaces.

Below you see a text sample before executing *Short Words*:

The superintendent and detective were also accused by the inquiry, headed by Mr Justice Frederik Morris, of lying to the tribunal

Now the same text after applying non-breaking spaces. The encircled word "Mr" jumped to the next line, because the normal space between "Mr" and "Justice" has been replaced by a non-breaking space:

The superintendent and detective were also accused by the inquiry, headed by Mr Justice Frederik Morris, of lying to the tribunal

5.7.5.3 How to Execute Short Words

Go to the *Extras* menu and choose *Short Words*.

Your options are:

- *Selected frames*: Applies non-breaking spaces to selected text frames.
- *Active page*: Applies non-breaking spaces to all frames of the current page.
- *All items*: Applies non-breaking spaces to the whole document.

5.7.5.4 Configuration

Short Words for Scribus provides a system-wide configuration file scribus-short-words.rc, which is usually located in the `~/lib/scribus/plugins directory` (the actual directory depends on where you or your distribution installed Scribus).

This configuration file is almost self-explanatory. Basically, it contains a list of short words for a given language, preceded or followed by a space and separated by commas. The position of the space, before or after a short word, indicates to the plug-in, where the non-breaking space should be put. Every line with configuration settings has to start with the language it is meant for, eg. en for English or cs for Czech:

```
#  English stuff STARTS here
   en=Dr. ,Dr ,Mr. ,Mr ,Mrs. ,Mrs ,Ms. ,Ms
,Prof. ,Prof ,Rev. ,Rev ,
   en= Kg, kg, g, mg, oz, lb, cwt, km, Km, m,
cm, mm,


#  Czech short words START here
## hanging conjunctions
   cs=K ,k ,S ,s ,V ,v ,Z ,z ,O ,o ,U ,u ,I ,i
,A ,
## physics and math
   cs= kg, g, m, cm, mm, l, hl, s, %,
```

If you want to create your own Short Words, eg. for a new language, you can create a scribus-short-words.rc yourself by using the Preferences. Just type your text into the field (it's up to you whether or not you want to remove the existing short words). Then click on the "Save" button on the right of the dialog. Use "Reset" to restore the default settings.

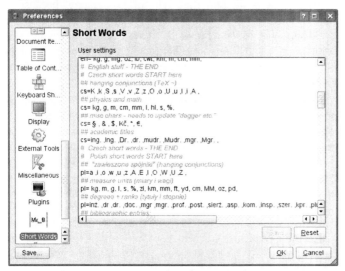

If you successfully created a configuration file for your language, you might consider sharing your work with others by sending it to one of the Scribus developers or by posting it on the Scribus mailinglist.

5.7.5 Hyphenation

HYPHENATION is an important part of typography, because a well-hyphenated text eases readability and doesn't disturb the eye of a reader by leaving white "holes" in it. The smaller the columns in a text frame are, the greater the importance of hyphenation, especially if the text is justified. Just take a look at a newspaper and you know what it means.

There are some rules of thumb you can apply if you want to produce a layout of higher quality. These rules are reflected in the default hyphenation settings in Scribus: don't leave less than two (or even) three letters at the end of a line, and don't use more than two consecutive hyphenations. Where many consecutive hyphenated lines occur, the resulting appearance is called a "ladder," and type people regard ladders as undesirable. On the other hand, if you are putting text in narrow columns, like, for instance, in a newspaper, and sharply restrict consecutive hyphens, you will get "loose" type, with wide interword spaces ("rivers") because you've limited hyphenation. And that's ugly too. Take your pick.

Hyphenator

☐ Hyphenation Suggestions

☒ Hyphenate Text Automatically During Typing

Language:	English ▾
Smallest Word:	3
Consecutive Hyphenations Allowed:	2

The hyphenator tab in the *Preferences* and the *Document Setup* offers you some more options that need an explanation. If you check "Hyphenation Suggestions," Scribus will ask you to confirm or change the suggestions derived from the hyphenation dictionaries. This may be annoying, since Scribus will ask for each word in the text. It may be necessary, though, as Scribus uses the same dictionary files as OpenOffice.org, and they are far from perfect.

A hyphenation suggestion in Scribus

If you agree with a suggestion, click "Accept," if not, you can place a hyphen with the "-" key elsewhere or add a new one. If you don't want this word to be hyphenated, click "Skip." To abort the hyphenation of your text, click "Cancel."

By default, Scribus doesn't hyphenate text. The regular way is to select a text frame and use *Extras > Hyphenate* Text. You can change this behavior by checking "Hyphenate Text Automatically During Typing" in the "Hyphenator" tab of the *Preferences* and the *Document Setup*. This means that each text that will be inserted after checking this option will be hyphenated automatically. Texts that are already there won't be affected.

Another important option is the choice of the standard language for your document, as each language has its own hyphenation rules. By default this is the language of your system. But if you create a document in another language, it's better to switch the standard language to prevent ugly or nonsensical hyphenations.

If you are working with a document in more than one language, you can apply different languages to text frames by selecting them and choosing another hyphenation language in the *Text* tab of the Properties Palette.

The result of automatic hyphenation may not be sufficient, and you might want to add some additional hyphens. You can do this, but don't use the "-" key – insert a smart hyphen instead. Smart hyphens are invisible in a regular text. They only become active if a hyphenation is actually possible. To insert a smart hyphen, use *Insert > Character > Smart Hyphen* or press Ctrl+Shift+- on the keyboard. The keyboard shortcut may not work in some environments, but you can assign another one in the *Preferences*.

Hyphenation can only be applied to one text frame or a chain of text frames at a time. Also note that hyphenation is not recorded by the Action History. Select a text frame and use *Extras > Dehyphenate Text* instead. Smart hyphens won't be removed by dehyphenating text, you have to delete them manually.

Sometimes applying hyphenation to a text chain may result in text frames that are rendered as if they were empty. If you run across this issue, don't worry. Just close your document and open it again. Your text will then be visible again.

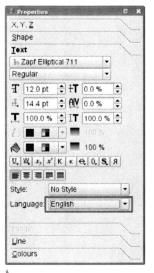

Changing the language of a text frame in the Properties Palette

5.7.6 Special Characters

5.7.6.1 Inserting Special Characters with the Character Palette

When you are in Story Editor or edit contents mode of a text frame, you will see these choices in the *Insert* menu. This allows to insert foreign language accented characters, special symbols not found on the keyboard, typographic symbols (such as typographic quotation marks, em dash, en dash, variably sized spaces, for example), and ligatures.

Selecting *Insert > Glyphs* brings up the dialog you see here, containing all available characters in your font. Which font will be displayed, depends on the formatting of the text in which the cursor placed, but you can select another font from the drop-down list in the upper left. Since the characters are displayed in your chosen font, if you see the character here, it should display on the page, which may or may not be true in Story Editor, depending on its display font.

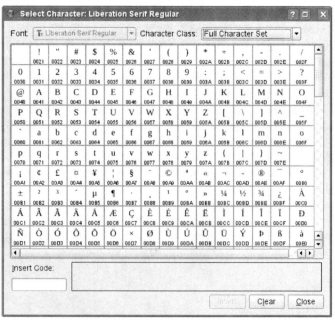

On the upper right you can choose if you want to display all glyphs of a font or subsets like "Basic Latin" or "Ligatures."

Each time you click on a glyph in the palette, it will be added to the gray field at the bottom. Thus, you can insert more than one glyph at once. To insert the selected glyph or glyphs at the cursor position in a text frame, click "Insert," and to clear the field, click "Clear."

You will note that the palette displays the Unicode string for each glyph. If you know this string, you can insert it directly in the field labeled "Code." That can be a big time saver, if you're working with huge fonts that contain hundreds of glyphs. While in Story Editor or Edit Contents of Frame mode, you can also press F12 on the keyboard, then the 4 digits of the Unicode number.

5.7.6.2 Inserting Selected Special Characters and Formatting from the Insert Menu

The *Insert* menu offers some submenus that can be used to insert selected special characters and special formatting. Let's have a look at these submenus and their entries, one by one.

Character

Of the first three entries only "Non Breaking Dash" needs an explanation, since "Page Number" and "Smart Hyphen" are already explained in the "Page Numbering" and "Hyphenation" sections. A non breaking dash is a dash that won't be accepted as a hyphen. Imagine you write "A–Z." You surely won't want a line break after "A–," and therefore you add a non breaking dash.

The "Copyright," "Registered Trademark" and "Trademark" entries don't need an explanation either, as their use is widespread. The following entries, however, might be less familiar:

- *Solidus*: The Solidus looks like a slash, but it isn't the same. It's used to denote the British currency Shillings and also in Mathematics to typeset fractions like 1/5 .

- *Bullet*: The Bullet point is used for unnumbered lists.

- *Middle Dot*: The Middle Dot can be used as a more reluctant version of a Bullet Point, but it can also replace a comma in continuous texts when used for enumerations. It can also be used as a symbol for multiplications in mathematical formulas.

- *Em Dash*: The em dash is mostly used in English typography. It represents a dash with the width of the letter "M" (uppercase). It can be used to typographically replace parentheses or parenthetical commas. The general recommendation is to use the em dash without spaces, like in this example: "all people—young and old, black and white—celebrated." However, this recommendation cannot be generalized, as many typographers use the em dash with Hair Spaces on both sides of the dash. Even in English typography, though, the use of the em dash is on the decline. Instead, Anglo-Saxon printers and tyopgraphers use the en dash plus regular spacing more extensively.

Outside the English typography the em dash is sometimes used as a replacement for double zero decimal places. For instance, 2.00 EUR can be represented by 2.— EUR. The em dash is also used as a replacement for the quotation dash (see below).

- En Dash: The en dash is a dash with the width of the letter "n" (lowercase) in a given font. It's smaller than an em dash or a quotation dash, but wider than a hyphen, a minus or a figure dash. The en dash is used for two purposes: First, it indicates a range between numbers or dates (12–14 °C). In this case, no space is added between the two values and the dash. The second use case is the same as the em dash, namely to replace parentheses or commas, but in contrast to the latter, it is used with spaces on both sides.

- Figure Dash: The figure dash isn't available in many fonts. It's a dash that represents the width of a digit in Monospace fonts. It can be replaced by a hyphen or a minus almost all of the time.

- Quotation Dash: Just like the figure dash, the quotation dash is rarely available in most fonts. It is used to indicate quotations, just like quotation marks. It can easily be replaced by an em dash, because even trained eyes won't notice the the difference.

Quotes

Apostrophe
Straight Double
Single Left
Single Right
Double Left
Double Right
Low Single Comma
Low Double Comma
Single Reversed
Double Reversed
Single Left Guillemet
Single Right Guillemet
Double Left Guillemet
Double Right Guillemet
CJK Single Left
CJK Single Right
CJK Double Left
CJK Double Right

There are many kinds of marks to denote quotations, some language-specific. In English, the proper typographic quotation marks will not be obtained directly from the keyboard, so here you have the ability to precisely choose the correct mark for your purpose.

- *Apostrophe*: This is actually not a typographic apostrophe, but a typewriter apostrophe. You shouldn't use it, unless you are trying to use it in connection with the "Straight Double Quote" in mathematics or to denote inches, like in: 5'45". Another use case is the emulation of typewriters. The "Apostrophe" name is derived from Unicode naming standards.

- *Straight Double*: The remarks made above also apply to the "Straight Double." Don't use it for quotes!

- *Single Left*: This name actually refers to English quotation marks. In English typography (and some others who adopted the English model), the single left quote is a comma, both horizontally and vertically mirrored, then used in superscript style. To describe the different uses of so-called curly quotes, typographers use the ciphers 6 and 9. The English single left quote is a 6-comma in superscript style.

- *Single Right*: Another English quotation mark. It is a 9-comma in superscript style. It's also used as a typographical apostrophe in most languages that use a European alphabet.

- *Double Left* is the double version of the English left quotation mark.
- *Double Right* is the double version of the English right quotation mark.
- *Low Single Comma*: This is the standard left single quote in German and Austrian German, Danish and in many Central European typographies.
- *Low Double Comma*: This is the standard left double quote in German and Austrian German, Danish and in many Central European typographies.
- *An additional note about "curly quotes": Afrikaans, Dutch, Polish, Finnish and Swedish use a mix of both systems: Low commas are left quotes, and the English double right mark is used for right quotation marks. In Greek it's the other way around: Left English quotes on the left and low single commas on the right.*
- *Single Left Guillemet*: This is the standard left single quote in Spanish, Portuguese, most Eastern European countries and in Switzerland. It's also the standard in French, but with an additional thin space between guillemet and text.
- *Single Right Guillemet*: This is the standard right single quote in Spanish, Portuguese, most Eastern European countries and in Switzerland. It's also the standard in French, but with an additional space between guillemet and text.
- *Double Left Guillemet*: This is the standard left double quote in Spanish, Portuguese, most Eastern European countries and in Switzerland. It's also the standard in French, but with an additional thin space between guillemets and text.
- *Double Right Guillemet*: This is the standard double right quote in Spanish, Portuguese, most Eastern European countries and in Switzerland. It's also the standard in French, but with an additional space between guillemets and text.
- *An additional note about Guillemets: In German and Austrian German and many Central European countries, guillemets are also frequently used as quotation marks, especially in books. They are, however used reversed, ie. a "left" Guillemet is a right quotation mark and the other way around.*
- Chinese, Japanese and Korean (CJK) use special corner brackets as quotation marks. These are only available in Asian font files

Special Characters in the Story Editor
If your special character fails to display, this most often means that it is not available in your chosen font. Just because it shows in the Story Editor does not mean it will show on the page – that only means it exists in the Story Editor's display font.

Spaces and Breaks

These are special size and purpose spaces. The first on the list, "Non Breaking Space," is actually a normal space with a particular behavior. One may have, for example, a couple of words like "Dr. Smith," so you would want a nonbreaking space between the two words so they do not get separated at a line break. See also Short Words.

Non Breaking Space	Ctrl+Space
En Space	
Em Space	
Thin Space	
Thick Space	
Mid Space	
Hair Space	
New Line	Shift+Return
Frame Break	Ctrl+Return
Column Break	Ctrl+Shift+Return

The rest of the upper section shows many different sized spaces which can be used. They will only be available if your chosen font includes them:

- *En Space*: Has the width of the letter "n" (lowercase) in the font.
- *Em Space*: Has the width of the letter "M" (uppercase) in the font.
- Thin Space: Has the width of one fifth (sometimes one sixth) of the letter "M" (uppercase).
- *Thick Space*: Has the width of one third of the letter "M" (uppercase).
- *Mid Space*: Has the width of one fourth of the letter "M" (uppercase).
- *Hair Space*: Is the thinnest possible space: 0.5 point.

The lower section first shows the ability to force a line break without creating a new paragraph – "New Line." The keyboard shortcut may not work in the Story Editor, however. A "Frame Break" will apply when you have linked frames – use this to force a break to the next frame in the linkage. Similarly, in a frame where there is more than one column, "Column Break" forces text to the next column.

Ligatures

Ligatures are special characters, representing the combination of two (or more) characters, such as "fi" and "fl" – they are not two characters close together, but one glyph. They must be present in your chosen font to be used. The OpenType format (OTF) provides some features for automatic replacement of two letters by the appropriate ligature. However, Scribus 1.3.3.x doesn't support them yet. To replace two letters with an appropriate ligature, you can use the "Search and Replace" feature described above, but be careful! The replacement of two letters may not always be correct. Therefore, you have to check each case. For instance, replacing "cufflink" with "cufflink" (to describe the effect of using a ligature) would be typographically wrong.

Entering Unicode Values Directly Into a Text Frame

While you are in Edit Contents of Frame mode in the main screen, or in the Story Editor, you can press F12, then the 4-digit Unicode string for a character and it will be entered into the frame. This is in hexadecimal format, so digit choices are 0 to f, and you will find these codes underneath the glyph in the glyphs palette. Example: press F12, then "00a9" for the Copyright symbol: ©

5.7.7 Lists

5.7.7.1 Numbered Lists

You may be familiar with the concept of automatically created numbered and bulleted lists from your word processor. Unfortunately, Scribus 1.3.3.x doesn't offer this feature yet. There is, however, an easy workaround, which has the advantage of giving you a maximum of control over the layout of your list.

First, create a new paragraph style for your list. In this style you create a tabulator at, say, 15 pt. This will be the distance between the number and the text. You also need to set the indent for the first line to a negative identical value to the tabulator, in our case -15 pt. This is almost all of the magic.

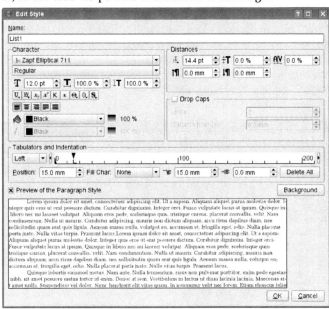

Create a text frame and write your list in the frame or in the Story Editor:

1. [tab key] First Topic
2. [tab key] Second Topic etc.

All you have to do is to apply the style to the list entries:

1. First Topic
2. Second Topic
3. Third Topic

5.7.7.2 Bulleted Lists

If you want to create a bulleted list, even with some unusual bullet points, you can do this easily and also with high precision. After creating your paragraph style as explained above, you have to use a unique combination of characters like &% as placeholders for your bullet points:

&% One Topic
&% Next Topic
&% Last Topic

Now you can choose a Dingbat font for bullet points. If you're not sure which symbol you should insert, you can use the preview of the *Insert > Glyph* dialog or *Extras > Font Preview*. Now open *Edit > Search/Replace*. Under "Search for:" insert "&%". Under "Replace with:" insert eg. "4" and choose a Dingbat font in the font selector:

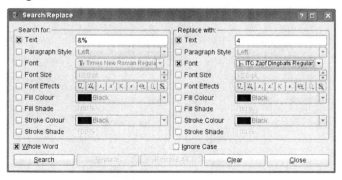

Now click "Search" and then "Replace All," and you're done:

5.7.7.3 Custom Lists

If you want to use your own symbols for list entries, you have two choices, namely inline graphics and the use of the *Multiple Duplicate* function.

In the example below, an arrowhead in SVG format had been imported into Scribus and then scaled down for use as a bullet point. You can see the result on top of the text frame. The next step was to copy the arrowhead with Ctrl+C, double-click on the text frame to enter the edit mode, move the cursor to the beginning of each line and then paste with Ctrl+V. As described in Working with Text, inline graphics can be resized and moved with the text formatting tools of the Properties Palette. If you know you need a certain distance between the bullet and the text, you can also create an invisible text frame or a shape of that size and group it with the arrowhead before you copy and paste.

If you need even more flexibility with respect to lists you can use the Multiple Duplicate feature, which is explained in its own section below. The downside of this approach is that you have to be sure that the text in your list doesn't change its formatting or its line spacing.

To create a list like the one shown below, you need to place the graphic you want to use as a bullet before the first item in the list. You are advised to do this at least at a zoom level of 400 %, because precision matters, and you will have to trust your eyes. Once the graphic is placed to your satisfaction, go to *Item > Multiple Duplicate*. Under "Number of Copies" enter the number of items in your list. Set "Horizontal Shift" to "0", and for "Vertical Shift" insert the value for line spacing as indicated in the Text tab of the Properties Palette or, in case you use a paragraph style for your list, the value set in the style. In the example below, the line spacing was 14 pt. Since there is an empty line between each item, it was necessary to double the value for vertical shift, thus, 28 pt. After clicking "OK," the list looks like this:

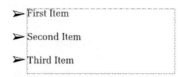

Note that you should group the bullets immediately after creation to prevent single bullets from being moved incidentially.

5.8 Placing and Moving Items with Precision

5.8.1 Measuring Tools

5.8.1.1 Measurements

THE BUTTON "Measurements" in the toolbar is a toggle button. If it's activated, a new window "Distances" appears. If you now click somewhere in your document and drag the mouse, the mouse pointer changes to a small cross, and a dotted line is drawn from your starting point to the current position of the mouse cursor, as long as you hold down the left mouse button:

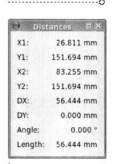

The measuring dialog

The unit for all values in the distances window is the standard unit of the document (in our example: mm). From top to bottom, it shows the following values:

- X1, Y1 and X2, Y2: These are the coordinates for the starting point (X1, Y1) and the end point (X2, Y2) of the line. As always in the Scribus coordinate system, the upper left corner of the document is the origin (0,0).
- DX and DY: The length of the drawn line in the X- and Y-direction.
- Angle: The angle of the line. A straight line from left to right with no shift on the Y axis is used as the starting point. Such a line has an angle of 0 degrees (as shown in the screenshot).
- Length: The absolute length of the line.

The image below demonstrates the use of these values: DX and length are the same, because there is no shift on the Y axis:

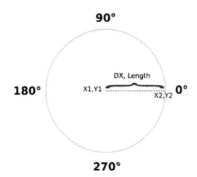

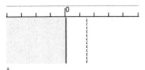

A ruler set relative to the page

5.8.1.2 Rulers

There are some viewing options for the rulers on the left and the top of the canvas. By checking/unchecking *View > Show Rulers or* with Ctrl+Shift+R you can show or hide the rulers.

If you choose *View > Rulers Relative to Page,* the left upper edge of each page becomes the origin of the rulers ("0").

You can also set a free point of origin by using the drag ruler. This means you drag your mouse pointer from the upper left corner to the new zero-point. To help you find the new point precisely, cross-hair lines indicate the position of the point in the rulers as long as you keep the left mouse button pressed.

In the status bar you can change the measuring unit of the rulers, as you can see on the left.

5.8.1.3 The Status Bar

At the bottom of the Scribus window, you can see the status bar. Here, the actual position of the mouse is always shown in the fields "X-Pos" and "Y-Pos":

5.8.2 The Properties Palette

ANOTHER utility for measuring sizes and for precise placement in Scribus is the Properties Palette. In the tab *X, Y, Z* it shows the geometry of the selected object. The display of the X and Y position depends on the chosen basepoint. The default basepoint is the upper left corner of a frame:

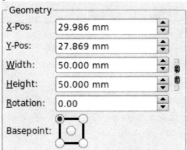

By using the X and Y Position spinboxes, you can place an item with extreme accuracy: Even if your default unit is point, Scribus allows you to place objects with a precision of three digits after the decimal point. But what if you want to add a value in a different unit than your default one? No problem at all. Just select the number in the spin box and overwrite it with the value you need. Let's assume your default unit is pt, but from calculations you know that an item hast to be placed somewhere by using centimeters. Enter the value in centimeters (for example, "3.5 cm") and the item will be moved exactly like you wanted, even though the value in the spinbox is converted to pt.

If you are using a wheel mouse, you can carefully move around or resize items. You can use the mouse wheel with the spin boxes instead of clicking the arrows. For small steps, put the cursor to the far right. Then spin the mouse wheel up and down to adjust the measurement or setting. This adjusts 10ths of a unit. For larger adjustments, put the cursor to the left side. For extra slow and precise adjustments 100th of a unit, hold Ctrl + Shift keys while moving the mouse wheel up and down.

But there's even more to it: Almost every spinbox where you enter values with measurements can do calculations for you. You can mix and match units as well. Special units are: pageheight, pagewidth, height, width.

Some Example Calculations

8.5in/3	Divide 8.5 inches by 3
pagewidth/4	Divide the page width by 4 (This only works with points).
width*2	Double the width of the selected object
5in+2p	Add 2 picas to 5 inches

5.8.3 Using the Keyboard

IF YOU use the arrow keys along with some modifier keys, you can resize or "nudge" items on a page with varying degrees of precision. Below is a list of the actions and the related keys. "Unit" refers to the unit of measuring you are using for your document:

- Move item 1 unit: Arrow keys
- Move item 10 units: Ctrl+Arrow keys
- Move item 0.1 units: Shift+Arrow keys
- Move item 0.01 units: Control+Shift+Arrow keys
- Resize item 1 unit outwards: Alt+Arrow keys
- Resize item 10 units outwards: Control+Alt+Arrow keys
- Resize item 1 unit inwards: Shift+Alt+Arrow keys
- Resize item 10 units inwards: Control+Shift+Alt+Arrow keys

5.8.4 Rotating Items

5.8.4.1 The "Rotate" Tool

THERE ARE two ways to rotate items in Scribus. You can do it manually by clicking on the "Rotate Item" button in the toolbar or by pressing R on the keyboard. The cursor will then turn into two round arrows. Now you can rotate a selected item with the mouse. The way the item is rotated depends on where you place the mouse pointer. If you place it on a corner of an item, the pivotal point will be the opposite corner, if you place it somewhere else, the center of the item is the pivotal point. By pressing the Ctrl key you can restrain the rotation to steps of 15 degrees.

There is no feedback as to angle of rotation. If you want precise control of rotation, use the Properties Palette instead.

5.8.4.2 The Properties Palette

The most precise way to rotate is using the Properties Palette. In the *X, Y, Z* tab you can enter values for rotation. Moreover, you can also change the way an item is rotated by using a different basepoint. Below you see a rectangle rotated six degrees by using different basepoints. From left right: no rotation, basepoint top left, basepoint bottom left, basepoint centre, basepoint top right, basepoint bottom right. Note that the distance between the rectangles was originally the same.

5.8.5 Multiple Duplicate

As YOU already learned in the Quick Start Guide, the Multiple Duplicate feature, which can be accessed via *Item >Multiple Duplicate,* can be used to copy items with a predefined and precise offset. One typical use case for the feature is the creation of tables that can be handled more flexibly than native tables in Scribus (see the section Tables). Below you will learn to use the features of Multiple Duplicate by creating a nicely formatted table.

First we create a single text frame (width: 25 mm, height: 10 mm), set the background color to "Grey88" and the line color to "Black":

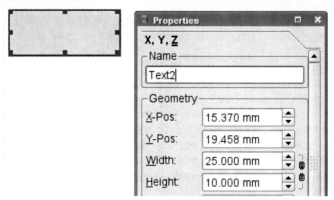

With the text frame still selected, we open the *Item > Multiple Duplicate* dialog. In the dialog we enter a number of 4 copies, so that we will end up with 5 cells in our first row. The horizontal shift will be the width of the frame (25 mm). The vertical shift will be zero, as we want all of our cells in one row:

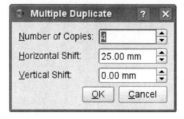

The result looks as follows:

Next we select all 5 "cells" with the "rubber band" method and bring up Multiple Duplicate again. This time we enter a number of four copies to get a table with 5 rows. The horizontal shift is now set to zero, while the vertical shift is the height of the row (10 mm):

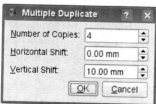

The immediate result is a good looking table:

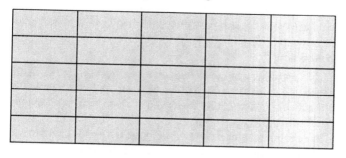

Of course you can do even more things with Multiple Duplicate and use horizontal and vertical shift at the same time, for instance to create a set of cells with a different background. Set the fill color of the last cell to "White," open the Multiple Duplicate dialog, enter a number of 4 copies, a horizontal shift of -25 mm and a vertical shift of -10 mm, and the result will be a diagonal line of cells with a white background:

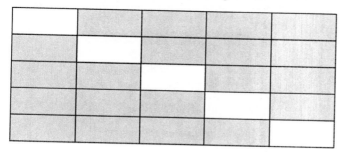

5.8.6 Aligning and Distributing Items

ALIGN AND DISTRIBUTE is a very powerful set of tools for arranging objects on a page. It is not available as a toolbar icon, only through the *Windows* menu.

You are more likely to use these tools in a "freeform" document such as a brochure or poster than in a more structured document like a book or manual. And its usefulness increases the more items you have to align or distribute. With small numbers of objects, manual placement may be faster; with larger numbers, Align and Distribute will speed the task and insure accuracy. Note that items which have been defined as locked will not be moved by Align and Distribute.

You are well advised to make yourself familiar with Align and Distribute – it will pay off sooner than later. Probably playing around with the options will help you more than lengthy explanations.

The first thing you will note when you brought up the dialog is that it's split into two parts. The upper region contains the "Align" commands, the lower the "Distribute" commands. What's the difference between those two? The main difference is that aligning an item or a group of items means changing its or their coordinates relative to a single reference point – an "anchor" in the terminology of Scribus – that need not be part of the item or the group. An anchor can be one-dimensional (like a guide or a page border) or two-dimensional (like a frame or shape). If a two-dimensional anchor is not a rectangle, Scribus will use the bounding box (see **Working with Frames**) to determine the coordinates. It also means that it's possible to align a single item to an external reference point. Distributing items on the other hand is a way to change the coordinates of items relative to other items, with no external references required.

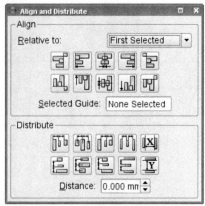

5.8.6.1 Aligning

The more complex part of the dialog is probably "Align." While the number of buttons is equal to "Distribute," the drop-down list in the upper right of the dialog provides access to its versatility, which is probably unequalled by most DTP and even vector drawing programs. If click on the list you can choose the options which allow you to choose an anchor to which the selected objects or a single object will be aligned:

- The first selected item (requires at least two selected objects).
- The last selected item (requires at least two selected objects).
- The page.
- The margins.
- A guide. This requires the selection a guide on a page by clicking on one with the mouse pointer. The selected guide will be indicated at the bottom of the "Align" part of the dialog.
- A selection of items.

Once you have made your choice, you can start aligning items with the buttons. Here's what they do (from left to right).

First row:

- Aligns the right sides of the selected object(s) to the left side of an anchor.
- Aligns the left sides of the selected objects relative to the anchor.
- Centers the selected objects vertically relative to the anchor.
- Aligns the right sides of the selected objects relative to the anchor.
- Aligns the left sides of the selected object(s) to the right side of an anchor.

Second row:

- Aligns the bottoms of the selected objects to the top of an anchor.
- Aligns the top of the selected objects relative to the anchor.
- Centers the selected objects horizontally relative to the anchor.
- Aligns the bottom of the selected objects relative to the anchor.
- Aligns the tops of the selected objects to the bottom of an anchor.

Note that for aligning to guides only the align left, center vertically and align right, or align top, center horizontally and align bottom are available, depending on the type of guide (horizontal or vertical). The other options will be grayed out.

The buttons themselves offer a good visual indication as to how the operations will work: the yellow rectangle is a symbol for the anchor, the red line for the axis along which the items (in gray) will be aligned.

5.8.6.2 Distributing

As stated above, distributing items requires at least two objects to be selected. Otherwise clicking on a button will have no effect. Once you have selected more than one item you can distribute them with following options.

First row:

- Distributes the left sides of items equidistantly.
- Distributes the horizontal centers of items equidistantly.
- Distributes the right sides of items equidistantly.
- Creates identical horizontal gaps between selected items.
- Creates identical horizontal gaps between selected items to the value inserted in the "Distance" field at the bottom of the dialog.

Second row:

- Distributes the bottoms of items equidistantly.
- Distributes the vertical centers of items equidistantly.
- Distributes the tops of items equidistantly.
- Creates identical vertical gaps between selected items.
- Creates identical vertical gaps between selected items to the value inserted in the "Distance" field at the bottom of the dialog.

5.8.7 Grids

THERE ARE three elements we are going to cover in this section: page grid, baseline grid, and page guides. Something all these have in common is that they do not become part of your printed output or PDF. They are tools you can use to assist your layout design.

5.8.7.1 Page Grid

These resemble the familiar graph paper used for many years to help place items easily, line one up with another, and also give some information about proportions. One could easily figure out the comparative area covered by content versus white space if that were desired.

More or less a page grid is always available, but the default is that it is switched off. Display it by clicking *View > Show Grid*. Like some types of graph paper, you can have darker major lines and lighter minor lines. Go to the chapter Customizing Scribus to see that you can change the spacing of major and minor lines, their colors, and whether they automatically are shown in a new document. If you save a document with them showing, they will show when the document is loaded, regardless of *Preferences* settings. The default settings for the page grid are 20 points between minor lines and 100 points between major lines, even if your dimensions are in other units. If you are using millimeters, for example, your defaults will be 7.056 mm and 35.278 mm respectively.

The page grid can be used merely as a passive background, but if you select *Page > Snap to Grid* from the menu bar, a frame or other object you are moving will have a sense of magnetism for the grid and will align itself with the vertical and horizontal lines. In *Preferences/Document Setup* you can choose to have the grid in the background of all objects, the default, or appear to be in front of them. There are also settings for the "stickiness" of the grid as it attracts objects – the snap distance and grab radius.

Also note that Snap to Grid does not affect objects already in place on the document, and only is in operation when you are moving an object by clicking on it and dragging with the mouse. If you create a new frame with Snap to Grid turned on, the new frame will align with and adjust its dimensions to the grid. Nonetheless your ability to make size and position adjustments in the *X, Y, Z* tab of the Properties Palette is not interfered with.

5.8.7.2 Baseline Grid

This is something like the page grid, but is used only for aligning text in a text frame. Similar to page grid, it is always available but turned off by default, made visible with *View > Show Baseline Grid*, and has settings adjustable in *Preferences* and *Document Setup*. The default spacing for baseline grid is the same as the default line spacing, which makes sense since this is what the baseline grid is used for. You can align to the baseline grid without it being visible.

Use of the baseline grid is a feature of text, and thus is controlled in the *Text* tab of the *Properties Palette* or with paragraph styles. To activate the feature, click and hold the icon to the left of the linespacing spinbox, where you will see the choices "Fixed Linespacing," "Automatic Linespacing," and "Align to Baseline Grid". Details can be found in the section on styles, under discussion of line spacing and offset to baseline of characters. Each text frame, and within each frame each paragraph style can have its own settings in regard to the baseline grid, even though the grid itself is always the same for a whole document. It is used for aligning lines of text from one frame to another, and from one column to another in the same frame.

5.8.8 Guides

A DRAWBACK of the page grid is the fact that, whether you want it to or not, it covers the entire page, and when you have "Snap to Grid" turned on, the stickiness to the grid can be problematic.

Guides are like individual horizontal or vertical lines from a grid which you create, as many in number and in as many positions on the page as you desire. Unlike the page grid and baseline grid, there are no default guides.

Create guides by clicking *Page > Manage Guides*, which brings up the guides dialog. This dialog will also appear if you right-click on an existing guide in a document.

Here is the guides dialog as it initially appears. When this screenshot was made, there was no content on the currently selected page, otherwise you would see a thumbnail version of any content on a page in the preview area:

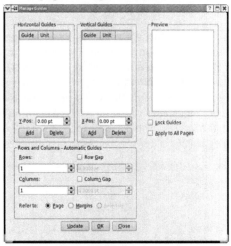

Begin making guides by clicking "Add" underneath the "Horizontal" or "Vertical Guides" areas. You immediately see a new guide in your list at 0.00 Y-Pos or X-Pos, depending on which type you have created. Now use the spinbox in any of the various ways you have become familiar with in other dialogs. Your adjustments will apply to whichever guide is highlighted, and as you do so, it will move across the page in the preview thumbnail.

Once you are satisfied, you have the option to lock guides and also apply to all pages of your document if you wish. Just as with the page grid, you can check *Page > Snap to Guides,* which incidentally will include snapping to margins.

Here we see a few arbitrary guides for this page. Note that both a horizontal and a vertical guide can be simultaneously highlighted and adjusted.

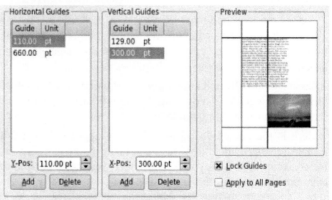

Finally, you can automatically generate collections of guides with this area of the dialog, dividing your page or a selected frame into rows and columns. Creating a gap between guides means that a single guide will be split into two with the gap value you inserted between them. The position of automatic guides can be calculated in relation to the page dimensions, the print space ("Margins") and a selected object. Note that you have to select an object before you open the guides dialog.

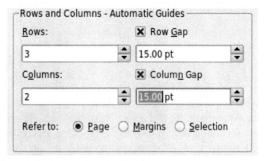

Once you have finished, clicking "Update" at the bottom of the dialog will add these to your lists above, where they can be individually edited. You can also lock all guides, thus preventing further editing of their position, or apply guides to all pages in a document.

If you prefer a less mathematical and more visual way to create guides, click in the rulers and drag horizontal or vertical guides with mouse to the canvas. You can move all guides with the mouse on the canvas by moving the mouse pointer over a guide. When the cursor turns into a double-sided arrow, click on the guide and move it to another position.

There are several ways to delete guides from a page or a document. The most obvious is to open *Page > Manage Guides*. Each guide is listed in the two guide columns, where you can select it and click "Delete." You can also remove a guide by selecting it with the mouse as described in the previous paragraph and dragging it to a ruler. Also be aware that the creation of guides is recorded by the action history, so that it can be undone in *Windows > Action History* or by right-clicking on a page and clicking "Undo."

5.9. Creating a Table of Contents

CREATING a table of contents is technically easy, but it's everything but obvious. The first thing to do is to create a paragraph style for the ToC. The distance between the entries of the ToC and their related page numbers is set by a tabulator. As with other tab stops, you can also choose a fill character between the entries, even though this isn't considered good style.

Once you have created your paragraph style, save it and open *File > Document Setup > Document Item Attributes*. Click "Add" and enter a name like "ToC" in the "Name" column. Due to a bug that's hard to resolve, you have to click in the "Value" or "Parameter" column once before clicking "OK." If you forget this step, Scribus won't save the value "ToC."

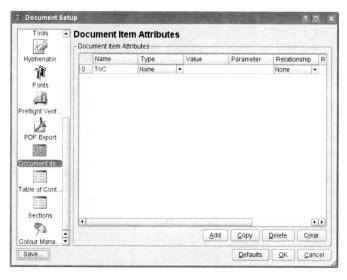

Next, create a text frame that will contain your ToC, and insert a unique name like "ToCFrame" for it in the *X, Y, Z* tab of the Properties Palette.

Open File > Document Setup > Table of Contents and Indexes. Click "Add" to prepare a new ToC. In the dropdown lists on the right choose the attribute we created before – ToC –, the name of the target frame – ToCFrame –, the position of the page numbers in the ToC – "At the end" will be the most natural option – and the paragraph style you created at the beginning. If you want to include text frames that are set not to print, check "List Non-Printing Entries" and click "OK."

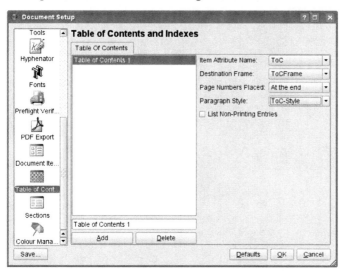

The next step is to tag the text frames that will appear in the ToC. For that purpose, you have to select "Attributes" in the context menu.

This brings up a dialog called "Page Item Attributes." In the "Name" column select "ToC," and under "Value" enter the text that is expected to be the entry in the table of contents. Click "OK" to finish the preparations.

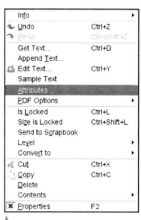

The "Attributes …" entry in the context menu

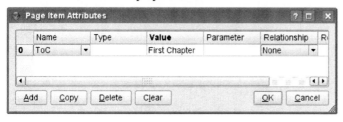

The final step is to use *Extras > Generate Table of Contents*:

First Chapter	3
Second Chapter	4
Third Chapter	5

If you want to add new entries to your ToC, repeat the steps described above and execute *Extras > Generate Table of Contents* anew.

5.10 Layers

YOU MAY know the concept of layers from drawing or image editing software. Layers are a powerful tool used to create complex documents. For instance, you can keep texts in another language on a separate layer and print versions in different languages from one file. Similarly, you might have different versions of images or graphics for different audiences. A single Scribus document can thus generate many different PDFs.

By default, a new document will have one layer, with the default name "Background." As you add frames and other objects, these will each be at its own level on this layer, so you may have many levels on one layer. For many documents, only one layer will be necessary, but for various reasons it my be desirable to add one or more layers.

5.10.1 Creating Layers

As frames and other objects are added to a layer, each object has its own level in relationship to others, above or below. As you see here, layers, containing one or more objects, also are above or below other layers. Just as an object's level can be changed in relationship to other levels, so can a layer's in relationship to other layers. Furthermore, an object can be moved from one layer to another.

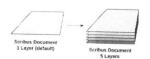

As described below, these different versions are created by using settings which tell Scribus which layers to use for printing directly from Scribus or creating the final PDF version.

The layers dialog can be opened via *Windows > Layers* or by pressing F6. It is clearly arranged, yet efficient:

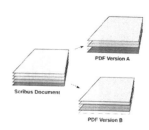

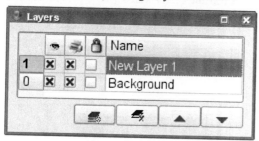

- Create a new layer by clicking the left-most button at the bottom, with a "New Layer" naming scheme as above.

- Remove whatever layer is highlighted by clicking on the second button from the left.

- The arrow buttons move the highlighted layer up and down in the stack.
- Change the name of a layer in this dialog by double-clicking its name, then editing with the keyboard.
- The checkboxes under the "Eye" icon, printer icon and lock icon will show/hide, enable or disable printing, and lock (not allow editing) the layer, respectively.

When you leave the *Layers* dialog, the highlighted layer will be the one you can edit. You can only edit one layer at a time, except for moving an object to a different layer.

In the main window, the layer which is being edited can be changed with a widget at the bottom, as you can see on the left.

5.10.2 Moving Objects from One Layer to Another

Use *Item > Send to Layer* from the menu bar (for whatever Item is selected), or right-click the object you wish to move for the context menu > *Send to Layer*.

5.10.3 Hints

If you're working with layers, you should consider the following:

- To make sure that a layer will be exported to another format, it has to be printable.
- An invisible layer will be printed or exported to another format only if it it's printable.
- Text flow around objects will only work if the text that is supposed to flow, is on a layer below the objects.
- If you're deleting a layer with objects on it, you will be asked if the objects on it should be removed as well. If you negate, all objects on the deleted layer will be moved to the background layer.

5.11 Managing Images

IF YOU click on *Extras > Manage Images* from the menu, you will bring up this dialog:

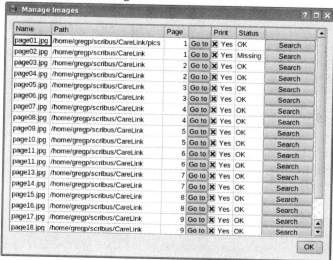

Name	Path	Page		Print	Status	
page01.jpg	/home/gregp/scribus/CareLink/pics	1	Go to ☒	Yes	OK	Search
page02.jpg	/home/gregp/scribus/CareLink	1	Go to ☒	Yes	Missing	Search
page03.jpg	/home/gregp/scribus/CareLink	2	Go to ☒	Yes	OK	Search
page04.jpg	/home/gregp/scribus/CareLink	2	Go to ☒	Yes	OK	Search
page05.jpg	/home/gregp/scribus/CareLink	3	Go to ☒	Yes	OK	Search
page06.jpg	/home/gregp/scribus/CareLink	3	Go to ☒	Yes	OK	Search
page07.jpg	/home/gregp/scribus/CareLink	4	Go to ☒	Yes	OK	Search
page08.jpg	/home/gregp/scribus/CareLink	4	Go to ☒	Yes	OK	Search
page09.jpg	/home/gregp/scribus/CareLink	5	Go to ☒	Yes	OK	Search
page10.jpg	/home/gregp/scribus/CareLink	5	Go to ☒	Yes	OK	Search
page11.jpg	/home/gregp/scribus/CareLink	6	Go to ☒	Yes	OK	Search
page11.jpg	/home/gregp/scribus/CareLink	6	Go to ☒	Yes	OK	Search
page13.jpg	/home/gregp/scribus/CareLink	7	Go to ☒	Yes	OK	Search
page14.jpg	/home/gregp/scribus/CareLink	7	Go to ☒	Yes	OK	Search
page15.jpg	/home/gregp/scribus/CareLink	8	Go to ☒	Yes	OK	Search
page16.jpg	/home/gregp/scribus/CareLink	8	Go to ☒	Yes	OK	Search
page17.jpg	/home/gregp/scribus/CareLink	9	Go to ☒	Yes	OK	Search
page18.jpg	/home/gregp/scribus/CareLink	9	Go to ☒	Yes	OK	Search

The first column, "Name," refers to the image file, "Path" refers to its location as saved in the Scribus file. If you happen to move a Scribus file without its images, in other words, did not use *File > Collect for Output* as recommended, this list will provide you an opportunity to try to find these image files again.

Clicking an image's "Go to" button will move you to the page indicated in the column "Page." The "Print" column gives you a single location to disable printing of as many images as you wish, which you might do to make a quick proof on a local printer and also to save ink.

The "Status" column shows "OK" if the image was found, "Missing" if not and also if the frame never had an image. In the latter case "Manage Images" won't help you to insert an image into the empty frame. You have to get it there as described in Working with Images.

"Search" gives you an opportunity to try to find any missing images. Clicking on the "Search" button brings up a normal file dialog. If you know where the image is located, you can navigate to the respective folder. You can also let Scribus search for the file from the file system root ("/") or a drive letter root ("C:\") or any other folder downwards – Scribus will search all subdirectories recursively for the file. Since Scribus is only searching for the file name, it will list all files that match the name of the image you're looking for. For instance, if you inserted an image called "dog.tiff," Scribus will find all images with the name "dog.tiff," even if their content is different. For users of Scribus on Linux and UNIX Systems (including Mac OS X) it's also important to know that the search for files is always case sensitive, so that a search for "dog.tiff" won't list "Dog.tiff." This may result in more found images on Windows and OS/2 systems, as these operating systems don't distinguish between uppercase and lowercase file names. While the search for an image is usually very fast, it may last too long if you have lots of images stored on your hard drive(s). You can abort the search by clicking on the "Search" button, which shows the caption "Cancel Search" while the search is running.

Once the search is finished, Scribus will show the results. If it can't find the image, it will show a failure notice:

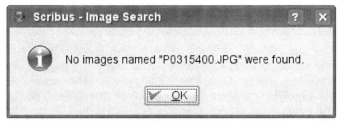

If it finds one or more matching file names, it lists all matches in a new dialog. By activating "Preview" and clicking on an entry in the list of search results you can find out if the found image is the one you need, or which of the matches is the one you've been searching for:

Clicking "Select" will reload the image into the frame and set the status of the link in "Manage Images" back to "OK"

5.12 Image Effects

IF YOU have imported an image into an image frame, you can apply some effects to the image. These effects are not a replacement for a specialized image manipulation program like The GIMP, but it allows for some quick enhancements. Moreover, the effects are non-destructive, ie. they are not applied to the image itself, but only to the image frame. This also means that the effects remain active if you load a new image into the frame. Note that the effects can't be applied to rasterized EPS and PDF files.

To apply one or more effects, right-click the image frame and select "Image Effects." You have the choice between 8 different effects:

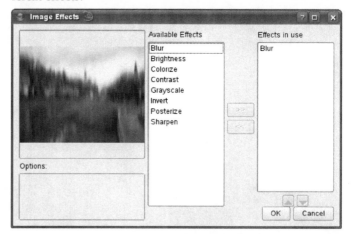

Select an effect in "Available Effects." With the arrow buttons (<< and >>) you can add or remove an effect. It's possible to apply more than one effect to an image. With the up and down buttons in "Effects in Use," the order of the effects can be adjusted. The latter will affect the result. Some of the effects can be modified under "Options," some cannot.

The image effects in detail:

• *Blur*: The blur effect reduces the sharpness of the image.

Brightness: Increases or decreases the brightness of an image.

Colorize: The dark/bright tones of the image are replaced by another color.

Contrast: The contrast is the difference between bright and dark parts of an image.

Grayscale: Converts the colors of an image to gray tones (No screenshot).

Invert: Inverts all colors in an image.

Posterize: Reduces the number of colors in an image.

Sharpen: Sharpens details and contours in an image

5.13 Extended Image Properties

5.13.1 Overview

ADOBE PHOTOSHOP is one of the world's best known software applications and widely used in professional graphics, both in print and for web work. One of the sources of its power is the native PSD file format. A PSD file can hold not only image data, but is more of a large container which can include meta-data, camera info, text, vector artwork and more. Most other programs only handle a small subset of its capabilities.

Scribus has native capabilities to import PSD files. Beyond importation, the support is quite extensive, including the ability to manipulate and adjust layer settings, and optionally enable and use masking along with the paths embedded in the file. In almost all cases, any embedded ICC color profiles which are not defective are detected and used when color management is enabled.

5.13.2 Layers

Like many other image editing programs, Photoshop can handle layers, and the PSD format stores them. The context menu for image frames containing a PSD file (or a TIFF file with layers exported from Photoshop) will show an entry which is not available for other image formats: "Extended Image Properties." The related dialog contains two tabs, "Layers" and "Paths." Let's have a look at the "Layers" tab first.

Similar to layers in Scribus, you can switch layers in PSD files on or off. This will not change the original file, but only affect its use in Scribus. In our example we have loaded a PSD file with three layers, as can be seen on the screenshot below. Scribus shows the name and a small preview of each layer:

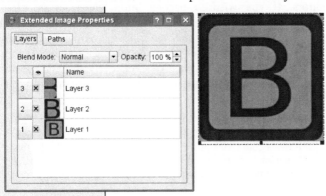

"Layer 1" is the background of the whole image, and we can switch it off by unchecking it in the row with the eye symbol:

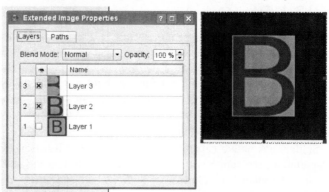

The utility of PSD files begins to show itself when you consider, for instance, that an image can contain layers for different slogans for the same image or different language or color versions. Many PSD files created by professionals contain dozens of layers, and you can easily switch them on or off in Scribus. Beware, though, that files with many layers may slow down the process of checking and unchecking single layers.

5.13.3 Blend Modes and Layers

Layers can interact with each other in different ways. These different ways are determined by so-called blend modes. A blend mode tells a program such as Photoshop or Scribus how a pixel on an upper layer will influence the matching pixel on the layer below. Blend modes can be used to improve existing images, but also allow for some fascinating effects. If you have a layered PSD (or TIFF) file, you will have the same blend modes available as in Photoshop, GIMP or other image editors. If you wish to become proficient in using blend modes, experience and experimentation are going to be your best teachers, since a manual, no matter how detailed, cannot beat experience in this area of image editing. Note that the use of blend modes requires a fast processor. If your computer has a slow CPU, you should expect some delay when you're applying them.

- **Normal**

   "Normal," while the default setting, is not exactly a blend mode. It treats both layers as if they were separate images. To let them "interact," you have to change the opacity of the upper layer, thus acting like you would with two overlapping image frames.

- **Darken**

  "Darken" does a pixel-for-pixel comparison between two layers and selects the darker pixel for display.

- **Lighten**

  "Lighten" does a pixel-for-pixel comparison between two layers and selects the lighter pixel for display.

- **Hue**

  This uses the hue (color) of the upper layer for the lower layer. Saturation and luminance remain unchanged.

• Saturation

"Saturation" uses the saturation of the upper layer for the lower layer. Hue and luminance remain unchanged.

• Color

"Color" uses the hue and the saturation of the upper layer for the lower layer. Luminance remains unchanged.

• Luminosity

"Luminosity" uses the luminance of the upper layer for the lower layer. Hue and saturation remain unchanged.

- **Multiply**

    This mode multiplies the value of the pixel on the lower level with that of the upper level, resulting in a darker image.

- **Screen**

    "Screen" multiplies the inverse value of the pixel on the lower level with that of the upper level, brightening the image.

- **Dissolve**

    "Dissolve" colorizes the lower layer with the colors of the upper layer. The degree depends on the level of transparency, as it only works for at least partially transparent pixels.

- **Overlay**

  "Overlay" combines features of the "Screen" and "Multiply" modes. It shows patterns or colors of the selected layer while preserving shadows and highlights of the underlying layer.

- **Hard Light**

  "Hard Light" also combines features of the "Screen" and "Multiply" modes. It's used to show highlights and shadows.

- **Soft Light**

  "Soft Light" combines features of the "Color Dodge" and "Color Burn" modes. It produces soft shadows and highlights.

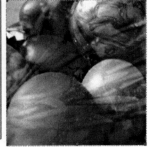

- **Difference**

  "Difference" subtracts the selected layer color from the underlying layer, depending on which is lighter.

- **Exclusion**

  "Exclusion" is similar to "Difference," but softer.

- **Color Dodge**

  The lightness values of the colors in the selected layer modify the underlying colors, by making them lighter. Black produces no effect.

- **Color Burn**

  The lightness values of the colors in the selected layer modify the underlying layers, by making them darker.

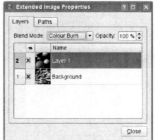 

4.13.3 Clipping Paths

Clipping paths are vector shapes which are stored in PSD files. They are mostly used to indicate the real shape (other than the rectangle of the image itself) of content. Scribus can read those clipping paths and use them. On the screenshot below you see a PSD file with a white background:

Opening the "Editing Extended Image Properties" dialog from the context menu reveals that the image file contains a clipping path called "Pfad 1," and it also shows a preview of its shape.

If you click on it, the path will be activated and the background is "clipped." Note that you can use only one clipping path per image.

To revert the clipping, click "Don't use any Path."

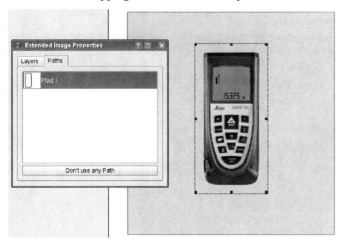

If you want to use clipping paths in PSD files by default, you can use the "Tools" tab for images in the *Document Setup*/the *Preferences* and check "Use embedded Clipping Path."

5.14 The Barcode Generator

BARCODE GENERATOR is a plug-in, which uses Terry Burton's award-winning Barcode Writer. [1] It creates barcodes in pure PostScript. The dialog is activated by selecting *Extras > Barcode Generator...*:

There is an extensive list of codes to choose from. Some, like the ISBN example shown here, have some limited information about the code, but generally you must know the appropriate use of the code from other sources. The information field in the lower left contains more information about the requirements and restrictions of different types of barcodes. When chosen, each code shows an example sequence of numbers and other characters.

For each barcode, there are some additional options available:

- *Include Text in Barcode*: This option will add the numbers of the barcode to the bars as can be seen in the screenshot above. If you don't see any text, make sure that Ghostscript is properly installed and configured.

- *Guard Whitespace*: This option will add arrows to the barcode which can help designers not to cover the code with other graphical elements.

- *Include Checksum* (if applicable): Some barcodes permit or even require a checksum. This option lets the barcode writer create such a checksum.

- *Include Checksum Digit* (if applicable): This option will add the checksum digit to the barcode, in other words: the checksum is visible.

You can also change the colors for the background, the lines and the text/the numbers. Currently, the color chooser only handles HSV and RGB colors.

When you click "OK," a code is generated according to your choices, and is then attached to the mouse cursor for placement as desired. The code itself consists of a grouped collection of polylines (the bars) and polygons (the characters). It is feasible to resize this grouped barcode, but caution is advised, since in general there are various specifications for bar widths which are important for accurate machine reading.

Since the barcode writer uses PostScript output, which is then converted to native Scribus items, you need a correctly configured Ghostscript available. Otherwise the feature won't be available at all, or it will display the error message "Barcode incomplete" if you check the option "Include text in barcode." See Importing Vector Drawings for more information.

[1] http://www.terryburton.co.uk/barcodewriter

6 Colors and Color Management

6.1. The Eye Dropper

THE EYE DROPPER is an interesting tool that will let you borrow a color from somewhere else on the screen and apply it to the fill color of a selected frame. Not only can this be a color from somewhere else on your document, it can be from virtually anywhere on your screen – a color from an image you have loaded, the background of your window manager, or various icons. If what you are clicking is a screen icon or button that produces some action, you may find this works less predictably, because colors picked from the Eye Dropper are always in RGB and also dependent on the color depth of the video mode.

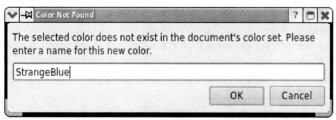

If the color you click on is not already in your list of available colors, you are presented with a dialog to give it a name, and it will then be added to your list. Thus, you can then apply it to text and lines thereafter.

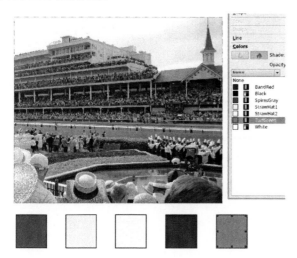

6.2 The Color Wheel

USING the color wheel in Scribus will help you to create or refresh your knowledge about the usage of color in a layout. The tool is placed in *Extras > Color Wheel* and it opens in a new window.

On the left you see the color wheel, on the right a live display of your actions, and the table below shows your instant results in plain numbers – the values for CMYK (Cyan, Magenta, Yellow, Black). The traditional RYB [1] color model, with red and green, blue and orange, and yellow and purple as complementary pairs, is a historical set of subtractive primary colors. This model is mainly in use by visual artists – in digital media it has been replaced by HSV and HSL within the RGB color model.

This does not mean that RYB has lost its significance as a design reference. Scribus, however, uses the RGB space and implements six different methods to specify color schemes. Below the color wheel you can select from a dropdown menu:

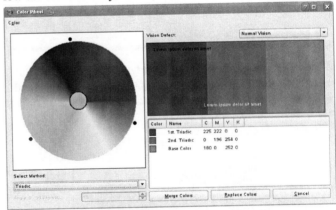

- Monochromatic
- Analogous [2]
- Complementary
- Split Complementary [2]
- Triadic
- Tetradic (Double Complementary) [2]

6.2.1 Monochromatic

A monochromatic color scheme is based on a single color with variations of lightness/shades. When you move your mouse over the color wheel, the red dot in the "orbit" indicates your base color. The Scribus color wheel does not include variations of lightness at this point. Thus, it does not matter if you move around inside the wheel. A monochromatic color scheme allows for paler or more saturated tints of the base color, also called the main color. While moving around, you will notice changing CMYK values for the base color, a monochromatic dark and monochromatic light in steps of 50% lightness. You can use other tints, shades, and tones of the key color to enhance the scheme.

6.2.2 Analogous Colors

Analogous colors are a palette of color combinations that are neighbors on the color wheel. If you stay in the color wheel below an angle of 60 degrees, the tool generates harmonious combinations. From 60 degrees on it begins to generate complementary pairs. First you will notice complementary pairs according to the RYB space and at 90 degrees you will find a full complementary pair within the RGB color space. While moving around you will notice changing CMYK values for a base color, the 1st analogous, and the 2nd analogous color. Avoid combining warm and cold colors.

6.2.3 Complementary Colors

Complementary colors correspond via opposite sides in the color wheel, in an angle of 180 degrees. They can be generated in any color value, even in different shades. Move around with the mouse pointer and observe how the contrast changes to more or less vivid combinations. When you move the pointer to a clear yellow, for instance, the opposite blue is dark and may need an adjustment by increasing its lightness to achieve a more vivid and at the same time a more harmonious combination.

6.2.4 Split Complementary

The split complementary schemes offers an alternative to the tension of the complementary scheme. Use the angle option to specify the range. At 0 and at 90 degrees, you will get a complementary pair, at 90 degrees you will also have a base color.

Between 0 and 90 degrees you generate two complementary pairs that go through the analogous color dimensions. In practice you may work with the base color and the 3rd and 4th split to create a soft complementary pair. If you use a base color and the 1st and 2nd split you will have an analogous scheme. Avoid dull warm colors – instead use a single warm color paired with two cold colors or vice versa.

6.2.5 Triadic Colors

Triadic color schemes are highly energetic color schemes based on three colors separated by 120 degrees on the color wheel. The primary (red, blue, and yellow) and secondary (purple, orange, green) colors are examples of triadic colors. This scheme is popular among designers and artists because it offers strong visual contrast while retaining balance, and color richness. This scheme has less contrast than a complementary scheme and will appear to be harmonious and balanced. It may be a good idea to choose one color as dominant and subdue the remaining by changing shade and saturation or by balancing color usage, distribution and accents in a layout.

6.2.6 Tetradic (Double Complementary)

Of all color schemes the tetradic (double complementary) is the richest. It employs four colors arranged into two complementary pairs. As you will see with the Scribus color wheel, the scheme is hard to harmonize because all four colors appear in more or less equal values. It may look unbalanced, conflicted, and you should choose one of the four colors to be dominant and subdue others. Although the color wheel suggests it, avoid using those colors in equal amounts. Think in terms of dominating, secondary and accent colors.

5.2.7 Vision Defect

The recognition of color combinations will be different for each human being. Aside from personal taste, customs and cultural backgrounds, not one human's eyes will see exactly the same colors. While the differences may be minimal in many, if not most cases, some people's color reception capabilities differ significantly to those of the majority. This phenomenon is referred to as "color blindness."

Designers may need to test their color combinations for people who suffer from color blindness, as, in extreme cases, they won't be able to tell the difference between some colors.

The color wheel provides an option to emulate some wide-spread forms of color blindness, a feature that, despite its usefulness, is rarely found in most graphics applications. It enables users to detect issues with certain color combinations before a document is published. To the best knowledge of the Scribus team, Scribus is the only DTP application with this as a built-in feature.

In the upper right corner you find a menu for "Vision Defect." Choose "Full Color Blindness," and you will see only gray values. There are also options to emulate protanopia, deuteranopia, tritanopia.

[1] http://www.digitalanarchy.com/theory/ryb-rgb.html
[2] Allows additional variations in angles from 0 to 90 degrees.

6.3 Spot Colors

SPOT COLORS are single ink colors, rather than colors produced by four (CMYK), six (CMYKOG) or more inks in the printing process (process colors). They can be obtained from special vendors, but often the printers have found their own way of mixing inks to match defined colors.

Spot colors may be desired for several reasons:

- Economy: If the document to print contains less than four colors, it may be less expensive to use ready mixed inks than to render them as a mixture of inks. The reason is that less plates are required. This is often used in newsprint, where advertisers may be able to use only black and red, for example. Another common use case is business cards.

- Accuracy: It isn't always possible to equal a certain color with a mixture of inks, especially when they are printed on different materials or with different machines.

- Spot colors allow for the printing of special colors that can't be mixed with the usual CMYK inks. The most common examples are out-of-gamut colors (like some very saturated blues and oranges) and metallic inks (gold, silver, copper print, etc.), but other inks, such as fluorescent inks, also exist.

The PDF specification supports the concept of spot colors. In terms of PDF information, a spot color is merely a color reference which is defined by a name. This name is supposed to be known by the printer and will determine which color will be used for printing. A PDF spot color also includes a RGB/CMYK information that may be used in cases where spot colors are not supported, for instance if viewed with a PDF reader. It is up to the user or the color vendor to choose a color that will approximate the spot color as closely as possible.

More on PDF and spot colors in the PDF reference from Adobe [1]

6.3.1 Spot Colors in Scribus

Scribus provides a way to generate PDFs with spot colors: it is as simple as going to *Edit > Colors > New* and checking the corresponding checkbox in the Edit Color window.

There are several industry standards for spot colors, some of which are only used in certain areas of the world. The most widely used color standard is produced by Pantone.

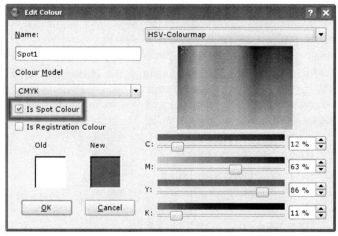

A spot color set is a list of colors maintained by a company. Each color corresponds to a number (and in some cases a name) assigned by this company.

In terms of software, Pantone (or another vendor's) colors are primarily used as spot colors. To produce a document with those colors, one has to:

1. Choose the color(s) from a spot color swatch (which is absolutely essential).

2. Create as many colors as needed in RGB or CMYK color space in *Edit > Colors > New*. You should try to match the color as closely as possible if you want to print a proof on an inkjet or laserjet (optional; it doesn't affect the final result that comes from the press ...)

3. Assign the the correct color names.

4. Go to *File > Export > Save* as PDF menu item, open the "Color" tab, switch the "Output intended for:" dropdown menu to Printer and uncheck the option "Convert Spot Colors to Process Colors."

5. Pass the PDF file to a print shop that supports the vendor's colors.

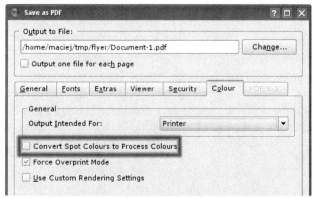

Even though most color tables contain RGB, CMYK and HTML values for each color, the way the color looks on screen (either in Scribus or a PDF viewer) is irrelevant in off-set printing, because it will be printed according to its name.

Since exact color matching requires real world color tables anyway, this is no real disadvantage. It can even turn out to be an advantage, because Scribus users are not mislead about the nature of built-in spot color swatches.

Other vendors of color standards are

- HKS, Germany [2]
- Trumatch, United States [3]
- ANPA, United States [4]
- Toyo, Japan [5]
- DIC, Japan [6]

6.3.2 Create Your Own Spot Color Sets

Some programs like QuarkXPress, InDesign or Illustrator come with built-in spot color swatches and their RGB/CMYK representations. In terms of workflow this feature eliminates the need for steps 2 and 3. However, since there is no real on screen representation, the most important step, which is step 1, is indispensable.

Since you don't need spot color swatches in your software, but rather a real color reference table, you may want to create a swatch yourself. To do this, you need to know how to include your colors in Scribus:

Open the file `scribus13x.rc` in your `$home/.scribus` directory under Linux/UNIX, or in `Documents and Preferences\username` under Win32. Open the file with a text editor (a real text editor, not Notepad!). At about line 40 you see the list of colors known to Scribus:

```
<COLOR Register="0" Spot="0" RGB="#f0f8ff" NAME="AliceBlue" />

<COLOR Register="0" Spot="0" RGB="#faebd7" NAME="AntiqueWhite" />

<COLOR Register="0" Spot="0" RGB="#ffefdb" NAME="AntiqueWhite1" />

<COLOR Register="0" Spot="0" RGB="#eedfcc" NAME="AntiqueWhite2" />

<COLOR Register="0" Spot="0" RGB="#cdc0b0" NAME="AntiqueWhite3" />

<COLOR Register="0" Spot="0" RGB="#8b8378" NAME="AntiqueWhite4" />

<COLOR Register="0" Spot="0" RGB="#7fffd4" NAME="Aquamarine" />
```

Copy the first line into a new document in your text editor. Next, you need a color reference. Search for the colors you need. For each color you write a line that looks as follows:

```
<COLOR Register="0" Spot="1" RGB="#40f822" NAME="MySpotGreen3" />
```

Note the changes: The value "Spot" is set to 1, and the color is the name that will be seen by your printing company. In actual practice, you will need to make sure this name has a meaning when your printer encounters it. Incidentally, you do not have to worry about placing your edited line in any precise location in the list, since Scribus will alphabetically sort this for you.

How do you find an approximate color now? That's easy. You can use KcolorEdit [7] for example, which will provide you the Hex digits to be inserted after RGB=#". Another possibility is the Wacker Art RGB Colour Mixer (English and German, requires Java) [8] that will do the same job. If you want or need to find a Pantone color that matches your RGB/CMYK values, try the Color Conversion Tool provided online by Peter Ferret [9]. EasyRGB offers a wide range of other color matching systems for online conversion. Once you have included all spot colors you need, save your file (just in case …). Then copy all lines to the clipboard and insert them right before or after the color list in scribus13x.rc. Now open Scribus, and voilà: Your spot colors appear in the list, marked with a red dot:

6.3.3 Obtaining Spot Color Palettes for Use in Scribus Legally

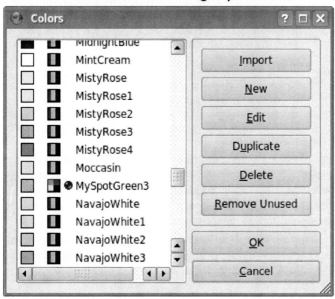

255

As long as no open standard for spot colors exists, Scribus users will have to buy a color swatch by one of the color vendors mentioned above and insert the values and names of spot colors directly into Scribus. As mentioned above, color swatches are a requirement for serious work anyway, but that's another topic. There is, however, another way to legally obtain commercial spot colors palettes and use them in Scribus. All you need is a commercial program that contains those palettes. Older versions of CorelDraw eg. contain Pantone, Toyo and more palettes from the major color vendors and can be obtained for a reasonable price. You can either run them yourselves under Windows or OS/X, install them on another PC you can access legally or even use another version – you have a license anyway.

In the drawing program:

1. Draw as many vector objects as one spot color palette contains.

2. Apply each spot color to one object – most palettes aren't huge, so this is feasible.

3. Export the drawing as EPS. Be careful not to convert the spot colors to CMYK during export.

In Scribus:

1. Create a new document and use *File > Import > EPS/PS*.
   You'll now see all the spot colors with their correct names listed in the color dialog after importing the file.

2. Now delete the imported drawing and save the file under an appropriate name, eg. spoteu.sla.

3. Next, close all docs again. Go to *Edit > Colors*, choose the palette "Scribus Small" from the dropdown menu. Remove all colors except Black (Scribus needs at least one color to work). Then click "Import" and select the spoteu.sla file. Now you can see all the spot colors in the color list. Finally, click "Save Color Set" and save your new palette (for example) as "Spot Solid Uncoated."

From now on your spot colors will be available for you in any project. If want to reuse your palette on another computer, just store the file "Spot Solid Uncoated" from your `.scribus` folder on a USB stick or a floppy disk and copy it to the respective directory on the other computer.

Some vendors, like Pantone or RAL, even offer free downloads of some or all of their color swatches. If the download contains EPS files, you can use these to import the colors as described above.

[1] http://www.adobe.com/devnet/pdf/pdf_reference.html, pp 234 and 532 of the PDF file.

[2] http://www.hks-farben.de

[3] http://www.trumatch.com

[4] http://www.anpacolors.com

[5] http://www.toyoink.com

[6] http://www.dic.co.jp

[7] http://docs.kde.org/development/en/extragear-graphics/kcoloredit/index.html

[8] http://www.wackerart.de/mixer.html

[9] http://web.forret.com/tools/color.asp

6.4 Color Management

6.4.1 Overview

THE OBJECTIVE of a color management system is to reduce the differences between the on-screen colors and final printing, as well as showing colors which are out of gamut, ie. beyond the color range of your selected output device. The caveat is you need to provide a profile of the printer and one for your monitor which is reasonably accurate. For new users, the default settings and descriptions can be quite confusing. Without prior knowledge of the terminology, it is very easy to choose the wrong settings. This can often make images look worse on screen or print. Then, the first time user simply says, "Enough!" and disables color management.

In a word, don't. Once you understand some basic concepts and know your final print destination, you will be able to predict and control more reliably how your document will look when printed. This is especially helpful when you will be sending files for later reproduction with four color printing or sending high-resolution PDFs. There are some commercial printers who specifically ask for files created with color management switched off, so that you better ask the printer *before* you start the job.

The steps to making color management work reliably (in other words, what you see on screen is what you print):

- Learn a little bit about color management concepts and terminology.
- Get the profiles set up properly. Most important is getting a good accurate monitor profile. Some profilers do an excellent job at creating monitor profiles. Without a properly created monitor profile, enabling color management will give you unsatisfactory results in printing and inaccurate previews on screen.
- Embed the image profiles properly in image editing applications where possible.
- The color management system within Scribus is designed foremost for enabling color managed "soft proofs" of the images within the document. Scribus can also show "out of gamut" warnings for colors which might not be accurately reproduced by printing. (Most printers have a narrower range of colors which can be printed, when compared to most monitors.) It does not embed or alter the profiles within your images. Some image formats, eg. PNG and TIFF, can have an embedded ICM or ICC profile within the file header – also known as files "tagged" with a color profile. Later on, we will describe how and when it

might be appropriate to use littlecms or Photoshop to apply a tag or embed a profile. If a file is tagged, Scribus will work with littlecms to read that profile within the image and use that profile to more accurately display the colors within an image. If an image does not have a tag, but you know the device profile which should be assigned to the image, you can still use the CMS settings to preview with the profile temporarily assigned within the document. Caution is advised not to assign the wrong profile unless you are absolutely sure of the image source.

The littlecms package that Scribus uses for color management has developed into a stable mature library. Independent tests vouch for its accuracy and littlecms is used within the printer firmware of some of the most expensive high end printers available.

6.4.2 What Are Color or Device Profiles?

ICC or ICM profiles are special types of files which describe the color characteristic of a device like a scanner, monitor or printer – basically any device which can create or display the color of a digital image. There are also color profiles which are known as device independent or working space profiles. These special files can be thought of as translators which are used to convert from one type of color profile to another. An ICC or ICM file is a set of tables which describes the mathematical values by which devices measure and describe colors. Fortunately, these are set by open international standards and work the same way on OS X, Windows, Linux or Solaris.

Device profiles are separate files which describe the way a device creates (scanner or digital camera), displays (monitor) or outputs (printer) colors. Users of Photoshop will be familiar with the choice of "Working Profiles" or "Working Spaces," which are color profiles not related to a particular device, but to assist in the conversion of color from one device to another. Well known RGB "working spaces" include sRGB, Adobe RGB 1998, Colormatch, Bruce RGB or CIE RGB. Users of Photoshop or similar programs may be wondering if this is a missing feature in Scribus, but littlecms uses its own internal color conversion process to make the transformation between color spaces.

6.4.3 Why "Soft Proofing"?

With the proper setup of device profiles, littlecms can adjust the colors of your monitor to more accurately represent how your document will actually look when finally printed. This can be doubly helpful if you are sending it to be printed commercially or for service bureau output. There are command line tools in littlecms to embed profiles with `tifficc` and `jpegicc`. See the littlecms docs for exact options [1]. You can also embed ICC profiles using Cinepaint, ImageMagick, Krita, GIMP 2.4 along with Adobe Photoshop or Corel Photopaint.

6.4.4 First Steps

Some initial requirements:

- Have accurately profiled input devices which create the images – scanners, digital cameras, and so on.

- Most importantly, have an accurately calibrated and profiled monitor.

- The first suggestion is to ease up on the eye candy – for example, you might want to switch to or come up with a "vanilla" theme setup. While KDE, Gnome, Windows, and Macs have gorgeous desktops, Scribus will like it plain and simple – no animation, no fancy graphics. For the most accurate color calibration set your desktop to a neutral gray or light color with no gradients or fancy backgrounds. We know that vibrant, saturated colors will affect the appearance of adjacent colors, so minimizing the contrast with screen features not an actual part of your work will help your eye to better judge color balance for images. For that matter, the same applies for GIMP or other graphics programs. What we are striving for here is to as accurately as possible mimic the way mixed inks look on paper.

Calibrating is setting the monitor to a known state. Most monitors are set to a default to color temperature of 9300 K or Kelvin, which is often too "cold" or bluish for accurate color work. Color.org has a multitude of color specifications for your reference [2]. Most color standards are set to 5000 K light temperature or "illuminant." For your monitor, 6500 K is recommended, which more closely mimics natural sunlight, as a starting point adjusting for your monitor. At first your eyes will think your monitor has a yellowish cast, but your eyes will soon adjust, especially if the brightness and contrast are set properly. 9300 K, which is the default factory setting for most monitors is fine for working with a word processor, but this will wash out colors and color will look less balanced with whites actually showing a bluish cast.

Each of the "working spaces" is based on certain settings for your monitor. Gamma and color temperature of your monitor should match the specs of the working space. For example, Adobe RGB and Bruce RGB specify 6500 K and 2.2 gamma, quite common for Intel based PC monitors and are the recommended defaults for users who are editing color critical images.

Printer profiles are highly dependent on the media chosen. Newsprint and uncoated stocks are grayer in appearance, so these profiles will have a narrower "gamut" or color range. They do not to produce the super vivid colors and saturation of coated stock or glossy photographic papers. A single print shop could easily have a dozen or more profiles, based just on differences in the paper color and ink absorbency.

6.4.5 Getting the Right Profiles (Or At Least the Best You Can)

Some profiles are "generic" and can be obtained from the device manufacturer, who generate them from a sampling of their units. A growing number of monitors, scanners and certain printer vendors will include these with any software bundled with the device. While these "canned" profiles are rarely a perfect match, this is a good first place to start. Go to the vendors website under drivers and see if there a profile available for your device. Another type of profile is a "generic" press standard profile. These are CMYK profiles which are defined to commercial press industry standards, such as SWOP, FOGRA, ECI and other print standards bodies.

6.4.6 Scribus Color Management Settings

The color management settings for Scribus can be found in *File > Document Setup > Color Management* for the current document and in *File > Preferences > Color Management* for future documents.

System Profiles: These dropdown boxes show the available profiles on your system. To enable Scribus to use profiles, they should be copied to the /usr/share/color/icc directory or you can put them somewhere in your home directory and point to this directory in your Preferences. On Windows XP profiles are stored in Windows\system32\spool\drivers\ color, and in Windows 2000 in WINNT\system32\spool\ drivers\color. Mac OS X uses */Library/Color-Sync/Profiles/ to store profiles. Color profiles are platform independent, thus files created in or available for Mac OS X or Windows are usable in Linux with littlecms as well. It is highly recommended to have the Adobe profiles, if you plan to do any type of cross platform or commercial printing, since most well-setup DTP workstations, as well as most commercial printers will be able to work with these profiles.

Activating "Color Management" enables color management globally within the document (or Scribus if set in *File > Preferences*). Scribus will remember the settings from file to file.

Note: Saving and closing a file with color management on will slow it down on reopening, as Scribus must not only open the files, but in addition littlecms must read and perform the corrections between the profiles. Color conversions make multiple floating point calculations for each color, so be patient.

There is another checkbox for simulating the printer on the screen. This tells Scribus and littlecms to do an on-the-fly conversion from the image color space to your monitor profile to simulate your chosen printer's profile. The checkbox to mark colors "out of gamut" will show warnings for colors that might not print accurately, based on the printer profile you have chosen. Typically, when colors are shown out of gamut, they will print darker, lighter or have a color shift when printing. The last option, "Use Black Point Compensation," is a way to help rendering shadows within color pictures. Experimentation will show if it improves your pictures.

6.4.7 Rendering Intents

The other puzzle for newcomers to color management is rendering intents. Your choice of rendering intents is a way of telling littlecms how you want colors mapped from one color space to another.

- *Perceptual*: This rendering intent maps color "smoothly," preserving relationships between similar colors. This prevents "gamut clipping" with its potential loss of detail and "tonal banding" problems. Gamut clipping happens when two or more colors that are different in the input image appear the same when printed. Perceptual rendering intent makes small adjustments throughout the image to preserve color relationships. It sacrifices some precision of colors in order to ensure pleasing results, usually the best choice for photographic images and scans. Perceptual intent will produce the most predictable results when printing from a wide range of image sources, for example, when printing RGB images on CMYK devices, or when trying to match CMYK devices that are radically different from each other. Consider this "foolproof" setting to be best for users who handle the wide variety of images that commonly enter large format printing facilities.

- *Saturation* is a good choice for logos, spot colors, etc. It tends to preserve the amount of or vividness of color, but it can make photos look ugly. If you are working with logos with a specific shade, saturation will bring better color matching, inasmuch as you give more importance to the color than to the image.

• *Absolute Colorimetric*: When a color is not printable within the "gamut" of the output device, this rendering intent simply prints the closest match. It reproduces in-gamut colors without compromise, as faithfully as possible. This produces the most accurate matching of spot colors. Unfortunately, it can also result in "gamut clipping" as mentioned above. White points are similarly clipped, then causing color relationship problems in the highlights of images. This type of clipping, and the resultant problems, typically make this rendering difficult to use with anything but spot colors. Some users will be disconcerted with a yellowish cast in their image, but this intent is measured in highly controlled lighting conditions with a D50 light box. This often has a "warmer" temperature than more typical viewing conditions. This rendering intent is almost exclusively used when a corporate logo or color must be matched exactly regardless of media. Kodak yellow would be a good example.

• *Relative Colorimetric*: When a color is not printable within the gamut of the output device, this rendering intent prints the closest match along with an adjustment that maps white to the paper of the output. This mapping of "white point" prevents the problems of "Absolute Colorimetric" when images except spot colors are concerned. When producing color proofs on RGB ink jet printers, while simulating CMYK printing presses you can use this intent, if you know the intended precise profile. Users of Adobe Press Ready will understand this concept quite well. This approach works well when you have accurate embedded profiles (typically scanner or more rarely digital cameras) in images being converted to CMYK space with printer profiles very precisely profiled with color measurement devices. This is most likely when someone has spent a lot of time and effort to finely calibrate and profile their equipment. It takes sophisticated (and expensive) color calibration equipment to measure the printer under fairly well controlled conditions.

6.4.8 Final Printing with Scribus

For Scribus users, there are a couple of options for printing with a color-managed intent. When printing, Scribus can optionally apply the printing profile you have chosen in the color management panel. This can be very useful, if you want to simulate a commercial printer profile with your inkjet printer via CUPS [3]. See Local Printing for more information about CUPS.

PostScript output would require having ICC profiles embedded in your images before being placed in Scribus files when outputting a Scribus document either as pure PostScript file or as individual EPS files. Scribus uses level 3 PostScript. Level 2 and level 3 PostScript can read and use ICC profiles within an image. Most color PostScript devices will read the embedded profiles and use them to render color within the PostScript file using something called a rendering dictionary.

6.4.9 PDF/X-3 and Color Management

Above, we covered the basics of getting color management working and configured properly. Now, let's consider using PDF/X-3 to optimize our output for commercial printing. PDF/X-3 is an advanced ISO standard for PDF files, and Scribus fully supports it.

The principal benefit of PDF/X-3 is the typically more accurate color conversion from RGB to a printer's CMYK output. The accuracy comes from working in RGB colors until very late in the printing process when the printer's own RIP does the RGB to CMYK conversion. The downside is that only the latest and most updated RIPs support PDF/X-3, although others may support earlier PDF/X standards. As the RIP engine has detailed knowledge of the exact color range and capabilities, it is thought to offer, in most cases, a more accurate conversion. PDF/X-3 does not preclude using CMYK images, but is ideal for maintaining your colors in RGB as long as possible in the process.

The major downsides to working in PDF/X-3 are twofold: You cannot use transparency natively. PDF/X-3 is based on PDF 1.3, which does not support transparency. The second is the limited, but growing number of printers who can support it. If in doubt, inquire.

The other issue is the question which printer profile one should use. There are two strategies: The first is to have an actual ICC profile from your printer for the matching paper type. The second is to use a well-known printing standard as SWOP, ECI or others. Using PDF/X-3 requires cooperation from your printer, but can really improve your print color matching. As always, a short visit to your printer in advance is strongly recommended.

[1] http://www.littlecms.com/TUTORIAL.TXT
[2] http://color.org/resource2.xalter
[3] http://www.cups.org

7 File Export

File > Export allows you to export files or items (as appropriate to their type) to plain text files, EPS, PDF, an image in a variety of bitmap formats, and SVG. Except for PDF, you do this solely to create something that can be used in another application (or even another Scribus document.)

Image and SVG export are implemented as plug-ins; they will not appear in the menu if you have disabled them in the *Preferences* under *Plugins*.

7.1 Text Export

There are two ways to save text from a Scribus text frame to a file:

1. Select a text frame and use *File > Export > Save Text*.
2. Select a text frame, open the Story Editor (Ctrl+Y), then go to *File > Save to File*.

In both cases a file dialog will be opened, and you can save your text as a plain text file (*.txt), which means all formatting will be lost. As described in Working with Text, you also have to choose an encoding for the text export.

Note that it only works for single frames or linked frames. To extract all text from a file in one go, you can use the script "Extract Text," which is described in the chapter The Scripter.

7.2 Bitmap Export

YOU CAN export your Scribus pages as bitmap images. Be aware, though, that the export quality depends on the preview settings for images. To create a high-resolution bitmap file, you have to set the preview settings for all images to "Full Resolution." Also note that color management is not applied to image export. This feature is best suited to produce some low-resolution images for web pages, eg. as a preview.

To export one or more bitmaps, use *File > Export > Save as Image* or Ctrl+Shift+E on the keyboard.

The names for your images are automatically generated, ie., the filename of the Scribus document is used and appended uniquely for each page. From the export dialog, you merely select the export directory for your files:

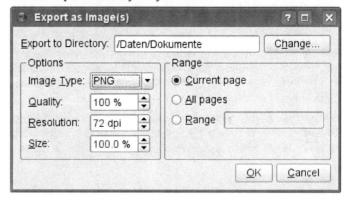

Under "Options" the following parameters can be set:

- *Image Type*: Scribus can export to BMP, JPEG, PBM, PGM, PNG, PPM, XBM, and XPM formats.
- Quality: The quality of the image can range from 1 up to 100%. The higher the quality, the bigger the file.
- *Resolution*: The resolution of your image can range from 72 to 2400 dpi. The higher the resolution, the bigger the file. Note that Scribus won't upscale any image in your document, ie. if an image has a resolution of 72 dpi, you can't improve the quality by exporting at a higher resolution.
- *Size*: Using more than 100% is not recommended, since even as much as 100% will result in a very large file.

Under "Range" you can determine which parts of your document will be exported, the current page, all pages or a range of pages. If more than one page is selected for export, Scribus will add a number to the resulting files, for instance: from flyer.sla, we produce flyer-1.png, flyer-2.png, etc.

Depending on the format, resolution, and amount of data, these image files can be very large and take a long time to create and later to open.

7.3 Vector Export

SCRIBUS offers several vector formats to export its documents to. In the menu *File > Export*, the following are available:

- Save Page as EPS (Encapsulated PostScript)
- Save as PDF (Portable Document Format)
- Save Page as SVG (Scalable Vector Graphics)

PDF export is covered in its own chapter. Beside the options in the menu *File > Export*, a Scribus document can be printed into a PostScript file. Please note that PostScript and PDF files are the only export formats which can contain more than one page, as the EPS and SVG specifications don't support multi-page files.

There is also a difference between EPS and SVG export. If you create an SVG file, Scribus will always export the whole page that's currently selected. If you export to EPS, the content of the created file depends on your selection. If no items are selected, Scribus will export the currently selected page. In all other cases, Scribus will only export the items on the page that are selected.

7.3.1 Some Limitations of SVG and EPS Export

The EPS and SVG formats are described in some detail in Importing Vector Drawings. What we want to show here are some limitations of these methods.

We'll start out with a simple page in Scribus, using sample text and an arbitrary image from a digital camera. The final DPI of this image in Scribus ended up to be about 420. The text is using a Gentium italic font, 13pt. size.

From this Scribus file, 3 separate PDFs were generated.

- The first was a direct export to PDF from Scribus, using the default settings.
- Next, an SVG was generated from this page. This SVG was then imported onto a blank document in Scribus, then a second PDF was generated.
- Finally, an EPS file was generated from this page, and the EPS then imported onto a blank document, then a third PDF generated

Note that these last two not only involve the exporting capabilities of Scribus but also subsequent importing.

7.3.2 The Text

These are screenshots of the PDFs with magnification at 200%. The text from the SVG is smaller since the SVG was not resized from its native export size. The EPS was also not rescaled.

quam erat quis   quam erat quis   *quam erat quis*
nulla, volutpat eı   nulla, volutpat eı   *nulla, volutpat eı*
eget, odio. Nulla   eget, odio. Nulla   *eget, odio. Nulla*

What is immediately apparent is that SVG export doesn't support all text features – we have lost the italicized style, and the placement of characters on the baseline isn't as expected, especially when there are descenders. The EPS looks better, yet there is some excessive thickness seen.

7.3.3 The Image

There is not a great deal of difference here, either in resolution or consistency of colors. One would need to check the final printed PDFs to better see any differences. The SVG uses a pointer to the original image, so it is not so surprising that image resolution is similar to that of the direct PDF export.

7.3.4 Behavior of Exported SVG/EPS in Other Programs

Problems with the display of exported SVG and EPS files are not necessarily problems with their creation. SVG is a relatively new format, and different applications have varying degrees of implementation of all its possible features, Scribus itself being an example. EPS unfortunately suffers from having such variability in what it can contain, that it is hard to accommodate all the possible information which might be included in the file.

Firefox 2 imported the SVG, with text displayed as well as with ImageMagick, but while the image was imported, it appeared onscreen only briefly. The EPS used an auxiliary program, in this case Document Viewer was used, with text faithfully reproduced, but the image was considerably darker.

GSView successfully imported the EPS. Like Document Viewer, the image was much darker.

ImageMagick successfully imported the SVG, with image intact, and interestingly, there was proper placement of characters on the baseline, but they were not in italics. Thus, we must conclude that the style is an export problem of Scribus, the baseline placement an import problem of Scribus. The EPS colors of the image were inverted, and the page was black, so it is unclear whether the text was displayed correctly in ImageMagick – applying "Negate" did not result in a complete fix of colors, and did not show text.

Inkscape failed to successfully import either the SVG or the EPS. It could not find the image for the SVG, which was especially curious since it was shown in the preview of the import dialog. The EPS also showed no image, and the text had the white areas of letters such as d, p, and b filled in with black.

Squiggle successfully loaded the SVG, image intact, and displaying normally. Appearance was at least as good as ImageMagick. Since Squiggle can be regarded as the reference viewer for SVG files (see the section Squiggle), this is a quite good testimony for Scribus's SVG export capabilities.

7.4 PDF Export

7.4.1 Scribus and PDF

THE POWER and versatility with the PDF (Portable Document Format) export in Scribus is one of its most notable features. Documenting all of its features requires almost a book by itself, since PDF really refers to a family of versions – we'll call them flavors. You are encouraged to read this introductory part thoroughly to become familiar with all the PDF features and options.

The Portable Document Format was developed by Adobe as the output format for its Adobe Acrobat application. The original intent was to produce documents from a variety of applications which could be read and printed on any modern computer. Another intention was to create structured forms which could be filled out and returned to the creator of the form.

The format has since grown to include such things as eBooks – books which can be read on a computer screen or specialized reader device. It is also increasingly popular for creating presentations similar to those from Microsoft Power-Point, which then can be projected from a laptop computer.

Initially, PDFs were created by writing a PostScript file, then passing it through Adobe's Distiller. Later, Adobe applications, and others, became capable of writing PDF files directly. Now, this capacity is widely available in non-Adobe and Open Source applications, including Scribus.

PDF also slowly became a mechanism for delivering content to a pre-press shop, instead of delivering the document in its native application format with all of the graphics and fonts accompanying it. That mechanism required a skilled application user at the pre-press shop and sometimes considerable time in tweaking it. PDF was initially regarded with suspicion by pre-press shops because of the enormous number of options involved in creating a PDF file – font handling, image resolution, compression and down-sampling, and much more. Tools from different vendors began to make it possible to pre-flight PDF creation and even to impose the pre-press shop's standards on the creator.

Finally a movement arose to develop even stricter standards – a movement initiated by major magazines interested in receiving advertising in digital formats which would end up in a variety of pre-press environments. This has blossomed into the internationally recognized set of PDF/X standards. We will focus later on PDF/X-3, which Scribus creates, but we'll first talk about plain PDF.

While PDF in one sense is a proprietary standard, it is also widely available on most every computing platform. It is also extremely well documented. The PDF abilities in Scribus allow one to repurpose a document. One document can be produced for printing, web download or for presentations similar to OpenOffice.org/StarOffice Impress or MS PowerPoint. That this is a future trend in publishing is indicated by the same strategy in Adobe's InDesign 2.0+ and the new PDF capabilities in Quark Xpress 6+ and Adobe Illustrator 10+. In electronic publishing and pre-press production, all of them have seen many enhancements to PDF, which often overcome the limitations of HTML and traditional PostScript, respectively.

Your best viewing/printing results will be with the newest version of Adobe Reader. Please also note, gv and derivatives are not suitable viewers for Scribus EPS or PDFs. Similarly, Adobe Reader on MacOSX is given preference over the built-in Preview app.

If any other PDF or EPS viewer you choose cannot display PDFs from Scribus, but they do view properly in Adobe Reader, file a bug with the upstream author. In almost all cases it is a limitation of the viewing application. Scribus PDFs are tested regularly with specialist pre-press software to validate their adherence to the published PDF specifications.

7.4.2 PDF Flavors – Which one is best for you?

Like many questions in DTP, this is an important yet not so simple one. Answering it brings up many additional questions and therefore is worthy of some discussion here of what the differences are in these different PDF versions. A later version does not necessarily produce a "better" PDF and in some cases works against you.

7.4.2.1 What is the Difference between Versions PDF 1.2 to PDF 1.5?

Each version roughly parallels the release of a major version of Adobe Acrobat. The short and overly simple answers are:

- PDF 1.2 = Acrobat 3.0 – relatively obsolete now.
- PDF 1.3 = Acrobat 4.0 – The first version of PDF which truly

had all the needed features to support "press-ready" PDFs, including color management, ICC profiles etc. It also added Java-Script, interactive and multimedia capabilities. This standard is probably the safest to send if you are unsure of the capabilities of the receiver of your file. PDF/X-3 and a number of commercial print work flows are based on PDF 1.3. Note that PDF 1.3 doesn't support transparency.

- PDF 1.4 = Acrobat 5.0, but actually introduced with Illustrator 9. The main difference to concern Scribus users is both transparency and alpha transparency capabilities. This makes a major difference in where a PDF with these features can be printed. It takes either newer commercial RIPs or certain Level 3 Post-Script printers to use these features properly. Even so, not all Level 3 PostScript printers will handle transparency. The latest versions of Ghostscript support the advanced PDF 1.4 features Scribus can create when exporting PDF. Note: Often, the only way you will be able to print exactly the transparency features viewed on-screen is to export PDF 1.4 and print from Acrobat Reader 5.x or newer.

- PDF 1.5 = Acrobat 6.0 – Among the most interesting for Scribus users: many improvements for "press-ready" PDF, the capability to have true layering within the PDF, PDF-X "pre-flight" capability, more security and interactive features, like the ability to add comments which are separate from the original doc. PDF 1.5 can also support more sophisticated compression options for images using JPEG 2000.

In deciding which version you choose for export, you need to consider the following:

- Where am I ultimately printing? If you are planning to have your files printed commercially, always try to ask the printer first.

- Does my document have transparency features? See above and ensure the rest of your equipment or workflow can support PDF 1.4.

- Am I exporting PDF forms? How do I know end receivers of my file can use it? Do you know the version of Adobe Reader your users will have? The safest is to use PDF 1.3 or 1.4.

- Do I need PDF layers? Only PDF 1.5 supports this. Be aware support for PDF 1.5 is not complete in most open source viewers. Ghostscript 8.5x does support some, but not all PDF 1.5 features.

7.4.2.2 What about PDF-X and PDF-A?

- In brief, PDF/X-1a requires the following: The color space to be CMYK/grayscale, all the fonts are embedded and the settings within PDF indicate whether it is either pre-trapped = true or not-trapped = false. Think of this as a blind hand-off, as there is no certainty of how it will output.

- PDF/X-2 is a looser standard, but with the requirement for more knowledge between the supplier and receiver of the file. Fonts are not required to be embedded and it is possible to use OPI (Open Prepress Interface). PDF/X-2 also allows device independent color spaces, like CIE L*a*b*, to be used.
- PDF/X-3 allows for color profiles to be resident in the PDF, as well as different output intents and "DeviceN" (spot color) color space – now supported in any version of Ghostscript 8.0+. This also allows overprinting colors.
- PDF-A is an ISO standard based on PDF 1.4 for long term storage of public documents in an open format.

7.4.3 PDF Export

A Scribus document can be exported to a PDF file via *File > Export > Save* as PDF or by a click on the button "Save as PDF" in the toolbar.

The Preflight Verifier will automatically check your document for errors like overflowing text or missing images. If everything is OK or if you choose to ignore the error messages, the dialog for PDF export will appear. See The Preflight Verifier for more information.

As you will see, PDF export in Scribus has a great number of options, which will be described in detail below.

Scribus will automatically assign a name, appended with .pdf, and if you haven't named your Scribus document, it will be something like Document-1.pdf. In "Output to File," at the top of the following dialog, you can enter a filename of your choosing. By default, a single PDF file is created containing all the pages of your document, but by checking "Output one file for each page," an individual PDF is created for each page of your Scribus document, each with a unique name. For example, if you enter example.pdf as the name of the file and check for single page PDFs, Scribus will create files named ex-ample-Page1.pdf, example-Page2.pdf, and so on. Be aware that this does add to the overhead – a 7-page all text document used as a test took up about 4 times the space exported as single pages compared with a single PDF of 7 pages.

Below you find a detailed description of the tabs of the PDF export dialog in Scribus.

7.4.3.1 General

- *Export Range*: Select all pages of the document or by page. Individual pages are separated by commas (1,2,4), a range with a hyphen (1–3), or you can use a combination (1,3–7). You can even use this in simple situations for booklet printing.

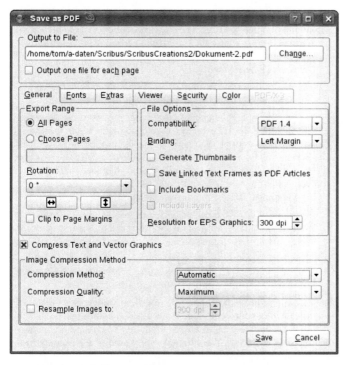

- *Rotation and Flipping*: The output can be rotated 90, 180 or 270 degrees and flipped horizontally (left button under rotation) or vertically (right button).
- *Clip to Page Margins*: Objects completely outside the margins you have defined for the page will not be printed or exported and objects partly outside the margins will be chopped at the margins on output.

File options

- *Compatibility*: There are several versions of the PDF specification. Scribus supports 1.3, 1.4, 1.5 and X-3. PDF/X-3 is only available if color management is activated. When PDF/X-3 is selected, the tab "Security" is not active. If your file contains transparencies, choose 1.4 or 1.5. If you produce a version higher than the Reader available to your audience, the PDF may not open or display properly.
- *Binding*: Binding refers to the side of the page where a book or booklet would be bound – for languages written left-to-right, binding will be left most of the time and that's the Scribus default.
- *Generate Thumbnails*: Creates small preview images of the pages, which can be displayed in Adobe Reader in the "Pages" tab. They help the reader navigate through the document.

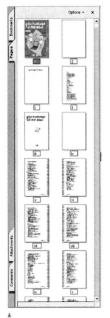

PDF thumbnails (above) and a PDF article (below) in Adobe Reader

- *Save Linked Text Frames as PDF Articles*: PDF Articles provide another navigation tool. Selecting this option will create "article threads." You can use them to read an article that is spread over two or more pages by clicking *View > Navigation Tabs > Articles* in Adobe Reader.

- *Include Bookmarks*: Bookmarks in Scribus can be exported to a PDF file and be used for navigation in a PDF viewer.

- *Include Layers*: If layers are used in Scribus, they can be exported to a PDF file. This feature is only available for PDF version 1.5 or later versions. You can use this feature in connection with Scribus layers. For instance, it's possible to create a layer that's invisible in a PDF viewer, but will print, like watermarks. Or you can set a layer to visible, but not printable if you want to prevent parts of the content from being printed.

- *Resolution for EPS Graphics*: The resolution which is used to render text and vector graphics in EPS files in image frames. It won't affect bitmap images.

- *Compress Text and Vector Graphics*: Text and vector graphics can be compressed, making the output PDF size somewhat smaller without serious compromise of quality.

- *Compression Method*: The ZIP algorithm compresses the images without a loss of quality; the JPEG methods results in smaller files, but also means a loss of quality. You shouldn't change the default setting "Automatic," unless someone else requires a specific compression.

- *Compression Quality*: Here you can select the level of the compression that will be applied to the images in the file. Note that if you chose the JPEG compression method, there will always be a loss of quality, even if you set the quality to "Maximum."

- *Resample Images to*: If this option is checked, the bitmap images in the file will be re-sampled to the resolution set in the spinbox. Note that Scribus will only downscale images, not upscale.

7.4.3.2 Fonts

- *Available Fonts*: All fonts used in the document are listed here (see The Scrapbook for an exception).

- Here the fonts are listed which will be embedded into the PDF.

- With the arrow buttons between "Available Fonts" and "Fonts to embed," you can choose which font will be embedded in the PDF file. The button "Embed All" selects all fonts for embedding. Embedding means that a copy of the font file(s) will be stored in the PDF file. This is important if you think it might be possible that the printer will have to do some minor corrections in the texts stored in the the PDF file, since the text characters will be contained in the PDF.

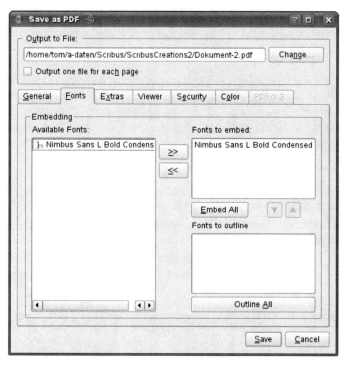

- *Fonts to Outline*: An alternative to embedding a font is to convert all glyphs to PostScript outlines. By using "Fonts to Outline," any glyph of a selected font will be converted to vector data, and the text as characters will be completely lost. With the arrow buttons beside the "Embed All" button, you can choose which fonts will be converted to outlines. By clicking "Outline All," all fonts in the document will be converted. Converting to outlines is an option if you have no license to embed a font (since embedding would mean distribution). It's also a viable option if you're unsure whether the quality of a font is sufficient for professional printing or when your printer might not have a new enough RIP or imagesetter to accept PDF 1.4. Beware, though, that text which has been converted to outlines can't be edited in a PDF editor anymore. It will also be impossible to extract text from the PDF you created.

OpenType Fonts and Unicode TrueType Fonts cannot be fully embedded by default, unless they are simple TrueType fonts that happen to have an *.otf extension. This greatly simplifies handling them in other applications. OpenType Fonts and Unicode TrueType Fonts can be quite large, some larger than 10 MB. OpenType Fonts/Unicode True Type Fonts are automatically converted to outlines in PDF. This allows them to be used in PDF, where often other applications cannot use them.

Text in PDF Files

While many programs export PDF files that can be searched or from which text can be copied to the clipboard, this may not be the case with Scribus PDFs. The reasons for this restriction are twofold: First, for Scribus, precise placement of glyphs in a document is more important than preserving the order of characters. Thus, the word "which" may look like "w hi c h" if copied and pasted into a text editor from a PDF viewer. For the same reason, a PDF created by Scribus may not be searchable.

The second reason is that some fonts will be converted to outlines automatically, as described in the main text. Outlines are curves and no longer text.

Moreover, embedding Open Type fonts is only supported in PDF 1.6+ (Acrobat 7.0.x), and this technology is quite new.

7.4.3.3 Extras

Like the established presentation programs StarOffice/OpenOffice.org Impress or PowerPoint, PDF files can be used for presentations. Graphical effects for transitions from page to page can be applied to every page. See PDF Presentations for more information.

7.4.3.4 Viewer

In this tab, you'll find some options that will affect the behavior of PDF viewer when it opens the PDF file.

"Document Layout": These options are controlling the page navigation in the PDF viewer:

- *Single Page*: The document is scrolled page by page.
- *Continuous*: The document is scrolled without considering page breaks.
- *Double Page Left and Double Page Right*: Two pages are dis-

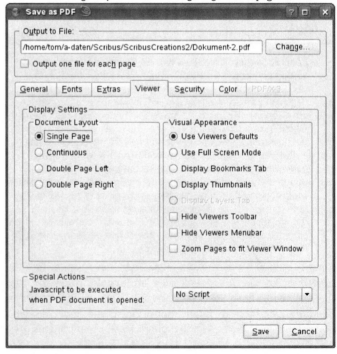

played simultaneously. The settings determine whether the first page of a document is displayed as a right or a left page.

"Visual Appearance": This controls how elements will be displayed in a PDF viewer:

- *Use Viewers Defaults*: The default settings of the viewer will be used
- *Use Fullscreen Mode*: The PDF viewer displays the file in full-screen mode, all menus of the PDF viewer will be hidden. This is particularly useful with presentations.
- *Display Bookmarks Tab*: The bookmarks are shown as a tree.
- *Display Thumbnails*: Previews of the pages will be shown in the PDF viewer.
- *Hide Viewers Toolbar, Hide Viewers Menubar*: These settings will hide the respective bars in a PDF viewer.
- *Zoom Pages to fit Viewer Window*: The PDF file is zoomed to the full size of the viewer's display window.

"Special Actions": Here you can select a JavaScript script which will be executed when the PDF file is opened in the PDF viewer. The script needs to be saved in the Scribus file to be embedded in the exported PDF file and to be executed.

Note that not all viewers are able to execute JavaScript code.

7.4.3.5 Security

PDF files can be protected with passwords, but be aware that there is no strong protection for documents. It can be bypassed easily, but might be effective for the general office user, who can disable the printing of a presentation. If you enable "Security" in the PDF export dialog, when you export PDF 1.3, encryption is 40 bit strength, with PDF 1.4 or later, encryption is 128 bit strength.

The PDF viewer will distinguish between an owner and an user. For both levels, passwords can be set in Scribus.

"Settings": These options are controlling the user permissions in a fine-grained way:

- *Allow Printing the Document*
- *Allow Changing the Document*
- *Allow Copying Text and Graphics*
- *Allow Adding Annotations and Fields*

Note: If you are producing PDF files for pre-press, you should always disable any security settings, because your printer most likely won't be able to use these files in his printing workflow.

7.4.3.6 Color

These options are very important. Here you can control which color space will be used in the exported PDF file.

- *Screen/Web*: the PDF file is created in RGB mode. Use this option if the PDF should be displayed on screens or will be printed to desktop printers.
- *Grayscale*: all colors are converted to grayscale. Note that for precise control of image conversions, you should use an image editor, especially when images come from different sources.
- *Printer*: the document will be color separated and the resulting PDF file uses the CMYK mode. This output intent offers some additional options:

"Rendering Settings:" This is really an advanced set of options, and it's only available if color management is switched on. You should only change the settings if your printing company expressly requires any changes. Basically, these are settings for a technology called screening. In CMYK printing, the illusion of continuous-tone colors is created by overlaying dots of ink in Cyan, Magenta, Yellow and Black. Each set of dots

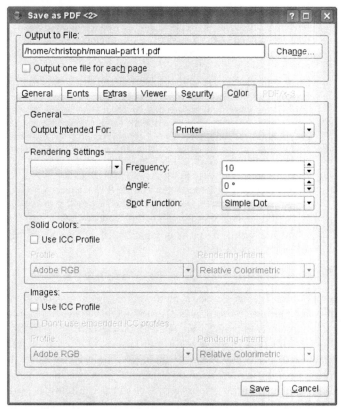

Working in RGB or CMYK?
For many programs, their vendors recommend to work in CMYK color space for output that's intended for offset printing and in RGB for other output. This means that users are advised to only import CMYK images into a document for offset printing.
This isn't true for Scribus. First, a graphic in CMYK may not print correctly even if it uses the CMYK color space. Depending on the ICC profile and the colors used in it, it may still show color issues when printed. Second, an RGB graphic may very well print correctly if correctly converted to CMYK at output time. Thus, Scribus will determine the appropriate color-space during PDF export, depending on the output target. You can mix RGB and CMYK images and colors in a document, you can mix images with embedded color profiles and those without. During PDF export, you can override the embedded profiles and apply a single profile to all images. This allows for more flexibility if a document is used for multiple purposes, for example offset printing and web display.

will be printed from a separate plate. To achieve the best results, each grid of dots on a plate uses a different angle. It's also possible to change the frequency of dots on plate, depending on the output media. For instance, a newspaper needs a lower frequency than a high quality offset print. It's also possible to change the shape of the dots. Note that the following values can be changed for each processs color separately.

- *Frequency*: The frequency of dots in lpi (Lines per Inch). For regular offset printing, 150 is a reasonable value.
- *Angle*: The angle of the grid on each plate. Do not change unless your printing company requires any changes! Sometimes the angles have to be adjusted to avoid moiré patterns, but in general this should be done by the printer.
- *Spot Function*: Contains a list of available dot shapes. The printing standard is "Ellipsis."

If color management is active, you'll see a different set of options:

- Under "Solid Colors" you can select an RGB color profile and a rendering intent for solid colors, both of which will be used for converting RGB colors to CMYK. This option is switched off by default. Use it only if your printing company requires such a profile.
- Under "Images" you have two options. If you check "Use ICC Profile," Scribus will use profiles embedded in the images. This only makes sense if all images in your document actually have a profile embedded. You can override the embedded profiles by checking the second option "Don't use embedded ICC profiles." In this case you can select an RGB profile and a rendering intent to convert RGB images to CMYK. The first option is active (and grayed out) only for PDF/X-3 export (see below), as it is required by the specification. For other PDF versions you need to switch it on yourself. The second option is switched off by default. Use it only if your printing company requires it.

If you are not going to print commercially, you'll be on the safe side with Screen/Web.

7.4.3.7 PDF/X-3

Support for PDF/X-3 was a major milestone in the development of Scribus. Scribus was the first page layout application to support a demanding, but open ISO standard: ISO 15930-3:2002. This type of support for high quality PDF creation had been exclusively the realm of expensive proprietary applications. Creating commercial press ready PDFs has historically been fraught with errors, especially for users unfamiliar with the nuances of PostScript, PDF distilling and varying capabilities of plate-setters or digital presses. The saying "It is hard to create a good PDF, but really easy to mess up" has a great deal of truth. The more common usage of the Adobe Acrobat Distiller family of applications for PDF creation has typically needed knowledge of at least some of the close to 100 Distiller parameters.

The creation of PDF/X, currently with 4 defined ISO standards, is, in part, an attempt to provide end users and creators with a vendor neutral measuring stick to vet files as suitable for professional printing or exchange with service bureaus. Scribus has easy to understand and use options which enable end users to create 100% PDF/X-3 compliant files. By judicious use of PDF options, end users can be assured their files, if required, to be 100% standards compliant. As always, be certain any PDFs you create can be used in the workflow of your printer's equipment or pre-press service bureau. Not all are equipped to handle the latest in PDF technology. Always consult with the commercial printer you are working with early into your production work. This is almost always good advice when working with commercial printers. This avoids trouble and makes for a much less stressful situation when deadlines approach.

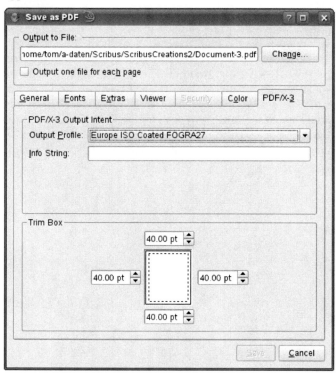

To export a PDF/X-3 file, you have to activate color management in the *Document Setup* first and then select "PDF/X-3" in the "Compatibility" list in the "General" tab of the PDF export dialog. You also need a color profile, preferably a profile provided by your printer. If you want to make your file 100% compliant with the PDF/X-3 standard, you also have to add the "Info String" (eg. the file name or a comment).

A Trim Box is one of several boxes defined in the PDF specification, and it's intended to specify the size of the document after trimming away what's not intended to be seen. By default, the numbers displayed are those of the margin guides as shown in *Document Setup*.

One of the outstanding features of PDF/X-3 is that it explicitly allows RGB objects to be tagged with ICC profiles. Scribus will use this feature when it's processing RGB layout elements, as this allows for better color-management when separations are created. Nevertheless, you should only export to PDF/X-3 if your printer explicitly asks for it.

Note that you cannot convert Type 1 and most TrueType fonts to outlines if your output target is PDF/X-3, as the specification requires that all fonts be embedded. You also won't be able to use any security features with PDF/X-3 files – the respective tab will be grayed out. The reason for this limitation, which is part of the PDF/X-3 specification as well, is that PDF/X-3 files are exclusively used for pre-press, so that your printer needs unlimited access to all parts of the file. As mentioned above, you also can't disable the use of ICC profiles for images – another restriction enforced by the PDF/X-3 standard.

8 Printing

8.1 The Print Preview

A SIMPLE use of print preview might be to just get a sense of how your document looks without all the non-printing objects visible, such as margins, guides, and frame borders.

The print preview initially generates the same process as printing, in which your document is sent to the preflight verifier and any errors or problems identified, according to your settings in *Preferences* or the *Document Setup*. If you have no problems or click "Ignore," then the document is processed as if being printed, but only a screen display is generated, with some limited ability to change the page display size.

There are some other view adjustments, the only one perhaps needing some explanation is the "Display Transparency" checkbox, which will remind you that what Scribus actually generates are instructions for printing on some medium, so now you see your frames and other objects, with their associated backgrounds if they are not also transparent. Partial transparency will also be shown.

Use on Windows
If you are running Scribus on the Windows platform, you need to install a PostScript printer driver to access the preview options. If you are only using a GDI printer, the checkboxes are grayed out.

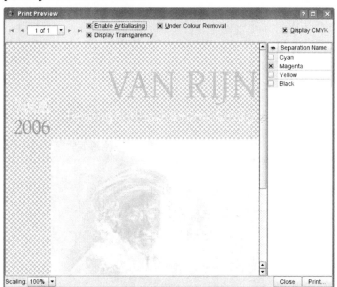

To see how it works, look at the screenshot on the previous page. It shows a print preview of our cover page from the Quick Start Guide. You may remember that the color we chose for the text "REMBRANDT" was white. Technically, "white" in CMYK has the values C: 0, M: 0, Y: 0, K: 0. In other words, it doesn't exist, and that's why we don't see anything of the white text in this preview. Why is this information useful? Because you can learn that if you print to anything but white paper, you'll need a spot color to actually print the color white

Among the settings is a chance to view your document in CMYK, and you can choose to view individual or collected color separations in case this is important before you send your PDF to your printer (local or commercial). If your document contains spot colors, Scribus will list each color with its name below the separation names.

If you are satisfied, you can either close or print.

8.2 The Preflight Verifier

WE'LL START our explanation of the Preflight Verifier by talking about its settings in *Preferences* and *Document Setup*, with the standard differences between those two repeatedly mentioned at this point. Here is a view of the "Preflight Verifier" section:

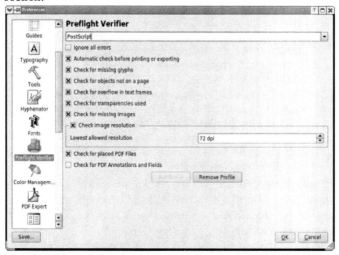

Now let's home in on the settings and cover them one-by-one.

- At the top in this view we see "PostScript." This is used for direct printing from Scribus, the print preview, and saving/printing to a PostScript file. Even if you don't have a PostScript printer, PostScript checks documents intended for your printer, as they are handled by Ghostscript. Other choices here are the PDF versions Scribus can export to: 1.3, 1.4, 1.5 and X-3. Each will have its own settings for all the checkboxes you see here. By selecting one of the preflight "profiles" from the dropdown list, you decide what will be the default file format that the Preflight Verifier will use for checking a document.

- *Ignore all errors*: Check this at your own peril, especially if you are taking your work to a commercial printer. As you will see, you can always ignore messages and process/export anyway.

- *Automatic check before printing or exporting* is straightforward.

- *Check for missing glyphs*: Checks if your chosen font does not include a glyph you are trying to print/export.

- *Check for objects not on a page*: Since you can freely slide objects from one page to another or even onto your scratch space, this will remind you if anything is even partially outside document boundaries.

- *Check for overflow in text frames*: One can easily to fail to see the overflow indicator in the lower right hand corner of a frame somewhere. Scribus will remind you if something's wrong with text frames.

- *Check for transparencies used*: Especially important if you are exporting to PDF 1.3, since this does not support transparency.

- *Check for missing images*: Any empty image frame will trigger this. It may be that no image was ever loaded, or it could be that when a Scribus file was loaded an image could not be found where it should have been.

- *Check image resolution*: For creation of a PDF for the web, 72 dpi is adequate, for most work that will be printed, 300 dpi is probably a desirable resolution. For some high-quality professional work, much higher values may be desired. You can let Scribus check for too low or too high image resolutions.

- *Check for placed PDF files*: What you are checking for is a PDF loaded into an image frame, where it will be rasterized or converted to a bitmap. Its resolution may be less than ideal.

- *Check for PDF Annotations and Fields*: These features are mainly intended for using them on a computer. They may cause issues in professional printing.

If you have checked in your *Preferences* to automatically check on print and export, you will surely run it then. You may also choose to run it at any time by clicking the "traffic light" icon on the toolbar.

The Preflight Verifier uses 3 different colors to indicate the status of an item in a document. Green means no problems. Red is used for errors like missing images, and yellow is a warning that will be triggered for problems like overflowing text frames. Note that an error message from the preflight verifier need not necessarily mean there is problem. If the error is something you can live with, such as an image of lower resolution than you've specified, this is a benign choice. But if you ignore attempts to put transparency into a PDF 1.3 document (which doesn't support transparency), you are asking for potential problems. To be sure you should at least check it by clicking on an object that's showing a yellow or red dot. Scribus will select this object automatically, so that inspection is easy.

8.3 Local Printing

ONE OF the challenges of an advanced DTP application like Scribus, is the ability to generate what can be referred to as "high-level" PostScript or PDF output. By high level, this is meant to describe things like transparency, blends, masks and gradients, usually created by professional grade DTP applications and illustration programs.

8.3.1 Linux/UNIX/OS X: CUPS

First, always make sure you have the newest updated versions of CUPS (Common UNIX Printing System) [1] and Ghostscript available for your distribution. Newer versions of CUPS and Ghostscript are much better at supporting the kinds of high level PostScript level 3 and PDF features Scribus can create.

If you compile Scribus yourself, make sure that you have the CUPS development libraries installed before you start building from source.

8.3.1.1 Basic Options

Print to any installed printer with the defaults, depending on your specific installation. You can also specify printing in grayscale, as well as select the pages or a range of pages. As in other printing dialogs, you can also set the number of copies that will be printed.

- You can choose different PostScript levels, the default is Post-Script level 3.
- You can open the print preview from the printer dialog
- You can also use an external print command, for example `xpp`, or `kprinter`, as shown below. In a KDE environment it is recommended to use the `kprinter` command, as the KDE printing manager provides access to a wealth of additional printing options.

Note: You will need to use an alternative printer command with some Linux distributions, notably recent versions of Fedora, including Fedora 8. A simple workaround is to enter `lp -d printername`, where `printername` is the specific name of the printer you wish to use.

On many Linux and UNIX distributions there are optional gimp-print or gutenprint drivers (gutenprint was known previously as gimp-print). These drivers can be used in any program to give you more exacting print control and in some cases much better output with photographs. Many printers on Linux are supported by more than one driver – typically an "ijs" driver and gimp-print/gutenprint. The main difference is the more refined color and ink density adjustments available in gimp-print/gutenprint. Often it will be slower than other drivers, but the higher output quality may be desirable.

To access setup and configuration for locally installed CUPS printers, there are 2 recommended methods to this with CUPS:

1. Type: http://localhost:631 in a web browser to use the CUPS web interface.

2. Use the KDE Print Manager (KPrinter). No other option will give you full access to all the features with CUPS.

You can also use KPrinter in combination with other programs which are not CUPS aware, but can benefit from high quality printing. As an example, Adobe Reader on Linux before version 7.0.5 does not recognize CUPS, but has a command line window to call KPrinter. Thus, you can, with the correct settings, print high resolution PDF's with the same high quality as Scribus. See Booklet Printing for more information about KPrinter.

When you are using true PostScript printers with Linux, especially more complex ones, which have multiple bins, sorting or advanced image and resolution settings, ideally you have the PPD file which comes on the driver disk with the printer. If not, try to download the latest from the manufacturer's site. A great many printer drivers come as windows *.exe files. For instance, any of the HP ones are simple WinZip self extractors. Any recent WINE [2] will open them easily. Then, it is strongly recommended that you run `cupstestppd` on the file to make sure it follows the PPD specification.

`cupstestppd` is a command line utility which you can use to verify the correctness of PPD files. A PPD file is a specially formatted text file which can be used on Linux, Mac OS X and Windows to install a true PostScript printer. On Linux in combination with foomatic and CUPS it is used for all printers to enumerate all the printer's capabilities. This command line tool verifies that the PPD file meets the specifications for PPD files. If there are issues, it will indicate how to remedy this. cupstestppd is most useful when using the manufacturer's supplied PPD on Linux.

8.3.1.2 Advanced Options

- You can "print" a separation. This enables you to create a 4 color separation of the CMYK inks used in process printing. Each of the inks will print on a separate page. This can also be saved to a PostScript file for later processing. Furthermore, you can also decide to only print single separations, eg. cyan.

- *Mirrored printing*: This option enables you to mirror pages on the printer. This is useful when printing things like card layouts, calendars or brochures to compensate for folds and cuts or when duplexing prints.

- *Set the Media Size*: This option will try to enforce a certain media size in the output device, such as US Letter. It may or may not work, as some printers simply ignore the command.

- *Clip to Page Margins*: If this option is enabled, objects outside the page margins won't be printed.

- *Apply Under Color Removal*: This is an option to both save ink and to improve the quality of some gray shades. UCR means that gray shades that are composed of cyan, magenta and yellow will be replaced with black.

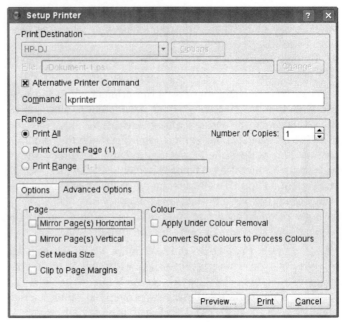

- *Convert Spot Colors to Process Colors*: Inkjet and laser printers can't print spot colors. Therefore, it's necessary to print process colors instead. This option will enforce the conversion. For further information, see Spot Colors.
- Apply ICC Profiles: This option will use embedded ICC profiles for printing. See Color Management for more information.

8.3.1.3 CUPS Hints

cups-calibrate is a command line program you can run as root to calibrate the printer. This only works with the gimp-print drivers – not other CUPS drivers. This is a step by step procedure which in some cases can improve the sharpness of your prints.

CUPS also has an escputil command line utility for cleaning the heads or checking ink levels on Epson printers. If you have KDE installed, this can be accessed via KPrinter. Otherwise simply type: escputil --help for options.

8.3.2 Exporting to a PostScript File

You can also use the print dialog to export your Scribus document as a PostScript file. Technically, the difference between printing and creating a PostScript file isn't huge: If you print on paper, a temporary PostScript file will be created and sent to the printer driver. However, if you export to a PostScript file, you create a permanent PostScript file, which can be opened or imported by other programs, or printed directly from the command line.

To create a PostScript file, select "File" in the drop-down list under "Print Destination." Just like in other file dialogs, you can insert a name for the file and change the output folder. The only difference is that you have to click on the "Print" button to "Save" the file.

Since you are actually creating a virtual print job when you are saving a PostScript file, all printing options are available to you. You should be aware that there is a technical difference between different PostScript levels. Scribus uses its own built-in PostScript engine to create PostScript level 3 files, which is the default. If a printer requires PostScript level 1 or, more likely, level 2, the export is handled by Ghostscript – yet another reason to have the latest Ghostscript installed.

8.3.2 Printing with Windows

The printing options on Windows depend on the capabilities of the printer driver, which may vary from printer to printer.

8.3.3 Printing with OS/2, eCOMstation

Printing support for OS/2 is not complete, but PDF export is. You can easily print via Adobe Reader or another PDF viewer as a temporary workaround.

[1] http://www.cups.org
[2] http://www.winehq.org

8.4 Booklet Printing

WHEN creating a document in Scribus, one typically is working in a very linear fashion, where page 1 is followed by page 2, then 3, and so forth. When you are getting ready to print this out, however, you may not necessarily create your final product in such a simple manner.

For example, let's imagine you have created an 8-page document, that you wish to print in a booklet form.

We might think of the Scribus document being created like this, with these large numbers simply indicating page number:

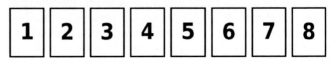

Since we want to print a booklet, however, we will want the output to have 2 document pages per printed page, printed on both sides, then stapled together so that when we flip through the booklet we flip in sequential order. The process of rearranging the pages so that this works correctly is called imposition. If you are taking your PDF to a commercial printer, they will have the ability to do this imposition for you. But what if you want to print this out on a local printer and do the imposition yourself?

There are various ways of doing this, several of which are documented on the Scribus Wiki, but here we will confine ourselves to small booklets in which the imposition might be accomplished just using Scribus and your PDF viewer/printer application. For our example we will use Adobe Reader 8.x, which has the ability to print in an n-up manner – putting more than one document page on each printed page.

8.4.1 Imposition Using Scribus and Adobe Reader

For an 8-page booklet, 2 pages per each side of a sheet of paper and printing both sides to assemble as a booklet, we only need 2 sheets of paper, but as we see here, if we maintain the original order, there is no way to make this work:

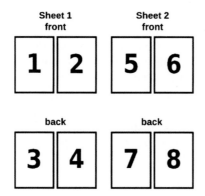

What we really want is this:

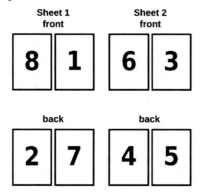

We can accomplish this using the "Save as PDF" dialog. Under "Export Range," check "Choose Pages," then in the selection list put 8, 1, 2, 7, 6, 3, 4, 5 – don't think about it too much, just do it.

Note here that you can still save your Scribus file in a normal order, and for that matter you can export different PDF versions, one with imposition, one without.

8.4.2 On to Adobe Reader (8.x+)

Now in Adobe Reader we can import this scrambled document and print. Bring up the print dialog and in the "Page Handling" area under "Page Scaling" choose "Multiple Pages per Sheet," "2 Pages per Sheet," "Page Order" is "Horizontal." Leave "Orientation" as portrait. In "Print Range" check "Pages," then enter 1, 2, 5, 6.

Now click "OK," and you will print the front pages above. Once this first print-run is finished, take the pages out, orient appropriately for your printer (make sure the sheet with pages 8 and 1 is on top), then print again as above, but this time under "Pages" enter 3, 4, 7,8.

Now assemble your booklet. Once you get the hang of this, you will be able to print multiple copies at a time. For example, you could print all, then rearrange the sheets and print all again – this of course requires keeping track of what needs to print with others.

8.4.3 Plan B

Once you see how this works, you may realize that you could have exported your PDF from Scribus without reordering, and simply used this same method in Adobe Reader with these two sets of groups: 8, 1, 6, 3 and 2, 7, 4, 5 – if you look at the diagram above you can once again recognize the pattern – front sides, then back sides. However, without the diagram, it may be easy to make errors.

Since each sheet will contain 4 pages with 2-up printing, multiples of 4 are possible.

The sequence for a 12-page booklet (3 sheets): 12, 1, 2, 11, 10, 3, 4, 9, 8, 5, 6, 7. Then using the first Adobe Reader printing method, print these two groups: 1, 2, 5, 6, 9, 10 and 3, 4, 7, 8, 11, 12.

And for a 16-page booklet (4 sheets): 16, 1, 2, 15, 14, 3, 4, 13, 12, 5, 6, 11, 10, 7, 8, 9. Then using the first Adobe Reader printing method, print these two groups: 1, 2, 5, 6, 9, 10, 13, 14 and 3, 4, 7, 8, 11, 12, 15, 16.

By now you should be able to see the simplicity of the pattern when printing from Adobe Reader, so that regardless of how many pages you have, you can envision: **1**, **2**, 3, 4, **5**, **6**, 7, 8, **9**, **10**, 11, 12, **13**, **14**, 15, 16 ..., where the bold style indicates the pages to print on the first pass, then the remaining ones on the second pass.

What about odd pages or a number not divisible by four? Simply add blank pages as needed at the beginning, the end, or wherever, to add up to one of these multiples of 4.

8.4.4 KPrinter

If you're working on a Linux/UNIX desktop with KDE as your desktop environement you can consider yourself lucky, as KDE's print control – KPrinter – will assist you in booklet printing.

The first thing you need to to in the Scribus print dialog is to check "Alternative Printer Command" and to insert "kprinter" (without quotation marks).

Then click "Print." Depending on the size of your document it will take a while until the KPrinter dialog appears, as Scribus is creating a temporary PostScript file first. Once you see the KPrinter dialog, click on "Properties."

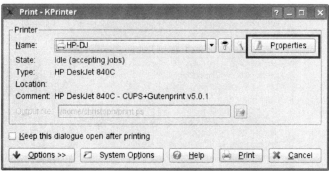

This will bring up the configuration dialog for your printer. In the last tab of the dialog, "Filters," click on the icon that shows a filter cone:

This will bring up another dialog, in which you can choose between many options, including those for pamphlet (booklet) printing.

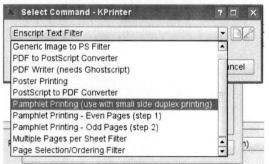

Once you have selected an entry, you can edit the underlying commands after clicking on the icon with the spanner. Editing those will require some familiarity with the commands, and you probably won't have to change anything here.

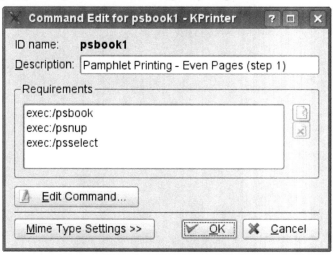

Click "OK," and the filter is available to the printer. In the configuration dialog you can also see which commands are used for the printing process and which file formats will be used for input and output. In this case PostScript is used for both, since Scribus creates a PostScript file that will be used by the printer, and the printing system will output a PostScript file, which is sent to the printer.

Click "OK" to save and close the configuration dialog, and in the KPrinter dialog click "Print."

8.5 Preparing Files for Commercial Printing

8.5.1 Printing Technology

IF YOU want to get hundreds, or thousands of copies of your Scribus document onto paper, both quality and economics dictate that at some point you will abandon your desktop printer or local copy shop and go to a printer – someone who owns printing presses.

This brief section cannot replace years of apprenticeship in the many arts and crafts that result in putting words and pictures on paper. Instead, it's intended to provide enough basic background to help you understand tools and terms used in Scribus.

When we talk about printing these days, we almost always are talking about "offset lithography," or just "offset."

There are other printing methods, including:

- *Letterpress*: Characters on the surface of (usually) metal blocks. Ink is applied to them, and transferred directly to the paper. The dominant method of printing from Gutenberg to the last half of the 20th century.

- *Flexography*: Characters on the inked surface of a flexible medium. Used for printing on surfaces such as plastic bags.

- *Rotogravure*: Letters engraved on the inked surface of a metal cylinder. Used for high-speed printing of both high quality magazines and lower-quality catalogs.

- *Screen*: Images on the surface of a screen. Used for printing T-shirts, etc.

- *Thermography*: Images indented in a metal surface, filled with ink. The resulting ink transfer to paper results in raised lettering, as seen, for example, on wedding invitations.

- *Engraving*: Images on the surface of a metal plate. Used for printing currency, expensive stationery, etc.

Offset lithography works like this: Images (type, photographs, line drawings, etc.) are applied to the surface of a plate (usually aluminum, but can be paper or plastic.). The plate is bent into a curve and put on a press cylinder. Ink (which is oily) and water don't mix, so the image areas of the plate retain ink and the non-image areas are washed clear with water. Ink is then transferred from the plate to a rubber "blanket," which in turn transfers ink to paper. The plate itself never touches the paper – hence the name "offset."

For each color, there is a separate press "unit," each with its own plate. Thus, to print color, one must separate a multi-color page into its constituent colors.

The conventional color offset printing job uses four process colors: cyan, magenta, yellow and black – CMYK. ('K' represents black, you can take your choice of a couple of reasons for this definition.) Theoretically, an image area consisting of 100 % cyan, magenta, and yellow should result in a black area, just as 100% red, blue, and green produces black on a computer screen. In fact, however, the result is a muddy brown; that's one reason black ink is used.

CMY printing is a subtractive process, meaning that the inks are transparent and act as filters for the light reflected off the surface of the printing paper ("substrate."). Black ink is not transparent. So in order to avoid that muddy-appearing black resulting from 100% CMY, real black ink is substituted. (Aside from producing better-looking results, it saves money because black ink is cheaper.)

To complicate things a bit, black is not always black. Printers and designers often prefer "rich black," which is 100 percent black ink with some lesser percentage of the transparent inks; as the name suggests, they produce a warmer, sometimes more pleasing look to solid black area. There are several semi-standard definitions of rich black combinations.

And there is also "registration color." While black is 100% black and 0% C, M and Y, registration color is 100 percent of all four. It is used to print registration and crop marks outside the margin of the printed page, and since it must appear on all four plates, must have 100% of all four colors.

Registration marks, which look sort of like bull's eyes, are used to indicate to the press operator that the several color plates print on exactly the correct place on the paper. Crop marks are used to guide the bindery in cutting printed sheets to the exact dimensions of the finished product. See Bleed and Print Marks in the Scripter chapter for more information about their use in Scribus.

All of this color stuff is irrelevant, of course, if your document is to be printed in black and white (including grayscale images). It's totally relevant if your document will have color on every page. Things get still more complicated if you plan to have color on some but not all pages (and pay only black and white rates for the black and white pages). This is where a visit to your printer becomes vital.

A book, magazine, catalog, etc. with a mixture of color and black and white pages is often printed on different presses, one for color, another for B&W. Depending on the size of the press, there may be as few as two and maybe as many as 64 pages on each side of a "signature," a press sheet that will later be cut and folded into a book. Registration is still important for B&W pages, but less so, as there are no separate plates to align, just pages on opposite sides of a sheet. The process of arranging pages on a sheet is called "imposition," and it's complicated enough to have produced university master's theses. But the bottom line is that the number of pages on a press sheet in a mixed color and B&W environment determines totally where color pages can appear in your document.

8.5.2 Be Prepared

If there is any generic advice we could give, it would be to please talk to your printing company before you submit a job to them. Preventing misunderstandings and discussing your goals will more than likely prevent 90% of the potential problems.

It always is a good idea to understand as much about the various parameters and requirements that your commercial printer may need to know or make use of with your print job. There are resources in this manual which you should be familiar with as you get your work ready for printing, namely: Color Management and Spot Colors, PDF Export, Fonts and Font Technology, Working with Images.

8.5.3 Ask Questions

- If they accept PDF, which level? PDF 1.3 (Acrobat 4), PDF 1.4 (Acrobat 5), PDF 1.4 (Acrobat 6) or PDF/X-3 (ISO Standard)? PDF/X-3 is the most advanced for commercial printing, and is expressly designed to assure good color fidelity between systems. If they can recommend specific ICC profiles to use, then all the better. You are more likely to encounter printers equipped to handle PDF/X-3 in Europe, where it has been more readily adopted.

- Will they be converting the PDF to other formats like EPS? Unless the printer's systems are using PDF 1.4, this is not a recommended solution, since not all page layout applications are capable of supporting some of the advanced PostScript Level 3 or PDF 1.4 features Scribus supports.

- Can they provide an ICC profile of their printing equipment if color fidelity is critical?

- What is the PostScript level of their RIP? This can be a determining factor in how you prepare the files. If their RIP is 3015.xxx+, there should be no problems in this regard.

- Do they require an additional bleed area for your documents? It's important for you to know this before you start laying out pages, as it will affect the way you work.

- If you are having trouble understanding the feedback you're getting, let your printer know. You can also ask on the Scribus mailing list or on IRC, since often there is someone knowledgeable who can answer your questions.

- In any case you should ask for a contact proof from the printer, so that you can see what the final print will look like. Many printing companies even require you to sign the proof, and you shouldn't hesitate to do this if it meets your expectations. Since this signed proof amounts to a contract, be sure to check the proof very carefully in all respects. It's an assurance for both sides, as in case of an alleged misprint, the result of the print can be compared to the proof.

9 PDF Forms

9.1 Introducing PDF Form Elements

SCRIBUS has the ability to create PDF forms with embedded JavaScript scripts. PDF forms are in some cases filled out by users on their computers and then printed out locally, but information in a PDF form may also be submitted online to a remote location for further processing. However, this online submission only works with Adobe Reader 8 or later; in earlier versions of Adobe Reader, the feature is only available if you are using the Adobe Reader plug-in for your browser, not with the standalone Reader application.

9.1.1 Start With OK

On your toolbar, find the icon with the default "OK" label, which by the way changes as you select from the list. Attached to its right side is an expander to generate a drop-down list of choices: *Button, Text Field, Check Box, Combo Box,* and *List Box.* By selecting one of these, you can then go to your document and click-drag to create a frame, which you will perhaps be disappointed to see merely creates a generic-appearing empty text frame.

What this shows is that simply making one of these form items does not do much of anything – each needs content, associated attributes, and actions to be useful in your PDF form.

9.1.2 Button

A button has several operations it can carry out. It might show itself as a text message, but you can also load an image for the button, and create your own tooltip. When clicked, you could go to a particular page of the same or a different PDF, submit data from the form, reset the form, run a short JavaScript command, or import some data to the form.

Submit Info

9.1.3 Text Field

A text field, not surprisingly, is for entering some keyboard input to submit with the form. You can set limits as to its length, perform some sort of testing of the input, make some calculation based on the input, and again, perform some action with JavaScript.

For privacy reasons, I prefer not to answer this.

9.1.4 Check Box

Clicking on this will, in the PDF Form, make or unmake a checkmark of some sort, the type chosen from a list in Scribus. Some JavaScript action can be carried out here also – see the section Emulating Radio Buttons for one such use of Java-Script.

9.1.5 Combo Box

For a Combo Box, create a list in the frame (with Story Editor for example), this simply being a column of possible choices, which can be editable or not. Any blank lines will not appear in the PDF form, and even if your frame height is much larger than the line spacing, only one choice appears at a time, until you click the right side feature to expand the list in a drop-down manner.

9.1.6 List Box

Like the combo box, a list box is a simple text list of items. There is no drop-down feature like a combo box, but instead use these scrolling arrows as seen here – you need to click the box to bring the scrolling feature in view. In contrast to the combo box, a list box will show as many choices as can be visible for the frame height chosen, with the actual choice to be submitted being highlighted.

9.2 PDF Form Features in Scribus

WHAT WE want to do in this chapter is to go through the process of creating a relatively simple PDF form with Scribus, incorporating at least the basic elements than can be used. Since there are many options, we will not plan to cover all of them, but some aspects of forms, such as JavaScript will be covered in later sections.

9.2.1 A Demonstration Form

Let's envision that we want to do a brief survey by collecting some basic biographical information, then some various opinions and other kinds of information.

We'll plan on collecting this information:
- The person's name
- Address
- City, Country
- Then ask them to make a series of choices

9.2.2 Text Field

Here is the beginning of our form. The frames outlined in black containing text are regular text frames. The others are special text frames called text fields," obtained by selecting "Text Field" from the drop-down list in the menu bar. PDF form elements will not be found in the menus.

Scribus Opinion Services

Name	
Address	
City	
Country	

For visual simplicity, we have kept the background plain, but depending on your preference, you might choose to use a grid or guides to assist with placement and alignment of these frames. A text field will be used to allow for filling out the space freely from the keyboard, rather than supplying choices.

When we right-click on each of these text fields, then choose "PDF Options > Field Properties" from the context menu, this dialog comes up. Instead of 'Text1," we will want to enter the variable name for each piece of data, so for our form, the text fields will have the variable names Name, Address, City, and Country.

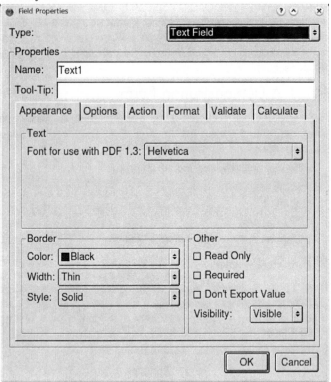

In our example, we will keep things simple, but for our "Name" category we might, for example, type "First, (MI), Last" as a tooltip so those filling out the form know our preferred entry order.

In contrast to regular text frames, we have limited choices for various features of our form fields. If we export to PDF version 1.3, for our font we can only choose regular, bold and italic forms of Courier, Helvetica, and Times, plus Symbols and Zapf Dingbats. The color of the border has a full range of choices, but the thickness can only be "None," "Thin," "Normal," and "Wide." Choices in Style are "Solid," "Dashed", "Underline," "Beveled," and "Inset."

In our "Options" tab, we have these checkbox choices, but for our example we will leave all unchecked. "Do Not Scroll" and "Do Not Spellcheck" will have no effect with PDF 1.3.

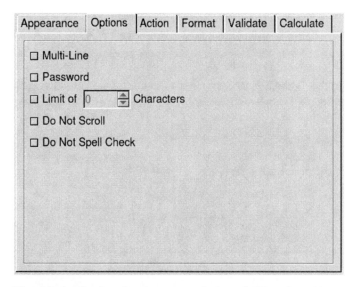

The "Action" tab only gives us a choice of "None" or "Java-Script," so this will not be shown further here.

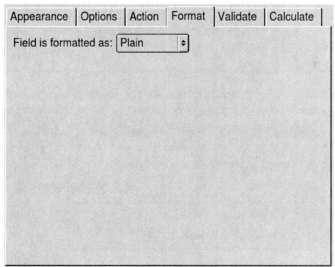

For our example we will leave the format as "Plain" (as in plain text). Other choices are:

- "Number," for which you can select number of decimal places, the character to use to indicate the decimal separator (period or comma), and whether to add a currency symbol.

- "Percentage," where again we can choose the number of decimal places and the character to show the decimal separator.

- "Date" – various date formats are possible.
- "Time" – again various format choices are shown.
- "Custom," where one must enter some personalized way of making a format for the entry.

In the "Validate" tab, we have a number of ways to check the entry into our text field. For our example, we will not make any changes.

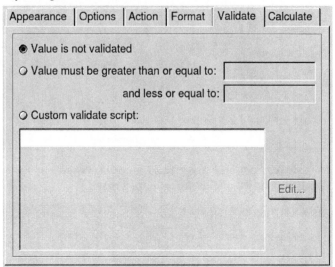

Finally, in the "Calculate" tab, we can change the settings to cause this field to be the sum, product, average, minimum, or

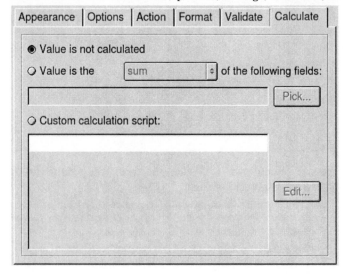

maximum of a set of other fields in our form. We can also have a custom method of calculation. For our example, we will choose "Value" is not calculated.

9.2.3 Check Box

Checkboxes are a relatively simple element, with only a few options. You must manually size your box, and you can choose between the choices you see here:

Enlarge the size of your mark with the font size spinbox in *Properties > Text* tab. Since you will not see this mark in Scribus, some experimentation will be necessary to balance the size of the check with the size of the box. The default can be either to have the box checked or unchecked. Each of these will of course have an associated text frame for the corresponding choice, and you must also align the text frame manually with the checkbox.

The *Action* tab for checkboxes also allows triggering of some JavaScript operation.

My favorite type(s) of checkbox are:

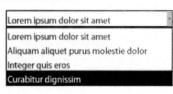

✓	Check
✗	Cross
◆	Diamond
●	Circle
★	Star
■	Square

9.2.4 Combo Box and List Box

In many ways a combo box is similar to a list box, so these will be described together here. Each allows you to choose an item from a list of choices, although the way these are displayed is somewhat different. A combo box will show only one choice regardless of its height as the default. In contrast, a list box will show as many as can be seen for the height of the frame.

Unlike the PDF fields mentioned thus far, you will see the contents of these boxes in Scribus. Create them to the desired height and width, then use the Story Editor to make the list of choices, each on a separate line. After saving and closing the Story Editor, now bring up the *PDF Options > Field Properties* dialog as we have before.

Here we see how the combo box appears in Adobe Reader after clicking the drop-down button. It may make more sense to use a combo box when the list of choices is long and especially when very different from one another, or for some other reason you want to be able to see all at once.

The funniest Lorem ipsum phrase is:

Lorem ipsum dolor sit amet
Lorem ipsum dolor sit amet
Aliquam aliquet purus molestie dolor
Integer quis eros
Curabitur dignissim

Here then is the list box sized to only choice show one at a time. List boxes can make more sense when the various choices occur in some natural order.

Completing this form was: 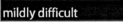 mildly difficult

If you look at the "Options" tab in Field Properties, it would appear that you can allow entries in a combo box and a list box to be editable, but you will find that only combo boxes can be edited in Adobe Reader. This may also be a reason to choose one over the other.

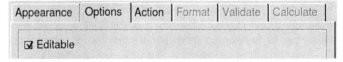

9.2.5 Button

Although button is the top choice in the *Insert PDF Fields* list, we're mentioning it last, since in many cases it will be something you click on after you have filled in or selected choices in other form elements.

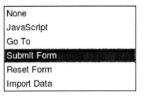

Let's focus on a particular type of button, a submit button. To the left we see this as one of the choices in the *Action* tab.

You can have your button say anything you like, but usually something simple works best.

When you select "Submit Form", you then need to enter the URL where your data will be sent. On the receiving end, you must have some way, such as a PHP file, to accept the information from the form.

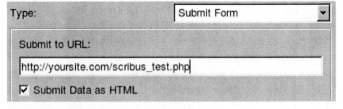

If your system is set up properly, you can alternatively enter "mailto:", then an email address for sending the information from the form.

In some cases, as shown here, you will want to check submit data as HTML. If you do not check this, the data will be sent in Adobe's FDF format. When submitting to a URL, your PHP file will need to be able to handle the appropriate data format. In either case, Adobe Reader must allow transmission of data, and the receiving site must allow for reception of this information.

9.2.6 Other Options

One thing you will not be able to do with a PDF form generated by Scribus is to save the data directly from Adobe Reader. You can, however, simply print the completed form on a local printer.

9.3 Enhancing PDF Forms with JavaScript

NOW THAT you have learned the basics of PDF forms in Scribus, you will probably be looking for more advanced features to customize your forms. One of the best ways to do so is by using JavaScript. JavaScript in PDF forms enables you to manipulate the appearance of form elements or even of the whole document, and to calculate and validate the contents of PDF form elements by attaching JavaScript code to events of its text fields, buttons, or even of the form itself.

As it is outside of the scope of the Scribus manual to cover all PDF-related JavaScript features, you are advised to download the JavaScript for Acrobat API Reference for a comprehensive list of available objects, methods and properties. [1]

9.3.1. Adding New Functions

Go to *Edit > Javascripts ...* and click on "Add." Choose a name for your new function and click on "OK" to launch the built-in JavaScript editor.

Let us call our first function "RunOnLaunch" and start with a simple alert that will be displayed on launching the PDF form in Adobe Reader:

```
function RunOnLaunch() {
  app.alert('Welcome to the Scribus Demo
Form!');
}
```

9.3.2 Launching JavaScript Functions while Opening Documents

Go to *File > Export > Save as PDF* and click on the "Viewer" tab. Choose the JavaScript to be executed from the "Special Actions" dropdown list. Save the PDF document and open it in Adobe Reader to see how it works.

9.3.3 Adding JavaScript Actions to Form Field Events

Let us make some text fields and text frames first. We will also need an optional check box and a button for performing some JavaScript actions.

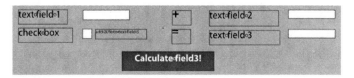

9.3.3.1 Validate Form Fields

First, we want to prevent users from submitting empty form fields. Right click on the button, choose *PDF Options > Field properties* from the context menu, go to the "Action" tab, choose "JavaScript" from the "Type" dropdown list and add the following snippet of JavaScript code to the "MouseDown" event:

```
if(!this.getField('field1').value) {
   app.alert('Please fill a number into field
1');
 } else if (!this.getField('field2').value) {
   app.alert('Please fill a number into field
2');
 }
```

9.3.3.2 Calculate Form Field Values

Now we would like to perform some simple calculations on form field values. In the following example, we will sum up the values of "field1" and "field2" and increase the result by 20%, depending on whether "checkbox1" has been checked or not. The final result will be displayed in the third form field. The code snippet below has to be typed into the "Mouse-Down" event of the red button.

```
if(!this.getField('field1').value) {
  app.alert('Please fill a number into field
1');
} else if (!this.getField('field2').value) {
  app.alert('Please fill a number into field
2');
} else {

  app.alert('Adding field1 to field2 and put-
ting the result into field3');
  this.getField('field3').value = this.get-
Field('field1').value + this.get-
Field('field2').value;

  app.alert('and now add 20% VAT to the res-
ult, if checkbox1 is checked ');
  var v = this.getField('checkbox1');
  if(v.value=='Yes')
    var vat = this.getField('field3').value
* 0.2;
  else
    var vat = 0;

  this.getField('field3').value = this.get-
Field('field3').value + vat;
}
```

9.3.3.3 Changing Field Properties with a Document Wide Script Executed on Button Click

First, let's create one combo box, one list box, a text field and a button. Use the PDF Tools icons to achieve this.

To add list items to a combo box or a list box, right-click on it and select *Edit Text …* from the context menu. Add one line of text for each list item and close the Story Editor.

The next step is to write a new JavaScript function. Go to *Edit > Javascripts …*, click on "Add," choose a name for your new function, eg. "SetFieldValues," and add the following snippet of JavaScript code to it. The code is meant to be self-explanatory, see the comments inside the function.

```
function SetFieldValues()
{
  app.alert('Running a document wide script
SetFieldValues. To see how it works, open the
source document in Scribus and go to
Edit/JavaScripts.');


  app.alert('Changing the values of the com-
bobox and the listbox');


  //setting combobox value to 12
  this.getField("combobox1").value = '12';


  //setting listbox value to option 3
  this.getField("listbox1").value = 'option 3';


  // Get the current date and time
  var rightNow = new Date();
  rightNow    = rightNow.toLocaleDateString();


  var fld = this.getField("date");
  //Change the date field border to dark blue
  app.alert('Changing the date field border to
dark blue, setting the date to current value,
and changing the date text color to purple.');
  fld.strokeColor = ["RGB",0.5,0.5,1];
```

```
//Change fill to light blue, won't work for
unknown reason
fld.Color = ["RGB",0,0,0.7];

//set the value of the date field to current
date
fld.value  = rightNow;

//Change text of the date field to purple
fld.textColor = ["RGB", 0.5, 0, 0.5];
```

9.3.3.4 Assign the New JavaScript Function to a Button Event

The function we have just written is now there, but it has to be tied to a PDF form element to make it really work. Right-click on the button, choose *PDF Options > Field Properties* from the context menu, go to the "Action" tab, choose "JavaScript" from the "Type" dropdown list and add the following line to the "MouseDown" event:

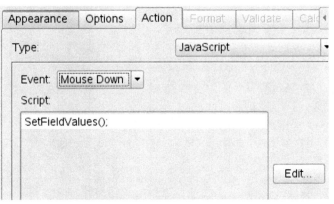

[1] http://partners.adobe.com/public/developer/en/acrobat/sdk/pdf/ javascript/AcroJS.pdf

9.4 Emulating Radio Buttons

CURRENTLY, Scribus cannot create real radio buttons in PDF forms, because the PDF specification for creating radio button objects requires a group of items with an identical name. Scribus does not support objects with an identical name, yet. Fortunately, a group of check boxes, each containing a little JavaScript, can be used to simulate a group of radio buttons.

9.4.1 The Method by Example

Select "Check Box" from the "PDF Fields" dropdown list in the toolbar.

In your document, create two or more check boxes and use a text frame to label each with suitable text. Each check box should also have a suitable name to reflect the purpose.

In our example we will have three check boxes called "Yes," "No," "Maybe" and three text frames containing "YES," "NO," "MAYBE." Be careful with the names when you are using JavaScript as Adobe Reader is case sensitive. You should end up with something like this on your page:

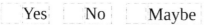

Right-click with your mouse on the "Yes" Checkbox (blue square). From the context menu select *PDF Options > Field Properties*. In the dialog, go to "Action Tab" and choose "JavaScript," then use the default "Mouse Up" event. Click on the "Edit" button and type the following code:

```
//this.getField("Yes").value = "Off"
this.getField("No").value = "Off"
this.getField("Maybe").value = "Off"
```

The initial "//" means that the first line will not be executed as a command, as it is not required for this field. Doing it this way makes it easy to copy and paste the complete code to all the check boxes and reduces typing errors. Click on "Save" and "Exit."

For the "No" check box, repeat the process with:

```
this.getField("Yes").value = "Off"
//this.getField("No").value = "Off"
this.getField("Maybe").value = "Off"
```

and then with the "Maybe" check box:

```
this.getField("Yes").value = "Off"
this.getField("No").value = "Off"
//this.getField("Maybe").value = "Off"
```

Save your Scribus document as a PDF file and view the PDF file using Adobe Reader. Now you should see the following fields that work like radio buttons:

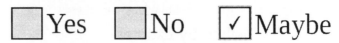

If you want to use traditional "round" radio button, you need to create an illusion.

For your check boxes use the following settings:

"Appearance" tab:

- Color: None
- Width: None
- Style: Solid

"Options" tab:

- Check Style: Circle

Now use the Scribus "Shape" tool to draw a circle around the check box. The resulting PDF should look like this:

9.5 Annotations and Links in PDF Files

9.5.1 Creating a PDF Annotation

PDF annotations can be useful for many purposes, and their advantages aren't limited to PDF forms. For instance, it's possible to send a PDF proof to customers and add annotations to get some feedback or to tell them you need a different file.

Here is a summary of what we need to do:

- Create a text frame, enter text
- Check context menu > *PDF Options* > *Is PDF Annotation*
- In the context menu, open *PDF Options* > *Annotation Properties*
- Select "Text" from dropdown list

To create a PDF annotation, create a text frame where you want the annotation to be displayed. Open the Story Editor and type your text. Note that you can't choose any text formatting for annotations.

In our example we want to tell someone that we need the image on the right at a higher resolution.

After typing the text, close the Story Editor. Don't be scared when you see unreadable text above the image. The text frame won't be visible in a PDF viewer, and it won't print either.

Next, open the context menu and check *PDF Options* > *Is PDF Annotation*:

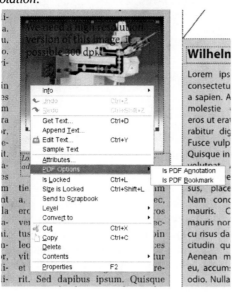

Open the context menu again and click *PDF Options > Annotation Properties*, then choose "Text" from the dropdown list:

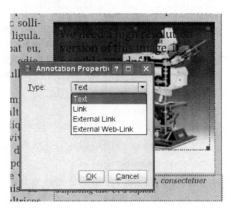

Now export your document as a PDF file and open it in Adobe Reader. There you see that the annotation is indicated by a page symbol. If you hover your mouse over the icon, the annotation is displayed:

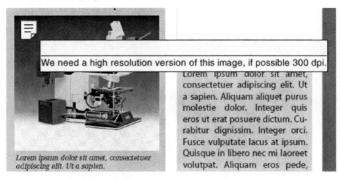

9.5.2 Internal Links

Another feature of PDF annotations is their use as links, like you are used to from web pages. You can create links within a document, links to external PDF files or hyperlinks.

To create a link within a document, select "Link" from the dropdown list in the *Annotation Properties*. Under "Destination" you can choose the page to which you want to link to. Scribus will display a preview of the selected page, so that you can easily select a destination with the mouse. If you need more precision, you can set the X and Y coordinates.

9.5.3 External Links

If you are using Scribus for presentations, it can be useful to link to another PDF file which could be opened in the same viewing application. Choose "External Link" from the dropdown list. Scribus will now open a file dialog from which you can choose the file. Once you have selected a PDF file, Scribus opens the "Annotation Properties," where you can choose the page to link to as well as the X and Y coordinates on the page.

Note that Scribus saves absolute paths to external files.

9.5.4 External Web Links

If you select "External Web Link," Scribus lets you insert a hyperlink. In most cases you will enter a web adress, like www.scribus.net, but you can also enter an email address. Just like in HTML pages you have to insert "mailto:" before the email address, eg. mailto:person@address.net. If properly configured, your email program will be opened through your browser.

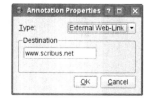

9.5.5 Some Additional Notes

• Regardless of the size of your annotation frame, the clickable area for the text type will be a small area near the page icon.

• In contrast, for a link, external link, or external weblink the clickable area is determined by the size of your frame – you will see the pointing hand icon appear.

• Consider these as special text frames, since any text frame can become an annotation or link. The text content becomes your annotation for text type. For links, any text is invisible. For all types, any background or line color is invisible.

• You can, of course, convert an image, shape, or polygon frame to a text frame, then to an annotation. The image will disappear in Scribus and in the PDF. For shapes and polygons Scribus will continue to show the shape and its associated colors. When you export to PDF, however, the colors disappear, and the clickable area is the rectangular bounding box, not just the shape or polygon.

9.6 Viewers for PDF Forms

THE BEST viewer for PDF forms is Adobe Reader, as it fully supports the whole PDF forms feature set. Moreover, Firefox can display forms with the Reader's "nppdf" plug-in. Okular in KDE 4 will support PDF forms as well.

CABAReT Stage [1] is proprietary, but freely available for personal use, and it has both Windows and Linux versions. It might have some problems (at least on Linux) with fonts, and perhaps some other factors for proper filling out of forms. The free versions have abilities for editing PDF forms, but will introduce a rather ugly "watermark" in the background while doing so – one must purchase a license to prevent this. However, the most important feature of the gratis version of CABAReT Stage is its ability to save the content inserted into PDF forms.

Linux users should be aware of the fact that CABAReT Stage may not work at all or even freeze your desktop (as experienced on OpenSUSE 10.3). As a workaround, you can open a PDF form in Adobe Reader, fill it out and print to a PostScript file. Then open the PS file in GSview and convert it to PDF. KDE users can also insert `kprinter` as an alternative printing command in Adobe Reader's print dialog and export directly to PDF.

[1] http://www.cabaret-solutions.com

10 PDF Presentations

10.1 General Remarks

CREATING presentation PDFs in Scribus is just as easy as using Scribus for its other purposes. In fact, using PDFs instead of traditional "presentation" applications has some significant advantages:

- They are portable. You can create a presentation PDF with Scribus and display it on almost any computer with Adobe Reader, available for free for almost every operating system. Other types usually require the application – or a special vewer – to be installed, and few are cross-platform.

- You can use all the drawing, text manipulation and image handling tools in Scribus, which are in many cases superior to those in other presentation applications. Few can import SVG or EPS files really well.

- You will have more precise typographic control of text. It is not likely your audience will comment about pixelated fonts, but even so, your presentation will have a decidedly less polished appearance – is this what you wish to portray?

- Because they are created in Scribus, you can export them with a higher resolution and they will print beautifully.

- Unlike other presentation tools, with use of the powerful form and JavaScript capabilities in Scribus you can make truly interactive PDFs which can take counts, ask questions with dialogs and more. You are only limited by your imagination and scripting skills.

10.1.1 Think Outside the Box

Don't let your previous experiences with digital presentations limit your ideas about what you can do. Here are a couple of ideas to get you started. Keep reminding yourself that you can create whatever Scribus can do, not just imitate existing presentation software.

10.1.2 The Non-Linear Presentation

The typical presentation will have a list of "slides" from first to last, and only in that order, unless you drop out of your plan and load another set. Let's imagine that somewhere around slide 8, you anticipate there will be questions from your audience (after all, Prof. Fussbudget may be in attendance), for which you would like to be able to take a detour from the presentation, show some additional information, then come back to where you were.

- If what you need to show is small, create a clickable annotation – showing additional data perhaps – then proceed as you would have.
- If it's several slides-worth of information, create a visible or invisible onscreen button which links to another PDF, then at the end links you back to where you were. You can even have serial links or forks to choose from, in case Prof. Fussbudget's brother also attends.

10.1.3 Multilingual/Multicultural Presentation(s)

It's hard to please your audience more than to have your presentation in their most familiar language. Whether you are presenting to serial audiences having different languages or a single multilingual audience, Scribus can help.

- With the ability that Scribus has to hide or show layers, a single Scribus file can generate all the presentations in whatever languages you might care to use.
- Taking a cue from the non-linear idea above, you can have onscreen buttons to show the same slide in another language as needed – talk about a crowd pleaser!
- We also live in a world where sometimes we must be diplomats. Changing certain images for some audiences might be desirable or necessary.

10.2 Hints

DOWN-SAMPLE all images to 72–96 dpi. Depending on the resolution of the displaying device, you might go as high as 120dpi, but higher will not gain you sharpness. But do this in an image editing program like the GIMP. Then import them into Scribus. A lower DPI value creates a smaller PDF and reduces screen update times.

Embed all fonts or convert them to outlines. This ensures the spacing and layout will remain the same, no matter which platform you are using.

You can use US Letter or A4 in landscape mode for your layout. This will most closely match the screen output of Adobe Reader in full screen mode. If you know the display size of your output device, use a custom page size to create a template of, say 800x600 points – using round numbers may help with proportions and setting up guides.

When displaying images like photos or screen shots, use a black or dark background on your page. They will make the colors more vibrant and give your viewers more contrast to see all the details in your slides.

Use RGB colors for your images and always use Screen/Web for Export. At the same time, use vivid colors sparingly! Use them to guide the eye to what you want your audience to notice, but don't tire them out with rainbows of color.

Load the PDF and run through each page once before giving the presentation, so the file is loaded in memory. This will make for smoother transitions on the screen.

10.3 Settings and Options

PRESENTATION EFFECTS and settings fall into two categories. The first is controlling the transition between pages when running a presentation PDF for example like you would when on stage. There are a variety of effects which are in the dropdown boxes and they are often not only supported in Adobe Reader, but in other PDF viewers like KPDF or Xpdf, for example. Moreover, each page can have its own transition, different from the others.

10.3.1 Effects

Select the page in the list on the left side and set the parameters of the presentation effect on the right side:

- *Display Duration*: Determines how long the page will be shown.
- *Effect Duration*: Determines how long the effect will be shown.
- *Effect Type*: Determines the effect type.
- *Moving Lines*: Sets the direction of moving lines for split and blend effects.

- *From the*: Determines whether the effect will start from the inside or the outside of a page.
- *Direction*: Determines the direction of an effect across the page.

Depending on which effect type is chosen, some of these parameters are not available. With the button "Apply Effect on all Pages," the effect can be applied to all pages instead of just the selected one.

Just because you have these effects, doesn't mean you have to use them. You cannot make an uninteresting presentation interesting with effects, and you risk visually fatiguing your audience. You may actually find that the best transition is a quick fade out of one slide, with quick fade in of the next.

10.3.2 Viewing Options

Viewer options also give you control over how the viewing application will open a presentation. Some of them will only work in Adobe Reader, as they are based on JavaScript commands in the PDF. "Special Actions" are more advanced ways of controlling the viewer on opening, but require custom JavaScript to work. The most important options to check are "Single Page" under "Document Layout" and "Use Full Screen Mode" under "Visual Appearance."

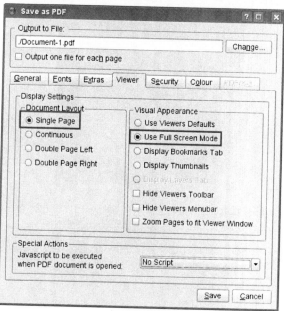

10.4 Graphical Elements for Presentations

MODERN presentations have some elements in common – here you'll learn how to create some of them in Scribus.

Create a rectangular shape with the main color and duplicate it. Round the corners of the duplicate – this is an adjustment in *Properties > Shape*. Fill it with another color (in our example: blue) and put it exactly behind the first rectangle with some offset at the top. The dialog *Windows > Align and Distribute* does a good job here. Duplicate it again, change the color to the color of the first rectangle and put it also behind the first rectangle – with a small offset from the bottom. Now we have got a textbox with rounded corners and a headline in another color. Group all three rectangles, duplicate the whole group and fill them with a shadow-like color. Put this second group behind the first one, with a small offset to the right and the bottom.

A bubble is nothing but a combination of a rectangle with rounded corners and a manually drawn Bézier curve.

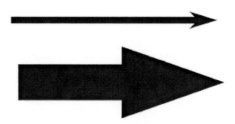

There are two ways to create arrows: a line with an arrow as its head/tail or using a shape. Among the different shapes you'll find some predefined arrows. Lines seem to be a little bit more flexible than the shape-arrows.

These, of course, are just circles with numbers above them, but can be done with a text box over a circle, or make a circle. Use *Convert to … > Text Frame* from the context menu, then insert the text. This might at first seem difficult, but first enter your number with the appropriate size, then in Properties > *Shape*, adjust the top and left distances to center it. Once you have done this, copy 9 times and edit the numbers in the copies.

Next, the header and the footer are placed on a master page of that document, so they are appearing automatically on every page. The page number (*Insert > Character > Page Number*) is also set correctly that way.

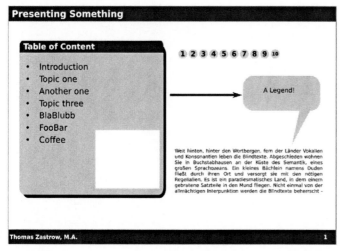

11 The Scripter

11.1 Using Scripts

11.1.1 General

THE SCRIPTER is a plug-in which allows for the use of the Python programming language to carry out a series of operations within Scribus. In general, one should consider using a script whenever there are a series of precise, repetitive tasks you want to do in Scribus, particularly when you will be doing this in a number of documents you create. Another advantage of the Scribus scripting engine – the Scripter – is that you can easily add a feature you are missing by using Python. Python is a powerful, yet easily learned programming language which is readily available for all current operating systems. [1]

There are a number of scripts included with your Scribus distribution which you may find useful for a variety of tasks, but also as examples which you can modify for customized purposes, as well as helping to understand Python syntax and associated Scribus commands. In addition, there are many more to be found on the Scribus Wiki. [2]

The requirements for being able to use Scripter are as follows:

- Python
- Python development libraries if you are going to compile Scribus with Scripter enabled.
- Tk and Tkinter – not always needed, but many of the scripts shipped with Scribus require Tkinter for the creation of various dialogs.
- Some 3rd party scripts may also require PyQt.

There are some fundamental differences between scripts and other functions of Scribus. For instance, a script will perform the task it is written for and then finish. Scripts that use dialogs will close them once they're finished. You have to re-run the script to use it again. Also, scripts can't be translated like other elements of the Scribus user interface. If you want a version of a script in your language, you have to edit the source file yourself. It's also impossible to add tooltips to scripts. Finally, Scribus uses Tk/Tkinter for building a user interface by default. As you will see in the examples below, this user interface toolkit has a different "look and feel" than the rest of the Scribus interface.

11.1.2. Using Scripts

There are three different ways to run a script within Scribus.

- The first is to go on the menu go to *Scripts > Scribus Scripts*, which will show you all of the scripts mentioned above.

Script	Windows	Help	
	Scribus Scripts ▶		BleedAndPrintMarks
	Execute Script...		CalendarWizard
	Recent Scripts ▶		DirectImageImport
	Show Console		DrawGrid
	About Script...		ExtractText
			FontSample
			ImageWizard
			InfoBox
			UnflipContent

- Under *Scripts > Execute Script ...* you will be presented with a file dialog to find your desired script. Some additional scripts can be found in /usr/share/scribus/samples or wherever Scribus is installed, and if you make your own, you can of course save them wherever you like.
- Once you have used a script, it will be saved in a list under *Scripts > Recent Scripts*.

Simply select a script in the file dialog, click "OK," and it will be executed. Be aware that each script will have certain requirements, which, if not met, will generate a failure, hopefully with a helpful error message. For example, some scripts require a document to be open or a frame selected. In case of a failure, the error message will be copied to the clipboard automatically, so that you can copy it into an email program and send it to the author of the script.

[1] http://www.python.org
[2] http://wiki.scribus.net/index.php/Category:Scripts_%26_Plugins

11.2 The Python Console

11.2.1. General

THE PYTHON CONSOLE is a helper tool for small Python code bits. Use standalone scripts when you need to perform complex or repeating tasks. This console might show some unexpected behavior in some cases. You can use the third party Extension Script (IDE) [1] from Henning Schröder in case you're facing some limitations or just when you like to have more functionality.

Since this is not a manual on Python programming, we'll cover just a few elements of console functions. As you see below, in the top of the Console window you enter one or more commands. If a command would result in output such as the `print` command, you will see the results in the bottom part of the window. Scribus commands resulting in changes on the main window produce them there, such as this text frame placed on the document to the left of the console window.

```
Script Console
File  Script

xpos = [ , , , ]
print xpos[ ] * xpos[ ]
print xpos[ ] * xpos[ ]
frame = createText(xpos[ ],xpos[ ],xpos[ ] * xpos[ ],xpos[ ] * xpos[ ])

16
80
```

This simple console is really mainly useful for small parts of a Python program for troubleshooting. It may have trouble interpreting blank lines or indentations, so error messages can sometimes be hard to understand.

11.2.2 The Python Console Menus

- *Open ...* opens a Python script in the console.
- *Save* saves the content of the console editor into a text file with the file extension *.py.
- *Save As ...* saves the content of the console editor into a text file with the file extension *.py.
- *Exit* closes the console window.

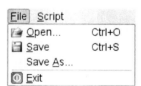

335

- *Run* runs the whole editor text or a selection as one Python statement.
- *Run As Console* runs the statement and waits for next one then. It's the same as in the Python interactive console mode.
- *Save Output ...* saves the current console output into a text file.

11.2.3 Console Configuration

Open *File* > *Preferences* > *Scripter* from the Scribus main window.

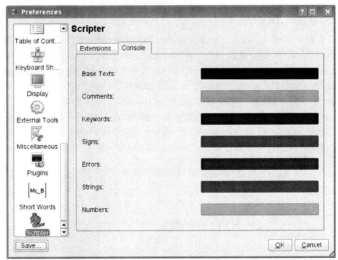

You can change syntax highlighting colors for the console editor in this dialog. There is no need to change it in standard environments, but it's very useful when you are using a dark desktop theme. You can set the console colors as you wish.

[1] http://henning.cco-ev.de/scribus/extensions/ide.py

11.3 Script Info

A programmer can use this feature to provide information about a script. If a user clicks on *Script > About Script* a file dialog appears, in which a Python script can be selected. After selecting a script and clicking "Save," the text will be displayed in the Help Browser.

Python scripts should contain the so-called Docstring. It's a general documentation about a program (script, module, etc.). Let's have a sample script foo.py:

```
""" This is a hello world example. """
if __name__ == '__main__':
    print "Hello World!"
```

The Help Browser will now display the following text:

```
Documentation for: foo.py
This is a hello world example.
```

It is recommended that script authors add the following information to the docstring:

1. Author(s)
2. Copyright and licensing informations
3. A short description of what the script does
4. Basic instructions on use

If the Python script doesn't contain any docstring, it will display the text "Script foo.py doesn't contain any docstring!" and the content of the script is shown instead.

11.4 Extension Scripts

EXTENSION SCRIPTS, like the one mentioned above, can enhance the functionality of Scribus, unlike regular Scripts that merely use the feature set of Scribus. For instance, it is possible to use them to create new palettes and dockable dialogs that can be used as if they were a part of Scribus.

Extension Scripts are mostly like normal Python scripts for Scribus. The most fundamental differences between normal scripts and extensions scripts are that:

- Extension Scripts can create Python objects that continue to exist after the script exits.
- Extension Scripts can create code that runs without blocking the execution of scribus, so it's possible to create floating palettes that can be present while the user works normally with Scribus.
- PyQt works correctly in extension scripts, unlike normal scripts.
- Extension scripts can make changes to the Python environment that will affect scripts run after it. Modules imported by one script can be seen by another, settings changed by one may stay changed, etc.

Since those scripts aren't controlled by the Scribus team, you need to permit their execution before you are able to use them for security reasons. Go to *File > Preferences > Scripter* and check "Enable Extension Script." Now you can load an Extension Script via *Script > Execute Script.*

If you want an Extension Script to be automatically started with Scribus, you can select one by clicking on the "Change ..." button in this tab. You will be presented a file dialog, where you can choose the Extension Script. Note that you can only set a default Extension Script in the *Preferences*, not per document.

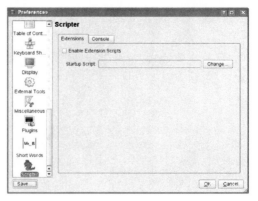

338

11.5 Scribus Scripts

11.5.1 Bleed and Print Marks

Bleed, printing marks, and color bars are currently only found natively in development versions of Scribus. In the meantime, this script provides a workaround for these features in the 1.3.3.x versions. This script gives you choices to independently allow for bleed, crop marks, registration marks, and also adds some information about the PDF outside the margins in the bleed area. It will take a multi-page Scribus document and create individual PDF files for each page. First let's explain a bit about the terminology.

11.5.1.1 Bleed

Bleed as a printing term refers to situations where you want some element of your final document to go completely to the edge of the paper. For example, this might be a photograph or a shape filled with color. The easiest way to ensure this is to print on a sheet of paper larger than your final desired size, after laying out your work, so that your image or shape extends beyond that future edge, then trim down or crop the paper after printing. Standard bleed amounts (the amount your object should extend beyond the final edge of the page) are 1/8 inch (9 pts) in the US and Canada, 3 to 5 mm in Continental Europe, but you should always check with your printer.

Your printing company may indicate it is unnecessary, but in some cases adding crop marks to the page to indicate precisely where you wish the paper to be cut can be useful.

11.5.1.2 Registration Marks

There are various meanings of this term in business and industrial processes, but in our printing context, registration marks are printed in the parts of the paper that will be cropped, and allow for alignment of the paper when a multicolor process is used – the paper will sequentially pass through the equipment for each color printed, and obviously one desires good alignment of these on the page. They are also used to align the print on opposite sides of a sheet of paper. (see Preparing Files for Commercial Printing for more information) It is important that these marks be printed using a color which will appear in each color separation. Here is one registration mark, along with an optional message the script will add.

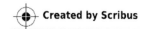 **Created by Scribus**

11.5.1.3 Color Bars

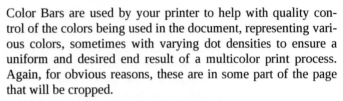

Color Bars are used by your printer to help with quality control of the colors being used in the document, representing various colors, sometimes with varying dot densities to ensure a uniform and desired end result of a multicolor print process. Again, for obvious reasons, these are in some part of the page that will be cropped.

As we see to the left in this partial example from our script, these have associated labels to indicate C, M, Y, and K values.

11.5.1.4 BleedAndPrintMarks.py

In preparation for using this script, make your document in Scribus with the final dimensions you wish it to have, in other words the size after cropping. The script works by creating new, temporary document pages, which are slightly larger than your original, while maintaining the size and relative positions of your original layout. Thus, the script does not modify your original document. Crop marks will be placed to mark your original dimensions. As we will see below, precisely where to place objects to get the result you desire will depend on various dialog entries.

When you run the script, with *Script > Scribus Scripts > BleedandPrintMarks* from the menu, you are presented with a series of dialogs. If you do not have a document open, the script will end with a message to that effect.

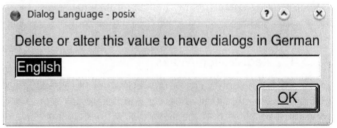

Properly running the script with a document first shows a dialog in which you can choose either the default English or German for dialog messages. Type "German" or "DE," if you wish, but actually anything other than the default chooses German. If you want to add another language, the script is structured so that you can easily add other language phrases – these are not built-in. Ask on the Scribus mailing list if you need help. The "posix" in the title bar is a message indicating this was run on Linux or UNIX – Windows would show "nt."

Next, you can choose a color for your registration and other marks. The default is a registration color – fully saturated in CMYK. You may choose your own if you are not using a four-color process, but importantly, make sure you have created the color and the name is correct.

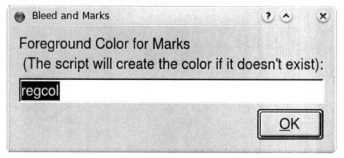

Now choose the directory where you wish your final PDFs to be saved:

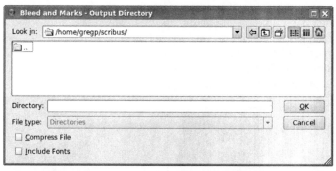

After this, you may edit the file prefix for your PDF files. The default names for your files will be "scribus_print_00001.pdf," "scribus_print_00002.pdf," and so on.

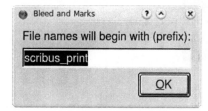

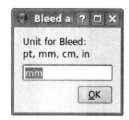

The next dialog will choose the units for your final document and the calculations for various parameters. The default is millimeters – you do not have to choose the units of your original document.

The following dialog will show a different default value depending on the units chosen. The default distance is equal to 20 points, but here we see this amounts to 7 mm. This is the amount to be cropped from the edges of the final paper size.

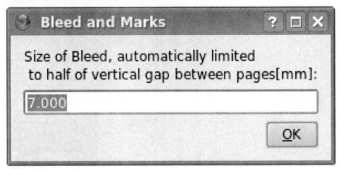

The page layout type will change the behavior of our script. For this script we may choose either a double page layout or single pages – see Opening, Creating and Saving Files, under "New Document Dialog" for more about this. In the script dialog we can choose "dr" for double-sided, first page a right page, "dl" for double-sided, first page left, and "s" for all single pages. Let's look at an artificial example to show what happens when we run our script.

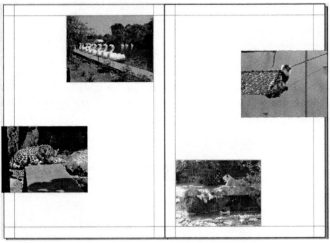

Above are pages 2 and 3 of an A4 document in Scribus where the images have been placed at the outer edges and inner margins of the original paper size. Note that it is up to the person using Scribus to place objects for the appropriate amount of bleed, the script does not do this for you. Here, the far left and far right images each extend 9 pts beyond the edge of the original page.

Here is the output as seen in Adobe Reader – these were individual PDFs from which a montage was created. These final pages are now 14 mm larger than A4 in both height and width, and are marked to be trimmed to A4 size. We anticipate that the left and right images will have about 9 pts trimmed from their outer edges.

Now you have choices for adding these various components individually. Again, ask your printer if these are necessary, useful, or perhaps a hindrance.

Finally, you have the opportunity to add a little message at the bottom of each page, and of course you want to proudly proclaim your use of Scribus, even though you can insert whatever message you prefer.

When you click this last "OK," the script transforms pages one by one, making single-page PDFs.

11.5.1.5 Limitations

- In Windows, a problem can occur if you run the script while you simultaneously have Adobe Reader running, and have opened a file of the same name that the script wishes to create –

the script will fail in this case. This is presumably related to the way Adobe Reader functions in Windows, and does not occur with Linux.

- It is important to use the "dr," "dl," and "s" options correctly for the layout, since results can be quite unexpected otherwise.

- The Scribus document that you begin with will be closed in Scribus, hopefully replaced by one called "tmp.sla," although this one will also not automatically be saved. Therefore, be sure that you have saved your original document before running the script, since there will be no warning or option to save once the script starts.

- There are quite a number of dialogs, and no way to go back or halt the script in the middle. Once you begin, if you should change your mind about an entry you will need to finish the script, then start from the beginning again.

11.5.2 Calendar Wizard

The Calendar Wizard allows you to create good looking calendars in a fast, flexible and comfortable way.

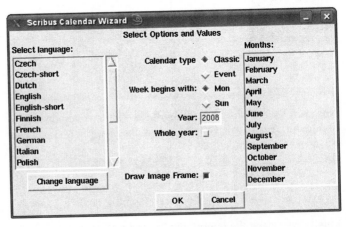

In the list on the left side, you can select the language of your calendar. Select a language and click "Change Language." The "Short" versions in Czech and English refer to the way the days of the week will be written, ie. "Mon" or "Monday" etc. The months in the calendar can be selected in the list on the right side. You can select one or more months by clicking on a name in the list. Clicking again will deselect a month. If you choose the option "Whole year," the script automatically selects all months.

In the field "Year" you can enter the year for which the calendar will be created. The default is the current year. With

"Week begins with" you can decide whether a week begins with Monday (European style) or Sunday (American style).

With "Calendar type" you can create two different kinds of layouts. See the screenshots below for a comparison.

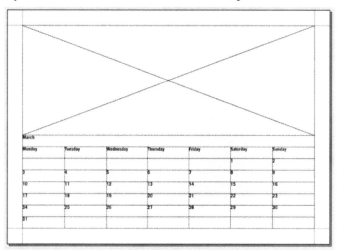

A classic calendar

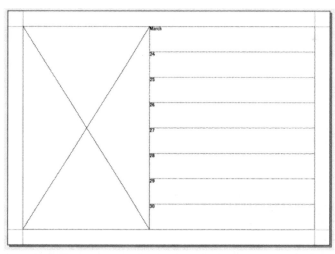

An event calendar

If "Draw Image Frame" is activated, the script will create an empty image frame in the upper or left part of each page, depending on the calendar type.

Clicking "OK" brings up the standard dialog for creating a new Scribus document. Select page size, margin guides etc. as

345

usual. Click "OK," and paragraph style dialog appears. Here you can select the font, its size etc. for your calendar text. Click "OK" again, and the script will create a new Scribus document with the settings you chose.

The resulting Scribus document consists of three layers, "Background," "Calendar Image" (if you decided to use an image frame) and "Calendar." This is important to know, as you have to switch between layers to edit either the image frame or the text frames.

11.5.3 Direct Image Import

If you want to import an image into Scribus, the normal way is to create an image frame and then load the image into this frame. For people who are unfamiliar with DTP programs, this is uncommon.

With this script, you can import an image into Scribus in a way that's more similar to a word processor: just execute the script, and it will open a file dialog, in which you can select an image. The image will be inserted immediately, as the script is drawing a frame and importing the image automatically.

The downside of this approach, compared to the regular procedure, is that you have no control over the size of the frame when it's created, even though you can change it later.

11.5.4 Extract Text

To extract all text from a Scribus file, you can use *Script > Scribus Scripts > ExtractText*. This script will allow you to extract all text from all frames from within Scribus. In addition, it will list all pathnames for images in image frames.

When you start the script, it will ask for a name for the text file to create. As soon as you enter this, it scans your document and creates the file.

Here is an example of the output from this script:

```
Page 1


header: Scribus
An Introductory Manual


body: A very brief intro
Scribus is an open source program for the production
of professional layout targeted toward press-ready
output, as well as other purposes PDFs may be used
for, such as presentations and online document dis-
tribution like this manual. Begun as a personal pro-
ject of Franz Schmid, it has attracted an increasing
number of developers and users. The main sources of
information will be found in the online manual in-
cluded with the Scribus distribution, at
docs.scribus.net, and at wiki.scribus.net. This manu-
al is meant to collect together selected information
from these sources in a format many have requested.
Because Scribus is rapidly changing and improving,
all of the sources of information, and especially
this one may have errors or incomplete instructions,
and in fact this is to be expected for develop-
ment/unstable versions of Scribus. In general this
manual will focus on the current stable version, now
in the 1.3.3.x series, but additional notes may be
included for 1.3.4+ when procedures and requesters
substantially change.
Orientation
Some detailed explanations of DTP (Desktop Publish-
ing) and its differences from wordprocessing can be
found on the Scribus sites. Here we will merely
point out that DTP is the design and layout of vari-
ous elements on the workspace. Your workspace, the
```

Document, is a 2-dimensional area on which you place
the content with high precision. In the screenshot
below, the blank white area whose border is lined in
red and has some light blue margin guides is the
workspace.

On this sample Document, two items or frames
have been placed. The one with a picture in it
is called an image frame, and to its left is a
text frame. To the right of our Document is
the Properties window, which you will find to
be one of the most important if not essential
tools for using Scribus. Note that the image
frame has been selected, since it is outlined
in a dotted red line. For whichever item is selected, the Properties window displays and allows the adjustment of its size, position, and
many other properties.

The display gives the appearance that the image frame is resting on top of the text frame -
- thus a workspace has its elements on various
Levels in relationship to each other. Any new
element added is laid on top of others, but
with the Properties window, one can move
frames and other items up or down Levels. Also
note that our text flows around our image --
this too is selected in the Properties window.
Furthermore, while not depicted in this screenshot, a Document may have one or more Layers,
each Layer being a collection of items on different Levels. This should begin to give you a
sense of the complexity of Scribus and DTP. If
we have Levels, why do we need Layers? A more
detailed explanation and demonstration is
found in the tutorial in the Wiki, but for
this manual let us sum it up by saying that
the Layers allow you to work on selected elements without disturbing others.

Image3: /home/downloads/Scribus/MainScreen.png

Page 2

Text4: Duplication, perhaps linked-to frame

348

11.5.5 Font Sample

The script "Font Sampler" allows you to create a Scribus document, which contains samples of some or all on your installed fonts.

Select the fonts you would like to include in the sample in the left list ("Available Fonts"). The button with one arrow in the middle of the two lists adds the the selected fonts from the left list to the right one ("Selected Fonts"). The button with the two arrows adds all the fonts from the left list to the right one. With the buttons "Up" and "Down" you can control the order of the fonts in the right list. The buttons with arrows to the left can be used to remove entries from the list of selected fonts.

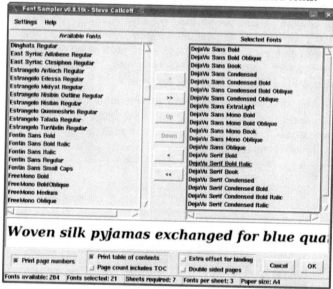

Under the list there's a preview field, where each selected font will be displayed with an English sample text, no matter if it's selected in the right or the left list.

Next you find some options for the layout of the sample document:

- *Print page numbers*: If activated, the Scribus document will contain page numbers at the bottom of each page.
- *Print table of contents*: A table of contents will be added to your document.
- *Page count includes TOC*: If selected, the table of contents will have page numbers too.

- *Extra offset for binding*: Adds some extra space to the left or inner margin for binding.
- *Double sided pages*: The document uses facing pages.

At the bottom of the window, a status bar provides information about the number of detected and selected fonts, the number of sheets required for printing, the number of font examples per page, and the paper size. The latter will be chosen automatically from your default settings.

If you have a great many fonts installed and decide to create a document with samples of most or all of them, executing the script may take a very long time!

11.5.6 InfoBox

Infobox.py is a script for creating smaller frames on top of a text frame, which horizontally exactly fill the space of one or more columns. You can add either a text or image frame, and by entering imageL for frame type, you are then presented with a file dialog to choose the image to load.

Other features are that you can determine the vertical size and vertical placement within the underlying text frame. The new frame also sets text flow around frames for all frames and scales all images to frames.

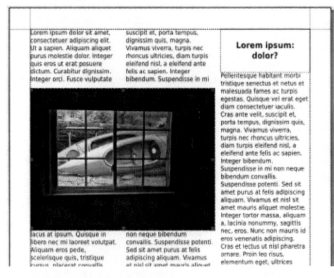

The example above illustrates two successive runs of the program, creating one image infobox, one text infobox (the text content was added afterward).

The script will fail with an appropriate message if you do not meet these requirements:

- You have to run this in Scribus.
- You must have a document open.
- A text frame is selected – it can have one or more columns, and does not have to have content.

After the script analyzes the frame, you then indicate via dialogs:

- How many columns you wish the infobox to spread across.
- If there is only one column this is skipped.
- Which column to start in.
- If there is only one column this is also skipped.
- What height you wish the infobox to be – default is entire height of selected frame. If you are going to load an image, there is no need to change this setting – it will be adjusted automatically.
- Where you want the top of infobox to be – default is top of selected frame, measured from the top of the document.

Now you are presented with a default name for the infobox, which you can change.

Next you select the frame type:

- `text` for text frame – this is the default.
- `imageL` for image frame and file dialog to load image.
- anything else (including blank) for an empty image frame.

At this point, the infobox is created and the script ends. You can run this script again on the same selected frame.

Although there is no Scripter command for "Adjust Frame to Image," the script has a workaround so that you can skip over specifying a height when you load an image from the script.

You cannot have your infobox extend outside your selected frame horizontally in the version that comes with Scribus, but you can do this vertically, depending on the parameters you enter for height and vertical placement.

11.5.7 Unflip Content

The "Unflip Content" script comes in handy if you have to make changes to your layout. Imagine you are working on a document with different margins for left and right pages, and your layout reflects the different margin settings. Imagine further that at some point you have to add a page, for instance to insert a one-page advertisement. You will now have to "flip" all content from left to right and the other way around. Look at the right page below, which then becomes a left page:

We can select all content on a page, group it and then "flip" it, but now the content is also flipped:

Here is where "Unflip Content" comes to the rescue. Select the group on the page (to work reliably, the content has to be grouped) and use *Script > Scribus Scripts > UnflipContent* and voilà: the images and the texts are displayed correctly again:

11.6 Scripting Basics

SCRIPTS are plain text files, and Python programs should have a .py extension – this extension is not a requirement per se, but for one thing, the file dialog uses this as a filter for its default behavior, and this is a general convention in Python script writing.

The first line of your file must begin with

```
#!/usr/bin/env python
```

or some equivalent, so that your operating system knows this is a Python script and where to find Python on your system.

The next line is strongly recommended, and if included must be the second line of the file:

```
# -*- coding: utf-8 -*-
```

which tells Python the character encoding for the file. Alternative choices to utf-8 might be latin-1 or ascii, which depend on your operating system and the editor which generated the script.

Individual comments can be inserted beginning with #. Use these to help others (and yourself for that matter) understand what the script is doing at certain points if it isn't obvious. In many cases, thoughtfully choosing variable names can avoid the need for comments.

Other than this, it is strongly suggested to have several comment lines, demarcated by """ at beginning and end, which indicate the author(s) of the script, its purpose and perhaps some brief instructions on use, since this will be displayed to users trying to understand what a script does and how it is used. If you look at *Script > About Script ... > ExtractText*, you will see how Scribus shows the following information:

```
"""

(C)2006.03.04 Gregory Pittman

(C)2008.02.28 Petr Vanek - fileDialog replaces value-
Dialog

this version 2008.02.28

This program is free software; you can redistribute
it and/or modify

it under the terms of the  GPL, v2 (GNU General Pub-
lic License as published by

the Free Software Foundation, version 2 of the Li-
cense), or any later version.
```

See the Scribus Copyright page in the Help Browser
for further informaton

about GPL, v2.

SYNOPSIS

This script takes the current document and extracts
all the text from text frames,

and also gets the pathnames to all images. This is
then saved to a file named

by the user.

REQUIREMENTS

You must run from Scribus and must have a file open.

USAGE

Start the script. A file dialog appears for the name
of the file

to save to. The above information is saved to the
file.

"""

After this, the actual Python commands begin. An important
and usually essential one in our context is to tell Python to also
look for Scripter commands in Scribus. We do this either with

```
import scribus
```

or

```
from scribus import *
```

The former is preferred, since the latter choice will load all of
Scripter's commands into Python, while import scribus only
loads them as needed, and also avoids confusion both to
someone reading the script and to Python when two modules
might have the same command. Be aware, though, that you
must indicate to Python that a command is from Scribus with a
prefix, and this includes predefined constants like ICON-
_WARNING:

```
import scribus
#
# other lines of code
#
if not scribus.haveDoc():
        scribus.messageBox('Scribus - Script Error',
"No document open", scribus.ICON_WARNING,
scribus.BUTTON_OK)
        sys.exit(1)
pagenum = scribus.pageCount()
```

where, for example, pageCount() is the actual Scripter command. Otherwise, we could have:

```
from scribus import *
#
# other lines of code
#
if not haveDoc():
        messageBox('Scribus - Script Error', "No docu-
ment open", ICON_WARNING, BUTTON_OK)
        sys.exit(1)
pagenum = pageCount()
```

A list of all Scripter commands is available via the Help Browser.

12 Tips and Tricks

12.1 Creating a Tiled Image

This tip shows how a collection of shapes can be used to create an irregular image frame. The techniques used are duplicate/multiple duplicate of shapes, combining them as polygons and then converting to an image frame.

- Create a rectangular shape. In the example, it has a width and a height of 16 mm. Of course, any other type of shape can be used.

- With the menu command *Item > Multiple Duplicate*, create 7 duplicates with a horizontal shift of 18 mm and a vertical shift of 0 mm.

- Group the resulting 8 rectangles.

- Multiply the resulting group again 5 times, with a horizontal shift of 0 and a vertical shift of 18 mm. This results in a two-dimensional group of rectangles, looking like a fence.

- At your option, ungroup the first row and change the position of the first rectangle. Resize it, rotate it, or whatever you like.

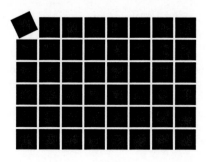

- Now, select all the rectangles and combine the polygons with *Item > Combine Polygons*.
- Apply *Item > Convert to > Image Frame*.
- Last, but not least, load an image into your new image frame.

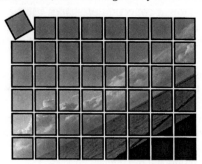

12.2 Creating a Circled Diagram

A diagram in circle style, often useful for presentations. It uses combined and grouped polygons and other elements, duplicating, a lot of rotating and the Attach Text to Path function.

- Create two round shapes, one of them a bit smaller than the other. Keep a copy of the smaller circle – you'll need it later for creating the text! To make an exact copy, select the circle, pressing Ctrl-C and then Ctrl-V, and now move the smaller circle. You will find there are two on top of each other. Hint: Holding down the Shift key as you make your circle keeps it from being an ellipse.
- Put one of the smaller circles in the middle of the bigger one. Now select both circles (you can do this by clicking and dragging a selection box around the two circles). Next, in the menu bar, use the command *Item > Combine Polygons*. This combines the two and creates a ring. Set the stroke color to "None" and the fill color to whatever you like.

- Now we build the arrows. Create a new triangular shape and use the same fill color you applied to the ring. Set the stroke color to white.
- Rotate the triangle, so that it points to one of the four directions we'll need.

- Place the triangle at its correct position above the ring.
- To hide the triangle's white stroke above the ring on the triangle's long side, just draw a small, filled rectangular shape without the stroke's color above the triangle.
- Group the triangle and the rectangle, create three duplicates, rotate the duplicates so that they are pointing to the four directions and place them above the ring.

- Now we add the text, using the copy of the small circle you made, but consider that you may want to go to Properties > *Shape > Edit Shape* to slightly enlarge it, since what you actually want is your text on an imaginary rim slightly larger than the smaller circle. Convert it to a Bézier curve. Create a text frame with your text and use *Item > Attach Text to Path*. Move this text until it has its correct position on the ring. You may need to adjust font size and spacing until it fits perfectly, and you can also further edit the circle after you have applied the text. See the section Attach Text to Path if you need more help.

- The text on the path is still editable – create three copies of the first text-on-path item, use the Story Editor to edit their content and move and rotate until the texts are all in the desired place above the ring. Once you have completed this project, select them all, then *Item > Group* to place the entire ensemble precisely where you want it.

- Now that you've gone through this process, remember that Scribus may offer more than one way to accomplish your end result. For example, you could have started with a single circle shape, made the fill color "None," made a copy for your text on path work, then increased line width of the original to a large number, say 40 to 50 pts, then added the triangles. You could also have done all the text at once in a long string, adding spaces in between word groups as needed to get them spaced properly around the circle. Neither one of the methods is inherently any better, though one may seem easier for you.

12.3 Creating Borders

For certificates, images or similar things sometimes complex borders are needed. This is a very simple trick that uses the duplicating functions for some shapes and – at your option – the combining of shapes. The results can be used in a lot of ways.

- We start with the creation of a polygon or a shape which will be the basis for the border. In this case, it's a polygon with four corners.
- Use *Item > Multiple Duplicate* and create 10 – or any other number of – duplicates with a horizontal shift that is slightly smaller than the width of the original shape. Vertical shift is 0.
- At your option, use *Item > Combine Polygons*.
- Duplicate the resulting object, rotate it and build a border for an image.

- With some white circles, combined with a paper-colored rectangle, you can build a memo.

- By the way, this seems to be the only way to build a dotted line from circles in Scribus:

⊙⊙⊙⊙⊙⊙⊙⊙⊙⊙⊙⊙⊙⊙⊙⊙⊙⊙⊙⊙⊙⊙⊙⊙⊙⊙ ⊙⊙⊙⊙⊙⊙⊙⊙⊙⊙⊙⊙⊙⊙⊙⊙⊙⊙⊙⊙⊙⊙⊙

12.4 Text Over Images

When placing a text frame over an image, the problem often occurs that the color of the text and the underlying images are interfering. Here are two simple tricks to avoid this.

- Create a rectangular shape with approximately the same size as your text frame, fill it with white or another color, set its opacity to 30% or another value smaller than 100% and put it under your text, but above the image:

- Create a text frame for your text, convert it to outlines by using *Item > Convert to Outlines*. Move it over a shape, for example a rectangular. Select both objects and use *Item > Combine Polygons*. If you move the new object over an image now , the image can be seen through the text:

- The "wave" has been produced in a similar way: I started with a rectangular shape. By using "Edit Shapes > Move Control Points" in the *Shape* tab of the Properties Palette, the points of the shape can be rearranged and changed to curves:

- In this case, a polygon with 7 corners and an applied factor of -45 was used to create a star. As described above, the price is "embossed" into the star and a duplicate of the result is used as a shadow:

And this is the result:

12.5 Filling Text With an Image

Please note that the effect probably needs a lot of computing power when it's applied to a larger text!

- Create a text frame and type your text, or load it from a file. Use a strong and bold font.
- Convert the text frame with *Item > Convert to* to outlines.
- Use *Item > Combine Polygons*.
- Change the new polygon via *Item > Convert to* to an image frame.
- Load an image into the new shape.
- At your option, play around with the fill and line color. In this case both are set to "none":

In a similar way, you can create "letters consisting of letters."

- Create a text frame and type one letter in it. Use a strong and bold font. Increase the size of that letter to a high value.

- Convert the text frame with the letter inside to outlines.

- Now, convert it back to a text frame.

- Double click it or use the Story Editor to add a lots of the same letters to that text frame:

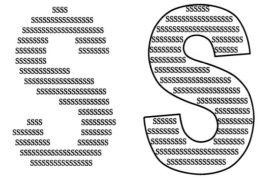

12.6 Custom Frames

At first glance, frames in Scribus are always rectangular. But that's not true: a frame in Scribus can have an arbitrary form. There are two ways to obtain a non-rectangular frame in Scribus:

- Create a (rectangular) frame in Scribus and edit it as described in Working with Frames.

- Create the outer form of the frame in an external application like Inkscape and import it into Scribus as vector graphic via Menu *File > Import*. SVG, PostScript (PS) or Encapsulated PostScript (EPS) are suitable for this purpose.

- Use the menu *Item > Convert to*, and choose either image frame or text frame

Now you can handle the new text or image frame in the same way as you do it with other frames:

The vector graphic you import into Scribus should contain only one path. If there is more than one path in the file, Scribus will convert only the first one.

12.7 A Rising Sun Text on Path

Here is an example of an interesting effect combining "Attach Text to Path" with other graphics.

Start out with a semi-circle – here, one of the shapes is used, but of course with Scribus there are many ways to get this result. Make a copy of this since we'll need it later – slide it off to the side. Take the original and in the context menu click *Convert to > Bezier Curve*.

Now for the rays for our sun, we'll use the inverted question mark: ¿

Make a text frame, then enter about 15 or so of those inverted question marks – find them in *Insert > Glyph*, or press F12, then "00bf" (without quotes). So now your have your text, your Bezier curve, so select both, then use *Item > Attach Text to Path*.

What you will find is that your question marks follow your path, but may not start at your sun's horizon. Also you see your sun has disappeared, and check "Show Path" in the *Shape* tab of the Properties Palette won't make it appear. This is where your copy of your semi-circle can now be slid into place. In Properties: *Shape > Start Offset* adjust to get your characters above the horizon.

You will probably need to adjust your font size – this example used Nimbus Roman Bold, 20pt – and perhaps kerning. Finally, make your background sky using a frame with a blue background.

This final example adds a radial fill gradient to our sun – and of course you could use a gradient for the sky as well.

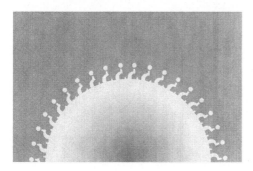

12.8 Footnotes

Scribus doesn't support footnotes yet, and unfortunately, loading texts with foot- or endnotes into scribus doesn't work with OpenOffice.org or ODT files. In Scribus versions prior to 1.3.3.12 the text ends after the last foot-/endnote, and the notes themselves appear in the text where the foot-/endnote mark is placed. Since 1.3.3.12 the situation has improved, but now all footnotes are stripped during import, so that one has to save and load them separately.

There is, however, an easy workaround for the problem. Write your text in OpenOffice.org/StarOffice and save it as a HTML file. Then import the HTML file into Scribus. All text is preserved, including foot-/endnotes, which are placed at the end of the text.

Note that you still have to place your footnotes manually if the text or the text frames are changing, but at least all of them are imported correctly and placed as separate items.

13 Your DTP Toolbox

13.1 GIMP

It's no stretch of the truth to call GIMP [1] the most versatile image editing application for Linux, and the latest version, 2.6, has added a very large number of significant improvements.

What we want to cover here are some of the adjustments in setting up GIMP for print work with Scribus.

- Make sure you have the latest 2.6.x stable version.

- GIMP now can work with CMYK colors. While the color model internally is still RGB plus alpha channels, you can use CMYK measurements and CMYK color definitions. To supplement this, there is a third party plug-in called separate+, which can export CMYK TIFF, using a neat trick with alpha layers. The separate+ plug-in can also embed ICC profiles into the exported file and create duotone TIFF.

- One of the really appreciated improvements is the text handling. GIMP 2.x uses fontconfig, so finding the fonts on your system is now much easier. Text can be kept in a separate layer to ease editing and correcting. In the 1.2.x versions certain type of handling were difficult, but there is little to complain about now. It is a pleasure to use the new text controls. In addition, there is also a separate freetype plug-in for GIMP, which allows you to manipulate type in the same means Scribus and Inkscape do. You can find this on the ftp.gimp.org site.

- Most recent versions of GIMP can export all paths as clipping paths in TIFF files and have much better support for clip paths in TIFF import as well.

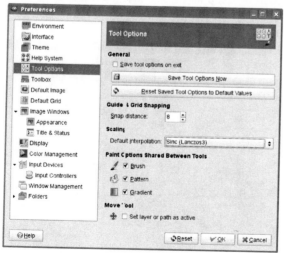

• The way that pixels are adjusted (interpolated) in filters and effects are applied use Linear as the default. While this is a good compromise for speed vs. accuracy, Lanczos should almost always be the default for print work. At the same time, expect many operations, (re-scaling, filter application) to run slower. Using Lanczos can sometimes create a dramatic difference in the perceived print quality of an image, so make sure GIMP is using it by default.

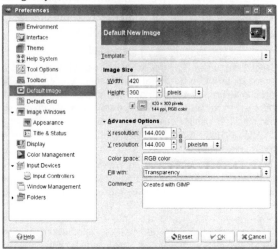

Like most image editors, GIMP's defaults are set up primarily for web site images, meaning too little resolution for print. So the first thing to do is set the defaults to a minimum of 144 DPI in resolution. Remember using these higher resolutions will result in much larger size files, so it may be necessary to adjust maximum settings for memory usage as well in GIMP preferences.

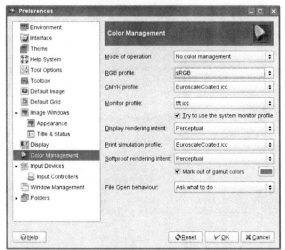

The other notable addition is the beginnings of some very basic color managed "soft proofs" of your images. This is available via littlecms, also used by Scribus, and you can set this in the preferences. It can help by allowing you to see how your image will look when transformed into a CMYK color space when it is printed or exported as PDF.

[1] www.gimp.org

13.2 Krita

Rising like Phoenix from the ashes, Krita [1], a part of the KDE Office suite, has become a wonderful application focused on natural painting. Using a brushes metaphor on screen, it has some innovative and quite interesting features like the ability to emulate the way watercolors dry on canvas, a filters gallery to display previews of each filter, adjustment layers, layer groups and tools to precisely manipulate brush strokes. That alone would be worth adding it to your publishing toolbox for the occasional artwork.

While it's not as versatile as GIMP with respect to image editing, it can also be used for many editing operations on existing pictures, partly thanks to its impressive collection of image filters.

The bonus for Scribus users is its versatile handling of a large number of formats and color spaces. Not only RGB, but CMYK, Grayscale (up to 16 bit), LMS, YCbCr and L*a*b are handled using the same littlecms color engine as Scribus. Krita fully supports RGB to CMYK conversion in a simple and easy to use manner, but can also convert 16-bit images into 8-bit to import into Scribus (Scribus 1.3.3.x doesn't yet support 16-bit images).

Notes:

- There is one limitation in the current 1.6.x Krita in the way resolution works when Krita writes an image to disk. Thus, Scribus
will always interpret the resolution as 72 DPI, which is not usually high enough for good quality print, so rescaling may need
to be done within Scribus.

- Krita is only available on BSD, Linux, MacOSX (via fink) and
UNIX. Krita 2 is expected to be available as a native Win32 and
OS X application.

- For importing into Scribus, exporting TIFF from Krita with
LZW compression should yield good results, and Krita reliably
embeds ICC profiles into the images to make color matching
from print to screen much easier.

[1] http://www.koffice.org/krita

13.3 digiKam

digiKam [1] is a tool for managing a large collection of images. It imports images from hard drives or via the integrated interface from digital cameras. Images are organized in hierarchical albums and can be tagged, which helps with abstracting content from particular collections.

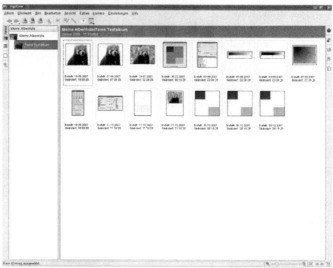

digiKam relies on both internal and external (KIPI plug-ins) tools to edit images. These tools include (but aren't limited to) contrast-brightness, color balance and hue-saturation adjustments, fixing white balance, sharpening, removing digital noise, cropping. digiKam uses DCRaw to process RAW images from over 200 camera models. It also handles meta information like EXIF and XMP tags and supports color management. Images can be shown as a slideshow and exported in several ways, including a function for creating calendars and web galleries.

While still young, digiKam is developing quickly, and it's on the way to become a viable Free alternative to Lightroom or Aperture.

[1] http://www.digikam.org

13.4 Gwenview

Gwenview [1] is an image viewer for KDE. It's fast, light-weight, and you can browse your images without importing them. Gwenview can display a variety of bitmap as well as some vector graphic formats (SVG, EPS).

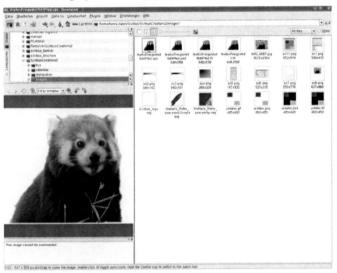

Gwenview handles EXIF information and can apply rudimentary manipulations to images. Collections of images can be displayed as a slideshow or exported in several ways – for instance an HTML gallery or a collection of several pages as one big image. Its functionality can be extended with plug-ins.

[1] http://gwenview.sourceforge.net

13.5. XNview

Considering that there are a number of image previewer/thumb nailing applications – even Konqueror and Nautilus have some of these features – why should anyone pick XNview [1], especially since it's not Free Software and only gratis for personal use?

Yes, its ugly, it uses old, Motif type libraries, but it has three very important redeeming qualities:

1. Its very fast, as fast as or faster than many similar applications.

2. It handles a wide array of image formats with very good conversion capabilities. There are even some very obscure file formats XNview can open and convert, and probably only ImageMagick and GraphicsMagick can handle a larger number.

3. It's an excellent batch converter.

It's very stable and worth at least adding to your graphics toolbox.

[1] http://perso.wanadoo.fr/pierre.g/xnview/enhome.html

13.6 IrfanView

Like XNview, IrfanView [1] is a versatile image viewer available as freeware for personal and educational use. It's only available for Windows, but runs without major issues in WINE on Linux.

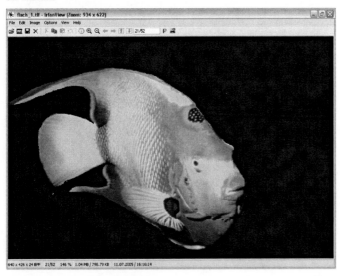

Some if its advantages are:
- Many supported file formats.
- Support for Adobe Photoshop filters.
- Multi-page TIFF editing.
- Support for embedded ICC color profiles in JPG and TIFF files.
- You can edit embedded IPCT data.
- You can change the color depth of images.
- Basic image editing features.

[1] http://www.irfanview.net

13.7 ImageMagick and GraphicsMagick

ImageMagick [1] and GraphicsMagick [2] (a fork of the former) are command line image converter processors. While there exists a UI display program called "Display," they are powerful in three ways:

- Batch conversion of image files
- Their ability to handle a wide range of image formats
- The newest versions understand color management and use littlecms, just like Scribus

Each program is something of a black box for image processing, but incredibly powerful when used properly. Versions for Linux, Windows and MacOSX are available.

[1] http://www.imagemagick.org
[2] http://www.graphicsmagick.org

13.8 Inkscape

Inkscape [1] is a versatile Open Source vector drawing program, which may be compared to Adobe Illustrator, CorelDraw or Xara Xtreme. It can be used to create simple shapes as well as logos, technical drawings or artistic pictures and is available for Linux, Mac OS X and Windows. Inkscape provides a user friendly interface, with extensive tooltips and a couple of really well done short tutorials on vector drawings. Almost every function can be accessed via keyboard shortcuts (the list of shortcuts is almost 10 pages).

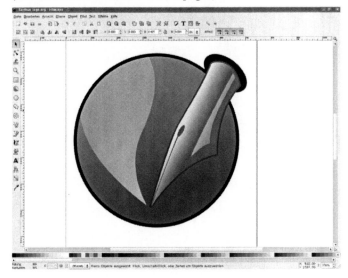

Originally a fork of the Sodpodi drawing program, Inkscape is primarily designed as an SVG editor [2]. Its main purpose is to produce files that are 100% compliant to the SVG specifications. The program is developing extremely fast, and despite its low version number already provides many features that commercial applications don't have. Among them is a very powerful tracing tool for the conversion of bitmap images to vector data, whose features and reliability are lacking in most equivalent commercial programs. The release notes of the current version 0.46 are a mere 43 A4 pages, if printed out. Some of its highlights are:

- SVG effects
- Blur effects for vector drawings
- Live path effects

- The ability to sculpt vector objects
- 3D boxes
- Enhanced text features
- Color management
- Bitmap effects (via ImageMagick)
- A paint bucket tool
- An engraver's toolbox in the calligraphic tools

Inkscape can also import several other vector (eg. PostScript, Adobe Illustrator, PDF or CorelDraw) and bitmap formats (eg. TIFF, BMP, PNG etc.). PDF export has seen major improvements in 0.46, thanks to the use of the Cairo graphics library.

[1] http://www.inkscape.org
[2] See Importing Vector Drawings for more information about SVG.

13.9 Squiggle

"Batik" is a collection of Apache XML modules for on the fly export/conversion of SVG. One of the really useful tools in the collection is Squiggle [1], a Java application for simply viewing SVG.

Why bother? Call it the sober judge of SVG. Of all of the SVG viewers, it is probably one of, if not, the one that complies with the SVG specification most. If you receive or create an SVG and it won't import properly, see how it views with Squiggle. If it does not display properly, it is more than likely an issue with the creating application. The one exception to this is SVG exported from Adobe Illustrator, which often has Adobe only extensions included in the SVG file, thus only viewable in Adobe SVG viewers or applications.

[1] http://xmlgraphics.apache.org/batik/tools/browser.html

13.10 UniConvertor

UniConvertor [1] is a universal vector graphics translator for the command line. It's based on Python and uses the sK1 [2] engine to convert from one format to another. One of its major advantages is its ability to convert various closed source formats, which are rarely supported by most Open Source drawing programs, especially CorelDraw 7–X4 (CDR/CDT/CCX/CDRX/CMX), Adobe Illustrator up to version 9 (Post-Script based AI files) and AcornDraw (AFF). These formats can be converted to SVG files, so that they can be used in Scribus.

To use UniConvertor, you have to install Python and the Python Imaging Library. Binary packages for Linux, Windows and Mac OS X as well as the source code are available.

The use of UniConvertor is simple. On the command line, enter the directory where the file you want to convert is located, then type:

```
uniconv drawing.cdr drawing.svg
```

This command will convert the CorelDraw file drawing.cdr into drawing.svg, provided it doesn't contain any text, as text can't be handled by UniConvertor yet.

The Scribus team is currently working on integration of Uni-Convertor into future versions of Scribus.

[1] http://sk1project.org/modules.php?name=Products&product=uniconvertor
[2] http://sk1project.org

13.11 Adobe Reader

Adobe Reader [1] 8.1+ is one of the essential tools to have when using Scribus. Although mostly a file viewer, it has some advanced features, which no other PDF viewer has: full support for JavaScript with a PDF and detailed information which is embedded in the PDF, but viewable only in Adobe Reader. Scribus is unique in the Linux/UNIX world for its ability to create scriptable, interactive PDF forms.

For judging colors or correctness, the Mac Preview application, KPDF, Evince or any other PDF viewer are definitely not recommended – this is where Adobe Reader excels.

13.11.1 Hints for Scribus Users:

It's strongly recommended to always use the latest Adobe Reader. Simply put, there is nothing else more capable of rendering PDF files correctly. Whatever your objections were to older versions (and there were some substantial ones, most notably on Linux), the later versions, especially those from 7.0.9 onwards, ameliorate the vast majority of them. It is far more stable, bug free, and loads quicker than earlier versions. On Linux it now has a modern look and feel. Versions after 7.0.9 also have direct support for CUPS, which allows many extra options for printing. Any PDF rendering issues with Scribus exported PDF in other viewers should be cross-checked with Adobe Reader before reporting bugs to the Scribus developers.

Some color mismatches may occur when viewing PDFs which have some kinds of transparency in PDF 1.4 files: Unfortunately, whenever there is an extended graphics state parameter dictionary present which contains any transparency blend space operators, Adobe Reader 7.x or later switches into CMYK mode showing incorrect colors. The issue has been confirmed even with files not generated by Scribus.

13.11.2 Tweaking the Viewer Preferences

You will find that getting the preferences right in Adobe Reader is important to improve the reliability when working with Scribus. There are many settings in the preferences in Reader 8, but the page display part is arguably the most important.

Please spend the time to set up this dialog properly for optimized viewing of Scribus-created PDFs.

Ensure "Smooth Text," "Smooth Line Art" and "Smooth Images" are enabled, since they apply a bit of anti-aliasing when viewing. In case you send someone a Scribus-created PDF and they complain that the text or gradients look like barbed wire or are "banded," advise them to enable these settings which are commonly available in Adobe Reader at least since version 7, and regardless of platform.

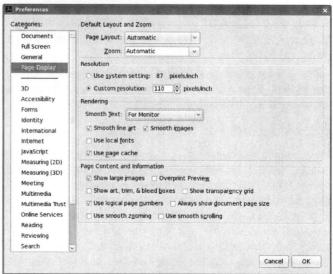

There is another option called "Use Local Fonts." What this choice does is enable Adobe Reader to use locally installed fonts which are named in the PDF, if it can find them in your font path. It's recommended to disable this for use with Scribus, because often PDFs you create in Scribus will be sent to other users. What you will want in most cases is a realistic view as it will be seen by anyone viewing this file. Thus, the only reliable way of ensuring your doc will view properly anywhere is to embed the fonts. You can also convert to outlines in the "Fonts" tab of the PDF export dialog to save file size. This is particularly important when you are using the Ghostscript fonts, like the Nimbus family. Adobe Reader does a poor job of simulating them with its own built-in fonts.

If you are creating Scribus files with transparency effects and export PDF 1.4 or higher (PDF 1.3 does not support transparency), you can enable "Show Transparency Grid." Be aware, though, that your page will also be displayed as transparent, unless you created a shape with a different color as a page background, just as we did in the Quick Start Guide.

Next, looking at the Reader window below, there are 2 features which can be useful:

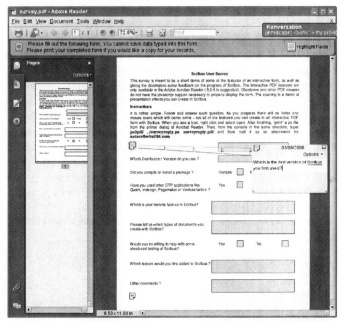

- Thumbnails are useful for navigating – Scribus can optionally embed these in the PDF when exporting.
- Notes which are non-printing can be used to give definitions or hints in a document. Most important is "Document Information." Within Scribus *File > Document Setup > Document Information* there is a panel to enter author and title of the document. See Customizing Scribus for more information.

[1] http://www.adobe.com/products/reader

13.12 GSview

The first thing to mention is that, according to Peter Linnell, a Scribus developer and professional pre-press consultant, GSview [1] is a superior replacement for gv and derivatives on Linux/UNIX. Moreover, for viewing PDF for print purposes, it is more reliable than any other open source PDF viewer. Although Adobe Reader is sometimes a better pure viewer for PDF, GSview is one of the most essential tools to have when using Scribus. GSview has a handful of extremely useful functions. For those unfamiliar with the program, it provides an easy to use "front end" to Ghostscript, as well as pstoedit for converting bitmaps into vector files. For those coming from the Windows/Mac world, it also has the functionality of Adobe Acrobat Distiller with a graphical front end for those applications which do not export PDF natively.

It is important that you have the latest version 4.7 or later (GSview migrated from the Windows world, where it has been excellent since the 4.x versions).

For use with Scribus, GSview has the following features:

- With the help of pstoedit, you can convert bitmap images or PDF content back into SVG and other scalable vector file formats (via *Edit > Convert to vector format ...*).
- The ability to preview, convert and add previews (TIFF recommended) to raw EPS (Encapsulated PostScript Files). This is done using epstool from the same author. Epstool can also fix EPS files with incorrect or missing bounding boxes. This is a separate tool to be installed and works as a plug-in like pstoedit.

- The ability to extract text from a PDF.
- An easy-to-use interface for creating PDFs in applications without the high level of export capabilities of Scribus. (You are still recommended to use the PDF export of Scribus, as it is optimized for Scribus files).
- It's an easy to use front end to Ghostscript's less well known features such as image conversion and re-sampling. There are others in Ghostscript including: converting between TIFF formats, changing the color depth of at TIFF, JPEG or the color space of an image.

One example where GSview can be used with Scribus is for troubleshooting/fixing EPS files which do not display correctly within Scribus. Although many applications can generate EPS files, some add their own quirks into the EPS, which can cause problems when used in other applications (like Scribus).

So, if you find difficulty with an EPS or PDF you wish to use in Scribus, open the EPS in GSview. Then, use the key command M to display messages from Ghostscript. The messages can indicate problems which cause display or printing errors. You can also use the epswrite "device" to re-save the EPS, which can help to strip out or fix issues with an EPS.

You can also rasterize an EPS image like this, by converting to PNG or TIFF and then resize, adjust colors etc. with an image editing program like GIMP or Adobe Photoshop.

Since version 4.3, GSView has been, in the experience of the Scribus developers, the most reliable and versatile PDF viewer along with Adobe Reader on Linux. For DTP with Scribus and Free Software, it's considered to be essential.

[1] http://pages.cs.wisc.edu/~ghost/gsview

13.13 KPDF/XPDF

KPDF [1] is the PDF viewer of KDE, and it's based On XPDF [2]. It's a very fast and lightweight alternative to Adobe Reader, and it will also view PS files by converting to PDF. KPDF contains most of the common functionality you need to deal with PDF files:

- Display of document properties and embedded fonts
- Navigating through PDF files via thumbnails
- A print preview
- Search for text strings
- Select a part of a PDF file as text or image
- Display options for PDF files
- Transparency support (PDF 1.4 or higher)
- Presentation effects

Don't forget to look through Settings and enable "aggressive" in the performance options, if you have the required memory. Enabling this makes a big difference in loading larger or complex documents. You still might want XPDF 3.02+ from Foolabs, as it includes some command line tools for converting PDFs to PS. To display properly embedded fonts with XPDF in all PDFs, not just Scribus ones, you should read the XPDF man page about setting up the fonts paths correctly via the .xpdfrc file. One known limitation is the inability to display transparency in Scribus generated PDFs.

In KDE 4, KPDF will be replaced by Okular [3], a versatile document reader. It uses the Poppler library [4] for PDF rendering. Among others, it can display many more PDF features than KPDF, and it can also read PostScript and XPS files.

[1] http://kpdf.kde.org
[2] http://www.foolabs.com/xpdf
[3] http://okular.kde.org/
[4] http://poppler.freedesktop.org/

13.14 jPDF Tweak

jPDF Tweak [1] is a Java application that can be used to join, split and modify PDF files. It uses the very robust iText [2] library for manipulating PDFs. While many features of the program are already available in PDFs generated by Scribus, others are not.

Here's an (incomplete) list of jPDF Tweak's additional features:

- Adding watermarks
- Changing page numbers
- Signing PDF files
- Shuffling pages for booklet printing and similar tasks

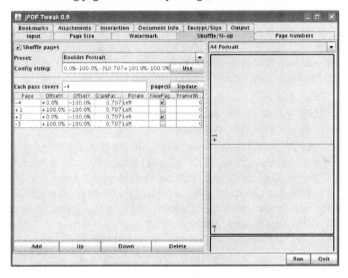

For more information about jPDF Tweak's features and instructions on use, see the online manual [3].

To run jPDF Tweak, you need Java 5 or newer.

[1] http://jpdftweak.sourceforge.net
[2] http://www.lowagie.com/iText
[3] http://jpdftweak.sourceforge.net/manual/index.html

13.15 OpenOffice.org

OpenOffice.org [1] and its commercial twin StarOffice [2] are both ideal complements to Scribus. In Basic Concepts the importance of a good workflow has already been mentioned. Text should ideally be prepared in a word processor, and OpenOffice.org/StarOffice Writer is one of the best programs of its kind. Moreover, its file formats, SXW and ODT (an open standard to which both office suites are reference implementations) are supported by Scribus (see Working with Text).

But there's more to it – both office suites can be regarded as digital translators, as they offer dozens of import and export filters for file formats that Scribus can't handle (yet), eg. WordPerfect, Rich Text Format, Lotus WordPro, Works, or DocBook. With OpenOffice.org/StarOffice you can also convert many proprietary graphics formats like WMF, EMF, or even old OS/2 Metafiles (MET) into formats that can be imported natively by Scribus, eg. SVG, EPS or ODG. See Importing Vector Drawings for further information.

Thus, OpenOffice.org or StarOffice are more than just full-fledged office suites for your workflow; they are also extremely powerful file converters.

OpenOffice.org is an open source project, which is supported by, among others, SUN Microsystems, IBM and Novell. SUN and IBM both sell commercial versions based on the OpenOffice.org source code, StarOffice and Lotus Symphony [3] respectively. While the latter is designed to integrate with the IBM application stack, notably Lotus Notes and Lotus Domino, StarOffice is almost the same as OpenOffice.org.

From the user's perspective, the additional value of StarOffice consists in better dictionaries, a printed manual and support by SUN. SUN also offers enterprise solutions for StarOffice, like the StarOffice document server. On the other hand, OpenOffice.org offers much better language support, having been translated to almost 100 languages, and OpenOffice.org is available for more platforms than StarOffice. Currently, Windows, Linux, Solaris, *BSD and Mac OS X are supported.

[1] http://www.openoffice.org
[2] http://sun.com/software/star/staroffice
[3] http://symphony.lotus.com

13.16 LProf

For those running *BSD, Linux or UNIX, LProf [1] is an essential tool for making color management work reliably in Scribus. Why is this? LProf is like sending your monitor to an eye doctor!

LProf is the only graphical tool available on Linux and UNIX that is capable of creating ICC monitor, camera or scanner profiles. It also works on Windows and, soon, Mac OS X. It helps to make color managed previews more accurate. Think of a monitor profile as a set of glasses which magically transform your eyes to see with perfect color balance. Within Scribus, a correct monitor profile can make a big difference in viewing accurately how your print or PDF will appear on a PostScript printer or when printed commercially. Without an individual profile of your monitor – no two monitors are alike – you have no real assurance the color transforms will be anywhere near close, when you are for example sending PDFs to a printer.

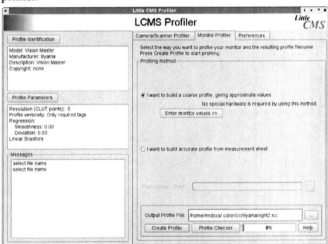

LProf has a simple step-by-step method to walk you through creating a profile of your monitor, which then can be used in Scribus. You should take the 5 minutes it takes to create a profile and then add this to your Scribus color management preferences. LProf can also create profiles for your scanner or digital camera. A look at LProf's documentation will give you a more detailed understanding of its capabilities.

The currently available released version doesn't allow using calibration devices yet. Adding this feature is a work in progress and a quite successful one: with the next version of LProf you will be able to use devices like X-Rite DTP94, Eye-One Display 2 and EyeOne Display LT to measure your display on both Windows and Linux.

On Mac OS X, you can also use the native built-in Color-Sync applet to create a monitor profile. On Windows, if you have installed Photoshop, InDesign or Illustrator, Adobe Gamma performs a similar, if more simplistic method of creating a monitor profile.

[1] http://lprof.sourceforge.net

13.17 FontForge

FontForge [1] is a program created to edit, create and convert fonts. Started as an editor for PostScript fonts in 2001, FontForge nowadays supports almost all vector and bitmap font formats. While its numerous options may be confusing for laymen, professional font artists appreciate its versatility. Among others, it's possible to use FontForge to extract embedded fonts from PDF files. It also provides access to the revolutionary "Spiro" technology [2] for curve and font design. Unlike a typical Bézier curve, a curve's behavior in Spiro resembles that of a coil. All points are on the curve, and there are no handles for editing nodes. Instead, moving nodes changes the whole curve relative to other points in a way that's more "natural." For many vector operations, especially in font editing, this works many times faster than traditional Bézier curves.

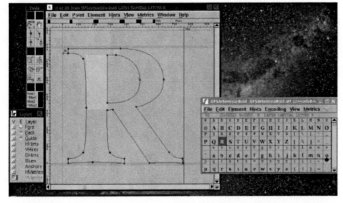

FontForge uses its own GUI toolkit, so that it doesn't integrate very well with any desktop environment. Nevertheless it should be considered a must on every computer which is used for layout work, as it can be very helpful if you're dealing with broken font files. FontForge is available for Linux/UNIX, Mac OS X and Windows.

[1] http://fontforge.sourceforge.net/index.html
[2] http://www.levien.com/spiro

14 Appendices

14.1 Installing Scribus from the Command Line on Linux/UNIX

BELOW you will find descriptions for the command line installation of Scribus, which is usually much faster than a graphical front-end.

All commands described below require root permissions.

AltLinux	`apt-get install scribus`
Ark Linux	`apt-get install scribus`
Debian/Ubuntu	`apt-get install scribus` `apt-get install scribus-doc`
Fedora	`yum install scribus`
Gentoo	`emerge scribus`
Mandriva	`urpmi scribus`
PC Linux OS	`apt-get install scribus`
PLD	`poldek -i scribus`
SimplyMEPIS	`apt-get -f install scribus`
Slackware	`installpkg scribus`
OpenSUSE/SLED	`yast2 --install scribus`
Zenwalk	`netpkg scribus`
BSD (as port)	`cd /usr/ports/print/scribus &&` `make install clean`
BSD (as package)	`pkg_add -r scribus`
Solaris/OpenSolaris	`pkg-get install scribus`

Additional Notes

Debian/Ubuntu

If you run Debian Unstable or Testing then you need not use special repositories as Debian packages for those branches are kept current.

However, the only way to run a current Scribus version on Debian/Stable and Ubuntu Edgy/Feisty/Gutsy is to use the Scribus Archive.

There are two identical repositories (debian.tagancha.org and debian.scribus.net) that provide bandwidth redundancy and failover capability. The repositories contain mainly i386 packages, but the Scribus team also occasionally hosts user-contributed amd64 packages when available.

Add the following lines to the file /etc/apt/sources.list:

Debian stable (Etch):

```
deb http://debian.scribus.net/debian/
stable main non-free contrib
```

```
deb http://debian.tagancha.org/debian/
stable main non-free contrib
```

Debian testing (Lenny):

```
deb http://debian.scribus.net/debian/
testing main non-free contrib
```

```
deb http://debian.tagancha.org/debian/
testing main non-free contrib
```

Debian unstable (Sid):

```
deb http://debian.scribus.net/debian/
unstable main non-free contrib
```

```
deb http://debian.tagancha.org/debian/
unstable main non-free contrib
```

Ubuntu edgy:

```
deb http://debian.scribus.net/debian/ edgy
main non-free
```

```
deb http://debian.tagancha.org/debian/ edgy
main non-free
```

Ubuntu feisty:

```
deb http://debian.scribus.net/debian/
feisty main non-free
```

```
deb http://debian.tagancha.org/debian/
feisty main non-free
```

Ubuntu gutsy:

```
deb http://debian.scribus.net/debian/ gutsy
main non-free
```

```
deb http://debian.tagancha.org/debian/
gutsy main non-free
```

Fedora

As of this writing, Fedora 8 and 9 will install the developmental and unmaintained 1.3.4 version. Therefore, you will need to find a binary version (see the notes regarding Open-SUSE Build Service below) and manually install, or compile from source.

Mandriva

Use http://easyurpmi.zarb.org and add "main" and "contrib" to your urpmi media database ("updates" and "plf" repositories are very useful, too).

Slackware

Download an (unofficial) package from the Italian Slackware Community website (http://www.slacky.eu) and install it with the command in the above table.

OpenSUSE Build Service

For some RPM based distributions like Fedora, Mandriva or OpenSUSE/SLED the OpenSUSE Build Service repositories provide the most current packages from the Scribus team. [1]

[1] http://download.opensuse.org/repositories/home:/mrdocs

14.2 Keyboard and Mouse Shortcuts

14.2.1 Keyboard Shortcuts

Entries in italics don't appear in any menu.

Menu *File*

New file	CTRL + N
New from template	CTRL + ALT + N
Open an existing file	CTRL + O
Close current file	CTRL + W
Save as	CTRL + Shift + S
Save as template	CTRL + ALT + S
Save as image	CTRL + SHIFT + E
Print	CTRL + P
Print Preview	CTRL + ALT + P
Quit	CTRL + Q

Menu *Edit*

Undo	CTRL + Z
Redo	CTRL + Shift + Z
Cut	CTRL + X
Copy	CTRL + C
Paste	CTRL + V
Select All	CTRL + A
Deselect All	CTRL + Shift + A
Search / Replace	CTRL + F
Edit Text	CTRL + Y
Copy Contents	CTRL + SHIFT + C
Paste Contents	CTRL + SHIFT + V
Undo	CTRL + Z
Redo	CTRL + SHIFT + Z

Menu *Item*

Duplicate	CTRL + ALT + SHIFT + D
Delete	CTRL + K
Group	CTRL + G
Ungroup	CTRL + SHIFT + G
Lock/Unlock	CTRL + L
Size is locked	CTRL + SHIFT + L
Level / Raise	CTRL + HOME
Level / Lower	CTRL + END
Level / Raise to top	HOME
Level / Lower to bottom	END

Menu *Insert*

Text Frame	T
Image Frame	I
Table	A
Shape	S
Polygon	P
Line	L
Bezier Curve	B
Freehand Line	F
Character / Page Number	CTRL + ALT + SHIFT + P
Character / Smart Hyphen	CTRL + SHIFT + -
Character / Non Breaking Hyphen	CTRL + ALT + -
Character / Frame Break	CTRL + RETURN
Character / Column Break	RETURN
Character / New Line	SHIFT + RETURN

Menu *Style*

Image Effects	CTRL + E

Menu *View*

Fit in window	CTRL + 0
100% Zoom	CTRL + 1
Show Rulers	CTRL + SHIFT + R
Zoom in	CTRL + Plus
Zoom out	CTRL + Minus

Menu *Tools*

Edit Contents	E
Edit Text Frame with Story Editor	CTRL + Y
Eye Dropper	Y
Link Text Frame	N
Unlink Text Frame	U
Rotate Object	R
Select	C
Zoom tool	Z

Menu *Windows*	
Properties	F2
Layers	F6

Menu *Help*	
Scribus Manual ...	F1
Others	
Hide/Bring up all Palettes	F10
Hide/Bring up all Guides, Grids etc.	F11
value	F12

Inside text frames or in the Story Editor, shortcuts are working as common in modern text editors:

Add the next character to the selection	SHIFT + Arrow right/left
Marks the current word	CTRL + SHIFT + Arrow right/left
Marks the complete text	CTRL + A
Move to the end / start of the line	END / HOME
Moves the cursor one word	CTRL + ALT + Arrow right/left

14.2.2 Changing Keyboard Shortcuts

In *File > Preferences* you can change all menu-related shortcuts and also set new ones.

To change or assign an action to a shortcut, select the action in the list. If a shortcut is assigned, it will be displayed in the gray field on the right. If the action has no shortcut assigned, the dialog will show the radio button "No Key" active. Click "Set Key" and type the new shortcut on the keyboard. If the shortcut isn't already assigned to another action, the radio button "User Defined Key" becomes active. In case the shortcut is already in use by another action, a warning will pop up.

You can also use your custom shortcuts on another computer. Just click on the "Export" button, and save a "Key Set XML File" using a file dialog. To use it on another computer, copy it to a USB stick or similar and load it with the "Import" button there. By clicking the "OK" button, you make the loaded set the shortcut set for your current and future documents. If you want or need to return to the default shortcut set, click on "Reset."

Another option is "Loadable Shortcut Sets." By default, it doesn't seem to be useful, as the only set in the dropdown list is "Scribus 1.3.3." You can, however, easily create your own shortcut set, eg. to mimic the behavior of another layout program you know. Just create a plain text file that looks like this:

```
<?xml version="1.0" encoding="UTF-8"?>
<shortcutset name="InDesign 2.x">
    <function name="fileOpen" shortcut="Ctrl+O"/>
    <function name="fileSave" shortcut="Ctrl+S"/>
</shortcutset>
```

"function name" denotes the action in Scribus, and since you probably won't know what all the functions' names are, it's probably better to open the file scribus13.ksxml in the install directory of Scribus under /lib/scribus/keysets (or \lib\scribus\keysets on Windows and OS/2) and use it as a template. If you edit the file, don't forget to save it under a different name, because otherwise you'll lose your Scribus default shortcuts. Once you've finished adding your desired shortcuts, save or copy the file to the "keysets" directory mentioned above, and the new shortcut will be available from the dropdown list. Please note that you'll probably need root/Administrator privileges to save the file in this directory. After selecting the new set from the list, you have to click the "Load" button and then click "OK."

14.2.3 Mouse Usage

Mouse usage in Scribus has some subtle, but once learned, very useful shortcuts:

- Click third button, or on two button mice ("chord" them by click left and right together) refreshes the view.
- Control+ Shift + left click for select through levels on the same layer.
- Control + left click resize/move for lower objects. Release + drag resizes. Hold down Control + drag moves.
- Left click + drag resizes frames. Add Ctrl, you get orthogonal movement
- Shift + left click + drag resizes frames proportionally.
- Ctrl + Alt + left click + drag resizes text frames and their content.
- Rotate tool + Ctrl + left click rotates an item in steps of 15 degrees.
- Right click: A context menu will pop up offering some choices.
- Ctrl + wheel zooms the view in and out.

• Shift + wheel adds a 10x multiplier to scroll wheel action.

• Ctrl + right button drag allows you to pan the document up or down and/or left to right depending on the zoom factor.

14.2.4 Other Shortcuts

• Space bar toggles the panning mode for the mouse if nothing is selected.

• With nothing selected, Tab will change between the open documents

• In normal mode we can:

   · Use backspace or delete to delete the item

   · Use PageUp to raise an item

   · Use PageDown to lower an item

   · Use the arrow keys to move an item or group around:

   - With no meta, by 1.0 unit

   - Ctrl, by 10.0 units

   - Shift by 0.1 units

   - Ctrl Shift 0.01 units

   · Use the arrow keys to resize an item:

   - Alt right arrow, move right side outwards (expand)

   - Alt left arrow, move left side outwards (expand)

   - Alt Shift right arrow, move left side inwards (shrink)

   - Alt Shift left arrow, move right side inwards (shrink)

• In edit mode of an image frame, use the arrow keys to resize the image:

   - Alt right arrow, move right side of image outwards (expand)

   - Alt left arrow, move right side inwards (shrink)

   - Alt down arrow, move bottom side downwards (expand)

   - Alt up arrow, move top side inwards (shrink)

14.3 Scribus, QuarkXPress™ and Adobe InDesign™ terminology

Scribus	QuarkXPress	InDesign
Align and Distribute	Space/Align	Align Palette
Collect for Output	Collect for Output	Package
Color	Color	Swatch
Convert to Outlines	Text to Box	Create Outlines
Default text properties	Normal Style Sheet	Default text attributes
Document	Layout	Document
(Double-click on image frame/Properties Palette > Image)	Content tool	Position tool
Edit Text (E)	Content tool	Type tool
Frame	Box	Frame
Get Image/Get Text	Get Image/Get Text	Place
Gradient	Blend	Gradient
Image	Picture	Graphic
Image Frame	Picture Box	Picture Frame
Item	Item	Object
Item Color	Background Color	Fill
Line	Frame	Stroke
Line	Line	Path
Line Spacing	Leading	Leading
Linking (text frames)	Linking (text boxes)	Threading (text)
Manage Pictures	Picture Usage	Links
n.a.	Project	Book
Page Display Color	White Color	Paper
Path Text Properties	Text Path Tools	Type on a Path Tool
Plug-in	Xtension	Plug-in
Preferences/Document Setup	Preferences	Preferences
Properties Palette	Measurements Palette	Control Palette
Properties Palette > X, Y, Z	Modify	Transform
Select Item Tool	Item Tool	Selection Tool
Shade	Shade	Tint
Shear	Skew	Shear
Story Editor	n.a.	Story Editor
Style	Style Sheet	Style
Table of Contents	Lists	Table of Contents
Text Flow (around a frame)	Runaround	Text Wrap

14.4 File Types and Resources Used by Scribus

14.4.1 Scribus File Types:

- .sla: Scribus document (Note that there are three different versions of sla: 1.2.x, 1.3 – 1.3.3.x and 1.3.4 or later. Older versions are not capable of importing files saved by newer ones)
- .sla.gz: Compressed Scribus document
- .scd: Scribus document (versions prior to 1.0)
- .scd.gz: Compressed Scribus document (versions prior to 1.0)
- .sce: (Scribus objects)
- .scs: (Scribus Scrapbook)
- .ksxml: (Keyboard shortcuts)
- .ucp: (Scribus Unicode character palette)
- .xml: (XML files with sample text; see the examples in ~share/scribus/loremipsum for correct tagging)

14.4.2 Resources Scribus can Use or Import:

- .dic: (OpenOffice.org hyphenation dictionaries.
- .gpl: (GIMP color palettes; additional ones need to be copied to the ~lib/scribus/swatches folder)

14.4.3 Image Formats:

- .jpeg: Joint Photographic Experts Group Format
- .tif: Tagged Image File Format
- .psd: Photoshop image files
- .png: Portable Network Graphics
- .gif: Graphics Interchange Format
- .xpm: X Pixmap Format
- .pdf: Portable Document Format (can only be imported rasterized)

14.4.4 Vector Formats:

- .eps: Encapsulated PostScript
- .odg: OpenDocument Graphics
- .ps: PostScript
- .svg: Scalable Vector Graphics
- .sxd: OpenOffice.org Draw

14.4.5 Text Formats:

- .txt: plain text
- .csv: comma separated value files
- .html, .htm: HTML documents
- .sxw: OpenOffice.org Writer 1.x files
- .odt: OpenDocument Text format
- .pdb: Aportis Doc files
- .doc: Word files

14.4.6 Special Files in the User's .scribus Directory:

- checkfonts.xml: Information about available fonts and if they are usable.
- prefs13.xml: Scribus preferences.
- scribus13.rc: 2nd part of Scribus preferences.
- scribus-short-words.rc: user configuration for Scribus's short-words functionality.
- tmp.ps: temporary file while printing, creating barcodes or using the print preview.

14.5 Useful Links

14.5.1 Official Scribus Links

- Project Website: http://www.scribus.net
- Official Documentation: http://docs.scribus.net
- Wiki: http://wiki.scribus.net
- Bug Tracker: http://bugs.scribus.net
- Scribus Developer Blog: http://rants.scribus.net
- Scribus Mailing Lists: http://lists.scribus.info/

14.5.2 External Resources

- http://www.kde-files.org: Scribus Templates, some of them very well done.
- http://openclipart.org: Open Clip Art is a steadily growing collection of free clipart in PNG and SVG format.
- http://www.openfontlibrary.org: The Open Font Library, a sister project of Open Clip Art. It collects public domain fonts, so that they can be used freely.

14.5.3 Miscellaneous

- http://www.fsf.org: The Free Software Foundation is a valuable source for licensing issues and other topics related to Free Software.
- http://creativecommons.org: Creative Commons provides free tools and licenses that let authors, scientists, artists, and educators easily mark their creative work with the freedoms they want it to carry.
- http://color.org: The International Color Consortium promotes the use and adoption of open, vendor-neutral, cross-platform color management systems. It's responsible for the ICC standard.

14.6 Copyrights and Licensing

CONTRARY to some common misconceptions, Free Software, Free Documentation and other Free Content rely on copyright protection in the same way their closed equivalents do. The major difference between Closed Source and Open Source licenses is the degree of freedom they provide for users, developers and authors. For Open Projects it's essential that copyrights and licenses are respected. Below you find details about the Scribus license, the license for this manual, as well as some hints about licensing and copyright issues with other people's content that will be used in Scribus.

14.6.1 Scribus

The Scribus license can be viewed in the Help Browser under "Other Information > Scribus Copyright."

14.6.2 This Manual

This copyright notice concerns the online and packaged versions of: "Scribus – Open Source Desktop Publishing. The Official Manual" (the "Scribus Manual") and its translations, originally created by Craig Bradney, Thomas G. Dorsch, Ivan Fetwadjieff, Cédric Gemy, Maciej Hanski, Riku Leino, Peter Linnell, Gregory Pittman, Craig Ringer, Christoph Schäfer, Petr Vaněk, Andreas Vox and Thomas Zastrow.

The Scribus Manual and the translations are distributed under the Open Publication License guidelines described at www.opencontent.org.

The following is the text of the license as it applies to this work:

I. REQUIREMENTS ON BOTH UNMODIFIED AND MODIFIED VERSIONS

The "Scribus Manual," including its translations, may be reproduced and distributed in whole or in part, in any medium physical or electronic, provided that the terms of this license are adhered to, and that this license or an incorporation of it by reference is displayed in the reproduction.

Proper form for an incorporation by reference is as follows:

Copyright (c) 2007/2008 Craig Bradney, Thomas Dorsch, Ivan Fetwadjieff, Cédric Gemy, Maciej Hanski, Riku Leino, Peter Linnell, Gregory Pittman, Christoph Schäfer, Petr Vaněk,

5. The original author's (or authors') name may not be used to assert or imply endorsement of the resulting document without the original author's (or authors') permission.

V. GOOD-PRACTICE RECOMMENDATIONS

In addition to the requirements of this license, it is requested from and strongly recommended of redistributors that:

1. If you are distributing Open Publication works, you provide email notification to the authors of your intent to redistribute at least thirty days before your manuscript or media freeze, to give the authors time to provide updated documents. This notification should describe modifications, if any, made to the document.

2. All substantive modifications (including deletions) be either clearly marked up in the document or else described in an attachment to the document. Finally, while it is not mandatory under this license, it is considered good form to offer a free copy of any hardcopy and CD-ROM expression of an Open Publication-licensed work to its author.

VI. ELECTED OPTIONS

Distribution of the work or derivative of the work in any standard (paper) book form is prohibited unless prior permission is obtained from the copyright holders. Other forms of distribution including CD-ROM, electronic, and magnetic media are permitted.

- Adobe, Adobe Reader, Adobe Acrobat, Adobe InDesign, Adobe Illustrator, Adobe PageMaker, Adobe Photoshop are trademarks of Adobe Corporation in the United States, other countries or both.

- Corel, CorelDraw and Corel Photopaint are registered trademarks of Corel Corporation in Canada, other countries, or both.

- HKS is a registered trademark of HKS Warenzeichenverband e.V. in Germany, other countries, or both.

- Mac, Mac OS, Mac OS X and Macintosh are trademarks of Apple, Inc. in the United States, other countries, or both.

- Microsoft, Windows, Windows 95, Windows 98, Windows ME, Windows NT, Windows 2000, Windows XP, Windows Vista, Microsoft Word, Microsoft PowerPoint, Microsoft Publisher and the respective logos are trademarks of Microsoft Corporation in the United States, other countries, or both.

- Motif is a registered trademark of The Open Group in the United States, other countries, or both.

- OS/2, OS/2 Warp, Lotus and Lotus Symphony are trademarks of IBM Corporation in the United States, other countries, or both.
- Pantone is a registered trademark of Pantone Inc. in the United States, other countries, or both.
- Quark and QuarkXpress are registered trademarks of Quark Inc. in the United States, other countries, or both.
- SUN, Java, Solaris and StarOffice are registered trademarks of Sun Microsystems Inc. in the United States, other countries, or both.
- UNIX is a registered trademark of The Open Group in the United States and other countries.
- Xara and Xara Xtreme are trademarks of The Xara Group, Ltd. in the United Kingdom, other countries, or both.
- All other company, product, or service names may be trademarks or service marks of others and are the property of their respective owners.

14.6.3 Other Copyright and Licensing Hints

The following is not legal advice. Please take time to learn the pertinent laws which apply to intellectual property/author's rights where you live.

When you are making some project for your own benefit or with some very limited distribution, copyrights and licensing may not be an issue. However, whenever you plan to distribute work widely, whether it may be via the internet or publishing a booklet or book, you must have a sense of whether any components of your work have restrictions.

14.6.3.1 Text

There is usually some allowance for small amounts of text borrowed from other works – one often sees indented paragraphs of quoted material with proper citation of its source – but when whole paragraphs and more are lifted from some copyrighted source you need to be aware of what rights you have to include this material. It may be as simple as contacting the author or publisher, in some cases there may be a fee, yet sometimes any use may be forbidden.

14.6.3.2 Images

Similarly, all kinds of graphic materials can be restricted, and this may include not just copyrighted photographs and computer-generated graphic materials, but also photographs of artwork of various types. In some countries, no art has a copyright beyond 75 years after the artist's death, thus many old paintings are freely available. Nonetheless, the owner of that art may impose restrictions based on access to reproductions or photographs.

14.6.3.3 Fonts

Though it may not be obvious, high-quality fonts represent a substantial amount of work to create, and thus there are those who make their livelihood in making and providing them commercially. Once again, licensing can sometimes be quite free, and an increasing number of freely available fonts are becoming available.

Some fonts are released freely for personal use, but may not be redistributed. In the case of Scribus, this redistribution will come about when you choose to embed the font in your PDF or by the use of Collect for Output for use on another person's computer. Make sure you know which fonts on your system you are allowed to embed or to distribute. In the case of commercially available fonts, embedding may be unnecessary, since commercial printers may have these fonts in their system and merely need the name (automatically included in the PDF) to use it properly when your PDF is published.

If you are not allowed to embed, converting to outlines may be a suitable workaround.

15 Glossary

Action History: Refers to an ongoing list of operations done in Scribus, which can be undone to some former state.

Arrow: One of the kinds of embellishments that can be created at the beginning of a line, end of a line, or both. In this manual, "arrow" may also refer to an arrow key on a keyboard.

Autosave: A built-in feature for automatically saving a → document at a specific time interval.

Barcode: A collection of bars which can be optically scanned by machinery, commonly used commercially for automated purchases, inventory tracking, and for postal codes.

Baseline Grid: A set of evenly spaced horizontal nonprinting lines which can be used to adjust the linespacing of text in → columns and in different → text frames.

Basepoint: As indicated in *Properties* > *X, Y, Z* tab, the reference point of the various position and dimension values of a → frame, also used as the center point for rotation.

Bézier Curve: A curve generated from a mathematical algorithm, initially developed by Paul de Casteljau and later employed by Pierre Bézier in the automotive industry. A Bézier curve is defined by four points, the starting and end points, as well as two → control points. The control points are used to change the curve. Two-dimensional shapes, like rectangles or circles will have more control points.

Bitmap Image: An image generated from and saved as a series of evenly spaced points, each of which is assigned a particular hue and saturation. Typically these are displayed on a device such as a computer monitor or used with a printer to generate a printed image. Examples of bitmap images include → TIFF, → JPEG, and → PNG, among many others.

Bitstream Fonts: Bitstream is a well-known foundry of commercial fonts. However, in the context of Scribus and this manual "Bitstream fonts" refers to the Bitstream Vera family, which has been donated to the Open Source community by Bitstream.

Black Point Compensation: Black Point Compensation is a method of improving contrast in photos.

Bleed: Space at the → margins of a layout which are meant to be trimmed away to create the finished product after commercial printing. Bleed allows the printed inks to go completely to the edge.

Blend Mode: Blend modes tell a program such as Photoshop or Scribus how a pixel on an upper layer will influence the matching pixel on the layer below.

Booklet Printing: A rearrangement and sometimes reformatting of pages of a → document so that when the printed sheets are printed front and back, then laid on top of each other, folded, then attached in the crease, a book is created which has the pages in proper order. Books are created by binding together a number of these booklets.

Bookmark: In the context of Scribus, a bookmark is an area of a page used as a reference point for quickly linking from one part of a document to another. Bookmarks can also be used in the Help Browser.

Bounding Box: A rectangular space on a page which will always have horizontal and vertical sides and which defines in boundaries of all of an → image's content, including → control points of a → vector drawing.

Building: In the context of computer software, this is the process of transforming human-readable software instructions to machine-readable instructions so that the software can be run on a computer.

Canvas: The working space for designing a layout in Scribus. This includes not only the area which represents the page on which the layout will be displayed or printed, but also the surrounding → scratch space.

Caps: An abbreviation for capitals or uppercase letters.

Chained Text Frames: If a text is too long to fit into a single text frame, it's possible to link this frame to one or more other text frames and let the text flow from one frame to the next.

Character: A symbol which has linguistic meaning, such as the letter A or the digit 1. This is differentiated from → glyphs, which are the very specific graphical representation of a character for a particular → font.

Checkbox: A small space, typically a square, which can be clicked on to visibly check or unchecked to indicate turning a feature on or off (also known as toggling). Checkboxes are used in the Scribus user interface, but they can also be created for → PDF forms.

Checksum: A computer-generated code using a mathematical algorithm based on a file's content. Currently, two commonly used checksums are the SHA1 and MD5 algorithms. Neither is an absolute guarantee, but both provide a high level of assurance that a file has not been tampered with or improperly downloaded. This is especially important for programs run on computers.

Cicero: Cicero is a typographic measuring unit. It consists of 12 Didot → points, thus 1 c is equvialent of 4.5 mm or 0.177 in.

Clipping: Clipping is a method to influence the → text flow. A → bitmap or → vector image can contain a separate vector → path, the clipping path. DTP programs like Scribus can read this path and use it for the text flow around an item.

Clipping Path: see Clipping

CMake: A small program used by Scribus prior to actually → building or compiling to check the computer's environment (the type of system, presence of necessary components), which then will make a list of instructions for the compiler program to use, or generate error messages when needed components are missing.

CMYK: A → colorspace based on the printing ink pigments cyan, magenta, yellow, and black, which is used in → offset printing.

Collect for Output: A method to collect together all of the various items used in a → document, including → fonts, so that a complete Scribus layout can be easily found and moved collectively. Often used for sharing a document from one person/computer to another.

Color Management: A process of "translating" colors between different devices and → colorspaces. It is used to match colors reliably in different media types like cameras, scanners, or printers.

Colorspace: A numerical system to describe colors. Not all colorspaces are 100% compatible. For example, it's impossible to "translate" all colors in the → RGB color space to the → CMYK colorspace.

Color Temperature: A typology of different light sources, for example daylight or a light bulb. The unit for color temperature is Kelvin (K). The different types of lighting have been defined in 1931 by the Commission Internationale d'Éclairage.

Columns: A property of → text frames allowing a large space of text to be broken up into smaller columns of text, commonly used in newsletters, newspapers, and textbooks.

Comma-Separated Values: A simple, text-based method of saving a table or database in a structured format. May or may not necessarily use commas, but can use some other character to indicate the jump to the next data value.

Compiling: See Building.

Context Menu: Obtained in Scribus by right-clicking on a → frame or other item to show a list of operations or settings which might be chosen by left-clicking.

Contour Line: An imaginary, editable space attached to an → item such as a → frame, which can be used to define the boundaries for surrounding content. Especially useful when these boundaries may need to have an unusual → shape or size.

Control Point: Used in → vector drawings as a visual tool connected to a → node to control the curve of a line from one node to the next.

Coordinates: In Scribus, these are X,Y values used to define the position of → items in a layout.

CUPS: Common UNIX Printing System, originally developed by Easy Software Products, now owned by Apple, Inc, to provide a common interface for → printing on UNIX-like systems, now employed by most Linux and UNIX distributions, including Mac OS X.

Cursor: The point of action, typically of the keyboard or the mouse. The keyboard cursor will be some version of a vertical line indicating where characters will be added or deleted. The mouse cursor is usually represented by an arrow graphic to indicate the point of action on the screen.

Dash: A horizontal line → character of variable length used as a separator in text. Typographically, the most common subtypes are en-dash and em-dash, whose widths should be the same as the letters n and M respectively. Dashes are differentiated from hyphens, and are not interchangeable.

Dependency: A term used in the → building of software, to indicate requirements for a software program to be compiled and run properly. These may be other programs or → libraries used as tools in the operation of a program such as Scribus.

Desktop Publishing: In a broad sense, desktop publishing (DTP) refers to everything related to publish with the help of a computer, including text editing, typesetting, image manipulation, or vector drawing. In a more narrow sense it means the assembly of all parts that are necessary for a (printed) publication, such as a book or a magazine with the help of a specialized program like Scribus.

Development Version: At all times, developers will be working not only on the current stable version, such as the 1.3.3.12 version of Scribus this manual is about, but also a more advanced version in which a number of new features are being added, or some major overhaul or rewriting of older features is taking place. Development versions will have variable and sometimes rapidly changing usability, and are therefore not recommended for critical work.

Directory: A metaphor for a special file which may be used to contain a collection of files for some type of orderly sequestering. On Windows and OS/2 machines, a directory as called a folder.

Distribution: All Linux versions and most Open Source UNIX variants (*BSD, OpenSolaris etc.) are created by companies or organziations who are responsible for the assembly of thousands of Open Source components. They are releasing the final product as a so-called distribution, which will be available for a fee or as a free download from the internet. Well-known distributions are, for example, Fedora, Debian, OpenSUSE, Ubuntu or FreeBSD.

Document: In Scribus, a document is the name for a project on which layout is done, consisting of one or more pages.

Document Outline: A dialog that lists all items in a file, sorted by page and level.

Document Setup: Found under the *File* item in the main menu, this allows changing various parameters for the → document which is currently open and active. See Configuration.

Drop Caps: An embellishment of text in which the first letter of a paragraph is enlarged, and its baseline rests below its original one. This capital may also use a different font face or color for further emphasis.

Dropdown List: A special widget in a computer program that contains a list of options which will unfold after clicking on an entry or an arrow.

Duplicate: A shortcut representation a combination of copying an item such as a → frame, then pasting a new identical version of the item at the same or a different location.

Emergency Save: In some situation of software failure (crash), Scribus will try to save the current → document using the name of the file appended with "emergency."

Encoding: The computer's numeric representation for collections of characters and special instructions like line breaks. The default encoding for Scribus is UTF-8.

EPS: Encapsulated PostScript. A file format derived from → Postscript to allow for the self-contained single page of PostScript.

Eye Dropper: A feature in Scribus for copying a → color from somewhere on the screen to be used elsewhere.

Fill Character: A → character used to fill in the space between items on a line of text. The (blank) space character would be commonly used, but periods or other characters can be used as alternatives.

Fill Color: The → color which fills the inside space of a → frame, a → glyph, or other graphic.

Fill Rule: When two or more closed spaces in a shape are superimposed, the fill rule determines which → color fills internal spaces, or whether the space may be transparent.

Flip: An action similar to that of flipping over a playing card, typically done either horizontally or vertically.

Folder: See Directory.

Font: A term that may refer to a file (or a set of files) which contains the informations to draw → glyphs on a computer screen or to print them. It may also refer to the specific look of a font, for example a "Garamond" font.

Font Face: A font may contain not just "regular" glyphs, but also bold, demi-bold or italic versions of those glyphs. These variants are called font faces.

Font Family: A collection of different → font faces.

Font Management: A collective term for previewing, classifying, installing/uninstalling and activating/deactivating → fonts.

Fontconfig: On Linux and UNIX systems, fontconfig is a special program that helps to keep track of installed fonts. It's essential for → font management on these platforms.

Formatting: In Scribus, this term is applied to the various features of text for a particular appearance.

Frame: An imaginary container representing a space which may contain text, images, or other graphical elements, placed with precision and having a collection of attributes (properties).

Freehand Line: A line drawn with the mouse cursor in a freeform fashion, beginning with depression of the left mouse button and ending when the pressure is taken off the button.

Freetype2: A → library used by Scribus and many other programs to access the internal informations of a → font.

Gamut: The part of a → colorspace which can be reproduced by a particular device.

Gap: In Scribus, the vertical space between columns of text. Gap is also used in the *Align and Distribute* dialog, where it means the distance between selected items.

GCC: The GNU Compiler Collection used in many UNIX-like environments for → compiling software.

GDI: GDI is an abbreviation for Graphics Device Interface. It's used for graphics programming and printing on the Windows platform. It has been enhanced with GDI+ on newer Windows versions (XP and Vista). Windows 2000 users have to install GDI+ separately to run Scribus.

Ghostscript: A utility program written to read or transform → PostScript or → PDF files to other formats.

GIMP: GNU Image Manipulation Program. A full-featured → bitmap graphic and photographic image manipulation program, which is very popular on many platforms.

Glyph: The actual graphical figure representing a → character for a particular → font.

Gradient: The gradual transition of one → color to another, typically seen in the → fill color of some item.

Grayscale: A → colorspace that uses only shades of black (B in the → RGB colorspace and K in the → CMYK colorspace).

Group: A collection of → items which have been selected together so that their relative physical relationships are maintained while they are moved about or modified in some way.

Grouping: The action of forming a group of items which will then be treated as a single item.

Guide: A non-printing line that helps to visually divide a layout.

Help Browser: Activated with *Help > Scribus Manual,* and contains much documentation about Scribus is its use.

HTML: The Hyper Text Markup Language is a → markup language mainly used by web pages.

Hyphen: Used as a separator when a word is broken into syllables, most often in fully justified text. This is found on standard keyboards, in contrast to en → dash and em dash which are used for very different purposes.

Hyphenation: The process of breaking a word on a line to produce a more even, visually pleasing, and legible arrangement of letters on a line.

ICC Profile: An ICC (International Color Consortium) profile is an international standard format to store the → Gamut values of a device.

Image Frame: A type of → frame into which a → bitmap image can be loaded. → EPS or → PDF files will be converted to bitmaps when loaded into an image frame.

Indentation: Displacement of the beginning word of a paragraph, and can be either to the left or to the right.

Inline Objects: Graphical items which can be used in a text frame, much as a glyph would be.

Item: Individual items which make up the content of a document, including various kinds of frames, shapes, and lines. Items can be grouped in order to move or edit them as a single item. In this manual the words item and object have the same meaning, while the user interface of Scribus only uses "item."

Item Action Mode: A special operating mode of the *Action History*. If activated, only operations for a single item are recorded.

Kerning: Applies to the horizontal spacing between two or more adjacent letters.

lcms: see LittleCMS

Letter: In typesetting and DTP the term "letter" may refer to a → character or a → glyph.

Library: In modern computing, many functions used by one or more programs are stored a separate file. The purpose of creating a library is to keep additional function separate from the core of the program or to share functionality with other programs. On Windows and OS/2, shared libraries use the file extension *.dll (dynamically linked libaries) on Linux/UNIX/OS X they end with *.so (shared object) most of the time.

LibTIFF: This is a → library used by Scribus for loading → TIFF images.

Ligature: A → glyph representing the combination of two or more adjacent letters. Two most common ligature → glyphs are those representing the combination of f and i, and the combination of f and l. A particular → font may or may not have ligature glyphs.

Linking: The process of connecting two or more → text frames so that a large amount of text automatically flows from one frame to the next in the linked sequence.

LittleCMS: An mature Open Source → library used by Scribus and commercial vendors like HP or Callas for → color management.

Locking: The process of freezing various characteristics of an → item, so that editing cannot be done until it is unlocked.

Lorem Ipsum: see Sample Text

Magic Wand: In Scribus and many other programs, the magic wand is a tool to copy and paste certain properties of an item.

Magnification: see Zoom

make: The command which tells → gcc to begin → compiling a program. Once compiling is complete, 'make install' will save the program and its various components to useable locations.

Man Page: An abbreviation for "manual page" on UNIX-like operating systems. The man page for a program can be read in terminal by typing the command 'man program' (without quotes), where "program" must be replaced with the actual name of the program, eg. 'man scribus.'

Margin: A zone at the edges of a page where none of the main text will appear. In some cases, it may denote areas at the edges of the page where a given printing device cannot print.

Margin Guides: Visual nonprinting lines used to help keep content within the → print space of the page.

Markup: Characters or collections of → characters, usually AS-CII, used to denote formatting commands to be interpreted by software. These can be standardized, such as the markup used in → HTML or LaTeX, or can be customizable by the user, such as textfile markup used in Scribus to select paragraph → styles.

Master Page: A customizable background repetitively used in several pages of a → document. Typical uses would be for headers, banners, and even → text and → image frames which appear on many pages. A document may have more than one kind of master page, but only one kind can be chosen for a given page. Once created, they will have the same uneditable appearance wherever they are used, except where → page numbering is included as a feature. Not to be confused with → templates.

Menu Bar: In Scribus and many other programs the menu bar is the first horizontally ordered list of entries that provide sub-entries for access to functions and dialogs.

Metadata: Information embedded in a → document which can contain a variety of information hidden in the standard display or printing of the document. Common uses might include the author, creation and revision dates, and other descriptions of content.

Mirror: see Flip

Mouse Pointer: see Cursor

Multiple Duplicate: In Scribus, *Multiple Duplicate* allows for one or more copies of an → item to be created, with a user-definable X and Y offset from one copy to the next.

Navigation: The process of moving from one page, an → item or a → bookmark of a → document to another.

Node: The connecting points of the lines drawn to define a shape or → Bézier curve.

Object: see Item

ODF: Open Document Format. A set of file formats for office applications maintained by the Organisation for the Advancement of Structured Information Standards (OASIS) and also an ISO standard. Currently Scribus can import OpenDocument Text (ODT) and OpenDocument Graphics (ODG) files.

Offset Printing: The process of using metal plates and rubber "blankets" to transfer color to a sheet of paper. It's the printing process used for most print products with huge print runs, such as magazines, books or newspapers.

Opacity: Refers to the degree of opaqueness. An item with 100% opacity will completely obscure what is behind it (see Layers, Levels). At 0% opacity, an item is invisible. Opacity is the opposite of → transparency.

OpenDocument: see ODF

OpenOffice.org: A powerful office productivity suite, whose source code has been donated to the Open Source community by Sun Microsystems, Inc. OpenOffice.org is also the reference implementation of the → ODF file specifications.

OpenSSL: Open Secure Socket Layer. A library of functions to encrypt information transmitted over the internet, to ensure privacy and validate the source of the information. OpenSSL represents an open source version of prior SSL technology.

OpenType: A → font format specification developed by Adobe Systems, Inc. and Microsoft, Inc. that combines the → Post-Script font and the → TrueType technology.

Package: On modern Linux and some UNIX distributions software is generally installed in the form of packages. Packages usually contain a particular program and a list of → dependencies, the advantage of this approach being that packages are much smaller than full-fledged installer files for Windows or OS X. Dependencies are resolved by a program called package manager like apt, urpmi, smart or zypper. The downside of this way to install software is that the package manager may not be able to resolve all dependencies, so that it can be hard to install a particular program. As a rule of thumb, using a popular distribution like Debian, Ubuntu, Fedora or OpenSUSE minimizes the risk of being unable to resolve a dependency.

Page Numbering: In Scribus, page numbering generally refers to the ability to add → special characters to a master page, so that pages can be sequentially numbered, using a starting point, an end point and a numbering system customizable by the user.

Pagination: see Page Numbering

Paragraph Style: see Style

Path: A word with different meanings. In an operating system, path is the whole hierarchy of → directories or folders that leads to a certain file. In Scribus, a path is either a → Bézier curve or a → clipping path.

PDF: The Portable Document Format, developed by Adobe Systems, is a standard format for the exchange of formatted content, which is the reason for calling PDF files "electronic paper." In DTP, PDF has become the standard file format to deliver data for printing. The PDF/X variants have been created with the requirements of pre-press in mind.

Pica: A typesetting measurement. One pica equals 1/6 of an inch or 12 → points.

Plug-in: A separate piece of software made to interact with some other, usually larger piece of software, designed to add some feature or function. As such, it is an option. Scribus is shipped with numerous plug-ins. For instance, the → color wheel is a plug-in. To learn more about Scribus plug-ins use *Help > About Plugins* from the Scribus → menu bar.

Point: The name for typesetting measurement unit. There are three kinds of points, the oldest being the Didot point, which has been introduced c. 1800 by a French typesetter. A Didot point is eqivalent to 0.375 mm or 0.01476 inch. Next is the → Pica point, which is mostly used in Northern America. A point in Scribus or other DTP programs is the desktop publishing point which is the equivalent of 1/72 of an inch or 0.353 mm. See also Cicero and Pica.

Polygon: In Scribus, this refers to a closed figure composed of equal connected lines arranged radially around a center.

PostScript: A programming language which is used to describe pages for printers and image setters. It's still a major part of modern printing technology.

PostScript Font: The first successful font format that replaced fonts described by → bitmaps with scalable vector fonts. PostScript fonts consist of two files, one describing the fonts themselves, and another that contains the font metrics, like distances between glyphs.

Preferences: A large collection of customizable features to be used whenever a new → document is created. These include page size, default → font, and numerous other features.

Preflight Verifier: A collection of tests run by Scribus either on demand or whenever a → document is to be printed or exported to → PDF. Designed to warn about potential errors, such as when an → item is off the printed page.

Presentation: In relationship to Scribus, an electronic document created to be used with a projector as a visual aid for an audience. Scribus allows for adding special presentation effects as defined in the → PDF specification.

Print Preview: A view of a → document generated to attempt to accurately depict the appearance after → printing. Limited by the screen resolution.

Print Space: The space on a page that contains the main body of text or the content. Some printable parts on a page, like page numbers or marginal notes, are often placed outside the print space. In Scribus, the printspace is denoted by a rectangle of → guides that separate the → margins and the print space.

Printer Margins: Denotes the areas outside of which a given printer cannot physically print.

Process Color: see CMYK

Project: Refers to all of the collected materials used in a → document, such as text and image files, in addition to the document file.

Properties Palette: An indispensable tool used to reposition and edit virtually every kind of → item that can appear in a → document.

PSD: The native file format of Adobe® Photoshop®, which is very versatile and wide-spread in desktop publishing.

Python: A modern programming language most often used in its plain text state, then compiled and run by an embedded interpreter each time it is called. One kind of a so-called scripting language, thus the source of the term → Scripter in Scribus.

Qt: Qt is a so-called toolkit for the development of programs like Scribus that use a graphical user interface. It is available under the GPL and a commercial license for use in closed source applications.

Quotation Marks: Sets of typographic symbols, used in some languages to denote spoken text, as well as other limited purposes. To be differentiated from the keyboard characters which would typographically be used to denote inches or geographic minutes.

Quote: A collection of text meant to be visually distinct from other non-quote text. Sometimes the term "quote" is also used as an abbreviation for → quotation marks.

Raster Image: see Bitmap Image

Raster Image Processor: Known as RIP for short, and the process may be referred to as ripping. Used by commercial printers for the final translation of a → document into instructions that the printing device can use to deposit ink on the printing medium.

Registration Color: A special color, usually consisting of 100% Cyan, 100% Magenta, 100% Yellow and 100% Black, which is used for printing → registration marks.

Registration Mark: Special printing marks, which are used to check if the → process colors covered exactly the same space on a printing sheet.

Regular Expressions: A standardized collection of → markup and abbreviations used in some programming languages and other software to simplify some iterative or sorting task.

Rendering Intent: A preset that tells a → color management system the priorities of the user when a file is converted from one → colorspace to another.

Repository: A location, often a server which can be connected to from the internet, where software and other files can be located and downloaded from or uploaded to. On a more limited scale, one might create a repository on a closed network or even an individual computer, perhaps a CDROM or DVD might also function as a repository. Modern Linix and UNIX distribution use repositories for the administration of software packages.

Resizing: see Scaling

RIP: see Raster Image Processor

Ruler: An optional marker at the borders of the → canvas to show dimensions in the chosen units.

Sample Text: A collection of arbitrary text generated to fill in a → text frame to help with choices of → font and its → formatting for a specific purpose. Lorem ipsum is a form of sample text in pseudo-Latin. Most languages have sample text available, some of which contain actual understandable text excerpts.

Scaling: In the context of graphics and layout software, scaling means resizing an item.

SCD: The Scribus file extension for Scribus files created with versions before 1.0

SCD.GZ: The compressed version of the → SCD format.

Scrapbook: A directory created by Scribus so that selected items can be saved, then later used in any document.

Scratch Space: The part of the → canvas or → workspace outside the actual → document → page margins. When a document is saved, these scratch space items will also be saved in their respective positions. They will not be included when the document is exported to → PDF, and will generate an error in the → Preflight Verifier.

Script: A script is a → Python program used to carry out a series of operations in Scribus, some with ongoing user feedback or selection of parameters.

Scripter: The Scripter is a → plug-in which permits the use of → scripts in the → Python programming language.

Selecting: The process of choosing an item to edit. When a → frame or other item is created, it is automatically selected. Left-clicking an item selects it, clicking outside the item deselects it.

SLA: The file extension of Scribus files. Even though all files created by Scribus since version 1.0 use the extension SLA or

SLA.GZ, the internals need not be be identical. While all current versions of Scribus can read any older file version, this doesn't work vice versa. In a stable series like 1.3.3.x, any older release within this series can read files created by a newer version.

SLA.GZ: The compressed version of the → SLA format.

Small Caps: A substitution of smaller capitals or uppercase glyphs for the standard lowercase glyphs. Scribus can create these artificially for most fonts, but the most visually appealing results come from fonts which contain small caps instead of lowercase glyphs.

Soft Proof: An emulation of the output of → color managed content on a certain device like an offset printing machine.

Sourceforge: A large internet repository for many active (and some inactive) software projects, including Scribus.

Special Character: In Scribus and also in this manual the term "special character" may have three different meanings. First, it may refer to a character which isn't contained in the basic Latin and English alphabet, like λ or ß. Second, it may refer to signs or symbols that aren't contained in any alphabet, for example dingbats. Finally, it can be used for so-called control characters, like a non-breaking space or a paragraph break.

Spinbox: The rectangular boxes containing numeric values for the setting of various item attributes. The name refers to the ability to use a wheelmouse to roll the values up and down.

Spread: In DTP a spread refers to two adjacent pages (left and right page).

Status Bar: The bottom of the Scribus workspace that contains the zoom tools, the page list, the progress bar and other elements.

Story Editor: The window brought up to directly enter text for a → text frame, as well as adjust its features, and apply and create paragraph → styles.

Stroke: The border of an → item or a → glyph.

Style: Styles are sets of features for certain parts in a document which are given a name, and thereby can be used and reused. Scribus 1.3.3.x supports paragraph and line styles. Colors work in a similar fashion and may also be called styles.

Subscript: → Characters printed below the → baseline to an adjustable amount, and typically smaller than the text on the baseline. Commonly used in chemical molecular notation and in mathematics.

Subversion: A version control system used for software development. It's a database that manages the codebase of a project like Scribus. Changes to the code as well as the developer who committed the code are registered, so that each change can be traced in case a problem occurs.

Superscript: → Characters printed above the → baseline to an adjustable amount, and typically smaller than the text on the baseline. Commonly used to denote mathematical exponents or footnotes.

SVG: The Scalable Vector Graphics format is a recommendation of the World Wide Web Consortium (W3C), which is maintaining the standard. It's an open, universal and extremely versatile vector file format.

Tab: Used for → indentation and alignment of text to a particular distance farther along the current line. The term also refers to elements of many dialogs in the Scribus user interface.

Tab Stop: One particular spot along a typewritten line for indentation.

Table of Contents: A list, usually somewhere near the beginning of a → document, which delineates the document's content by chapter name and sometimes in more detail, such as sections and subsections. May also contain associated page numbers and synopses.

Tabulator: The section of the → Shape tab in the Properties Palette used to set and edit tab stops for text frames. The tabulator key can also be used to switch between buttons, field and other elements in dialogs.

Template: In Scribus, a template is a file which is stored with all its related content (images, fonts, profiles) in a hidden folder. Templates can be opened with the command *File > From Template*. They can be added via *File > Save as Template*. They should be used to save documents recurring content, eg. magazine layouts or menus.

Text Frame: A container for formatted text in Scribus and most other DTP programs.

Theme: In graphical desktop environments for computers like Gnome, KDE, OS X or Windows a set of colors, icons, and fonts used for the display of the desktop environment and applications running inside the environment.

Thumbnail: A small version of an image, typically used in a dialog to help recognition of the file. In Scribus, the term can also refer to a special shortcut for the display size (→ zoom) of a → document.

Toolbar: In many programs for Windows and Linux/UNIX that use a graphical user interface the toolbar is a row filled with icons for commands. In general the toolbar is the second row under the → menu bar. The latter contains dropdown menus.

Tooltips: Small messages which transiently appear on hovering over some icons or other screen features as indicators of their names or functions.

TrueType: A font format developed by Apple and Microsoft as an alternative to the → PostScript font format. In contrast to PostScript fonts, TrueType fonts consist only of one single file. See OpenType.

Type 1: see PostScript Font

Typography: A collective noun for everything related to the creation and the use of fonts, as well as typesetting. There are also some overlaps with spelling, for example hyphenation, quotes or dashes.

Ungrouping: see Group

Unlinking: see Linking

Uppercase: see Caps

URW Fonts: URW is an established font foundry, which is well-known for its high quality fonts. However, in the context of Free Software in general and Open Source DTP, the term URW fonts sometimes refers to the set of fonts donated by URW under an open font license for distribution with Ghostscript.

Vector Drawing: An image or a graphic that's described by co-ordinates and mathematical formulas.

Workflow: The overall process involved with a project for the ultimate layout, creation and final output of a → document. Workflow thus not only includes the layout itself, but the creation of text and image content, and even includes the printer who makes the final product. Workflow can be a process only involving a single person, but in many cases is the work of a team.

XML: An abbreviation for Extended Markup Language. The purpose of XML is to describe any data structure by using plain (unformatted) text. XML uses tags in a hierarchical and nested order. Scribus, OpenOffice.org and →SVG files are XML files.

Zoom: Visually enlarging or shrinking the appearance on the screen, much as one might do with a zoom lens. Thus, one can either zoom in or zoom out.

16 Credits

WITHOUT contributions from many people, this manual wouldn't have seen the light of day. In recent years, documentation mostly took place in three ways: First, there was (and is) the official Scribus online documentation, almost entirely written by the indefatigable Peter Linnell, a professional pre-press and publishing consultant, who generously gave permission to re-use some of his texts in this manual. If you have a déja-vu while reading some sections of this manual, you probably read his texts in the Scribus Help Browser before.

The second way to make information about the use of Scribus available to its users was (and is) the Scribus Wiki. Almost all of its content has been written by users for users. Probably the most important part of the Wiki documentation is the tutorial "Get Started with Scribus," which is an update to the masterpiece written by Niyam Bushan for an older Scribus version – at a time when the Scribus project lacked the infrastructure it has today. If you studied the documentation on the Scribus Wiki carefully, you will also note that some of the content of this manual has been prepared there some time ago, most notably some of the "Working with ..." sections. This is no coincidence, as the main authors of this manual also belonged (and continue to belong) to the main contributors of the Wiki. Thus, at least a part of this book has been prepared in another medium, which is probably one of the reasons for our quick progress.

On top of the documentation efforts by the Scribus team and the Scribus users, other authors created their own documentation, some of them even as commercially printed books. Since we're not tracking every published book about Scribus, we recommend to check your native language book market to see whether there are products that suit your needs better than this one. Also note that many printed computer magazines publish Scribus tutorials.

List of Contributors (in alphabetical order):

CRAIG BRADNEY (Australia/Luxemburg): IT manager for a global e-commerce company, Scribus developer, Scribus webmaster, created a separate Wiki for documentation purposes, in which large parts of this manual have been written collaboratively, helped finishing the manual by proofreading the whole text and by providing many useful hints. He also wrote the preface.

Louis Desjardins (Canada): Owner of a professional design and pre-press company in Montréal, a long-time contributor to Scribus, and the celebrated organizer of Libre Graphics Meeting 2007. He helped proofreading the texts and provided countless useful hints.

Thomas G. Dorsch (Germany/U.S.A.): Professional musician, artist and designer. He wrote the initial version of the "Color Wheel" section.

Ivan Fetwadjieff (Russia/Australia): A PDF forms expert, who agreed to relicense his contributions to the Wiki for use in this manual.

Cédric Gemy (France): Lecturer for layout and design at French universities and Technical Colleges. Author of books about graphics design and layout. He wrote the initial version of "Importing Vector Drawings."

Maciej Hanski (Poland/Austria): IT Manager for an Austrian government agency, long-time Scribus contributor, account manager for the Scribus Wiki, PDF forms expert, Scribus translator. He helped finishing this manual by providing some texts about PDF forms, by proofreading the PDF forms chapter and by providing many useful hints.

Riku Leino (Finland): IT Manager for a Finnish non-profit organization, Scribus developer. He wrote the initial versions of "Opening, Creating and Saving Documents," "The Action History," and "Importing Text with Custom Text Filters."

Peter Linnell (U.S.A./France): Professional pre-press, publishing and web consultant, Scribus developer, main author of the Scribus online documentation. He generously permitted the re-use of some of his texts in this manual.

Oleksandr Moskalenko (Ukraine/U.S.A.): Molecular biologist, Scribus developer, maintainer of Scribus Debian and (K)Ubuntu packages. He contributed the texts about installation of Scribus on Debian and (K)Ubuntu.

Gregory Pittman (U.S.A.): Neurologist, long-time Scribus contributor and experienced script author. One of the main authors of the manual.

Daniel Prien (Germany): Professional printer. He contributed the artwork for the cover.

Vladimir Savić (Serbia): Professional designer and printer, Fontmatrix developer. He contributed some graphics for this manual and wrote the initial subsection about Fontmatrix.

CHRISTOPH SCHÄFER (Germany): Historian, germanist, works for a museum and also as a freelance-writer and layouter, Scribus developer. One of the main authors of the manual.

PETR VANĚK (Czech Republic): Professional software developer, Scribus developer. He generously permitted re-use and editing of his "Short Words" instruction.

ANDREAS VOX (Germany): Mathematician and professional software developer, Scribus developer. He contributed the subsection about Mac fonts.

THOMAS ZASTROW (Germany): Computer linguist at a German university, long-time Scribus contributor and a gifted tinkerer. He wrote initial versions of many sections or subsections, most notably those in the "Tips and Tricks" chapter and also created useful info-graphics.

Aside from the particular persons listed above we have to thank the Scribus development team for creating this wonderful piece of software. But without the many Scribus users who pestered the developers and the contributors on the mailing list and in IRC, this manual wouldn't exist.

We also want to thank Jos Buivenga [1] for making available the Fontin font, which has been used on the title pages, free of charge, Bitstream [2] for releasing the Bitstream Vera Sans font, also used on the title pages, under a Free font license, and Red Hat, Inc. [3] for releasing the Liberation Serif font used for continuous text in this manual under an Open Source license. Other fonts used for this manual are commercially licensed, so that the vendors are credited by paying the license fees.

Finally, we have to thank Anduin.net/Øverby Consulting [4] for the hosting of the documentation Wiki. This manual wouldn't exist without their willingness to support the Scribus project.

[1] www.josbuivenga.demon.nl
[2] www. bitstream.com
[3] www.redhat.com
[4] www.anduin.net

A

Abbreviations *see* Short words
Action history 159ff, 223, 411
Adjusting *see* Scaling
Adobe Reader 144, 272f, 290, 294, 305, 322ff, 320, 324, 343, **381f**
Aligning items **216ff**
Alignment of text 80f, 87, 146, 220
Annotations *see* PDF – *annotations*
Arranging pages 55, 61, 294ff
Arrows
  • *as feature of line* **113ff**, *149, 331*
  • *as shape* 115, *331*
Attributes 70, 97, 150, 195, 225
Autosave **46ff**

B

BAK (Backup files) 49
Barcode generator **244ff**, 403
Baseline grid 80, 83, 97, 113, 146f, 220
Basepoint 65, 213, 411
Bézier curves 108, **116ff**, 129, 157, 162, 359, 364, 411
Black point compensation 262, 411
Bleed 304, 373, 411
Blend modes **263ff**, 412
BMP (Windows Bitmap) 266, 378
Booklet printing 291, **294ff**, 412
Bookmarks **56ff**, 70, 412
Borders 15, **359ff**
Bounding box 67, 107, 126, 216, 412
Building *see* Compiling

C

Calendars, **344ff**
Calibrating devices **258ff**, 292
Canvas (definition) 35f, 412
Caps 83, 412
Chained text frames *see* Linking/unlinking text frames
Character encoding 78, 354, 416
Checkbox 306, 311, 315f, 319, 412
CID fonts 176f
Cinepaint 152, 260
Clipping paths **242f**, 367, 413
CMYK 32, 98ff, 120, 128, 248ff, 252ff, 261ff, 273f, 280ff, 291, 340f, 367ff, 370, 413
Collecting for output **47f**, 229, 413

Color
  • *bars 337f*
  • *color blindness 250f*
  • *color management 123, 140,* **258ff**, *273ff, 283, 368f, 413*
  • *color profiles* see *ICC profiles*
  • *color sets 68f, 118,* **121**, *254ff*
  • *editing/adding ~ 119f, 252ff*
  • *line and fill colors 27,* **118f**
  • *separations 285f, 291*
  • *spot colors* see *Spot colors*
  • *temperature 260f, 413*
Color wheel **248ff**
Columns 45, 52, **79ff**, 148, 413
Combo box 306
Command line 2ff, 10, 292, 393ff
Comma-separated values **73f**, 134, 403, 413
Compiling **3ff**, 412
Configuration
  • *files 141, 168, 196, 254f, 388f, 403*
  • *see also* Document – *Setup*, Preferences
Context menu
  • *general 27, 62ff, 228, 364f, 399, 413, passim*
  • *image frame 19, 96f, passim*
  • *polygons, shapes 105*
  • *text frame* **70ff***, 225, 307, 331, 358ff, passim*
Contour line 67, 109, 413
Control characters 53
Control point 106ff, 414
Converting items 71, 105,119, **157f**, 193, 331, 358ff, passim
Coordinates 107f, 209, 414
Copying item properties *see* Magic wand
CorelDraw 256, 377, 380
Crop marks 302, 337f
CUPS 2, 263, **289ff**, 414
Customization *see* Document – *Setup*, Preferences

D

Dashes **201f**, 414
Development versions 5ff, 415
Dfonts *see* Mac fonts
Diagrams **358ff**
DigiKam **372**

Distributing items **218**
DOC *see* Word files
Document
  • *display* **50ff**
  • *information* **144ff**
  • *layout* **58ff**
  • *loading* *41f*
  • *new* *14f,* **39f,** *153, passim*
  • *outline* *55, 415*
  • *preview* *53*
  • *saving* **46f**
  • Setup *27f, 45, 50ff, 60, 103,* **141ff,** *189f, 220f, 224, 243, 261f, 283, 287ff, 292*
  • *viewing options* **51ff,** *266, 268*
DPI (dots per inch) 102, 368
Drop caps
  • *advanced* **193f**
  • *simple* **88**
Duplicating items 63, 357, 415

E
eCOMstation 188, 292
Emergency save 49, 415
Encoding *see* Character encoding
Endnotes 365f
Enhanced Metafile (EMF) 130
EPS 32f, 40, 47, 96, 100, **125ff,** 130f, 134, 325, 362, 373, 402, 416
Export
  • *bitmap* **265ff**
  • *EPS* **268ff**
  • *PDF see PDF – export*
  • *PostScript* **292f**
  • *text* *92, 94,* **265,** *268*
  • *SVG* **268ff**
Extended image properties **235ff**
Extension scripts, **338**
External tools 152
Eye dropper **247,** 416

F
FDF 312
File formats
  • *fonts* *174ff*
  • *images* *402*
  • *Scribus* *402*
  • *text* *265, 403*
  • *vector* **123ff,** *402*
Fill
  • *characters* *88, 148, 416*
  • *color* *14f, 68f,* **118ff,** *148, 330, 416*

  • *rules* *110*
Flipping items 351ff, 416
Fondu 117
FontForge 175f, 186
Fontmatrix 186f
Fonts
  • *conversion* *174ff*
  • *embedding* ~ *127, 189, 273f, 276f, 327*
  • *installation* **184ff**
  • *legal download* *173,* **179ff**
  • *Mac see Mac fonts*
  • *management* *149,* **188ff,** *416*
  • *outlining* *327*
  • *preview* *92,* **183ff**
  • *types* *149,* **173ff**
  • *subsetting* *183*
  • *substitution* *77, 153, 189*
Font sampler **349ff**
Footnotes **365f**
Formulas **129**
Frames
  • *boundaries* **359ff**
  • *conversion* **157f**
  • *custom frames* **357f**
  • *general* *25ff, 51,* **62ff**
  • *geometry* **63ff**
  • *image* *15, 69,* **96ff,** *147, 195, passim*
  • *shape* *66f, 149, passim*
  • *text* **70ff,** *passim*
FreeBSD 371, 388, 393, 415
Freehand lines 119, 416

G
Gamma **258ff,** 417
Gamut **261ff**
Ghostscript 2, 8f, 100, 127f, 130, 245, 273, 289, 293, 324, 417
GIF 32, 96, 98, 402
GIMP 96, 152, 232, 236, 260, 287, 327,**367,** 402, 417
Glyphs 178, **200ff,** 277, 417
Gnome 186, 260
GPG 3
Gradients 121f, 417
GraphicsMagick **376**
Grayscale 273, 280, 417
Grid 51ff, 146f, **219ff**
Grouping items 64, 330, 357, 417
GSview 32, 127f, 270, **384**
Guides 51ff, 80, 146f, **221ff,** 417, 419
GwenView **373**

H

Help
- *Help Browser* **37ff**, *337, 356, 405, 417*
- *on the web* **405**
- *Tooltips* **38ff**

HSL 248
HSV 120, 245, 248
HTML 28, 74f, 165, 170, 254, 272, 312, 323, 365f, 373, 403, 417
Hyperlinks 312, **323**
Hyphenation
- *applying* **198f**
- *settings 142, 149,* **198f**

I

ICC profiles 98ff, 142f, 235, 258ff, 273, 281ff, 303, 371, 375, 404, 418
Illustrator 125f, 254, 272f, 378ff
Image
- *compression 276*
- *direct import 346*
- *effects 19f, 96,* **232ff**
- *extended image properties* **235ff**
- *formats* **98ff**
- *loading 16ff, 96, 101*
- *managing* **229ff**
- *paste 97*
- *paste absolute 97*
- *preview 18, 96, 98, 235*
- *resolution 53f, 96, 266, 268, 327*
- *scaling a frame to image size 97*
- *scaling an image to frame size 101*
- *visibility 53ff*

ImageMagick 260, 269f, **376**
Importing
- *colors 121, 256f*
- *master pages 137*
- *pages 59*
- *PDF 288*
- *scrapbooks 156*
- *styles 89f*
- *text 73ff,* **165ff**
- *vector graphics* **123ff**

Imposition 244, 303
Indentation 89, 401, 418
InDesign 254, 272
Info box **350f**

Inkscape 123, 131, 270, **377ff**
Inline objects 71f, 207, 418
Installation 1ff, 393ff
IRC (Internet Relay Chat) 304, 404
IrfanView **375**
Item action mode **160**, 418

J

JavaScript 272, 279, 305, 309, 311, **314ff**, 325, 328
jPDF Tweak **387**
JP(E)G 32, 96, 99f, 266, 375, 402
Justification *see* Alignment of text

K

KDE 185, 260, 289, 292, 324, 373
Kelvin see Color – *temperature*
Kerning 83, 87, 94, 175
Keyboard shortcuts 28, 53, 151, 212, **396ff**
KPDF 328, 386
KPrinter **289ff**, 297ff, 324
Krita 152, 260, **370f**

L

Layers 26, 71, 96, 105, 227f, 235ff, 273, 276, 326
Leading *see* Line spacing
Levels 17, 26, 65, 71, 96, 105, 227
Licenses 173f, 176, **405ff**
Ligatures 204, 418
Lines
- *colors 133, 149*
- *creating 113*
- *edges 68, 113, 149*
- *endings 68, 113, 149*
- *styles 68, 114, 149*
- *width 68, 113, 149*

Line spacing 82f, 87, 147f
Linking/unlinking text frames 53, 78f, 412, 418
Linux 1ff, 152, 177, 184ff, 230, 254, 259, 288, 297, 324, 340, 343, 371, 376f, 388, 393, 415, 421
List box 306, 311f
Lists **205ff**
LittleCMS 2, **259ff**, 419
Locking items 16f, 66, 71, 97, 105, 369
Lorem ipsum *see* Sample text

M

Mac fonts 177, 184f

Mac OS X 8, 99, 127, 152, 177, 187f, 230, 256, 259f, 288, 297, 371, 376f, 388, 421
Magic wand 69, 419
Mailing lists 404
Managing images **229ff**
Margins 14, 44f, 51f, 222, 275, 291, 419
Master pages
• applying *29, 31, 55, 58, 61,* **137ff**, *143, 331, 419*
• converting pages to ~ *137*
• creating *31,* **135ff**
• deleting **136**
• duplicating **136**
• editing *55,* **135ff**
• importing **137**
• renaming **136f**
Measuring tools **209ff**
Measuring units *see* Units
Menu bar 35, 420
Metadata **144ff**, 420
Mirroring pages 291
Multiple duplicate 16, 63, 207, 214, 420
Multiple Master fonts 176, **214f**, 357f

N
Named styles *see* Styles
Names of items 65
Navigation **55ff**, 420
Node 106ff, 420

O
ODG 40, **128ff**, 191, 402
ODT 32, **76f**, 190f, 365, 403
Offset printing 301f
Opacity 115, **118ff**
OpenDocument format (ODF) 28, 32, 76f, 123, 128ff, 420
OpenOffice.org
• *Calc 134*
• *Draw* **128ff**, *131, 191*
• *Math 129f*
• *Writer 128, 134, 191, 198, 365*
OpenType fonts 82, **173ff**, 189, 277f, 421
OS/2 188, 230, 293

P
Packages (Linux/UNIX) 393ff, 421
Pages
• adding **58ff**
• arranging *55, 61*
• converting ~ to master page *137*
• copying *59*
• deleting *58f*
• importing *59*
• list *55*
• margins *14, 44, 51f, 143, 222, 275, 291*
• moving *59*
• numbering *55, 135, 139f, 151, 331, 349, 421*
• orientation *14, 44, 58, 143, 295, 327*
• properties *44, 61, 143*
Pagination *see* Page – numbering
Paragraph styles 85ff, 91ff, 165, 178, 191, 205
Paste absolute (images) 97
PBM 266
PDB files 78, 409
PDF
• */A 273*
• articles *276*
• annotations *70,* **321ff**, *326*
• bookmarks **56f**
• display settings **278**
• encryption **279f**
• export *28, 32f, 47, 50, 56f, 68f, 81, 128, 143, 148ff, 157f, 173, 183, 189, 227f, 253, 258, 265f,* **271ff**, *287, 294ff, 303, 337, 340, 367, 378*
• forms *65,* **305ff**
• importing *96, 100, 232, 378, 402*
• links **321ff**
• presentations *278,* **325ff**, *422*
• versions *68f,* **272ff**, *303, 308*
• viewers *272, 278f, 324*
• *X-1a 273*
• *X-2 274*
• *X-3 149, 204,* **272ff**, *303*
PGM 266
Photoshop *see* PSD
Plug-ins 154, 156, 195, 265, 377, 421
PNG 32, **98f**, 156, 258, 266, 377, 404
Polygons
• combining *110f, 358ff*
• editing *104ff*
• inserting *104f*

• *splitting 110f*
PostScript 9, 28f, 32, 125ff, 130,
    149, 173, 183, 189, 245, 263f,
    268, 271ff, 282, 285, 287, 289,
    292f, 297, 299, 304, 324, 363,
    378, 402, 422
PostScript fonts *see* Type 1 fonts
Preferences 9, 27f, 50ff, **141ff**, 190,
    196, 220f, 243, 261f, 287ff,
    336, 338, 398, 422
Preflight verifier 34, 149, 274, **287f**,
    422
Pre-press 271f, 279, 282
Presentations *see* PDF
Preset layouts 144
Preview settings 95, 98, 148, 151,
    153
Printer margins 144
Printing
    • *booklets **294ff***
    • *commercial 34, 260ff, 273,
        277, 282ff, **301ff**, **337ff***
    • *disable/enable printing of
        objects 66, 228*
    • *local 89, 149, 263f, 273, 282,
        285, **289ff***
    • *marks 337*
Print preview **285f**, 422
Print space 52, 60, 422
Process colors 292, 302, 422
Progressive JP(E)G files 32, 99
Properties Palette 14, 35, 55, 62ff,
    73, 82ff, 85f, 97, 101, 105,
    117f, 132f, 147, 157, 163, 178,
    193, 207, 211, 213, 220, 224,
    311, 361, 365, 423
PSD 28, 96, **100**, **235ff**, 402, 423
PyQt 1ff
Python 2, 142, 380

Q

Qt 2ff, 10, 142, 423
QuarkXPress 254, 272, 401
Quotation marks **202f**, 423

R

Radio buttons **319ff**
Redo 70, 105, 159f
Registration color 120, 302, 341,
    423
Registration marks 120, 302, **336ff**
Regular expressions **170ff**, 423
Rendering intents **262ff**, 423

Revert to saved 43, 47
RGB 100, 120, 245, 248ff, 252ff,
    262ff, 280ff, 327, 370
Rich black 302
Rotation of objects 109, 213, 357ff
Round corners **66**, 330
Rulers 36, 210, 223, 424
Runaround *see* Text – *flows around
        frame*
RYB 248ff

S

Sample text 70, 78, 153, 424
Saving
    • *as template 45ff*
    • *autosave **46ff***
    • *documents 23, 34*
    • *emergency 49f*
    • *items (Scrapbook) 155f*
Scaling
    • *free scaling 101*
    • *images to frame size 101, 148*
    • *frames to image size 84, 148*
SCD, SCD.GZ 29ff, 402, 424
Scrapbook 71, 97, 105, **155f**
Scratch space 35
Scripting
    • *basics **354ff***
    • *extension scripts **338***
    • *scripts shipped with Scribus
        333, **336ff***
Search and Replace (text) 92, **161**,
    206
Shade **118ff**
Shapes
    • *editing 15, **106ff**, 133, 157*
    • *fill rules 110*
    • *inserting 15, 104*
Shortcuts *see* Keyboard shortcuts
Short words 154, **195f**
sK1 **380**
Skewing 109
SLA, SLA.GZ 28, 39ff, 59, 159,
    402, 424f
Small caps 83, 147, 178, 425
Smart hyphens 199
Smart text selection 92
Solaris 259, 388, 393, 415
Squiggle 270, **379**
Spaces *see* Special characters
Special characters
    • *dashes 201f*
    • *inserting 92, **200ff***

- *ligatures 204*
- *quotation marks 202f*
- *spaces and breaks 203f*

Spot colors 120, **252ff**, 263f, 274, 286, 292, 303

Status bar 35, 55, 425

Story Editor 71, 200ff, 306, 311, 321, 363, 425

Styles
- *import 89f*
- *menu 35*
- *line 27, **114f***
- *paragraph 27, 71, 75ff, 85, 91ff*

Subscript 83, 425

Superscript 83, 426

SVG 28, 40, **123ff**, 130f, 265ff, 306, 311, 363, 373, 377f, 380, 402, 425

SVN 2ff

SXD 40, **128ff**, 365, 402

SXW 76f, 190f, 403

T

Tables of contents **150**, **224ff**, 349, 426

Tables
- *complex tables 134, 214f*
- *converting cells 133f*
- *editing 72, **132f***
- *importing 75*
- *inserting 132f, 214f*

Tabulators 81ff, 88f, 205, 426

Templates 34, 45ff, 165ff, 327, 404, 427

Text
- *alignment 84, 87*
- *appending text 70*
- *attaching text to path **162ff**, 157, 358, 364f*
- *effects 83, 87, 93f*
- *extracting 265, 342f*
- *fields 305f, 314f, 319*
- *filters 78, **165ff***
- *flows around frame 66f, 82, 193, 278*
- *formatting 74ff, 82ff, 86ff, 91ff, 147f*
- *height 83, 86*
- *import 70, 73ff, 165ff, 190*
- *indentation 89*
- *kerning 83*
- *width 83, 86*

Text frames
- *automatic creation 45, 70*
- *editing text in ~ 71ff*
- *inline objects in ~ 71f, 207*
- *inserting 70*

Themes 142, 426

TIF(F) 32, 96, 98f, 107, 236, 258, 367ff, 375, 378, 402

Tk/Tkinter 333

Toolbar 35, 427

Tooltips 38ff, 333, 427

Transparency 273, 275, 285, 288

Trim box 283

TrueType fonts 82, **173ff**, 277, 284, 427

Type 1 fonts 82, **173ff**, 189, 284, 422

Type 3 fonts 174

Type 42 fonts 174

Typography 165ff

U

Under color removal 291

Undo 70, 105, 159f, 223

Unflipping content **351ff**

Ungrouping 64, 132

UniConvertor 380

Units 45, 141, 212, 219, 341, 411ff

UNIX 2ff, 126, 177, 184ff, 230, 245, 288, 297, 340, 371, 393, 413, 421

Unlinking frames 79, 412

V

Vector drawings 106ff, **123ff**, 427

Vision defect *see* Color – *color blindness*

W

Wiki 333, 404

Windows
- *cascading 50*
- *tiling 50*
- *Windows 2000/XP/Vista 9ff, 100, 125, 127, 130, 152, 176f, 187, 230, 245, 288, 297, 324, 340, 343f, 376f, 388f, 421*
- *Windows Metafile (WMF) 130f*

Word files 28, 77f, 402

Workflow 28ff, 427

Workspace 35ff

X
XBM 266
XML 28, 123, 128, 170, 427
XnView 374
XPDF 328
XPM 96, **99**, 266, 402

Z
Zoom **54**, 148

Inkscape

- import PDF ~~save as svg~~
- Select AD   (or modify)
- export Bitmap @ 300 dpi

Lightning Source UK Ltd.
Milton Keynes UK
19 October 2009

145142UK00001B/223/P